CRITICAL ACCLAIM
FOR *FOOD*

"Sterling's themes are nothing less than human universality, passion, and necessity, all told in stories straight from the gut."
—Maxine Hong Kingston, author of *The Woman Warrior*

"Here are feasts for the hungry: a vast, buttery range of writing wrapped around our stomachs, our hearts and our sense of place…nightstand reading of the first order."
—*Los Angeles Times*

"The stories are bound to whet appetites for more than food."
—*Publishers Weekly*

"The 350-page collection of heart-warming, funny and sometimes frightening true stories will make your mouth water while helping you better understand other cultures."
—*Chicago Herald*

"If you're looking for a foodie book to satisfy both appetite and wanderlust, curl up with *Food.* Edited by Richard Sterling, this beguiling collection of travel tales takes you around the world."
—Angelina Malhotra-Singh

Travelers' Tales Books

TRAVELERS' TALES

FOOD

A TASTE OF THE ROAD

TRAVELERS' TALES

FOOD

A TASTE OF THE ROAD

Collected and Edited by

RICHARD STERLING

Series Editors
JAMES O'REILLY AND LARRY HABEGGER

TRAVELERS' TALES, INC.
SAN FRANCISCO, CALIFORNIA

Cover design: Michele Wetherbee/doubleu-gee
Interior design: Kathryn Heflin and Susan Bailey
Cover photograph: © Jochem D. Wijnards/Getty Images/FPG
Illustrations: Nina Stewart
Map: Keith Granger
Page Layout: Cynthia Lamb, using the fonts Bembo and Boulevard

Distributed by Publishers Group West, 1700 Fourth Street, Berkeley, California
94710.

Library of Congress Cataloguing-in-Publication Data

Travelers' tales food : a taste of the road / collected and edited by Richard
Sterling.
  p.cm.
Includes bibliogaphical references and index.
  ISBN 1-885211-77-5
 1. Food—Anecdotes. 2. Travel—Anecdotes. I. Title: Taste of the road
II. Sterling, Richard. 1952

TX357 .T67 2002
641.3—dc21   First Edition   20020011764
       Printed in the United States
       10 9 8 7 6 5

In food, as in death, we feel the essential brotherhood of man.

—VIETNAMESE PROVERB

Table of Contents

Part Two
SOME THINGS TO DO

Part Three
GOING YOUR OWN WAY

Part Four
IN THE SHADOWS

Part Five
THE LAST WORD

Preface

TRAVELERS' TALES

Just as there are many different places to which we can travel, there are many different ways we can travel. We can experience life and the road through any of our senses, any of our faculties. For some people travel takes the form of museums and works of high art; for some it is hotels or resorts; a friend of mine, and not a macabre sort at all, visits cemeteries wherever she goes; another runs rivers the world over. But there is one universal constant in travel, and it is the subject of this book.

Any number of people will tell you that they travel, in large part, to eat. To break bread with strangers and leave the table with friends. To discover the world through the medium of cuisine, deepen their understanding, broaden their horizons, and to make their travels the richer. This collection furthers the proposition that humanity is revealed through cuisine just as surely as it is through any other art or social activity. Through the personal experience of the writers, in rollicking adventure, humor, and even pathos the reader will agree that, as Napoleon said of the army, we travel on our stomachs.

I think you will not put this book down and think of food, or travel, or travel literature, in quite the same way again. And you will say, "Yes, of course. It was there all the time, in all my journeys, I simply never acknowleged it. These are my stories, too." And I think you will know intimately, even if for the first time, these words of Rudyard Kipling:

> I have eaten your bread and salt,
> I have drunk your water and wine.
> The deaths Ye died I have watched beside,
> And the lives Ye led were mine.

There are a multitude of journeys in those brief words. They are the distillate of half a life's wanderings, by one who knew the road as well as any ever could. And they are the distillate of the many appetites of a man who hungered greatly: for life, love, food, drink, the open road, the next horizon. All of us have our several hungers, and they are all intertwined. And those of us who hunger most, I think, hunger best. Welcome, Reader, to the literature of Gusto. As you navigate these pages, I wish you a good journey and a good appetite.

RICHARD STERLING

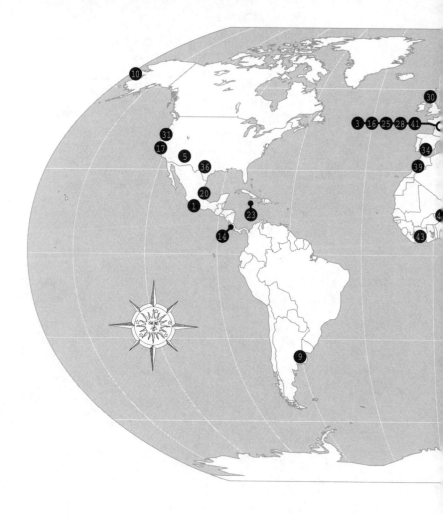

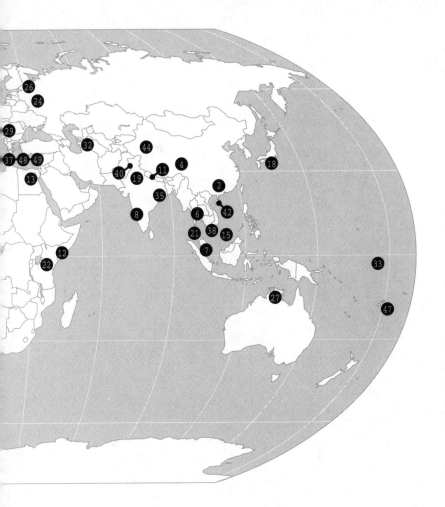

Food: An Introduction

BY MARGO TRUE

One warm, moon-bright evening about ten years ago, I was standing in a square beneath the majestic bulk of the Red Fort in New Delhi, transfixed by what I was eating. The shy street-vendor behind one of the dozens of carts parked there had just handed me, fresh and hot from a pot of bubbling oil and carefully stacked inside a newspaper cone, several tiny, golden puffs. I put one between my teeth and bit down. Instantly the frail crust gave way, flooding my mouth with cool, cilantro-flavored water spiked with chili. It was great fun, like popping edible balloons. I remember what a surprise it was—and how well it characterized my experience of traveling in India: Practically everything about India surprised me, most of those surprises were either wonderful or amusing, and my senses felt flooded nearly all the time. In the witty little *pani poori* I ate that night—for it surely seemed to me they'd been created by a cook with a subtle sense of humor—I found an expression of all three.

For me, and for the other contributors to this book, a memorable meal—or even a snack—on the road has to do with more than just the taste or the sight or the smell of the food. It has to do with the way food can carry you into the heart of an experience, how it can become the means of the journey. In "A World Without Latkes," for instance, the narrator gradually warms to his chatty middle-aged seatmate on a flight to Chicago and discovers, as she gives him a lesson in making latkes, an unexpected and profound empathy with her. Over a plate of spicy dumplings in a restaurant in Northeast India, the lonely writer of "*Momos* at Tashi's" has a laughter-filled exchange with a little girl that becomes, she says, "a connecting thread thrown across borders of culture and language."

Sometimes food makes you realize the nature of the road you're taking—as in "Liberation Day," when the narrator sees that the farther she and her lover drift apart, the more they eat to fill the void.

Giving food away, depending on the needs of the giver and the receiver, can be an emotionally charged act. In "Give unto Others," a student at the Ritz Hotel's cooking school in Paris distributes her class's creations—rich tarts and sables, croissants and eclairs—to the poor, with poignant results. The young man in "Night of the Oranges," set in impoverished Romania, stands in line for hours to buy his little brother a bag of oranges, a deed that so thrills him he feels it will be the best Christmas of his life. In "*Si, Simpatica,*" an American tourist dines by happenstance with a burly, hirsute, transsexual prostitute in Florence—and accepts a bite of what turns out to be transcendentally good salad.

All of these stories evoke far more than gustatory anticipation, relish, and post-prandial satisfaction. Here are tales of maternal love, guilt, sensuality, spiritual comfort, generosity, brutality, and camaraderie, and of food that can stave off death, addiction, and loneliness. In "Etiquette Soup," food becomes a cultural challenge that, once crossed, leads to a most pleasant discovery; in the aptly titled "Pass on the Primate" it forms an unbreachable barrier.

The destinations included in the book span the points of the compass. You'll read stories set in Kenya, India, Spain, Romania, Mexico, Japan, Costa Rica, Italy, Morocco, Texas, Micronesia, France, Tibet, Alaska, Egypt, and China. Most of the contributors are American, but not all; and while many are professional food or travel writers, others have very different backgrounds—a plant conservation biologist, a couple of musicians, a filmmaker, a sociology professor, a retired telephone engineer, an 18-year-old exchange student. One writer was, until recently, homeless. (His wise, articulate, and thoughtfully written story about scavenging for food makes it clear why he's been dubbed the "Thoreau of Dumpsters.") And, as you would expect with such a diverse group, their voices are hardly uniform. One of the pleasures of reading these pages is the journey, if you will, of moving from prose that is spare and straightforward to that which is densely poetic, or from a contemplative, peaceful story to one that makes you laugh out loud.

Stories written about food in this way, especially if the writer has been afforded total freedom of expression, are—like life—not always appetizing. Some are downright nauseating, such as Brett Allen King's account of his companions sucking down offal in Madrid, or shocking, as in Zhang Xianliang's vivid description of food-collection strategies in a Maoist labor camp in the late 1950s. M. F. K. Fisher, the grand dame of American food writing, tells a heartbreaking, beautiful story about traveling with her dying lover by train through Italy on the eve of World War II; their safe haven is the dining car—for a while.

A word on the chapter headings: They are meant to correspond to different facets of gastronomic travel. Hence, "Essence" contains stories that introduce the idea of food as journey, of a window to some sort of discovery and transformation of self. "Some Things to Do" tells of events that the reader, should he or she visit the place the writer describes, might feasibly be able to recreate for him or herself: An Indian train trip with friendly, food-giving fellow passengers, or a meal at Mexico City's Cafe Tacuba, or an aromatic, memory-triggering trip through your own kitchen cupboards (stocked, ideally, with spices you picked up while traveling). The stories in "Going Your Own Way" could only have happened to that writer in that particular time and place: Here you'll encounter a young American woman who made a mint selling brownies to the Scots (it comes, as do several of the stories in this book, with a recipe) and of a crew of U.S. Navy river men in Vietnam who go duck hunting with machine guns and fishing with grenades—anything to get an alternative to the infamous C-rations. "In the Shadows," describes the darker side of travel food—from offensive edibles to downright dangerous ones—and of times when eating fails to bring pleasure. Only one story falls under the book's final heading, "The Last Word," and it sums up what every traveler hopes to find when dining in a foreign land.

As I crunched my *pani poori* that night in New Delhi, smiling at each delicious little explosion, I realized something else through my haze of bliss. The Indians eating with me were smiling too, and together we enjoyed our snack. It is moments like these, when a bite of food turns into a larger, richer event, that the writers in this book bring to us.

Currently an editor at Gourmet *magazine, Margo True grew up traveling around the world as the daughter of a foreign service officer. Her earliest memories are of eating (rice, beans, and bananas in Brazil).*

PART ONE

ESSENCE OF FOOD

Apron Strings

We must all eat to live;
some more urgently than others.

THAT FIRST DELICIOUS DRENCHING OF HOT, PUNGENT MEXICAN air as I stepped off the plane in Manzanillo made me realize I had been unconsciously seeking the tropics all my life. What a sensation—as if the stewardess had opened the door of a blast furnace fueled by jasmine, corn husks, bacon grease, and Clorox bottles rather than the door of a rickety DC-9. The tarmac below was liquid and shimmering, even at 9 p.m. As Salman Rushdie says, fantasy grows best in the heat.

My son Jonathan and I were on our way to a small fishing village about 40 miles away called Barra de Navidad for a celebratory vacation, my gift to him for graduating from college. A friend had offered to let me use his house there on the condition that I make curtains for all the windows, a task that would end up taking just about the whole vacation, handstitching being slower than I'd imagined. But the price was right and Jonathan and I were looking forward to lounging like lizards on the beach and getting to know each other as adults, both of us having grown up quite a bit during his years away at UCLA.

We took a cab from the airport, as my friend George had instructed. The ride was a misty, dreamlike passage through a banana

and coconut tree corridor, punctuated by occasional blurred spec-
tral shapes on the side of the road, some four-legged, some two. I
amused the driver with my attempts at casual conversation in
Spanish, half-remembered from a small repertoire learned long ago
from a Peruvian lover.

After hurtling for an hour or so through a headlight-lit lush
green tunnel of sorts, we turned off the main highway onto a dusty
cobblestone road. The driver announced we had arrived in Barra.
The town, George had told me, was named for the sand bar (*barra*)
on which it had been built in the 16th century. His decidedly 20th
century house was in a sparsely developed residential area on the
outskirts of town. It was called Casa Amarillo (Yellow House), but
was in fact white and blue. Tiny, boxy, plain, and nearly charmless,
save for a brick-walled back garden dripping with electric purple
bougainvillea in which stood a papaya tree hung with almost obscenely gonadal green and yellow fruit. The garden was to come as
a surprise the next morning, however, for we had arrived during a
power blackout. All George's instructions about "opening" the
house would be of no use until daylight: how to turn on the electricity (throwing a giant switch that made me feel like the warden
at San Quentin) or how to light the zeppelin-shaped propane hot
water heater, a terrifying contraption that is essentially a bomb attached to the outside of the house.

After fumbling with many keys and chains and wrought iron security gates, Jonathan and I managed to get inside the front door.
Searching for candles in a strange, dark house quickly proved fu-
tile, so, hungry, eager to begin our vacation in earnest, and to see
the village that was to be our exotic home for the next three
weeks, we dumped our luggage on the floor and set out into the
moist tropical night in search of a good restaurant. We were
equipped with a crude map George had drawn for us.

Uncertain of what kind of bathroom facilities the village restaurants might offer, Jonathan had decided to do his insulin shot
before we left the house. It had been several months since we'd
discovered he was diabetic, but watching him stick a needle in his

abdomen still made me wince and flush with sorrow, fear, and guilt (his disease a legacy of my family genetics).

He had handled his diagnosis well, after an initial period of "Why me?" and was not letting his insulin dependency stop him from living pretty much as he had before. I applauded his gumption and tried to keep my own maternal terrors and concerns in check. He, in turn, developed a facade of bravado and nonchalance, partly for my benefit, I think, but mostly to quell his own newfound inklings of mortality. Consequently, after those first few nightmare weeks post-diagnosis—when we struggled together with learning to manage the disease itself, as well as with our lack of health insurance and our sadness—we now hardly ever spoke of it. "It's my body, Mom," he'd say, if I inquired when he had eaten last, or asked if he had the requisite emergency candy bar with him when leaving the house.

The short and long term consequences of diabetes are brutal. Childhood memories of my grandfather slipping into a coma at Thanksgiving dinner, or my uncle acting weird and abusive when his blood sugar level was high were hard to erase. I feared falling into my grandmother's role, monitoring every morsel and c.c., always worrying and always on the verge of pushing the panic button. After twenty years of encouraging my son's independence, suddenly I found myself obsessed with his safety, worrying when he went out with friends for a beer, or when he exhausted himself on the basketball court. Food intake, exercise, a head cold—for the diabetic, all these things affect insulin dosage in mysterious and difficult to calculate ways. A mistake can mean organ damage, heart failure, blindness, even death.

Now, many months after finding out he had diabetes, Jonathan was still learning, by perilous trial and error, how to factor these variables into his regimen; I was still learning how to swallow my fears and let him make the mistakes that would teach him what he needed to know in order to survive. This was proving difficult for me, although I had years of training when the stakes were a little lower. Raising Jonathan alone since his father abandoned us when he was three, I had tried hard not to be overly protective, fearful of cultivating what my mother had always called a "Mama's boy."

"Don't tie him to your apron strings," she admonished, filling my child-bride head with fears that, as I matured, seemed unnecessary and misguided: I am all he has in the world for now, I came to reason, he should know that he can count on me to be there no matter what.

By the time Jonathan reached adolescence, I had achieved an uncertain balance of mother love and distance, offering advice and help if asked, but encouraging self-reliance, if not something akin to unbridled freedom. So far, it seemed the tack was working: except for a few weeks in junior high school when he eschewed school for handicapping at the race track (giving it up when his paper route savings and his luck ran out) he had not taken unfair advantage of my rather laissez-faire approach to single parenting. I had always thought he probably learned more at the track than he would have in a classroom, anyway.

Now in his twenties, he was an uncommonly direct and sweet young man, kind to women, children and animals, ambitious, but not driven, with a charming and diverse circle of friends, and a characteristic northern California easy-going approach to life. We were just getting used to a new kind of adult relationship with each other when diabetes entered the picture and created new dependencies and fears for us both, tangled us up in heart strings and apron strings, a scared Mama and her boy once again.

I had hoped our trip would help us untangle this emotional mess, the challenge of travel being an almost surefire catalyst for confrontation, change, and revelation. We are never more nakedly ourselves than when removed from routine and familiar comforts. The road *itself* is an unflinching ally on a journey of any sort, it had always seemed to me.

So there we were below the Tropic of Cancer for the first time, Jonathan and I, navigating around a strange town in total darkness with a cigarette lighter and a map that looked as if it had been drawn by Captain Hook. Clearly, the beach area of the town would be our best bet for finding something open late. Upon examination, George's map seemed useless, so we decided to head toward the smell of water. It was a Friday night and Barra was a weekend resort for city dwellers from Guadalajara, so we thought we'd have no problem finding something open along the waterfront. My Spanish was good enough, I thought, to ask which way to town— *"¿El centro?"* But after walking along a promising looking path for half an hour or so, we hadn't encountered anyone to ask. Once, thinking we heard voices in a field, we plunged off the path into the darkness, only to find a mule grazing on tall grass.

Trying to get our bearings, we stopped to listen for the sound of the surf, which seemed to be coming from all directions. Deciding to continue following our noses instead of our ears, we

or most diabetics, traveling is not difficult. As for all travelers, however, preventive health planning is important. Diabetics should be especially attuned to preventing some of the common travel-related health problems—motion sickness, heat exhaustion, travelers' diarrhea—because these temporary maladies can cause an otherwise well-controlled diabetic to become poorly controlled.

While diet is a fundamental way of controlling diabetes, culinary adventures are often a fundamental part of travel to foreign lands. Brush up on your food exchanges before you leave: bread is bread; meat is meat; and so forth. Use discretion, but don't be afraid to sample the local dishes.

—W. Scott Harkonen, M.D.,
Traveling Well:
A Comprehensive Guide
to Your Health Abroad

wandered on, ebullient, still confident we were nearing *el centro* and not yet realizing we were lost. Houses were sparse in this part of town, separated by overgrown lots. Many were in a state of either being built or torn down, it was hard to tell which, with partially finished or demolished second floors porcupined with rebar and wire. Piles of lumber and debris seemed to be everywhere. Even houses that appeared intact looked uninhabited, most of them sitting dark and quiet. Here and there we'd see the glow of a candle or the sweep of a flashlight beam, but mostly it seemed as if everyone was either out of town or gone fishin'. I later learned that, indeed, most of the houses in this part of town were empty, used in season by Guadalajarans, and that taxes are lower on unfinished dwellings, hence, many houses in Mexico remain "under construction" forever. As it turned out, we had inadvertently headed toward the lagoon, rather than the beach (our noses unable to distinguish the smell of fresh water from salt) and were roaming through the deserted streets of Nuevo Barra, a rather unsuccessful real estate "development," about as far from *el centro* as it could be.

Disoriented, but still unconcerned, we ambled on, chatting, delighting in the vibrant and warm night air. Finally, just as we were beginning to worry about our chosen course, we reached the water. Instead of crashing onto the beach, it was lapping quietly at the shoreline: we had smelled our way to the lagoon.

At this point, Jonathan began to get anxious. "I need to eat soon, Mom. I already did my shot."

"We'll find the village soon," I reassured him. "At least now we've identified one landmark on the map. If this is the lagoon, then the ocean must be over there somewhere," I gestured into the darkness hopefully and off we ambled along a footpath that hugged the water.

We hadn't gone far when an old woman (or more precisely, her gleaming white teeth) materialized before us on the narrow path. We set upon her like the desperate, lost, hungry tourists we were. *"¿Por favor, señora, donde está el centro, restaurante, comida?"*

With a quiet *"Derecho,"* she passed us and was quickly swallowed up by the night. *Derecho,* to the right. Heartened and with new confidence and direction, we headed off the path and into what seemed to be a meadow of some sort.

The unfamiliar terrain in total darkness presented us with a variety of surprises, most of them sudden and some quite frightening—muddy ditches, holes big enough to swallow a cat, tethered goats, the crunch of a mouse-sized dead beetle underfoot, and the craggy, silhouette of a tree that came alive with bats as we passed. Lone birds cried out from invisible perches; now and then a gecko screeched. Our warm evening stroll was taking an ominous turn, it seemed.

I began nervously calculating the effects of the insulin coursing through Jonathan's bloodstream in search of calories. He was beginning to exhibit some of the early signs of insulin shock—giddiness, irrationality, aggressiveness. He did not have his emergency candy bar with him, he explained testily, because he was afraid it would melt in his pocket. Oh-oh. For every traveler, the uncertainty of where one's next meal is coming from is a challenge and at times an inconvenience, but for the diabetic traveler (particularly in out-of-the-way areas), it can be life-threatening.

Just as the maternal alarm bells were going off in my head, I spied a welcome green glow in the distance. Someone out there had power on and I intended to use my limited Spanish to beg for food, if it turned out to be a private house. We hurried toward the light. "It must be the town, Jonathan. Look!" His response, or lack of it, sent me into near panic.

As we got closer, I realized that there would be no food for us at the source of this particular green glow. We stood at the edge of an enormous field, lit by thousands of fireflies, flickering on and off, creating a canopy of luminescent mist that hovered over a seemingly endless expanse of dew-covered grass. The effect was almost ET-like—otherworldly, comforting, magical. My panic was momentarily suspended as we watched in silence. "I wonder what you call them in Spanish," I thought to myself.

"Luciernagas," someone answered.

A sweet-faced young girl was standing at my elbow, smiling up at me.

"Luciernagas...fireflies," she repeated.

English! "Please, which way is town, *muchacha,*" I began and within minutes we were on our way *derecho,* straight ahead, not *derecha,* to the right, a linguistic distinction I will never again fail to apprehend.

Soon we reached the back streets of Barra, dusty cobblestone lanes dotted with jumbled gardens in which sat small, crumbling adobe and cinder block houses, all the more welcoming in their candlelit coziness. Voices, guitar strains, and laughter wafted out to greet us as we passed, headed for a blue and white-tiled arched entrance near the end of the block, Los Arcos. We could have found no finer haven in all of Barra, if not all of Mexico. The restaurant was, in fact, closed when we found our way to its doorstep, but Mario and Cuca, the owners, took us in without hesitation. *"¡Bienvenidos a Barra de Navidad!"* they both chimed. It was as if we had been expected.

Mario and Cuca spoke no English, but quickly understood the immediacy of Jonathan's need for food, as well as my anxiety. They set about comforting us. Jonathan was given tortillas, cheese, and salsa right away and quickly regained his equilibrium. Mario seated us at one of the four turquoise tables covered with red oilcloth inside the tiny whitewashed room and suggested we try the dorado (a local mahi mahi-like fish) and the chicken *mole*. Cuca set to work by candlelight behind the white tiled counter, smiling over at us from time to time reassuringly. As I began to relax, I noticed the cheery, whimsical decorations on the walls: a 3-D painted plaster turbaned head with a panther, a bumper sticker in Spanish suggesting that I "Visualize World Peace," a painting of snow-capped mountains, a Christmas wreath. Hanging down from the center of the big archway and from various spots overhead were small plastic bags filled with water, which Mario explained were to keep insects away. When I raised an eyebrow to this Mario pointed out that, although the restaurant was open to the street, there were no insects, a fact that may have had more to do with the stealthy geckos I spotted once or twice on the wall than with the plastic bags, but who am I—a city *gringa*—to judge?

The street in front of Los Arcos, viewed through the big arch that took up the entire front of the building, seemed like a stage or a movie screen: one's attention was demanded somehow, even though at this hour (or at any hour we later found) not much happened. Every now and then a skinny dog might slink by, or you might see a man pushing a wheelbarrow, or a pair of lovers, perhaps, snuggled together on their way home.

In no time at all, Mario brought our food. He presented it to us with much formality and pride, while Cuca beamed from behind her counter. We attacked our plates as if it had been days, rather than hours, since our last meal. At the time, I thought that perhaps Cuca's food tasted almost preternaturally delicious because of the desperate quest that preceded it. Having eaten her food for years now, I know that it always tastes that good: in our serendipitous wandering about that first night in Mexico, Jonathan and I had stumbled into the kitchen of the acknowledged best cook in Barra de Navidad. And like all good cooks, she liked to watch people enjoy her food. She and Mario glanced at each other knowingly as Jonathan and I swooned over every mouthful. The *mole* had over thirty ingredients in it and I could swear that I was tasting every one of them. To soothe taste buds sent almost 'round the bend, she brought me a flan for dessert and, thoughtfully, a fresh fruit compote of mango, papaya, coconut, and bananas for Jonathan.

It seems to me that our three basic needs, for food and security and love, are so mixed and mingled and entwined that we cannot straightly think of one without the others. So it happens that when I write of hunger, I am really writing about love and the hunger for it, and warmth and the love of it and the hunger for it…and then the warmth and richness and fine reality of hunger satisfied…and it is all one.

I tell about myself, and how I ate bread on a lasting hillside, or drank red wine in a room now blown to bits, and it happens without my willing it that I am telling too about the people with me then, and their other deeper needs for love and happiness.

There is food in the bowl, and more often than not, because of what honesty I have, there is nourishment in the heart, to feed the wilder, more insistent hungers. We must eat. If, in the face of that dread fact, we can find other nourishment, and tolerance and compassion for it, we'll be no less full of human dignity.

—M. F. K. Fisher,
The Gastronomical Me

We ended up all sitting together like family, jabbering away. I understood about a third of what I was hearing, and tried to translate for Jonathan, who had struck up a friendship with Monica, Mario's mischievous parrot who nibbled at our toes under the table. With patience and determination, over the course of the evening, the four of us managed to tell each other our life stories. Mario and Cuca had raised eleven children in Mexico City and decided to "retire" to Barra, where they now worked twelve hours a day, seven days a week running Los Arcos. They loved their new lives (and clearly, each other), went swimming every day, and saw their children and multitudes of grandchildren regularly.

As we sat talking after dinner, the electricity came back on, causing a cacophony of rooster crowing throughout the village, as if to herald its return. It seemed a good time to try to make our way back to our house, so Jonathan and I said warm and mushy goodbyes to Mario and Cuca, our new friends who felt so much like old friends.

We made it home without incident and collapsed into a pair of hammocks strung up in the living room. Jonathan fell asleep almost instantly. I stayed awake for a while, listening to the distant surf and a remarkable cricket chorus, which sounded for all the world like an orchestra of 101 *maracas* playing Latin favorites. There would be too few nights in my life, I knew, that I would fall asleep with the soothing sound of waves as my lullaby, precious fewer still ahead when my son's steady breathing nearby let me know he was safe.

How perverse, I thought, that—as I prepared to send him out into the world alone, to "cut the apron strings," so to speak—I should feel such an intense closeness, akin to what I felt when he was in the cradle. Awash with emotion, Cuca's flan resting happily in my belly, Jonathan's sweet snore singing in my ear, I soon fell asleep and added my contented breath to the tropical nighttime symphony.

Pamela Michael is a freelance writer, radio producer, and education consultant. She is the editor of The Gift of Rivers, *co-editor of* A Mother's World *and* A Woman's Passion for Travel, *as well as the author of* The Whole World is Watching. *Currently, she is the director of* The River of Words *Project, which she co-founded with U.S. Poet Laureate Robert Hass. She lives in Berkeley, California.*

⋆

Friday I tasted life. It was a vast portion.

—Emily Dickinson

CUCA'S FLAN QUESO PHILADELPHIA

5 eggs	2 t. vanilla
8 oz. cream cheese	6 T. sugar
6 oz. evaporated milk	4 cinnamon sticks

The Custard: Put eggs, cheese, vanilla, 2 tablespoons of sugar, evaporated milk and an equal amount of water in a blender. Blend until smooth.

The Caramel: Put 4 tablespoons of sugar and the cinnamon sticks in the top part of a double boiler. For this step, however, don't cook over boiling water, but directly over a very low flame. Stir constantly with a wooden spoon until the sugar melts and turns into a syrup the color of cinnamon. Remove syrup from the burner, take out the cinnamon sticks and discard. Then dip the bottom of pan in a bowl of cold water to harden the syrup.

Pour the blended custard mixture on top of the hardened syrup. Cook, covered, over boiling water for about 1 hour or until a knife inserted in the center comes out clean. You will probably have to add water to the bottom of the double boiler occasionally. Be careful not to jiggle the top pan too much during this procedure; you don't want the (now liquid) caramel and the custard to mix.

Note: Both cream cheese and evaporated milk come in low fat versions. I'm sure Cuca wouldn't mind the substitution.

Feast of the Pig

The perfect host puts his guest at ease.

CHOU EN-LAI WAS AMUSED BY MY PREOCCUPATION WITH THE folklore of Chinese warlord politics; and he enjoyed himself, sometimes for hours, by his tale-telling and his instruction of this novice. Chou had much time then, for the six- or seven-man staff of the Chinese Communist headquarters in Chungking was a lonesome group; and the visit of a malleable young American reporter gave them an opportunity, as they saw it, of influencing *Time* magazine.

However it was, after a year of growing friendship, Chou invited me to a banquet in my honor. His headquarters had, presumably, a budget for reaching American opinion; and they would use *Time's* correspondent as a pretext to eat a meal grander than the noodles, rice, vegetables, occasional chunky meat stews they normally ate at their own mess. So we went to the finest restaurant in Chungking, the Kuan Sun Yuan, to dine—Chou, the Communist headquarters staff and myself, the only Westerner.

The reader must remember now how far I had come from home. I had learned to drink. I had had my first experience in bed with a woman and that was behind me. I knew I had been for months eating nonkosher food, but always tried to delude myself that the meats I ate were lamb, beef or chicken. This habit was my last link to family practice. I was still so pinned to Jewish tradition that to eat pig outright seemed a profanation. Chou En-lai's banquet, however, was extraordinary—first the Chinese hors d'oeuvres, both hot and cold; then the bamboo shoots and chicken; then the duck livers. And then the main course—unmistakably pig, a golden-brown, crackle-skinned roast suckling pig.

"*Ch'ing, ch'ing,*" said Chou En-lai, the host—"Please, please," gesturing with his chopsticks at the pig, inviting the guest to break the crackle first. I flinched, not knowing what to do, but for a moment I held on to my past.

You shall not eat any abominable thing…and the swine is unclean for you. Their flesh you shall not touch.

—*Deuteronomy 14:3*

I put my chopsticks down and explained as best I could in Chinese that I was Jewish and that Jews were not allowed to eat any kind of pig meat. The group, all friends of mine by then, sat downcast and silent, for I was their guest, and they had done wrong.

Then Chou himself took over. He lifted his chopsticks once more, repeated, "*ch'ing, ch'ing,*" pointed the chopsticks at the suckling pig and, grinning, explained: "Teddy," he said (as I recall it now, for I made no notes that evening), "this is China. Look again. See. Look. It looks to you like pig. But in China, this is not a pig—this is a duck." I burst out laughing, for I could not help it; he laughed, the table laughed, I plunged my chopsticks in, broke the crackle, ate my first mouthful of certified pig, and have eaten of pig ever since, for which I hope my ancestors will forgive me.

But Chou was that kind of man—he could make one believe that pig was duck, because one wanted to believe him, and because he understood the customs of other men and societies and respected them.

The late Theodore H. White was born and raised in Boston and graduated from Harvard with a degree in history in 1938. He worked most of his life as a journalist, and wrote the seminal works, The Making of the President.

★

If you accept a dinner invitation, you have a moral obligation to be amusing.

—Duchess of Windsor

A Language for Food

Eat your words.

HUBERT, LIKE ALL FRENCHMEN, TAKES FOOD VERY SERIOUSLY AND likes it fresh, so I go shopping every day on the rue Rambuteau, in the shadow of the Centre Georges Pompidou. This street runs through the no-man's-land between Les Halles (a faceless, modern shopping district, much of it below ground) and the upscale area of the Marais, the heart of aristocratic Paris in the seventeenth century and now the closest thing to a gay ghetto to be found in France. Despite the chic museum landmark, Rambuteau couldn't be more typically French (France, don't forget, is a country where the people spend a quarter of their income on food). There is a small supermarket, but since I'm always with Fred, my dog, and he's not welcome, I avoid it. All the other stores either open onto the street or are actually in it, like the little old flower man with his cart.

First Fred and I go to the fish man, who drives me mad because he insists on speaking English. Not that he knows anything *useful* in English, such as the names of fish or pounds instead of kilos. In a weak moment he once confessed to me that he hates the English (that was after he found out I was American), but then when the trade talks were going badly with the Americans and

17

irate French fishermen were throwing their catch back in the
ocean just to spite everyone, he announced he hated Americans,
too, and was boycotting EuroDisney. He preferred to take his kids
to something educational, such as that theme park outside Paris
devoted entirely to scale models of important French châteaux.
Not my idea of a fun family outing, but the French can't enjoy
themselves if they don't think they're learning something. Ever notice how they crowd in front of the long, written explanations at
the beginning of a museum show and whiz past the paintings
themselves?

But he does have nice fish, and in the best French didactic
manner he'll even write out recipes for me if I ask him. There he
reverts to his native language and uses lovely expressions such as "a
tear of wine" (*une larme de vin*), "a suspicion of ginger" (*un soupçon
de gingembre*), "a cloud of milk" (*un nuage de lait*) or "a nut of butter" (*une noix de beurre*). The best recipe he gave me was for mussels: "Brown two chopped onions and a piece of garlic in a thread
of butter, then when they're transparent add two cups of dry white
wine and a cup of water, salt and pepper, and a bay leaf. Let them
bubble nicely while you clean a quart of mussels for each person.
With your fingers pull off the beard (it rips off easily if you're
pulling in the right direction). Throw away the mussels that are
open when uncooked. Now put the good mussels in a casserole,
cover with a lid, after five minutes shake them well to change their
position and in five more minutes lift them out with a slotted
spoon onto a waiting dish with a cover and pour the juice through
a strainer lined with cheesecloth to remove the remaining grains
of sand. Serve with a baguette for a hearty first course."

All in all Fred prefers the butcher, who is fat and red-faced,
with an attractive scar that runs from chin to temple, and wears a
dubiously bloody apron. He always remembers to give Fred a big
bone. Fred gazes at him admiringly as he cuts the fat off steak,
chops off a chicken's head, digs out the giblets, sews up the cavity
and passes the trussed bird under the blowtorch to remove the last
feathers. The word for "torch" is the most beautiful in French,
chalumeau, a close rival to Edgar Allan Poe's proposal for the most

beautiful sound in English, *cellar door.*

The fruit and vegetable man is young and handsome and an incorrigible skirt-chaser. If an attractive woman comes to his stall he tells his downtrodden assistant, "I'll take this one." Of course it would be sacrilege to palpate or even touch any of his produce; he's always shouting at Americans who can't read the warning sign—naturally, since it's written in French. His prices and stormy temperament are worth it, however, given that he can tell by smell alone the exact degree of ripeness for a melon, never sells rotting raspberries or fungusy blueberries, has eight kinds of lettuce, crisp tarragon, heavily perfumed basil, the subtlest chervil and even courgette flowers for deep-frying.

The cheese store smells either intriguing or repulsive, depending on your mood or health. There are so many cheeses—little "turds" (*crottins*) of goat cheese, runny Brie made from yummy unpasteurized milk, nightmarish rotting pyramids wrapped in leaves that remind you of nothing so much as vomit, even divinely bland cottage cheese made specially for the local Americans. I'm always reminded of de Gaulle's remark that it's impossible to rule a country that makes 250 kinds of cheese.

The Italian shop (the Casa di Pasta), the bakery with its irritating dog which always mounts a chagrined Fred, the wine store—

The linguistic philosophers of France, especially the late Roland Barthes, understood how French cuisine and French culture are related, and how both fit with structuralist philosophy. A Parisian dinner is meant to be a single elegant statement, like a well-turned sentence or an outfit from Yves Saint-Laurent. The Anglo-Saxon view of a banquet can be expressed in terms of the history of the world. You begin with soup—water with things swimming in it—then move to the aqueous kingdom, then to flying creatures, then to mammals. Finally you celebrate man in cheeses and desserts, both products of sophisticated culture. This is the diachronic view, which the French reject. They prefer to see the various courses as syntagms, or sentence components—soup adjective, fish noun, chicken adverb.

—Anthony Burgess, *But Do Blondes Prefer Gentlemen? Homage to Qwert Yuiop and Other Writings* at last we're heading home. Since I invariably forget my carryall, my hands are turning red, cut and strangled by dozens of little blue plastic bags biting into them, and Fred is now fully awake, excited by the smell of the upcoming bone, and pulling feverishly every which way.

And to think my publisher wonders how I spend my days.

Edmund White has taught literature and creative writing at Yale, Johns Hopkins, New York University, and Columbia, and served as executive director of the New York Institute for the Humanities. In 1993 he was made a Chevalier de l'Ordre des Arts et Lettres. For his book Genet: A Biography *(1994), he was awarded the National Book Critics Circle Award and the Lambda Literary Award. His other books include* The Married Man, Nocturnes for the King of Naples, The Flaneur: A Stroll Through the Paradoxes of Paris, A Boy's Own Story, *and* Our Paris: Sketches from Memory *from which this story was excerpted. He lives in Paris.*

✳

Onions are a noble vegetable in France, figuring as importantly in the French language as in the cuisine (the French produce some 145,000 tons each year, most of them cultivated in Provence, and import more than 1.5 million tons, largely from Italy, the Netherlands, and England). Like the bite of their fumes, their use tends to be insulting.

If someone gets a bit nosy, you tell them to "*occupe-toi de tes oignons,*" or "mind your own business." Someone who dresses in multiple layers of clothing is said to be "*vetu comme un oignon,*" while those who wait in line, whether to get into the theater or to kiss the bride at a wedding, are said to be "*en rang d'oignon.*"

If someone creates a scene in France, it is called "*un spectacle aux petits oignons.*" On the kinder side, if you make something with particular care, you will be complimented for making it "*aux petits oignons.*"

—Patricia Wells, The Food Lover's Guide to France

A Tibetan Picnic

As the belly fills, so fills the heart.

THE LAND CRUISER LABORS ITS WAY ACROSS THE COUNTRYSIDE, followed by the baby blue supply truck. We are in the remote stretches of Tibet to do field work, and it is two 16,000-foot passes since breakfast. Time is of little consequence in this immensity, and the decision to eat will be made by place, not by the clock. Open pasture stretches out on either side of the dirt road that passes for Tibet's major highway out here, and in the distance a girl is collecting yak dung in a basket to bring back to her village for fuel. Suddenly the Land Cruiser veers off the road and bumps across the sparse grass towards the river we have been following for hours, the blue truck lurching behind like a drunken dinosaur. We have arrived.

Dawa is out of the truck in moments, and climbs up the side bars to unlash the canvas top. He is a giant of a man, with a heart as huge as the sky and a wacky, Jackie Gleason sense of humor that can shake the road weariness out of us in moments. He reaches into the hold of the truck and drops three lumpy burlap sacks and the wooden tea churn to waiting arms below. Small fireplaces sprout across the grass like mushrooms, built of round stones packed with clay from the nearby river, and you realize why this spot was chosen above all the other promising sites you had passed, although how they could tell this or remember the distinguishing characteristics that mark this particular bend in the road remain a mystery, to be stored with many others that have filled your head since entering this beautiful enigma of a place. Phurbu the cook bends over the sticks and dried grasses he has gathered in one of the fireplaces, coaxing flames into life, and within moments the blackened tea kettle is set on the fire. Life does not continue without tea.

We are in a campsite used by countless people before us; nomads following their flocks down from summer pasture, traders walking their goods to the town that lies two days journey to the east, families making the long pilgrimage to Lhasa to honor the deities that protect their country. The sacks are untied; from one comes a full leg of a sheep. Refrigeration is both unavailable and redundant here; the dry air and the cold of the high plateau take care of it for you. From another sack a plump pillow of roasted barley flour and a large wooden bowl are pulled out, from the third a small rosewood bowl, its top tied with a leather lace. These are the ingredients for a Tibetan picnic.

We sit on the sun-warmed grass, sweaters around our shoulders against the promise of winter that haunts the wind. Shamba returns from the riverbank, his face and hands bright red from their scrubbing in the frigid water. He holds the tiny branch of a bare bush, which he sets down gently beside the teapot without saying a word, then joins our circle on the grass. Phurbu is kneading the barley with the first of the tea, working the flour around the edges of the bowl to make a dough. As each handful comes to the right consistency, he squeezes it in his fist and passes it to one of us, a tube of roasted grain imprinted with the mark of his sure hand. Dawa is at work on the leg of the sheep; he draws the dagger-like knife which every Tibetan man and most Tibetan women keep hanging from their waists for just such occasions. Everyone else pulls their daggers out as well; Dawa's is simply a big flattened steel bar, ground to an edge with a massive handle fitted on the end. We will make do with our Swiss Army knives, which look fragile as matchsticks in the company of all this serious metal. Dawa slices off chunks of mutton, throwing most of them onto the grass in the center of the circle; the irresistible chunks he pops directly into his mouth. When he has cut a good-sized heap he sets the leg down beside him. The rosewood bowl has been opened to reveal ground red pepper, which we tip into the lid as a serving bowl. There isn't a fork in sight, nor a plate or napkin for that matter. However, it is time to eat.

We fall onto the food as if it is the first we have seen in days, or the last we will see for days to come—and in truth you never know up here. Between bites of *tsampa*—the roasted barley flour dough, we reach into the pile of meat, dipping our pieces into the red pepper either on just one side or two, depending on how hot you like it. As the meat pile diminishes, the leg of mutton is passed around and we take turns cutting off more and throwing it into the pile, usually while we are both chewing and talking. Manners do count out here, but they are a different set of manners, and you get to break every rule that was drummed into you as a child. (This may be the real reason that people fall in love with Tibet.)

Meanwhile, Phurbu has poured the black tea into the wooden churn, and hooks his leg around it as a brace. He adds a knife-blade full of yak butter and a small handful of salt, then with the gesture that is rhythmic and graceful and practiced a thousand times over, he churns the *sö cha,* or butter tea, regular as a metronome. The tea is poured, thick as cream and the color of caramel, back into the black kettle, its smoky flavor interwoven with the scent of melted yak butter. Phurbu reaches over to the twig that Shamba had brought back from the river and fits it into the spout, a perfect strainer. Our cups are ready, always ready for tea: there are silver-lined traditional wooden tea bowls alongside plastic thermal mugs, and the kettle is lifted time and again—no cup gets drunk to the bottom before being refilled, and the brothy mixture is warming from deep within. Here it is quite proper, expected even, that you will make a lot of noise when you eat. In fact, if you have no appetite but don't want to offend your hosts you can get by with a lot of smacking of your lips and swallowing sounds; they don't no-

It was comfort in those succeeding days to sit up and contemplate the majestic panorama of mountains and valleys spread out below us and eat ham and hard-boiled eggs while our spiritual natures reveled alternately in rainbows, thunderstorms, and peerless sunsets. Nothing helps scenery like ham and eggs. Ham and eggs, and after these a pipe—an old, rank, delicious pipe—ham and eggs and scenery, a "downgrade," a flying coach, a fragrant pipe and a contented heart—these make happiness. It is what all the ages have struggled for.

—Mark Twain, *Roughing It*

tice as long as you keep drinking your tea.

And so we sit, nine human beings in a circle, encircled by a wall of mountains that swallow up our laughter and tiny voices. We tell jokes and stories while we eat, tossing any unwanted bits over our shoulders until we are surrounded by a necklace of gristle and bone. Amidst the talk and jokes there is a sudden sharp crack. Dawa raises his dagger arm again and slices across the bone, taking the whole top off this time. For all their congeniality, Tibetan picnics can have a decidedly Neanderthal flavor to them. With the point of his ten-inch blade Dawa reaches into the bone for the marrow, eating it straight off the knife tip, the yellow sash swinging like a jaunty exclamation point from the handle. We wait our turn, knives ready.

Suddenly, without a spoken signal, the picnic ends. Burlap sacks are cinched closed and tossed back into the belly of the truck. Jackets are folded to once again provide seat cushions against the rutted road. The last of the tea is swung in an arc across the grass; the twig strainer is carefully removed from the spout and left by the fireplace for the next set of pilgrims. We pile into the vehicles and set off in silence, the spell of our meal together still hovering over that tiny spot in the immense Tibetan land.

Barbara Banks has been traveling since age five, when she ran away from home because her brother ate all of the ice cream. She has built wooden boats in France, driven a freight train across Turkey, and sailed across the North Sea. More conventional work has been as a documentary filmmaker and writer for an adventure travel company. She lives in Berkeley, California.

Before setting off on an overland trip from Lhasa to Mt. Everest, we were treated to a yak feast in the Holiday Inn, to be prepared, we were told, by a man who had been the Dalai Lama's chef many years ago. Thus we arrived to banquet full of anticipation, and the awareness that we wouldn't be eating well on the road in the days ahead (and indeed would soon enjoy a meal cooked with a blowtorch). In addition we were hungry from a day of hiking in the hills around Lhasa.

The first courses were promising—yak broth, morsels of meat washed down with tea—but we soon came to the grim realization that every course was going to be yak, that we were going to eat *nothing but* yak from snout to tail and everything in-between, and that we would be doing so for hours. The timid diners among us paced ourselves, taking modest portions, but others less temperate wolfed down enormous portions of black meat and swilled great draughts of every beverage offered. One woman in the group raved about each dish as though it were Manna, causing a peevish guest to comment, "Put a bowl of shit in front of her and she'd say the same."

After the feast wound mercifully to a close, a crispy old man was brought out from the kitchen and introduced with pride by our host, to which an ungrateful diner muttered *sotto voce,* "String him up!"

The meek among us were healthy the following morning, but the immoderate suffered intestinal discomfort for the next couple of days, as their bodies faced the challenge of digesting a large mammal.

—James O'Reilly and Larry Habegger, "A Banquet in Lhasa"

DICK BEESON

✶ ✶ ✶

A Man and His Chile

He really knows his beans.

IN THE DECADES OF THE 1950S AND '60S IN ALBUQUERQUE, NEW Mexico, there existed a culinary phenomenon that I have come to believe is unique in the cultural history of the Southwest. It was a small café located in the 1200 block of Rio Grande Boulevard NW called Videz. Its owner and sole cook was Pete Benavidez, hence the name. During this time a wide variety of Albuquerque residents would make their obligatory weekly visit to this small café to partake of what can only be called a special excellence in Southwestern cuisine.

In fact, for dozens of its clientele, these visits were more on the order of a cult experience. I have a friend who is an airline pilot who told me in all seriousness that once, as a private passenger, he made a flight from Washington, D.C. to Albuquerque just to have a "bowl of red" at Videz. I believe him.

In 30 years of traveling the American-Mexican border and the Rio Grande Valley searching out small Mexican family cookeries, I came to believe that Videz was, for its kind, simply the best in the world. Other than the food, however, there was little about the café Videz that was imposing. The building was a small white stucco type that could have been a neighborhood barbershop in earlier days. The floor was covered with linoleum. There were perhaps eight four-place tables with varying colors of pastel oilcloth, each adorned with a salt shaker and a metal dispenser of small paper napkins. Water came in vertically-ribbed plastic glasses undoubtedly purchased in a 1950s variety store. Wall decor was a single framed Mexican beer advertisement showing a plate of food and the words, *"Muy Sabrosa."* Plain stuff indeed.

The café could have been the dining room of any of the hundreds of houses surrounding Videz, squeezed in as it was between the ancient barrios of Barelas and Los Duranes from which it drew its ethnic inspiration. The food was family fare. Here one didn't find the uptown gloss of stuffed *sopapillas* nor the watery *menudo* of the steamy-windowed all night café. The food at Videz was found on the tables of the community. Not all of it, of course. Mexican-American family cooking is enormously varied and includes not only those items often poorly copied in popular Mexican restaurants but also *caldos* (broths), *cocidos* and *quisados* (stews), *sopas de seca* (dry soups) of every description, *carnes* (meats) of beef, pork, lamb, and kid, and *legumbres* (vegetables) of many types. Almost all of these dishes used chile of one type or another. The mainstays of Rio Grande cooking, as it was at Videz, are beans, corn, and chile. Videz was famous for its bowl of red, its beans, its tacos, and its red and green chile enchiladas.

In the back of the café was a walled partition with an open door and restaurant window where one could watch the ample-bodied Pete Benavidez glide in slow motion between his pots. Pete, for whom a starched white shirt and a girdling white apron were *de rigueur*, never did anything in haste. This quality seemed almost an extension of his philosophy of food: keep it simple but do that which is simple right; and right usually entailed infinite care. In my early days of cooking I had the puerile tendency to want to add every spice on the shelf. "No," said Pete. "The object is to enhance the natural flavor of the food, not mask it." This and many other lessons I gathered over the years in ten-minute conversations after

I had finished my meal. Mostly I listened. Pete was the expert. Pete would talk to God and if I behaved myself, I was sometimes permitted to eavesdrop.

Wish I had time for just one more bowl of chili.
—Kit Carson's last words

Pete Benavidez was passionate about his food. Pete knew that one of the most important things about food was its quality, and that often depended upon where and how something was grown. He also impressed upon me that in the actual preparation, little things done at the proper time could make a big difference in the finished product. "Red chile," Pete insisted, "should be cooked for a long time." How long? Pete did not deal in quantities of anything and if you insisted, he let you know you belonged on the other side of the counter. Pete said that the best red chile came from the area around Chimayó in the northern part of the state. That is what he used at home but not at the restaurant. This chile tended to be somewhat hotter than the typical Number 6-4 medium and would not be suitable for some of his customers.

Pete's red chile came from the North Valley in Albuquerque; it was, in fact, the same chile he used in its green form, only sun dried on the plant. And the green chile? "Well," he shrugged his shoulders, "it doesn't make that much difference. It is important with the red," he explained. "Red chile is a concentrated flavor and different plant characteristics are very evident." Over time—decades and even centuries—red chile varied from one Northern New Mexico valley to the other. Native farmers would select certain qualities in their chile that appealed to them and this selection process can be tasted to this very day in land races such as Chimayó and Velarde. I have often bragged to others that you can taste the high altitude and the sunshine in northern New Mexico red chile. That is probably utter nonsense, but this chile does have unique qualities. It is this taste depth that will be missing if red chile is simply purchased off the supermarket shelf in most places in the country; it's worth doing but it will not have the bouquet found in reds from the northern valleys.

Nothing so much furrowed Pete's brow than when the topic of beans came up. He had apparently isolated a considerable number of variables that affected the cooking of pinto beans. It made a difference whether the beans were cooked indoors or out, on a woodstove or modern appliance, and yes, the water made a difference too. Most of all, good beans depended on the quality of the beans. For Pete, the only bean to use was a dry land New Mexico or Colorado pinto bean of the current year. These beans he called "new beans" and his own came in 100-pound burlap sacks from Dove Creek, Colorado. The "new" new beans, two or three months after harvest only, were the best and are noticeably distinctive in both flavor and consistency. They are light in color with considerable differentiation between light and dark spots and cook quickly into a grayish-pink soupy texture. A "plain ole new bean" is a batch from the current year. Nothing else was worth cooking. Pintos whose light spots had darkened because they had remained on a supermarket shelf for two or three years were good only for making paperweights.

Pete knew that many of these variables could not be controlled by the average person so his instructions to other people were amazingly simple: take several cups of new new or just new beans and spread them out on a table and pick out the small rocks (no longer necessary). "Never soak beans in water before they are cooked," he insisted, "it dilutes the flavor." Wash the beans well, put them in a pot, fill with three or four times their volume of water, cover, and cook slowly until done. After they have expanded, the cooking liquid should never be higher than the very top of the beans. Too much water weakens the flavor and will not produce the proper texture in the finished bean. Add small amounts of hot water as the cooking proceeds. The beans are done when they are soft, with most of them retaining their individual shape but all of them held together in a thickened soupy texture. Salt is never to be added until the very last when a final rough ten-second stirring produces the soupiness. Pete Benavidez could analyze every food item on his menu, and dozens more besides, with this exact grasp of principle and detail.

✳

The last time I saw Pete was in 1971 while walking out of the café at his new location far out on north Fourth Street. In the late '60s, construction of the east-west freeway passed exactly over the roof of the old Videz. It occurred to me that there was a small irony here—the best little restaurant I had ever found, whose roots went back hundreds of years, being taken out by a modern slab of concrete whose function was to move people at 65 miles an hour. The two sets of values, the café and the freeway, were exactly opposed. The one, the timeless pursuit of a rational ideal and its excellence. The other, dedicated to expediency, often without the guidance of any notion of excellence whatsoever.

As I left, I saw Pete sitting on the stoop of an adjoining house, apron drooping between his legs, eyes staring at the ground. If this suggested a hint of dejection, Pete soon confirmed it. The restaurant was soon to close, he told me. Yes, it made a living but it was not like the old days before the freeway. Many people did not want to drive five or six miles to the new location. The clientele had changed too. "Some of these people," Pete muttered, "want saltine crackers with their chile." Pete Benavidez had moved too far away from the mother lode of his creativity.

Dick Beeson is professor emeritus of sociology at the University of Idaho and a writer of stories on such varied topics as hydroponic gardening, bicycling, outdoor sports, and food. He is currently touring the country with his wife, Claire, on their tandem bicycle "Big Blue," pulling a bicycle trailer called "Bob." He lives in Moscow, Idaho.

✳

The kitchen was a beehive of activity. A wood fire blazed under a large pizza-sized metal disc balanced on three stones. The mother ground the corn in a hand-grinder giving the dough to Olympia, the oldest daughter, to grind on the *metate*. Then Elsa, her younger sister, took a pinch of dough and patted it expertly into round tortillas. As she pinched, patted, and shaped, I thought of the Mayan belief that man was made by the corn god, Chakh, using yellow and white maize. After the tortilla was properly thin and round, Elsa dropped it onto the metal disc. One or the other of the girls flipped it over at just the right moment. They were sorcerers working in unison. As each tortilla was cooked just right—golden with a few black flecks—Elsa would sail it into the cloth-lined basket. It was an extravagant gesture for such a shy girl. But the second and third tortilla were delivered with the same regal thrust. And then I realized that it was just the way the tortilla, the end product of all the families' effort, had been honored for centuries. The tortilla couldn't have been tossed with greater care had it been a disc of pure gold, for it represented the labor of not only the father in the planting, the children caring for the corn, the mother treating it and passing on the skills to her daughters, and the community as well. A tortilla was not to be taken casually. It was to be celebrated. It was the ultimate gift of the gods.

—Dorothy Aksamit, "Dinner on the Rio Dulce"

PETE'S RED CHILE

6 dried red New Mexican chiles, stems and seeds removed, or a
   blender container packed loosely with the dried chiles
1 clove garlic
1 teaspoon ground Mexican oregano
1/2 pound pork, either cubed from a roast or chops, or even bones
   with meat
1 to 1 1/2 pounds very lean ground beef

Cover the chiles with very hot water and soak for 20 to 30 minutes or until limp and partially rehydrated. Place the chiles back in the blender (they should loosely fill 3/4 of the container, if more, make two small batches). Fill the container to near the top with water. Drop in the clove of garlic and sprinkle the top with the oregano. Add a little salt at this stage if you wish. Blend for 2 to 3 minutes on high or until a homogeneous or orangish-red mixture is obtained.

Pour the mixture into a saucepan and add the pork. Cook, covered, over a very low heat, or uncovered at a slight bubble, for 2 to 3 hours. If cooked uncovered, periodically add water back to the original level to maintain the proper consistency, which I can only describe as medium soupy.

Remove the pork pieces and save for another meal such as *carne adovada*. Place the chile sauce in the refrigerator and cool. Remove any fat that congeals on the top.

Season the beef with a little salt and pepper and sauté until the meat is no longer pink. Combine the sauce and beef and simmer, covered, for an additional 30 to 45 minutes.

The question of consistency in the preparation of red chile and its de-rived sauces is crucial. The final product should be the consistency of a medium thick soup but thick enough to retain form and flavor. If the sauce is too thin, the meat flavor is weakened; if too thick, the raw chile flavor dominates. It is better if the sauce is on the thin side; it can always be thickened with flour and water paste and cooked for an additional 10 minutes.

Serves: 4 to 6

Heat Scale: Medium

Breakfast Without Toast

There's more than one way to start the day.

BREAKFAST IS A FUNNY THING. SOME PEOPLE SKIP IT ALL TOGETHER, and they should not be trusted. Others inhale a bowl of cereal while standing at the kitchen counter. I knew a man like that once, in fact lived with him, but we couldn't breakfast together.

I am ritualistic about early mornings, almost never stepping outside what is for me the prescribed, correct way of doing things. Correct means thin, properly toasted bread cut from a fresh loaf, with grapefruit juice, still pulpy, on ice. Coffee isn't important. In the city where I live there are very good European-style bakeries that understand the fine art of toast, and both are used to me showing up at the back door for my morning feed, while the world sleeps around us.

It takes a special breed of cat to serve my toast and juice; fools are not tolerated well at any time of the day, and certainly not before breakfast. After the meal, I am like a happy dog and will lick your hand in gratitude, but don't cross me before I've eaten. I have cast a witch's eye on servers who chat with me while my toast is cooling, and am happiest with just a cordial greeting. Leave me alone with my breakfast and *The New York Times*, and ask about the weather later.

The only place in the world I abandon this ritual, even gladly, is in Thailand, a country so deep with mysteries and seeming incongruities that it seems rather logical my toast isn't a part of it. In Thailand I eat rice gruel loaded with tiny, dried shrimp every morning, much like the Chinese consume their *congee*. Sometimes a raw egg is broken into it, and poaches as the hot rice holds it beneath the surface.

Once I stayed with a Thai family who own the Volvo truck dealership in Nakhom Pathom, and slept among them on the floor of a room overlooking their showroom of mechanical wonders. Before going to sleep my first night there, the woman of the house, who knew no English, pulled the slatted window to the backyard shut, blocking my view of the coconut trees in moonlight, and carefully said to me, "Moss Kweetos."

That woman garnished her rice soup with sautéed broccoli, a few pieces of warmed meat, bits of pork, and rice sausage with lemongrass, and occasionally big plump river shrimp. She was wealthy and kind. I ate well and constantly while I was with her family, but it is the soup that I remember. We inhaled great quantities of it at a magnificent table—between two Volvo trucks—set with elaborate placemats and carved chairs.

Here at home, I occasionally go to a breakfast place that has existed for 35 years. The Greek owner hugs and pats me, and sends me off to work with bowls of cut fruit so exquisite that each is worthy of a still-life artist. In northern Thailand, where I have stayed with friends for many happy visits, I was taken to their town's equivalent of this café, when it comes to discussing the merits of its soup. She cross-examined me on what possible additions I wanted topping the rice, then ordered in a conversation that lasted a good ten minutes and sounded remarkably like gunfire from an automatic weapon. But those troughs of food that were set before us were perfect, and the cement café, with its seven metal tables and rickety chairs, seemed a cool respite to the seductive, sweltering day organizing itself outside the front door.

I learned the way to this restaurant, and would pedal there on my friend's bicycle through the dusty streets, respectful of the orange parade of saffron-robed monks parading by. I found a bamboo bicycle rack against the side of the shop and leaned my bike into it as the Thai customers did theirs. I spoke every day to the cat sleeping in the spirit house on the property, and brought small treats (lychees, rambutans, huge strawberries on the stem) to the café owner. I never asked why her servers were all gay men, astonishingly beautiful in their women's sarongs and immaculate lace tops. It didn't bother the Thai people, nor did it come between me and my soup, and the one time I asked my friend about these men and their customs, she smiled and answered, "they prefer our way."

I did my early training on grits, a food so comforting that I have wept in gratitude over it on an otherwise horrible day. It seems right that the rice which sustains vast nations of the East should make such a grand appearance at breakfast, evoking the same soothing effect on those who eat it. I may have toast here, but in a world of fish sauce and hot chilies, steaming gruel seems a fine alternative.

Every Thai house or building has to have a spirit house to go with it—a place for the spirits of the site, or Phra Phum, to live in. Without this vital structure you're likely to have the spirits living in the house with you, and that can cause all sorts of trouble. Spirit houses look rather like a birdhouse-sized Thai temple mounted on a pedestal. At least your average spirit house does—a big hotel may have a spirit house as big as an average house.

—Joe Cummings, *Thailand - a travel survival kit*

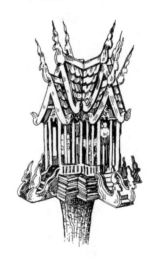

Terrell Vermont was Southeastern regional judge for the James Beard Restaurant Awards and cuisine editor for Creative Loafing *magazine. She was beautiful and charming, a woman of taste, a southern belle who ran*

marathons, rowed competitively, knew how to party, and enjoyed a good cigar. She died of a brain tumor January 3, 1996 at the age of 41. She is sorely missed.

★

Toasts were first drunk in France at the time of the Revolution. The name comes to us from the English, who, when they drank anyone's health, put a piece of toast on the bottom of the beer pot. Whoever drank last got the toast.

One day Anne Boleyn, then the most beautiful woman in England, was taking her bath, surrounded by the lords of her suite. These gentlemen, courting her favor, each took a glass, dipped into the tub, and drank her health. All but one, who was asked why he did not follow their example.

"I am waiting for the toast," he said. Which was not bad for an Englishman.

—Alexandre Dumas, *Alexandre Dumas' Dictionary of Cuisine,*
translated by Louis Coleman

PATRICK PFISTER

Hungry Ghosts

What is the fate of the mean-spirited?

In the first day of the Seventh Month of the Chinese lunar calendar, the gates of Hell open and insatiable spirits rush out to roam the land of the living. In former lives these wretched souls were humans consumed by greed and unholy desire; now reincarnated as Hungry Ghosts, they are spirit creatures with tiny mouths, narrow throats and enormous stomachs, doomed to a constant and desperate search for food. And they never find enough.

Hungry Ghosts take advantage of humans and stir up trouble in the most tranquil neighborhoods. They are mischievous, bring disease and torment, and may even devour children. To keep them under relative control and ensure spiritual law and order, an elite emissary also comes forth from Hades, Phor Thor Kong, the King of Hungry Ghosts. He is a kind of supernatural sheriff, a fierce demon-god empowered to detain and arrest any spirits engaging in criminal behavior.

I first saw him on Cintra Street in George Town as I was hurrying back to my new hotel. I had arrived on Penang late the previous night—too late for dinner or a choice of rooms—and had grabbed at the first available place, a traditional Chinese flop-house that, like most others on the street, doubled as a brothel. I spent the night listening to ladies in high heels and their clients in bare feet clicking and slapping down the halls; doors opened and closed, cries of ecstasy came through the walls. Around three o'clock a squadron of bedbugs started chewing on my arms and legs and I decided that I had had enough. First thing in the morning I found a new hotel, went out for something to eat—delicious roast duck at the Yi Kim Restaurant down the street—and was now on the way back to my room for a shower and a nap.

As I neared Campbell Street I happened to glance to the right. There stood the King of Ghosts. He had long pink-and-white-nailed hands, a terrifying red-and-black face and was dressed in a vermillion-blue-and-gold-sequined robe.

I stopped instantly. He was a huge paper effigy set up just off the street in an area called Rumah Pangsa People's Park, an expanse of blacktop that looked like a parking lot except for several bright canopies covering temporary shrines and altar tables. Rows of giant joss sticks smoldered in front of a large stage. As I walked into the makeshift compound, a contingent of Taoist priests and mediums, all of them chanting and ringing small bells, came forth leading a procession of two hundred people.

There were no other Westerners in sight. I had no idea whether it was a private ceremony, so I stuck to the outer edges of the crowd. Music—cymbals and stringed instruments—started up. The priests marched toward the King of Ghosts and began a series of preliminary rituals. I moved in under the main canopy, keeping to the rear, craning my neck over bony shoulders. Other paper effigies, many no more than a foot or two tall, some almost as large as the King himself, stood next to claw-brandishing dragons. The head priest anointed the King of Ghosts, dabbing vermillion ink on his eyes, nose, mouth, ears, hands and navel to open his senses to the world, then moved to anoint the other effigies. The chanting continued.

I glanced around again to make double-sure I wasn't intruding. Most people were watching the priests, but just then a short man with thick glasses and large white eyes spotted me, hurried through the wafting incense smoke and grabbed my arm. He shook my hand so enthusiastically I bounced up onto my toes. He said his name was Andrew and, speaking on behalf of the entire neighborhood, he officially welcomed me to the Festival of Hungry Ghosts. Before I could say a word, he pulled me over to the King of Ghosts himself and introduced me, adding that the King was also called Tai Su lah (The Great Intellect).

"You believe or you don't believe," Andrew said, "that's all." He was still pumping my hand; his teeth were a set of radiant piano keys. Next he led me toward the other effigies and told me that the King of Ghosts had brought assistants with him from Hades and established a temporary government to rule over the neighborhood during this difficult period. One by one he presented the assistants. There was Tua Pek (Grand Uncle), the Chief Inspector of Hades, armed with handcuffs and foot shackles; Jee Pek (Second Uncle), who wore a tall red hat and waved a fan; Phor Kua (Secretary of Hades), equipped with an inkbrush to jot down good and bad deeds; and Thor Tay Kong, the local Earth God or supernatural district officer, a personage invited to almost every festival.

"They can all be bribed," Andrew said cheerfully. He pointed to a stack of fake gold ingots, then to Second Uncle's tongue, smeared with black opium; but he was quick to add that most of the offerings were to compensate the temporary government for the hard work of protecting the neighborhood and ensuring spiritual law and order. An immense banquet had been set out on several tables: roast duck and chicken, giant wicker baskets brimming over with pineapples and bananas, apples, pears, grapes, oranges and rambutan; there were cakes and pastries, bottles of stout and Otard cognac, an enormous roast pig, noodles and rice, and dragons stuffed with wheat muffins. In addition to being fed, the gods had to be entertained.

"Rock concert tonight" Andrew told me, "and comedy."

I tried to concentrate. I was still dizzy with tiredness and the heat and the priests were still ringing their bells. My mind wandered to the Hungry Ghosts, beings eaten by greed in former lives. The word greed meant "to hunger." Did I hunger for anything? Perhaps some more roast duck, but I didn't need the Goddess of

Mercy for that—I could simply return to the Yi Kim Restaurant for dinner.

Twenty minutes later I arrived at my hotel, a white, semi-colonial building in a recessed courtyard just off Chulia Street. On the terrace beneath the entrance archways sat two ancient Chinese men sipping tea and, farther along, an elderly Norwegian couple fanning themselves with postcards. As I passed by Reception, Mr. Chen, the manager, rapped the desktop with his knuckles.

"You come here," he said.

"You rent bicycle this afternoon?" Mr. Chen asked.

"I'll be taking a nap this afternoon," I answered.

"Where you go next? Thailand?"

"Sumatra, I think."

"You buy ticket from me."

It was an order, not a question.

"Maybe…" I answered slowly.

"You stay here tomorrow night."

Another order.

"Maybe…"

"Better you pay now."

Better for him, he meant. I studied Mr. Chen for a moment. About fifty years old, he was shirtless and had a blue dragon with a red tongue tattooed onto the knob of his shoulder. The corners of his mouth had fallen downward, exhausted from a lifetime of never curling upward into a smile. He hadn't yet looked me straight in the eye, not from shyness or unease, but because he was ignoring everything about me except what most interested him, my money. He drummed his fingers on the desktop.

I was about to tell him I might or might not pay tomorrow one second before checkout time, but then thought better of it. Why pick fights? Instead I reached into my pocket and started counting out Malaysian ringgits. Happily, I found that with the change from the restaurant I had M$16.85. The exact price of my single room was M$16.87, but the missing two sen was such a small sum—less than half of an American penny—that I was sure it would be waved aside. In Kuala Lumpur I had seen a ragged beggar grumble at receiving five sen. Still, I was tactful and told Mr. Chen I would give it to him that afternoon or evening, as soon as I got more change. There was a moment of silence. Mr. Chen grimly regarded the M$16.85 on his desktop.

"Better you pay now," he said.

The only other bill I had was a fifty ringgit note. I showed it to him, certain he wouldn't want to break it. With a quick tug he removed it from between my thumb and forefinger. He opened his money drawer and started counting, but soon found he didn't have enough change. He called an assistant, then another, and finally the man in charge of the kitchen. All three looked at me suspiciously, then emptied their pockets, but together they couldn't break the bill. Mr. Chen dismissed two of the men with a grunt and sent the third to the Indian moneychanger around the corner. About fifteen minutes passed before he returned. Not once during all that time did Mr. Chen look my way as I stood waiting beside his desk, let alone murmur any apologies.

Now he counted out my change with the same stoney expression that had been on his face since the beginning of our exchange. But as I picked up my money his dark eyes momentarily glinted with triumph. He had not allowed me to cheat him. He had gotten his two sen.

I nodded and went to my room feeling I knew Mr. Chen a little better. He was a sure bet to be reincarnated as a Hungry Ghost.

For dinner that evening I returned to the Yi Kim Restaurant for another plate of roast duck. If anything, it was even more delicious than the serving I had eaten for lunch. The outer skin was perfectly browned, the meat so tender I barely had time to savor it before it melted in my mouth. As I paid my bill and left, I wondered if I would have the will power to avoid coming back for lunch tomorrow.

Andrew met me when I arrived at People's Park. The giant joss sticks smoldered in front of the stage, as did thousands of smaller ones on the altars beneath the canopy, and the clouds of incense smoke stung my eyes. Andrew introduced me to other committee members who took turns explaining the work they had done on the festival. Tomorrow and the following night there would be official seating for the opera, but tonight I could stand anywhere I wanted.

As soon as the concert began, the stage burst into a display of special effects: strobes, multicolored lights, billowing smoke screens, flashing bulbs; the set decorations mirrored the ornamentation and chaos of the religious ceremony next door. Two snake-dragons loomed over a pretty girl in a miniskirt and high heels as she belted out a note-perfect version of "Material Girl" in Cantonese. Two songs later, a wiry guy in a turquoise zoot suit did "Johnny B. Goode" in Hokkien dialect and with Chuck Berry strut. At the end of each number I struggled against reflex and forced my hands not to clap together. Not only do Chinese audiences never applaud, they yawn, chat and scratch, wander about and spit as if nothing were happening in front of their eyes. The performers filled the tortuous void between songs with cheery patter and band introductions, but watching them do it after every number made me grit my teeth.

About twenty feet in front of the stage a small, rectangular area had been roped off and five empty chairs placed inside. I didn't need anybody to tell me that Phor Thor Kong and his ghostly assistants from Hell were seated there. Everyone who walked by kept a wary distance. Even dogs sniffing about the ground instinctively shied away. Periodically Andrew or another festival organizer came up to a table in front of the five chairs and lit a joss stick or set out an offering bowl. Midway through the show an old woman poured five cups of tea and served them to the Hungry Ghosts. Armed with automatic weapons, I wouldn't have gone near one of those chairs to save my life.

Under the canopy behind us devotees were praying; every time someone made a donation a bell rang and more chanting began. Nobody seemed upset at the rock music blaring out next to them; likewise, neither the rock stars nor their audience seemed to mind the religious activities. Most of the people were from the neighborhood, shopowners and their families. Cintra Street was well endowed with tailors and merchants and there was also the Poh Tai Medical Hall, a cake shop, a computer center, the Hock Hwa Trading Company and a shoe store. The street around the corner, Campbell, was lined with jewelry stores and shotgun-toting guards, but most of the neighborhood was inhabited by simple people out to enjoy the music and pray for the Hungry Ghosts.

They pray for the Hungry Ghosts because as good Buddhists they must attempt to relieve the suffering of all sentient beings, human or not. It is impossible to rescue the Hungry Ghost from Hell, but prayers might ask that their gullets be opened slightly so that they can eat a little. It is said that having the throat of a Hungry Ghost is like being hung upside down, and the Buddhist ceremonies that assist the Hungry Ghosts are called Yi Lan Pen Hooi, or "saving those who are hung upside down."

Mr. Chen was standing rightside up the following morning when I told him I wanted to rent a bicycle. His eyes were filmed over and three pillow lines ran down his left cheek, but he quickly snapped alert.

"You pay now," he said.

"First I want to see what I'm paying for," I told him.

We walked around the side of the building and found the bike in a small garage. I checked the brakes and bell, adjusted the seat, and then waited as he pumped up the rear tire which was low. As he worked, the dragon on his shoulder jiggled and its red tongue lashed about. Finally Mr. Chen stood, I handed him the two ringgit rental fee and he gave me my final instructions.

"If accident you pay, if bike broken you pay, if bike stolen you pay, if—"

"Mr. Chen, you're making me afraid to go anywhere," I told him. "Okay, but no refund."

He wasn't joking. He already had a grip on the handlebars and I had to give a little yank to get the bike away from him. I swung my leg over the seat and pedaled across the courtyard and out into George Town traffic.

George Town was slow and steamy on the surface and full of activity underneath. The stench of open sewers mixed with the tangy aroma of spices. In the overwhelming Chinese atmosphere, mainland Malaysia seemed a world away, but the beauty and mystery of Southeast Asia always felt close. I rode past the Goddess of Mercy temple where devotees were tossing Banknotes from Hell into rusty furnaces, then to the Kapitan Kling Mosque, and afterwards out to The Esplanade, where white waves sprayed over the old retaining wall. By the time I pedaled down to Wat Chayamangkalaram, the Thai "Temple of the Reclining Buddha," I had worked up a sweat and an appetite and although there were plenty of restaurants in the area, my thoughts—and soon afterwards the front wheel of the bike—pointed to the Yi Kim for more roast duck and rice.

An hour and a half later I left the restaurant with my stomach full and my throat slightly constricted: the roast duck had again been delicious, but my conscience now demanded to know if desire had a stranglehold on me. Greed takes many forms and Mr. Chen wasn't the only one with a chance to be reincarnated as a Hungry Ghost.

I rode around for another couple of hours, saw a few more sights, chatted with a trishaw driver for a while and finally headed back to the hotel. As soon as I coasted the bike to a stop, Mr. Chen appeared, took the key out of my hand, locked the bike and started to pocket the key. He did it so quickly that a moment passed before I realized what was going on. Technically, I had rented the bike for the entire day. I probably wouldn't go out anymore but that was for me to say, not for him to assume. At the least he should have asked before grabbing. Instead he was scowling at me as if I were one of the hotel workers slow to jump at his tyrannical grunts. I told him I wanted the key back. He muttered something, reluctantly handed it to me and started inspecting the bike for damage. I was about to walk off when he pointed to the rear tire.

"Puncture here in tire," he said. "You pay."

I looked at the tire. It was a bit low again. I reminded Mr. Chen it had been like that in the morning. "You pumped it up yourself before I left," I added.

"Different now," he said. He stooped down and squeezed the tire. "Before tire low. No air. Now tire flat. Have puncture. You pay."

"Where's the hole if it's a puncture?" I demanded. "Do you see a hole? Is there a nail or a piece of glass somewhere? I don't see anything except a tire low on air like it was this morning."

"Hole too small to see because nail small," Mr. Chen countered. "Small nail make small hole. This small puncture. You pay."

"If you can't see the hole or the nail how do you know it's there?" I said, growing hot. "Even a small nail would leave—" I stopped myself. Why was I bothering to argue with this guy? "Look, Mr. Chen," I said suddenly, "you rented me a bike in bad condition. I might've been killed. Even a discount wouldn't make up for that. I want my money back right now. All of it."

He stared at me in stupefaction for ten seconds, then turned and walked off, muttering over the dragon on his shoulder "Tire have puncture...you lucky I no charge this time..."

In ancient Greek mythology Hell was populated by people like Sisyphus. He was condemned to roll a huge stone to the top of a hill. But whenever he reached the crest of the hill, the stone would roll back down and he had to start over yet again. Among his fellows in perdition, one was eternally thirsty, but whenever he reached for nearby water, it receded. Still another suffered hunger, and food ran away from him. The name for this place was Tantalus, whence we get the English word "tantalize."

—RS

The crowd was slightly different tonight. Older, wealthier Chinese, especially women, watched the stage with stern concentration. It was my first live Chinese opera, and I sat, totally mesmerized, in the front row seat Andrew had reserved for me. The three principal performers wore brilliant red, yellow and blue robes, their pancake-white faces heavily rouged at the cheeks and their great black eyebrows arching up to their temples. In their heavy robes under the fierce lights, they had to be losing a pound a minute, but they swayed and drifted about the stage as if floating on a cool breeze on a spring day.

To my left sat Mr. Yap, a fat and serious seventeen-year-old, kindly trying to fill me in on the nuances of the story line. His chubby face was partially paralyzed and his mouth twitched as he spoke. Three kings want to marry a queen, he explained, but they learn she is already married to the tallest king. The other two kings become furious. The queen tells them, if you really want to marry me then you must have a war. "But nothing is the way it seems," Mr. Yap added. "Everything is the opposite. Understand?"

The last act was full of action: sword and spear fights, blades flashing. The tall king and the queen had a terrific battle until the king finally prevailed and the curtain came down to dead silence, a magnificent four-hour performance ending without even one hand clapping. The scratching, burping, yawning audience rose to its feet, stretched and headed home.

"You see the queen wasn't really the queen in the end," Mr. Yap explained. "Everything was the opposite."

Andrew and four other festival organizers came over to learn if I had enjoyed the show. I told them I had enjoyed it very much even though I might have missed a few things. They explained that every movement and color had a symbolic meaning, then admitted they hadn't understood it all either. They went on to say that the troupe would be paid 3000 ringgits a night. The money, like everything else, came from donations and ticket sales. The Cintra Street neighborhood had sponsored the entire festival. "Lots of preparing, lots of people," they said.

"It must have been very difficult to organize," I replied. "Lots of people means lots of different ideas."

They stared straight ahead smiling cheerfully, comprehending nothing. Finally a light flicked in Andrew's eye and he gently corrected me.

Units of the U.S. Marine Corps served for many years in China where individuals often picked up a bit of "Gringo Chinese," words or phrases commonly used in everyday life, and well mispronounced. The most famous bit was the Chinese for "work together." The Marines pronounce it "Gung Ho!"

—Captain Robert Callahan, U.S.M.C.

"Chinese people not have this problem," he said. "Everybody think together, everybody work together."

We all nodded together, shook hands and said goodnight.

The following morning I awoke with memories of two incidents. The first involved Mr. Chen. When I had arrived at the hotel after the opera I had ordered a coke, paid him with a one ringgit coin and watched in amazement as he carefully inspected the coin, doing everything short of biting into it. Most surprisingly, the action wasn't vindictive. Rather than trying to get even for the bicycle, he was just conducting business as usual, taking precautions against counterfeit coins ever slipping over the counter into his money drawer.

The second incident occurred around four or five in the morning. I had been dreaming about roast duck but suddenly found I was awake; a ghostly wailing had shaken me out of sleep. I had never heard a sound like it in my life. What was it? I concentrated and my muddled brain finally gave it identity: the Chinese hotel dogs were howling as the *muezzin* howled louder, calling the faithful to prayer.

After a shower and a shave, I went out to the terrace for a breakfast of sludgy coffee and toast. I scanned a few articles in both the *Straits Times* and the *Star*, talked for a few minutes to the elderly Norwegian couple, and then went up to the desk to pay for another night. I handed Mr. Chen a twenty-ringgit note. He wrote up the bill and got change out of the money drawer, then pushed both the bill and the change across the counter. I started to scoop them up. Then stopped. He had mistakenly charged me M$18.87 for a double room instead of M$16.87 for a single. I pointed out the error. He bent forward to look.

It wasn't intentional, I had no doubt. I paid the same thing every day and would have to be a real fool to miss it. So it was just a simple mistake, but the kind for which a client is due a minor apology. And I wanted mine. I waited for it.

And might have gone on waiting for years. Mr. Chen's jaw tightened; his arms stiffened until the red-tongued dragon turned to stone. In an instant the tension at the counter grew so electric that two backpackers behind me scurried out to the terrace for safety.

Mr. Chen took the bill in his hands as if it were an enemy's neck. He glared at it. Greed turns a man into a tyrant first, a Hungry Ghost later; and tyrants can't stand to be told they are wrong. When you are never wrong you never have to apologize. Now Mr. Chen was not so much choking a paper as on the words in his own mouth. In his next life his throat would be so narrow he wouldn't be able to get food down it, in this life he couldn't get an apology out of it.

For a second I hesitated. "Just let the damn thing pass," I thought. But the coin incident was still on my mind, and so was the scene with the bicycle and the fifteen minutes I had spent waiting while the assistant had run off to the Indian money-changer because of two sen. On top of it all there was Mr. Chen's superior, you-come-here, you-pay-now attitude, flung not just at me but at every guest in the hotel. A chance like this might not come for another century. I rapped my knuckles on the counter.

"This is a serious mistake," I said. "I was almost overcharged." My voice was loud enough to carry to the Norwegian couple and the two backpackers. Mr. Chen smiled, the sure sign of a Chinese burning with embarrassment. I tried not to let his wide grin throw me off. I didn't know the exact rules for losing face but his was disappearing before my eyes. His skin paled, his forehead seemed to shrink, his eyes retreated into two dark slits.

"You pay now," I told him.

He winced as if bitten by dragon's teeth.

"No problem, give refund," he mumbled murderously.

It was as close as he would ever get to an apology, I knew, and knew further that people who never apologize are the same ones who never say thank you. Everything is one direction: they take, never give. With only a single exception: orders, which they give and never take.

That was Mr. Chen, I thought, always taking the key, the bike, the money out of my hand, never giving even an inch.

"Two dollars," I insisted. "I was overcharged two dollars."

His body shook so violently that for a second I was physically afraid, as if he might come leaping over the counter and do a Kung Fu dance on my head. But instead he crumpled the bill, pulled back the incorrect change from in front of me and began writing out another bill. Of course he could simply have scratched out the 18 on the first bill and filled in a 16. There was nothing official about the bills, they were just scraps of paper. But that was not Mr. Chen's way. Now every fiber, every atom and every blood cell in his being were concentrated on making out the revised bill. There would be no mistakes on it, no little errors for me to point out, nothing out of the ordinary, and above all, nothing wrong. He would regain his lost face without even squeaking out a little "sorry about that."

As he finished, color came back into his cheeks, his glinty eyes slowly opened, and his spirit reasserted itself. He stood taller, then tried to lower himself off the hook. But I was ready for him.

"This not big problem," he said offhandedly.

"Maybe not for you," I replied. "But it's my money. Why should I have to pay more than the fair amount?"

He waited a moment, then muttered:

"Not so much difference in bills."

"If that's true then charge me two ringgits less for tonight."

"Maybe I no give refund."

"Maybe I call the Tourist Police."

His face paled again and his eyes retreated. He would kill me if he ever got the chance, but he wouldn't say anything more. He pushed the bill and my change across the counter. I picked them up and stuffed them into an empty pocket of my jeans. When I walked past the people on the terrace, one of the backpackers winked at me, but the victory gave no satisfaction; if anything it had left me feeling dirty. And I was sorry to see, as I started across the courtyard, that my thoughts had already turned to lunch, and my steps were already taking me to the Yi Kim Restaurant for more roast duck.

That night when the Chinese opera ended, the audience rose,

did not applaud, stretched and moved off to the side. Instantly, twenty teenagers appeared and gave a stunning example of "everybody think together, everybody work together." As Taoist priests chanted in the background, one folding chair after another was scooped up, smacked together and stacked in a heap by the giant joss sticks. Another team scrambled up to the canopy roofs and tore them down. Thirty boys with brooms beat at the ground and within ten action-packed minutes the entire area had been disassembled and cleaned.

Mr. Yap guided me out toward Cintra Street where a crowd had formed in front of a large ring of burning joss sticks. In the center lay a great pile of paper artifacts and paper money, a funeral pyre. Most people held joss sticks in their hands in attitudes of prayer. Professional photographers had set up their gear on the roofs of nearby buildings. Festival organizers began to pull the giant effigy of Phor Thor Kong, King of Ghosts, toward us.

"Now ghosts go back down," Mr. Yap explained as the crowd pressed in for a better view.

"Down?" I asked.

"Down to that place."

"To Hell?"

"Yes, back down to Hell place."

I felt tired as I watched the King of Ghosts come toward us. It had been an emotional day and the scene with Mr. Chen had not ended at the hotel. After my lunch of roast duck at the Yi Kim Restaurant, I had reached into the pocket where I had stuffed the bill and change and drawn out M$2.13, one ringgit short of what Mr. Chen should have given me. Seething, I clawed my pocket again and again before finally admitting that I had not even checked the amount and Mr. Chen was probably snickering to himself at that very moment.

The festival organizers maneuvered Phor Thor Kong onto the funeral pyre and the Taoist priests chanted louder. The photographers readied their cameras as Andrew and four other men lit torches. The rest of the temporary government, the assistants from Hell, were brought forth: Tua Pek (Grand Uncle), the Chief

Inspector of Hades; Jee Pek (Second Uncle); Phor Kua (Secretary of Hades), still holding his inkbrush; and finally Thor Tay Kong, the local Earth God. Mr. Yap grew excited at my side.

As the Hungry Ghosts prepared to depart this world, I examined my own greed. One thing slightly in my favor was that I had not eaten roast duck for dinner that evening, not for entirely honorable reasons such as a refusal to give in to desire, but rather because I had finally grown sick of roast duck. It was abstinence in reverse. Any of the Taoist priests could give the sermon: the things of this world never really satisfy. Have enough of something and instead of filling you up it will leave you empty. Hungry Ghosts never learn this lesson so they must come back to be taught it again and again.

Five torches met paper and flames blazed upward toward the towering effigy of Phor Thor Kong. In an instant the King of Ghosts and his supernatural assistants imploded in a ball of fire, lighting up the Cintra Street neighborhood, and then they vanished, trailing smoke, returning to their regular jobs in Hades.

Born in Detroit, Michigan, Patrick Pfister has lived and traveled all over the world. A self-described "Jack of all trades," he has been engaged in numerous occupations, ranging from carpenter to ice cream man to assistant softball coach. He is presently employed as a translator and language instructor in Barcelona, Spain, where he has lived for the past twelve years. When he is not traveling, he spends his time in his studio staring at a blank wall and trying to write a sentence someone might be interested in reading. This story is excerpted from his book, Pilgrimage: Tales From the Open Road.

*

> Your citizens named me Ciacco, The Hog:
> gluttony was my offense, and for it
> I lie here rotting like a swollen log.
>
> Nor am I lost in this alone; all these
> you see about you in this painful death
> have wallowed in the same indecencies.

—Dante Alighieri, *The Divine Comedy*, verse rendering by John Ciardi

Goan Feast

The food chain has no limits.

THE MONSOON WAS WANING OVER GOA AND THE BEACHES WERE blissfully empty. My lover and I rented a stone cottage on Anjuna Beach. A sagging bed and tepid wash water were the only amenities. Neither windows nor doors locked, and there was no electricity. A veteran of Goan beach culture, my lover immediately embraced our rustic digs.

Across the field, a congenial Goanese sold meals from home. She sent over huge platters of spicy fried mackerel, prawn curry rice, *dal,* vegetables, yogurt, *roti,* salad, beer. The flavors were stunning. We fed each other urgently, then pushed the food away. I climbed onto his lap. He smelled of Goa already: salty, humid, ripe.

The heavy petting halted abruptly as the first mosquitoes attacked. They swarmed through the air. We dove under the bed sheet, peppered with holes. The springs pierced like cacti. The pillows were rock hard. Sand chafed against my skin. The mosquitoes returned. I lost my concentration. We had to stop.

I lay awake late into the night with my partner snoring blissfully. A muffled clang emanated from our metal dinner plates, then the scraping of little feet across the sandy floor. We had mice. I turned on my flashlight, aiming it at my feet. I didn't care for company. Some time around dawn I finally fell asleep.

The days flew by; Goa insinuated herself under our skins. We tasted every fish dish in our neighbor's repertoire and sampled all the local *feni*. But the hostile bed had spun its curse and incredibly when it came time to leave we hadn't made love once. Next time, we vowed, we'd check into a hotel.

On our final morning I realized that several pairs of my underwear were missing. I roamed the small cottage, searching diligently. Then I stepped out and examined the exterior. Half-buried under the porch, I spotted a pair. And then the others, jammed between various stones in the cottage wall.

I shook out the sand from each one, wondering how they got there. I reached in for the label to double check that they were indeed mine. I kept looking, blinking in confusion. I wondered if I'd lost my mind. There were three holes for legs instead of two. Suddenly I understood, and froze in shock. The crotch had been neatly excised from every single pair.

Who could have done this? Some sexual deviant? A panty fetishist? A repressed local? My boyfriend? As I wondered, a mouse wiggled its way through a hole in the wall, and scampered across the sand. I burst into laughter, clutching my precious trophies. I'd been paid the highest rodent compliment.

Ginu Kamani is the author of Junglee Girl, *stories on the sensuality of Indian women. She has contributed to* On a Bed of Rice: An Asian American Erotic Feast *and the forthcoming* Dick for a Day *and* Herotica 5. *She lives with her husband and mice in Northern California.*

*

The ancient practice of alchemy produced many love philtres, often made with some connection to body parts. One formula required a woman to sit naked in a barrel of grain. She then moved herself and the grain about in such a fashion that the maximum number of grains would come into contact with her pudenda. She would then grind the grain, make it into bread, and feed it, unbeknownst, to her intended.

—RS

✳ ✶ ✳

Burnt Offerings

Fire and meat, salt and smoke:
what more do you need?

THE RESTAURANT IS CALLED LA ESTANCIA—THE RANCH—AND there are many like it in this city, in a country where campfires are a national obsession. Join the Argentines on their evening *paseando* down Lavalle, one of the glitzy pedestrian thoroughfares in downtown Buenos Aires, and eventually you'll come upon a most unusual gastronomic tableau, crackling with incongruity in the cosmopolitan night. A beautiful bouquet of flames, a roaring campfire. Behind glass, but a campfire nevertheless. The fire is centered on the tiled floor in the front of the restaurant, in a dirt and ash pit, stoked with fat, round plugs of logs you couldn't reasonably ask a 12-year-old to lift. The flames rise chest high, spurting higher; it's a fine campfire, one of the world's simple wonders.

Encircling the flames are the sizzling carcasses of perhaps a dozen sheep, each crucified on an *asador*, a cross-shaped iron spit, staked vertically and leaned toward the heat, the legs of the animals splayed outward, mounted like grisly butterflies, succulent pennants of roasting flesh, golden and greasy. It's not so much the idea of food that intrigues as the idea of the campfire itself, I suppose you could call it a gimmick, a tourist attraction, but the *porteños* think of it otherwise, and so do I. A *parrilla*—an Argentine grill—

is an entirely ubiquitous and portable affair. But that's not what this is: this is an *asado*, a camp-style outdoor barbecue brought indoors, as if on a dare. Not country come to town, but city escaped to the countryside, a nostalgic gastronomic journey meant to evoke the lasting vitality of the Argentine romance with the pampas, *el campo*, life in the camp, camaraderie and freedom, love of the earth, an endless horizon. The aesthetic of survival, out here at the bottom of a hemisphere.

I had come to Buenos Aires for the first time from a friend's ranch, Estancia La Susana, in the province of Santa Fe, a place as midwestern to my eye as Iowa or Nebraska. We had ridden through unending pastures and paddocks, the two of us mounted on handsome but lazy horses, inspecting my friend's herd of Aberdeen cattle. The day before, the *gauchos* had fixed us an *asado*: a martyred sheep, *chorizo*, long strips of spare ribs, blocks of beef tenderloin. They had spread the meat on a raised grill that looked like a metal bedframe, then rigged a sheet of tin over it as a roof, so that they could cook the *asado* slowly and tenderly from above and below. The ranch manager built a campfire off to the side and, when the flames had retreated, shoveled coals beneath the grill and atop the tin, so that the heat came from two directions and radiated through the meat, leaving it juicy and delicate, fragrant with woodsmoke, not carcinogenically seared but not rare either. That is how they like their meat in the Argentine, unseasoned except by salt and smoke.

The day was cold and cloudy, a wintry summer in the southern latitudes, with a storm threatening to blow in from Patagonia. I ap-

> *Once we domesticated fire as if it were some beautiful temperamental animal; harnessing both its energy and its light, it became possible for us to cook food to make it easier to chew and digest, and, as we found out eventually, to kill germs. But we can eat cold food perfectly well, too, and did for thousands of years. What does it say about us that, even in refined dining rooms, our taste is for meat served at the temperature of a freshly killed antelope or warthog?*
>
> —Diane Ackerman, *A Natural History of the Senses*

preciated the fire and its virtues, its warmth, its antecedents that echoed forth from the timelessness of Argentine history, the common denominator it seemed to present among us gathered round: the *gringo,* the Anglo-Argentine *patrino,* the Yugoslav overseer, the two *gauchos,* one young and cheerful, the other old and dark and a bit gloomy, each wearing a crushed-felt hat and wide silvered belt, a *facone*—wedge-shaped knife—tucked into their waistbands at the small of their backs.

We began with the *chorizos.* We ate as much as we could—almost everything, washed down with plenty of good local red wine. Argentines eat meat and little else: some fried potatoes, a small salad. Sometimes their intestines block up. Stomach cancer is a problem. Vegetarians are regarded as a screwball cult, like anarchists.

I had crammed myself to the top of my gunnels, so full that the heaviness stayed with me throughout the following day and made horseback riding all the more uncomfortable, though no less exhilarating. By the time I arrived in Buenos Aires, I had begun to fantasize about pasta. In Argentina for only five days, I had already consumed my yearly quota of livestock, even indulging in offal—sweetbreads and kidneys (but resisting udder and intestines). Nevertheless, walking down Lavalle, I stepped inside La Estancia, seduced by the campfire. Not to eat, mind you, though it was in fact dinnertime. I wanted only a pungent whiff of woodsmoke. I wanted to feel the warming of the flames on my face, I wanted the olfactory trigger that would propel the dream into my senses—a horse and rider cantering sweatily down the fenceline, the bulls scattering, the breeze autumn-sweet, the Andes barely visible off over the horizon. The magically real, latent in a campfire. All these smells and tastes of a heritage for those citizens of Buenos Aires who come through the door of La Estancia. It's like a visit home after a period of exile, which is the best way I know to describe the power of a campfire.

We hardly need Iron John or the Boy Scouts to tell us campfires connect us with what is primal and universal in our lives. Fires lure people this way; they are agents of artificial bonhomie, inspirers of metaphysical drift. They ask that we eat and sing; they want us to interpret life. They make love more fierce, solipsism more impenetrable; they make strangers risk revelation. They are soothsayers, fires are, and crystal balls reflecting a past that will always be mysterious. I suspect any fool bored around a campfire would find Pavarotti equally tedious.

Bob Shacochis counts among his honors and awards a James Michener Award, an American Book Award, and Playboy's Best New Fiction Award. This story is excerpted from his book, Domesticity: A Gastronomic Interpretation of Love.

＊

As you see, within our bodies each of us has the elements needed to produce phosphorus. And let me tell you something I've never told a soul. My grandmother had a very interesting theory; she said that each of us is born with a box of matches inside us but we can't strike them all by ourselves; just as in the experiment, we need oxygen and a candle to help. In this case, the oxygen, for example, would come from the breath of the person you love; the candle could be any kind of food, music, caress, word, or sound that engenders the explosion that lights one of the matches. For a moment we are dazzled by an intense emotion. A pleasant warmth grows within us, fading slowly as time goes by, until a new explosion comes along to revive it. Each person has to discover what will set off those explosions in order to live, since the combustion that occurs when one of them is ignited is what nourishes the soul. That fire, in short, is its food. If one doesn't find out in time what will set off these explosions, the box of matches dampens, and not a single match will ever be lighted.

If that happens, the soul flees from the body and goes to wander among the deepest shades, trying in vain to find food to nourish itself, unaware that only the body it left behind, cold and defenseless, is capable of providing that food.

—Laura Esquivel, *Like Water For Chocolate,* translated by Carol Christensen and Thomas Christensen

Salmon Head

The author learns the true meaning of "delicacy."

OUR GROUP STOOD OUT FROM THE OTHERS LIKE THE CAST OF A drag show at a Rotary Club luncheon: a wood carver, a marine biologist, two Dutch cousins, a lawyer and his mother, a young female cook, a long-haired captain, and me. We were wandering in Southeast Alaska's inland passage in a graceful, old, 65-foot wooden schooner among the professional fisherman in their utilitarian fishing boats. We were on a seminar of sorts, searching for evidence of Tlingit village sites on Prince of Wales Island: remnants of mossy, decaying totems, shards of china dishes, bent tea kettles.

The fishermen must have been amused by us. They treated us kindly, though with a bit of condescension. And nearly every day we received a gift of a fish or two from one of them. When it was salmon, and it often was, I asked the cook if the head was included. No, the fishermen were always "so kind" and gave the fish to us cleaned and dressed.

I continued to ask, to hope, because I love to eat salmon heads, especially the eyes. I enjoy the cheeks, soft and flavorful, though tiny compared to a halibut's. The bones are fun to suck, yielding a rich gelatinous substance. But the eyes are special.

I gently remove each eye, a fatty bulb with smooth rich tendons that reach deep into the skull. I suck until only a tiny, hard, chalky white sphere remains.

On that boat, I was the butt of many jokes for my eccentric culinary desire, but I knew I had plenty of company. I'd seen the fish heads for sale in markets in Filipino neighborhoods and I knew that, traditionally, in Chinese families eating the fish's head is a privilege reserved for the patriarch.

The last day of our trip was spent in Wrangell inspecting Chief Shakes House with its exquisitely carved house poles set with abalone. Local Tlingit women danced in button-trimmed capes—a special performance for us.

When we returned to the boat, the cook had good news for me. Finally, a whole salmon had been given to us. "You deal with the head," she told me and handed me a nearly three-foot-long package.

With reverence, I unwrapped it, sliced the head from the body, scaled the head, washed and dried it, placed it in a pan, and slid it under the broiler.

Earlier, we had invited the dance leader for dinner. She arrived with a man who created exquisite silver bracelets with whale and eagle and bear symbols wrapped around them. He brought soapberries so he could show us how to smash and whip them into a foamy suds, and mix them with sugar for a delicious, airy dessert. She brought a foul tasting rancid oil from the tiny eulachon fish which looks like

We cruised into a world of steep granite cliffs and densely forested hillsides with glaciers coursing down the valleys.

Suddenly a call rang out for whales, and there they were, just ahead, two majestic humpbacks. Their black backs sliced the surface, a graceful slow-motion dance, but nothing compared to their huge tails lifting slowly out of the water and thrusting down into the sea. We followed them for a long time, spellbound by the clouds of mist they blew high into the air, a mist so fine it took ten seconds or more to drift back to the sea, a dazzling cloud of spray hanging in the air against a backdrop of trees.

—Larry Habegger,
"The Marine Wonders
of Kenai Fjords"

smelt but is oilier and, to our uninitiated tongues, quite unpalatable. To be polite, I asked them if they would like to share my treasure as an appetizer.

"How wonderful," the dancer cried.

"Oh yes, thank you," said the jeweler. No one dared laugh as the three of us sat down at the galley table and began to divide the prize.

The Dutch cousins were sitting at the table too, having their pre-supper glasses of wine. They watched us sucking on spiky translucent bones, peeling silver skin away, smacking our lips with pleasure. Though both were fluent in English, they often spoke their own language with each other. Suddenly they were engaged in an animated private conversation.

Then they turned to us and spoke in English: "Salmon has been extinct in our rivers all our lives, but we have an expression in Holland for delicacy. We just realized, literally it means 'head of a salmon.'"

A shiver ran up the back of my neck. I don't know which is the older culture, Tlingit or Dutch, but I know I was blessed to be present for this moment of meeting.

Sandy Polishuk is a poet, oral historian, and political activist. In former lives she has been a textile artist, librarian, and radio producer. She has savored delicacies on five continents. She lives in Portland, Oregon.

★

"Try one of these," said the beautiful princess. Having announced to her my interest in Lao foods and cookery, I had to suppress the suspicious expression with which I would otherwise have regarded the platter, and do as invited. "Delicious."

"Yes, they're deep-fried grasshoppers, and their nutritional value is quite high."

"Oh, really? That's good." So saying, I casually manoeuvred myself in the direction of a platter of fried chicken. The piece I picked up was a gizzard, and it brought a foot with it, which I vainly tried to shake off with seemingly casual motions of the wrist. The kind Princess Marina had followed me. "Ah," said she, "you know which are the best parts of the chicken."

—Alan Davidson, *A Kipper with My Tea: Selected Food Essays*

RAJENDRA S. KHADKA

* * *

Food for Thought

Who will serve?

I WAS WORKING AS A "PRODUCTION ASSISTANT" WITH A BRITISH film crew that was making a documentary for a British multinational firm about deforestation in Nepal. We were based in Trisuli, a small but bustling town named after the well-known river, which is about 85 kilometers north of Kathmandu. My job as the production assistant was to find "extras" from the surrounding villages where we were filming; I negotiated their pay, explained the "terms and conditions" of being employed for a few hours, and even had to instruct them on how to "act," per directions given by the British director. It was not a pleasant job because I was caught in the middle between the demands that led to misunderstandings between the Nepali villagers and the five-man British crew. My primary job was to placate each group or individual, if not make him or her happy.

One hot, steamy afternoon in a forested area alive with vicious red ants, we stopped shooting for lunch. We found a sunny, flat spot in that hilly terrain. Our lunch, packed in various pots by the kitchen staff at the guest house in Trisuli, was in the two rented Land Rovers that were parked nearby on a narrow, dirt trail that passed for a road.

There were a dozen villagers, our "extras" for the day, with us. There were no tea shops nearby and the villagers were not close to their homes. They had nowhere to go so they watched us as we, the *sahibs,* spread plastic sheets over the ground, unpacked our lunch of lentil soup, rice, curried vegetables and meat, and *chapatis.* The English crew and our two Nepali drivers began to eat, but I declined, saying I was not hungry. But the real reason I did not eat was because I did not feel comfortable eating while a dozen hungry people watched.

In our large, extended family, it was considered rude to eat alone in front of others, especially uninvited guests who happened to drop by just as you were about to have lunch or dinner. You immediately offered to share your food with the guest, even though there may not be enough for all. The guest always declined because he or she knew that there was just enough food for the family. So you delayed your lunch or dinner until the guest left. If it was bad manners to eat alone in the presence of others, it was worse to watch others eat.

Attached to this idea of civility, there was a darker concept of what may be described as the "evil eye." I had first learnt of this as a child when I visited my grandparents who lived in a small town in the southern part of Nepal that bordered India. Occasionally, a servant would be sent out to buy some hot *jelabi* or *samosa* to accompany morning or afternoon tea. And the servant would always be told to cover the snacks when he was bringing them back. The idea was that when he was returning with the food, and if it was uncovered and thus available for all to see, then someone could cast a spell and we could have stomach trouble, or worse, after we ate the food. Of course, the educated person knows that when the food is uncovered, it immediately attracts flies and such, and one is likely to get sick eating such unsanitary food. But the concept of the "evil eye" has remained deeply buried in my modern psyche, dislodging more rational explanations about food and people.

After the film crew and the drivers had finished eating, there was still food left. The director said to me, "Perhaps these people

would like to eat. It would be a
shame to throw food away." I answered I was not sure. Again, I
was aware of the delicate etiquette of food and guests.
Leftovers were given to servants;
among certain orthodox Hindu
families, I was aware of a practice
where the wife ate what the husband left on his plate after he had
finished eating. In most homes
women ate after the men. But
these villagers were neither servants nor our family members. I
was in danger of insulting them

*The British nearly lost India
in 1857 during the Sepoy
(native troops) mutiny because of
gastronomic taboo. The muzzle
loading rifles then issued to the
army employed a paper-wrapped
cartridge, one end of which had to
be bitten off before loading. The
paper was coated with grease to
make it waterproof. Hindu soldiers
thought the grease was fat from the
sacred cow; Muslim soldiers were
convinced it was from the abominable pig. Neither would bite.*

—RS

by offering them leftover food, especially food first eaten by foreigners, who are perceived as untouchables and outcasts in the eyes
of certain Hindus. Yet, like the Britisher, I did not want food to go
to waste. And I had noticed some of the villagers had that unmistakable look of hunger. So I asked them if they would like to eat
some of the food that remained. There was an audible but garbled
murmur. Some wanted to eat, others didn't. Some of the men, feeling insulted, broke away from the circle of villagers, muttering,
"*Jutho khadaina.*" They were not going to eat food already "polluted" by foreigners. But the majority surged forward. Yes, they
were hungry, they wanted to eat.

I asked a woman near me to ladle out the food. She was squatting close to the pots. She was elderly with kind, gentle features. I
felt that she would share the leftover food equally. She hesitated,
and before she could do anything, a young woman aggressively approached the pots of food. She said loudly, "Here, let me do it. I'll
take care of it." Her aggressiveness annoyed me. I said to her, "No,
you sit down. I've already told this old lady here. She can do it."
The young woman stopped in midstep and slowly stepped back
into the circle. Then a man called out, "No, sir, let the young
woman do it." I ignored him and requested the elderly woman to

begin serving food. Suddenly, looking shy and avoiding my eyes, she said, "No, sir, I shouldn't do it." Still squatting, she began to shuffle away from the gathered villagers.

"But why not?" I asked, totally perplexed. I was now more concerned about who should serve food than their hunger. Now several men spoke up, even those who had first refused food. There was a chorus of male voices urging me to let the younger woman take over. And before I could say anything more, she purposefully strode forward, squatted by the pot of rice and began to ladle out food on the unused paper plates. The rest followed suit, crowding around the food and the young woman, hands outstretched for the plate of food. All except the old woman who remained squatting, just outside the sheets of plastic on the ground. She had a pine needle stuck between her teeth, as if she were picking her teeth after lunch. She looked on calmly, as if a mother watching her happy children crowd around bountiful food.

Within the Jewish community, one finds extraordinary variations in the way Jews observe the dietary laws. The most observant will eat only in their own homes, in the homes of people they know to be scrupulously kosher, or in restaurants under rabbinical supervision.

Some Jews keep kosher at home; "outside," they will eat in nonkosher homes and in restaurants those foods that are kosher, even when they have been prepared in pots and pans that also are used to prepare unkosher foods. These people believe that the use of such utensils does not render kosher items unkosher.

—Rabbi Joseph Telushkin, *Jewish Literacy*

Intrigued by her, I approached her and asked her why she did not serve the food. Was she not hungry? But she simply repeated, "No sir, I shouldn't." And then a man, in between mouthfuls of rice, told me that she was not of the right caste. If she had even touched the pots of food, other villagers wouldn't have eaten.

But of course! I knew that! Yet it had not registered. My encounters with untouchability had occurred in my grandparents' village. Yet it had been in an intimate, family situation. Thus, the Muslim farmhands never entered the kitchen and they always ate outside in the open veranda. In the sacred part of the kitchen, where rice and lentils were cooked, only a Bramhin man or woman cooked and no one, not even my grandparents, were allowed to enter beyond a certain invisible line that separated the "sacred" from the "profane." Meat and vegetables, especially those cooked with onions, garlic, and other spices, were cooked in a separate part of the kitchen, accessible to all, except Muslims and untouchables, such as those whose caste duty it was to clean the outhouses and open drains. As a child visiting my grandparents, I had taken such separations for granted. There were degrees of discrimination, and everyone was discriminated at a certain level, including my grandparents. But at our home in Kathmandu, there was no practice of "untouchability"; my father rejected such ideas and attitudes as "backward" and "undemocratic" and actively encouraged us to disregard such traditional practices. So I grew up in an environment where outcasts and untouchability were not on daily display. Thus my failure to recognize the aggression behind the young village woman, as well as the calm dignity (or fatalism, if you will) behind the older woman's retreat during lunch above the town of Trisuli.

The young woman called out to me. She had noticed that I had not eaten and asked me if I wanted some food. I asked her if she had had her share. "Not yet," she replied. I told her to help herself and then I would eat if anything was left. She said there was plenty of it. Then she ladled out a plate of rice, meat, vegetables, and one *chapati* and brought it over to the older woman. "Next for you?" the young woman asked me.

"No, after you."

But she didn't listen to me. She brought me a plate of food too. Seeing that everyone had been served, she finally helped herself.

The old woman began to eat, and I sat down next to her and began my lunch too.

Rajendra S. Khadka was born in Nepal, educated by the Jesuits in Kathmandu and Yankees in New England. His desultory career pursuits have included freelance journalism, managing a movie theater during the pre-VCR days, and a chef-on-call. He is now a writer, editor, and researcher living in Kathmandu. He is the editor of Travelers' Tales Nepal.

★

Let us sit down soon to eat
with all those who haven't eaten,
let us spread great tablecloths,
put salt in the lakes of the world,
set up planetary bakeries,
tables with strawberries in snow,
and a plate like the moon itself
from which we will all eat.

For now I ask no more
than the justice of eating.

—Pablo Neruda, "The Great Tablecloth," *Extravagaria,*
translated by Alastair Reid

P. J. O'ROURKE

All Guns, No Butter

We have met the enemy and he is indeed us.

WE DO NOT, IN THE MODERN WORLD, HAVE FAMINE, PLAGUE, AND war caused by a population crisis; we just have famine, plague, and war. Of these, war is the easiest to condemn, plague is the most frightening, but it's famine that makes us squirm.

Famine is too close to dieting. We snap at our spouses, jiggle on the scale, and finish other people's cheesecake. If we're turned into angry, lying thieves by a mere forgoing of dessert, what must real hunger be like? Imagine a weight-loss program at the end of which, instead of better health, good looks, and hot romantic prospects, you die. Somalia had become just this kind of spa. I went there in December 1992, shortly after U.S. troops had landed in Mogadishu.

I was hoping famine would prove to be a simpler issue than overpopulation. Population alarmists have forgotten that each numeral in a census represents an individual human with as much interest in living and as much right to do so as a population alarmist. Hunger alarmists are professional worriers, too, but they don't wish the rest of humanity dead. Quite the contrary. And in Somalia the good intentions that professional worriers forever profess were being combined with—how rare this mixture is—good deeds.

Food was being shipped to the country and international peace-keepers were being sent to deliver the food.

"Feed the hungry" is one of the first principles of morality. Here it was in operation. So where *were* the starving children of Mogadishu? Where were the pitiable little fellows with the gone-away expressions, faces already turned to some less painful world, limbs as thin as the lines of type in a newspaper obit column and bellies gravid with death? A glance at these tykes racks the soul. They are the emblem of Third World misery, the inevitable cover of news magazines, the constant subject of videotape on *Eyewitness News.* I half-expected to be met by a delegation of them at the Mogadishu airport.

What I met with instead were guns. Arrayed around the landing strip were U.S. guns, U.N. guns, guns from around the world. Trucks full of Somalis with guns came to get the luggage. These were my guns, hired to protect me from the other Somalis with guns, and they all had them. And I thought I might get a gun of my own besides, since none of these gunmen—local, foreign, or supranational—looked like they'd mind shooting me.

Everything that guns can accomplish had been achieved in Mogadishu. For two years the residents had been joining, dividing, subdividing, and rejoining in a pixilation of clan feuds and alliances. Previously Somalia had been held together by the loathsome but stable 22-year reign of dictator Siad Barre. But

Hunger is not an unavoidable phenomenon like death and taxes. We are no longer living in the seventeenth century when Europe suffered shortages on an average of every three years and famine every ten. Today's world has all the physical resources and technical skills necessary to feed the present population of the planet or a much larger one. Unfortunately for the millions of people who go hungry, the problem is not a technical one—nor was it wholly so in the seventeenth century, for that matter. Whenever and wherever they live, rich people eat first, they eat a disproportionate amount of the food there is and poor ones rarely rise in revolt against this most basic of oppressions unless specifically told to 'eat cake.' Hunger is not a scourge but a scandal.

—Susan George, *How the Other Half Dies: The Real Reasons for World Hunger*

Barre gained loathsomeness and lost stability, and when he took a walkout powder in January 1991, all and sundry began fighting each other with rifles, machine guns, mortars, cannons, and—to judge by the look of the town—wads of filth.

No building was untouched, and plenty were demolished. It was a rare wall that wasn't stippled with bullet holes and a peculiar acre that lacked shell damage. Hardly a pane of glass was left in the city.

There was no potable water and no electricity. At night the only illumination was from tracer bullets. Mogadishu's modern downtown was gone, the steel and concrete architecture bombarded into collapse. The old city was deserted rubble, a no-man's-land between two envenomed clan factions. Rubbish was dumped atop wreckage everywhere and goats grazed on the offal. Mounds of sand had blown through the streets. Sewage welled up through what pavement was left.

The destruction had squeezed people into the roads, where they built market stalls from pieces of scrap wood and flattened olive-oil cans—market stalls which seemed to sell mostly pieces of scrap wood and flattened olive-oil cans. Young men waving AK-47 assault rifles pushed among the crowds. Rusted, dent-covered, windshieldless pickup trucks with gun mounts welded into their beds sputtered down what remained of the right-of-way, outnumbered by donkey carts and overtopped by pack camels.

It was a scene of Paleolithic ruin except for the modern weapons. The Somalis used to paint the outside walls of their shops with crude pictures of canned goods, television sets, photocopiers, and the like. Cartoon murals on abandoned storefronts were the only evidence that the twentieth century had produced anything pleasant.

Compared to Mogadishu, starving children would be cute. In fact, somewhere in the psychic basement of the sob-sister sorority house, in the darkest recesses of the bleeding heart, starving children *are* cute. Note the big Muppet Baby eyes, the etiolated features as unthreatening as Michael Jackson's were before the molestation charges, the elfin incorporeity of the bodies. Steven

Spielberg's E.T. owes a lot to the Biafran-Bangladeshi-Ethiopian model of adorable suffering.

It's easier to advertise our compassion for innocents in misery than it is to face up to what happened in a place like Somalia. What happened was not just famine but the complete breakdown of everything decent and worthwhile. I spent two weeks in Somalia and never saw a starving child, not because they didn't exist but because they were off somewhere dying, pushed into marginal spaces and territories by people with guns. Going to Somalia was like visiting the scene of a crime and finding that the murderer was still there but the body had fled....

In order to go to Somalia, I took a job as a radio reporter for ABC news. It wasn't someplace I could go by myself. News organizations had to create fortresses for themselves in Mogadishu and man those forts with armies.

ABC sent in its most experienced fixers, men known in the news business (and not without respect) as "combat accountants." The accountants hired 40 gunmen and found a large walled house that used to belong to an Arab ambassador. The house was almost intact and close to the ruins of the American embassy, which—the accountants hoped—would soon be occupied by U.S. Marines.

Satellite dishes, telephone uplinks, editing equipment, half a dozen generators, fuel, food, water, beer, toilet paper, soap, sheets, towels, and mattresses all had to be flown in on charter planes from Nairobi. For some reason we wound up with 500 boxes of a Kenyan chocolate chip cookie that tasted like bunion pads. Cooks, cleaning people, and laundry men were employed, as well as translators—dazed-looking academic types from the long-destroyed Somali National University.

Some thirty of us—journalists, camera crews, editors, producers, money men, and technicians—were housed in this compound, bedded down in shifts on the floor of the old audience hall while our mercenaries camped in the courtyard.

It was impossible to go outside our walls without "security" ("security" being what the Somali gunmen—gunboys, really—

liked to be called). Even with the gunmen along, there were always people mobbing up to importune or gape. Hands tugging at wallet pockets. Fingers nipping at wristwatch bands. No foreigner could make a move without setting off a bee's nest of attention—demanding, grasping, pushing crowds of cursing, whining, sneering people with more and worse Somalis skulking on the fringes of the pack.

One of the first things I saw, besides guns, when I arrived in Mogadishu was a pack of thieves creeping through the wreckage of the airport, sizing up our charter cargo. And the last thing I saw as I left was the self-appointed Somali "ground crew" running beside our taxiing plane, jamming their hands through the window hatch, trying to grab money from the pilot....

Mogadishu is almost on the equator. The sun sets at six, prompt. After that, unless we wanted to mount a reconnaissance in force, we were stuck inside our walls. We ate well. We had our canned goods from Kenya, and the Somalis baked us fresh bread (made from famine-relief flour, no doubt) and served us a hot meal every night—fresh vegetables, stuffed peppers, pasta, lobsters caught in the Mogadishu harbor and local beef. Only a few of us got sick. We had a little bit of whiskey, lots of cigarettes, and the pain pills from the medical kits. We sat out on the flat tile roof of the big stucco house and listened to the intermittent artillery and small-arms fire.

Down in the courtyard our gunmen and drivers were chewing qat. The plant looks like watercress and tastes like a handful of something pulled at random from the flower garden. You have to chew a lot of it, a bundle the size of a whisk broom, and you have to chew it for a long time. It made my mouth numb and gave me a little bit of a stomachache, that's all. Maybe qat is very subtle. I remember thinking cocaine was subtle, too, until I noticed I'd been awake for three weeks and didn't know any of the naked people passed out around me. The Somalis seemed to get off. They start chewing before lunch but the high didn't kick in until about three in the afternoon. Suddenly our drivers would start to drive straight into potholes at full speed. Straight into pedestrians and livestock, too. We called it "the qat hour." The gunmen would all begin talking at once, and the chatter would increase in speed, volume, and intensity until, by dusk, frantic arguments and violent gesticulations had broken out all over the compound. That was when one of the combat accountants would have to go outside and give everybody his daily pay in big stacks of dirty Somali shilling notes worth four thousand to the dollar. Then the yelling really started.

Qat is grown in Kenya. "The Somalis can chew twenty planes a day!" said a woman who worked in the Nairobi airport. According to the Kenyan charter pilots some twenty loads of qat are indeed flown into Mogadishu each morning. Payloads are normally about a ton per flight. Qat is sold by the bunch, called a *maduf*, which retails for $3.75 and weighs about half a pound. Thus $300,000 worth of qat arrives in Somalia every day. But it takes U.S. Marines to deliver a sack of wheat.

I went to the Marine Corps encampment at Mogadishu Port on the day before Christmas. The docks and quays and warehouses had been so heaped with wreckage and muck that the first pieces of military equipment the marines landed were bulldozers. The marines plowed away the debris and sprayed the wharves with fire-fighting equipment from the U.S. Navy ships. It took three scrapings and hosings before Mogadishu was only as dirty as an ordinary seaport. Then the marines built a twenty-foot wall of cargo containers around the space they'd cleared, not so much for military reasons but to make a sort of citadel of hygiene.

Only one of the port's warehouses had enough corrugated tin left on top to provide shelter, and this was pinked with galaxies of bullet holes. Somalis must have stood inside and fired through the roof for the sheer noise of it. Seven or eight hundred marines were sleeping here, their mosquito net-draped cots in rows as close as auditorium chairs. It was 100, 110, 115 degrees every day in Mogadishu, with air so humid that the wind felt like shaving lather. Even in our thick-walled, shaded house the only way I could sleep was to lie naked on the mattress with an electric fan pointed at me. There were no fans in the warehouse and not even much of that hot, sopping breeze.

A branch of some reasonably firlike plant had been set up by the warehouse doors, its needles decorated with miniature Tabasco bottles, Chiclets, and other of the less-esteemed items from the MRE ("Meal Ready to Eat") ration packs. In place of a star was a plastic envelope of beef stew. The Navy claimed it would try, the next day, to get some turkey in from the ships' galleys. And satiric carols had been composed:

> On the first day of Christmas,
> The Marine Corps gave to me
> Forty injections for tropical disease...

The troops were crabbier than they'd been in the Gulf War. They were sticky and dirty and bored. They had no showers, no hot meals, and, even with female military personnel all over, no private place to take a crap. But all these conditions had existed in Saudi Arabia and for months on end. The problem in Somalia was more abstract. This was the first large-scale military operation in history to be launched for purely altruistic reasons. Nobody knew how to go about such a thing. In a war against hunger, what do you do? Shoot lunch?...

So here we were on another crusade, this time one of compassion (though Richard the Lionhearted thought his cause was compassionate too). Enormous stores of food aid were arriving in Mogadishu, food donated by international governments and by private charities. Armed convoys were being formed to deliver that food. It takes a lot of weapons to do good works (as Richard the Lionhearted could have told us). And this is not just a Somali problem. We have poverty and deprivation in our own country. Try standing unarmed on a street corner in Compton handing out twenty-dollar bills and see how long you last.

I went with an ABC camera crew on the first convoy to Jalaaqsi, 120 miles north of Mogadishu up the Shebeli river. For the sake of making America's allies look less worthless, the Italian army was given the escort job. A company of Italians in Fiat jeeps and troop

carriers led a dozen aid-agency food trucks. Two U.S. Army pla-
toons in Humvees brought up the rear.

The convoy was not a work of logistical genius. It left town a
day late because (my American military sources swear this is true)
the Italians lingered too long over lunch. Then the Italians, who in
their own country are homicidally fast drivers, insisted on a
twenty-mile-per-hour convoy speed. They also took three meal
breaks. Then one of the Italian drivers fell asleep at the wheel and
ran into practically the only tree in the Somali desert. After the sun
went down, the convoy got off course somehow. I'm not exactly
sure what happened, but I believe the lead driver saw what he
thought were the lights at the Jalaaqsi airstrip and headed toward
them, but those were actually the lights of the last vehicles in the
convoy. Anyway, we wound up with an enormous merry-go-
round of trucks, jeeps, and Humvees circling in the desert.

The trip took fourteen hours. Then, with thousands of square
miles of parched sand in every direction, the Italians found a mud
flat for us to camp in.

The Somalis had been busy, too. Before we even left
Mogadishu, the Italian colonel in charge of the convoy had caught
one of the Somali drivers draining the radiator of his own truck.
That way he'd have a "breakdown" en route and his cargo would
be "stolen." A number of other such sabotages were detected. The
Somalis were also quarreling with each other, and their qat-addled
driving was bad even by Italian standards. Then, during meal break
three, the Somalis decided they couldn't eat Italian rations and they
couldn't eat American MREs. They would have to leave the convoy, go to a local village, and get Somali food.

"This is a famine, goddammit," said an American sergeant.
"There *isn't* any Somali food. If
there *was* any Somali food, we
wouldn't have to fucking *be*
here."

The Italian colonel said he
wanted to shoot all the Somali
drivers.

> *For expiation he shall
> feed poor persons, or
> the equivalent thereof in fasting,
> that he may taste the evil conse-
> quences of his deed.*
>
> —Koran

An American lieutenant commented, "I'm quitting the army. I'm going on welfare. I'll sell the cars to my folks, sell the house to my sister, and get benefits. This thing sucks—helping people who don't give a shit."

ABC's Somali employees had also claimed they needed special food. The Kenyan canned goods we were going to pack for them might have pork inside. They wanted a million shillings. Which they got. But they didn't buy any food with it. And, when we weren't looking, they ate all of ours. We had to get the ABC satellite phone out, set it up in the mudflat, and trade soldiers long-distance calls to Mom for MREs.

We didn't have any camping gear either, and when we got ready to go sleep in our trucks, we found our gunmen already stretched out on all the seats, roofs, and hoods. I took three Halcion tablets and lay down in the mud, and I understand the entire U.S. military presence in Jalaaqsi was kept awake all night by my snoring.

When the sun came up, we could see a refugee squatter camp stretching for a mile along the Shebeli river. These people were not starving; that is, they weren't starving to *death*. Their misery had not quite reached the photogenic stage. But they were living in huts no bigger than the houses children make by putting a blanket over a card table. These homes weren't even hovels, just little humps in the landscape formed with sticks bent in half-circle hoops and covered with grain sacks and pieces of scrap cloth.

The refugees had none of the proud shyness...found among the nomads. You could approach these people at random, and they were only too glad to talk. They had nothing to do but talk.

I talked to a woman named Habiba Osman. She had fled from the fighting in someplace called "Burrui," which I cannot find on a map. She was a Hawiye, a member of the Hawadli subclan, and had been chased away from her home by other Hawiye, members of the Abgaal subclan. She had nine children, she said, holding up four fingers, and she was forty-five. Her husband, Muhammad, stood in the background. They were getting one portion of coarse cornmeal a day. It was hard to eat. They made it into porridge.

I counted her possessions: a wooden bowl, a long pestle for

cracking grain, an empty two-gallon olive-oil can, an aluminum pot, a few aluminum dishes. The goats and camels had been stolen.

I went to watch one of our convoy trucks unload food for the Save the Children charity in Jalaaqsi. The town itself hardly existed anymore, though it hadn't been ruined by the war or abandoned by its population. It was just—like the rest of the Somali nation, citizenship, and culture—a neglected, entropic, crumbling mess. The Save the Children headquarters was a tumbledown school sitting in a small yard inside the high walls with which everything needs to be surrounded in Somalia. The food we'd brought to them was something called Unimix, a sort of Purina Famine Chow made of 50 percent corn, 30 percent beans, 10 percent sugar, and 10 percent oil, all ground together. It makes a nourishing gruel when stirred into water, if you can find clean water. A great number of Somalis had to be hired to unload the food: some to carry the 50-pound sacks, more to stand around yelling commands, and even more, armed with long switches, to argue with the others and take swipes at townspeople who gathered in a nosy cluster around the truck.

Save the Children had managed to keep some food coming into Jalaaqsi. In the midst of the worst chaos they had eight kitchens operating to feed kids. They were able to do this, they said, because they worked closely with clan elders. More importantly, there isn't much of a thieves' market for Unimix. Save the Children was losing only 10 percent of its food shipments. But, even so, as many as ten children a day were dying in the refugee camp where I talked to Habiba Osman.

Several reporters were interviewing a Save the Children aid worker. One of the reporters must have flunked journalism school because he asked a question that went straight to the point. "Who cares?" he said, looking around at the wretchedness, squalor, muddle, and despair. "Back in the United States, in the rest of the world, who really cares about these people?" The man from Save the Children started to laugh. He was possessed of Christian charity—or Muslim or Jewish or whatever. The idea that someone could look at this suffering and not care was absurd to the aid worker, utterly ridiculous. So he laughed, the only laugh of kindness I've ever heard.

Much uglier jokes were available. About food, for instance. It was all over the place. In fourteen hours of travel the previous day, we'd never been out of sight of the stuff. The American sergeant yelling at the Somalis for trying to grocery-shop in a famine was wrong. Just as I'd been wrong about parched sands when I'd seen our bivouac area. The Shebeli river valley is wet and fecund and contains the richest farmland in Somalia. The road from Mogadishu traversed miles of corn and sorghum, the fields marked out with animal skulls set on stakes. (Scarecrows, maybe, or scarepeoples. I saw a human skeleton beside the pavement.) Even in the drier areas, away from the river, there were herds of cows and goats. We'd been carrying thousands of pounds of food relief through thousands of acres of food.

It was not a supply-side problem they had in Somalia, as our drivers and gunmen pointed out to us that afternoon when they refused to take us back to Mogadishu. They said they'd be robbed and shot. "But," we said, "you knew we were coming to Jalaaqsi, and you knew we'd have to go home. We talked about this before we left. We asked for volunteers. You weren't afraid then," we said. They said they'd changed their minds.

So we left the little army that our corporation had hired with the larger army that our tax dollars pay for and hitched a ride to Mogadishu on a relief agency plane.

Somalia is amazingly roofless. Almost every building we flew over had its ceiling off. How much of this was from neglect and artillery and how much from looting of corrugated tin sheets I don't know, but you could look right down into the rooms and hallways, and it made the entire country seem like a gigantic game board of Clue. Probable correct answer: Everybody. In the toilet. With an AK-47.

Beautiful beaches, however. As we came into Mogadishu we could see miles of tawny sand with not a hotel or time-share condominium in sight. At this very minute some real estate developer is probably saying, "We got your two baby-boom major obsessions here: oceanfront property and weight loss. Bingo, it's the new Hilton Head."

On New Year's Eve I went with another convoy west a hundred miles to Baidoa, this time with U.S. Marines in the lead. We made the trip in three hours despite long sections of road that weren't there anymore. Marines drive like qat-influenced Somalis except they don't litter. American troops in Somalia were scrupulous about not tossing empty water bottles out Humvee windows or scattering MRE trash on patrol. They policed their areas and always left the campground cleaner than they found it. We tried to explain to the marines that the locals *wanted* those water bottles and MRE scraps. Somalia is so bad that making a mess improves the place.

The land was less fertile here than in Jalaaqsi. Western Somalia is one great thorn scrub savannah gradually rising toward the mountains of Ethiopia and utterly featureless except for two gigantic limestone rocks, Bur Acaba and Bur Eibi, which jut out of the surrounding plain as big and steep and out of place as ski resorts. But, although this was desert, it had wells and irrigated fields, and between the fields was grazing land dotted with cows, goats, and camels. Again, we were never out of the sight of food. And never out of the sight of hunger either.

Children were begging frantically by the roadside, pointing to their bellies and making terrible faces. Older boys twirled rags to attract attention. That they had enough energy for theatrics meant they were among the better-off. We weren't going to stop for them anyway. The road was famous for bandits....

We went on the trip to Baidoa to see George Bush, who was making the kind of high-speed kiss-and-promise tour of Somalia that seemed, I thought, indistinguishable from presidential campaigning—as though the man had suffered complete memory loss, forgot he was beaten the previous November, and forgot he was in the wrong country besides.

Baidoa had been completely destroyed: "Somollified," as we'd taken to calling it. And it stank with the same smell poverty has around the world—stale smoke and fresh shit. The only buildings left intact were the fortified charity offices. The charities also had the only vehicles left running, all filled with gunmen and sporting the flags and logos of various relief agencies. A total innocent, set down in these environs, would say by the look of things that Baidoa had been conquered and pillaged by the Red Cross, OxFam, and CARE.

We found lodgings of a sort in Baidoa at the Bikiin Hotel, named not after the bathing suit but, very approximately and very unaccountably, after the capital of China. The Bikiin was a disintegrating thatch-and-cement establishment that served dirty plates of spaghetti and warm Kenyan beer. But it had the one thing you want most in Somalia—a high wall. It also had an antiaircraft gun and a howitzer outside the front gate.

No rooms were to be had, not that we wanted one of the dank little cubicles. And there were no bathrooms that we would go into more than once voluntarily. We commandeered an empty hut at the back of the compound, made pallets on the floor, and draped mosquito nets around as best we could. We got our gunmen squared away, fed on the spaghetti and staked out around our trucks. Then we found a table and some chairs and set these out under a palm tree.

There were four of us ABC employees: a reporter from New York, a South African soundman, a cameraman from Cairo, and me. We'd requisitioned two bottles of scotch from the ABC emergency larder. Huge red clouds rolled through at sunset like blood pouring into water. The sky turned ruby then maroon then mahogany then black. A breeze came up. The temperature went down to only 90 degrees. The clouds blew away again and there was a moonless equatorial sky undimmed by the lights of civilization or anything resembling it. The sky was so clear that the starlight cast shadows, and so many sparkles and glitters and glints appeared above us that it looked like something really expensive had been dropped and shattered in heaven—God's Steuben ashtray, maybe.

We began to drink and think big thoughts. What the hell were we doing here? We thought that, for instance. And we thought, well, at least some little bit of good is being done in Somalia. The

director of the Baidoa orphanage had told us only one child died
in December. Before the marines came, the children were dying
like..."Dying like flies" is not a simile you'd use in Somalia. The
flies were prosperous and lead full lives. Before the marines came,
the children were dying like children. Would this last? No, we
thought. Everything will slip back into chaos as soon as the
marines are gone. But to do some good briefly is better than doing
no good ever. Or is it always? Somalia was being flooded with
food aid. The only way to overcome the problem of theft was to
make food too cheap to be worth stealing. Rice was selling for ten
cents a pound in Somalia, the cheapest rice in the world. But what,
we thought, did that mean to the people with the fields of corn
and sorghum and the herds of goats and cattle? Are those now
worth nothing too? Had we come to a Somalia where some people sometimes starved only to leave a Somalia where everybody always would?

*W*ho is the slayer, who
the victim? Speak.
—Sophocles

We had some more to drink
and smoked as many cigars and
cigarettes as we could to keep
the mosquitoes away—mosquitoes which carry yellow fever,
dengue, lymphatic filariasis, and four kinds of malaria, one of
which is almost instantly fatal. Was this the worst place we'd ever
covered? We thought it was. We had, among the four of us, nearly
forty years' experience of journalism in wretched spots. But
Somalia...tiresome discomfort, irritating danger, amazing dirt, prolific disease, humdrum scenery (not counting this night sky), ugly
food (especially the MREs we were chewing), rum weather, bum
natives, and everywhere you looked, suffering innocents and thriv-
ing swine. True, the women were beautiful, but all their fathers,
brothers, uncles, husbands, and, for that matter, male children over
twelve were armed.

Still, we thought, this wasn't the worst New Year's Eve we'd ever
spent. We had a couple more drinks. We certainly weren't worried
about ecological ruin, shrinking white-collar job market, or fear of
intimacy. All that "modern era anomie" disappears with a dose of

Somalia. Fear cures anxiety. The genuinely alien banishes alienation. It's hard for existential despair to flourish where actual existence is being snuffed out at every turn. Real *Schmerz* trumps *Welschmerz*. If you have enough to drink.

But what do you do about Somalia? We had even more to drink and reasoned as hard as we could.

Professor Amartya Sen says, "There has never been a famine in any country that's been a democracy with a relatively free press. I know of no exception. It applies to very poor countries with democratic systems as well as to rich ones."

And in *The New York Times* article featuring that quote from Professor Sen, Sylvia Nasar says, "Modern transportation had made it easy to move relief supplies. But far more important are the incentives governments have to save their own people. It's no accident that the familiar horror stories…occurred in one-party states, dictatorships or colonies: China, British India, Stalin's Russia." She notes that India has had no famine since independence even though the country suffered severe food shortages in 1967, 1973, 1979, and 1987.

Says Professor Sen, "My point really is that if famine is about to

he Chinese Confucian philosopher Mencius… held agriculture to be China's basic industry, with crafts, manufacturing, and trade less important, and he made bold to criticize the policies of the Chou emperor whose court he graced: "If you do not interfere with the busy season in the fields, then there will be more grain and the people can eat; if you do not allow nets with too fine a mesh to be used in large ponds, then there will be more fish and turtles than they can eat…. Now when food meant for human beings is so plentiful as to be thrown to dogs and pigs, you fail to realize that it is time for garnering, and when men drop dead from starvation by the wayside, you fail to realize that it is time for distribution. When people die, you simply say, 'It is none of my doing. It is the fault of the harvest.' In what way is that different from killing a man by running him through, while saying all the time, 'It is none of my doing. It is the fault of the weapon.' Stop putting the blame on the harvest and the people of the whole empire will come to you."

—James Trager,
The Food Chronology: A Food Lover's Compendium of Events and Anecdotes, from Prehistory to the Present

develop, democracy can guarantee that it won't." And he goes on to say that when there is no free press "it's amazing how ignorant and immune from pressure the government can be."

Well, for the moment at least, Somalia certainly had a free press. The four of us were so free nobody even knew where we were. But how do you get Somalia one of those democratic systems Amartya Sen is so fond of? How, indeed, do you get it any system at all? Provisional government by clan elders? Permanent international occupation? U.N. Trusteeship? Neo-colonialism? Sell the place to Microsoft? Or...Or...Or...

We were deep into the second bottle of scotch now, and boozy frustration was rising in our gorges along with the MRE entrées. It's all well and good to talk about what can be done to end famine in general. But what can be done about famine specifically? What the fucking goddamn hell do you do?

There's one ugly thought that has occurred to almost everyone who's been to Somalia. I heard a marine private in the Baidoa convoy put it succinctly. He said, "Somalis—give them better arms and training and seal the borders."

Author, commentator, and humorist P. J. O'Rourke has written for publications as varied as National Lampoon *and* Rolling Stone. *He is the author of numerous works, including* The CEO of the Sofa, Eat the Rich, Holidays in Hell *and* All The Trouble in the World: The Lighter Side of Overpopulation, Famine, Ecological Disaster, Ethnic Hatred, Plague and Poverty, *from which this story is excerpted.*

★

Some three hours, eight or nine shared pounds of prawns, and two thick steaks apiece later, we had gluttonized ourselves comatose. Unable to rise from our seats, we stared at each other glassy-eyed over hugely distended bellies, trying somehow to will our digestive systems into action. At last, after another hour of torpor, Suhoski emitted a thunderous belch and heaved himself to his feet. Groaning with gut-ache, I struggled up, and we waddled out of the restaurant.

The same lunch, identical in all its particulars, became as regular a feature of our trips to Calcutta as did postprandial sex—alfresco or in the shelter of a taxicab—with the city's contingent of Chinese whores. We abruptly lost our appetites for further gorging at the restaurant, however, when after a typically disgraceful pig-out, we staggered from the table to the revolving door, which was jammed by what I took to be a bundle of dirty rags. On closer inspection, the impediment turned out to be the body of some poor wretch who had starved to death, apparently with his nose pressed to the glass while watching us stuff ourselves.

I never again returned to Firpo's. Or perhaps I did, decades later and thousands of times, when fifteen years of my days and nights were spent consuming rarefied delicacies while Ethiopia starved, much of the rest of the Third World went hungry, and some elderly Americans subsisted on cat food.

—Jay Jacobs, *A Glutton for Punishment: Confessions of a Mercenary Eater*

ROBERT GOLLING JR.

A World Without Latkes

The author finds continuity and
history in a simple dish.

On a flight to Chicago I settled into my seat located on the left side of the plane, on the aisle. I was looking forward to a good solid block of reading time. A steady stream of people bumped their way down the aisle, finding seats, looking for carry-on luggage space. A lady with a Nordstrom bag smiled at me. "Oh, thank you," the lady said as I stood out of her way. She slipped across my row to the window seat. "So many people have no manners these days, thank you." I helped her put her bag into the overhead storage.

Plumpish, not fat, she looked to be in her late fifties or early sixties. Her face was round with hints of wrinkles next to her mouth and eyes. She wore an exercise suit that was dark blue with large white stripes on the jacket. The material was of some crinkly, shiny fabric. Beneath the jacket she wore a dark red blouse. A thin gold chain flashed around her neck, diamond studs glittered on her ears. She wore white tennis shoes. Practical traveling wear; the effect was fancy casual.

She settled into her seat and I back into mine. "Good morning," she said. Trying not to be too friendly and displaying my book, "Good morning," I said; but I couldn't help but smile as I saw her perched next to the window, wiggling to get comfortable before take off.

"My name is Esther." Her right hand was undeniable as she grabbed just the fingers of my right hand. "I'm Bob." I got the feeling that the next four hours were not going to be my own.

"Would you like a Tic Tac?" she offered. As I declined she began a monologue. She'd been out visiting her daughter in San Jose, California. "Where do you live Bob?…Campbell? Is that near by?" She was on her way home now. She'd had to take a taxi; the daughter and son-in-law were at work; she didn't mind. "You're going to Chicago on business? Oh, training for your company."

It wasn't a frantic jabber, but a kind of continuous chatter. Like air is for breathing, for Esther, words were always in her mouth. "I transfer in Chicago. My home is in Allentown, Pennsylvania…" She told me about her husband, Jerry. He owned a small furniture store; he was always working; she didn't mind.

Being curious and courteous, I had been looking at her over my left shoulder. "Oh, Esther, I have to turn away. I have a cramp in my neck." I said. "That's O.K." she said and continued on. She'd left a week's worth of dinners frozen for Jerry. "He'll eat the meat loaf and the latkes," she said "but he won't touch the casseroles."

"Latkes?" I asked. I had heard of them, but I wasn't quite sure what they were. Like one of those words you vaguely know in context, but when asked to define you are at a loss. So was I with latkes.

"Latkes?" she looked slightly incredulous and bemused. "A simple dish, really, made from nothing. A treat. They're a traditional Chanukah dish. Pancakes, that's all they are. Latke means pancake in Yiddish. They are made with potatoes, onions, salt and pepper, or just about anything else you want to throw in. Fried golden brown, topped with sour cream and applesauce. They're like a dessert. A world without latkes is a world without light." As she spoke a look of great distance and time came over her face.

Even though my neck hurt like hell there was something more I wanted to find out about Esther and latkes. What was that look about? Stretching and rubbing my neck I asked, "So tell me, Esther, about latkes and light."

"Would you like to know?" one eyebrow arched. "Oh, I should be cooking them for you. Some people, they're such purists they won't change a thing. True, there are certain stages…well, if you don't do them right the latkes won't turn out as good; but you can do lots of different things too."

"Start with potatoes. Everybody has potatoes. In the old days that's all you had to eat. My mother, God rest her soul, always insisted, grate the potatoes with the small holes on the grater, and the onions with the large holes. But I've used a food processor and it works just fine. Into a bowl first grate onions then potatoes, then onions, then potatoes, and so on. You do this so the potatoes don't turn brown. A little lemon juice doesn't hurt either. Drain as much water as possible into a bowl. This is key, the less water the better. After a while a sediment will settle into the bottom of the bowl. Pour off the water, and add the sediment back into the potatoes and onions."

> *Anyone who has visited Hirschhorn, in the sweetly romantic Neckar Valley, and who has climbed the hill to the partly ruined castle that dominates the little village, will remember being confronted by a "Potato Monument" dedicated piously "To God and Francis Drake, who brought to Europe for the everlasting benefit of the poor—the Potato."*
>
> —Irma S. Rombauer and
> Marion Rombauer Becker,
> *The Joy of Cooking*

Esther was so animated telling me her recipe I could almost see her bustling about in her kitchen. I imagined the phone to her ear. Talking, talking, talking as she grated, poured, and squeezed. Maybe a neighbor sat at the kitchen table drinking tea and kibitzing.

"The traditional way, Mama always insisted, is to add flour or matzoth meal, a couple of slightly beaten eggs, salt and pepper, and that's all. Then you just fry them up quick as that. Aaaahh, but what is life without a little spice. Look around your kitchen. Aunt Birdie used to add bits of mushrooms and a little garlic."

I nodded my head thinking that anything else you could do to potatoes would probably be good on latkes. Nodding my head helped relieve the cramp in my neck.

"Aunt Birdie?" I asked.

"Mama's youngest sister, her name was Bertha. But my sisters and I called her Birdie. She was small and used to eat little amounts, a cracker, a piece of cheese, a slice of apple all throughout the day. She was always eating but she never gained a pound. We were never allowed to call her Birdie. It was our private name for her. Now it doesn't matter."

"No, why not?" I asked.

"They've passed on. My sisters too. They're all gone now," she said.

"I'm sorry." My apology seemed not enough, but it was the best I could do.

"It's O.K.," she said "It was all a long time ago."

We sat quietly for awhile. I had recently lost my mother to cancer. Our respective losses, except for time, seemed the same. "How much flour should I use with how many potatoes and onions?" I asked.

"Portions shmortions, who knows from portions? Its been so long since I looked at a recipe. Use three or four potatoes, one onion, one slightly beaten egg and one half cup flour until mixed up it looks like applesauce, salt and pepper to taste. Then add what ever spice you like. Parsley is good. Garlic, basil, and parmesan gives you a real pesto flavor."

"I like pesto." I said thinking pine nuts would be good in them also. "What about cooking them?"

"To cook them, first heat your pan, then add one-quarter inch of oil. Use good vegetable oil. This is how latkes are connected to Chanukah. Oil is light."

"Oil?" I asked.

"Yes, Chanukah is the celebration of a great Maccabean victory that rescued Judaism from annihilation. Judah the Maccabee celebrated the victory by lighting the lamps of a great menorah. In those days their lamps were fueled by oil. So heat your oil, medium high heat, spoon out and flatten a latke, a few minutes on each side, until golden brown. That's all it takes."

She continued telling about this person or that relative that had used zucchini, sweet potatoes, or dill with cucumber/yogurt sauce.

As she talked she rocked ever so slightly forward and back as if in prayer. Her words were ginger, cinnamon, nutmeg, and thyme, but her voice was something else.

The flight hadn't seemed half over and we were being told to prepare for landing. As I packed my unread book away... "Bob, would you like a Tic Tac?"

"Why yes I would, Esther."

The candy box was in her left hand. As she reached across the empty seat between us, her sleeve inched up her forearm. There, tattooed in black were a series of numbers from a time long ago, a time without latkes.

As we departed the plane, I said, "When I get home I'll make your latkes Esther."

"*Kaddishel,* Bob," she responded, "*Kaddishel.*"

I was to learn later that a Jewish son is affectionately referred to as "my *Kaddish,*" the one who will say Kaddish, the Jewish prayer for the dead, for me.

Bob Golling is a U.S. Navy veteran of the Vietnam War and a retired telephone engineer. He no longer travels on business. He does practice his culinary skills every day on his two sons.

★

Passover is a gastronomic holiday whose main point is to teach children about the privation of flight and exile. The protracted preprandial service forces the young to sit and be hungry, to experience directly the pangs their ancestors felt in the desert. During that service, they are from time to time allowed to consume small amounts of wine and symbolic antifoods—salt water and horseradish and haroset (chopped fruit and nuts)—culinary eccentricities never eaten at any other time in quite this way, even during the Passover week. For an hour or so, the children wait and listen to an incomprehensibly scholastic and nonnarrative analysis of the historical events described in the book of Exodus. They grow hungry and then they are fed a very full meal, but a meal which is itself circumscribed by a set of prohibitions unique to the occasion.

So there are two systems of paradox at work. The first is that of the anti-meal of the service; the second is that of the special dietary restrictions of the Passover meal itself. The first paradox—the service of the Haggadah—is an object lesson in history taught through mortification of the flesh and a subversion of normal eating. This service is a fast in the form of a meal. The second paradox of the Seder embodies an even more fundamental paradox. It is the opposition between normal eating, whose most basic act is the consumption of bread, and the special festivities of the Seder, whose basic act is the consumption of unleavened anti-bread, matzo.

—Raymond Sokolov, *The Jewish American Kitchen*

LATKES

3 medium russet potatoes	1 teaspoon baking soda
1 large onion	1/2 teaspoon salt
1 egg (slightly beaten)	pepper to taste
1/2 cup all purpose flour	1/2 cup vegetable oil, as needed

Peel and grate the potatoes and onions alternately into a bowl. Press out as much liquid as possible and reserve the starchy sediment at the bottom of the bowl. Return the sediment to the mixture. Add the egg, flour, baking powder, salt, and pepper. Mix ingredients until it looks like applesauce. Spoon, drop and flatten into medium high oil in frying pan. Fry until golden brown on both sides (2–3 minutes). Serve immediately with sour cream and applesauce.

MARK GRUBER, O.S.B.

Breaking Bread

A desert encounter reveals the brotherhood of man.

I REMEMBER, WHEN I WAS IN EGYPT, I WAS MAKING THE JOURNEY in a Land Rover from one desert monastery to another. These monasteries were very remote. They could not be approached, in many cases, by roads—just across the unmarked sand. And as luck would have it, during this one journey, the land rover broke down. I was in a rather precarious situation—much like the movies in which you see a poor soul dragging himself across the desert sand under the hot Sahara sun, desperate for water. Well, I wasn't quite so desperate, but in my imagination, I was playing out every such movie scene I had ever seen.

I had traveled quite a distance looking for some help or some resting place in the shade, when finally, I noticed a goat. I realized that there are no wild goats in this desert, that it must belong to an encampment of some kind, and so, without disturbing it, I followed the beast from a distance until it led me to the tents of its owner, an encampment of Bedouins, nomads. I presented myself to the first tent where the father of the dwelling, burly and larger than life, lavishly welcomed me in the custom so well known in the Arab world. He sat me on pillows and with the precious water of his house washed my feet and my hands and gave me to drink. His children went out to gather a variety of delicacies from the neighboring tents, and his wife prepared for me a gracious meal.

Part of the reason for this hospitality is that people who live in the desert so seldom find strangers to entertain and it provides for them great social interest to have an occasion of receiving someone generously and even excessively. It is also a mark of nobility in their society to be extravagant with hospitality. And finally, it's a kind of safety for them to make the desert a place of hospitality rather than fear for it might happen to any of them in various times in their life that they may find themselves alone and in the search for welcoming and for assistance.

So, according to the dictates, the norms of their culture, I was received with great kindness. And part of the hospitality of the father of that house, of that tent, was to pour out at my feet the equivalent of a bushel of cakes of bread! It's marvelous how the nomads in this region bake their bread because water is scarce between the oases of their journeys. They must do all of their baking during those relatively few times when they are close to a generous supply of water. So they make a lot of bread and carry it with them as they travel.

The trouble is, of course, that it would tend to become quite stale on the long journey, and so they bake their bread with a thick and, if you will, a hermetically sealed crust keeping the contents of the bread moist and fresh because of the hard, stiff shell. Once you break open a cake of bread in the Bedouin camp, you must eat the inside more or less all at once because you cannot save it. No plastic wrap, no tinfoil, no tupperware here. Their means of preservation is a thick crust in its integrity. Once broken, all the contents must be eaten or lost.

So the father of the tent picked up a cake of bread at my feet and broke it open for me. I thanked him and said I would be full now, but he urged me to a third one, even if I was only nibbling the second. And I told him that I was really filling up now and that I would be needing to leave soon and could he help me back to the jeep, or could he take me to the monastery because I couldn't linger for long. I was expected somewhere else....

He broke a third cake, and urged me to have a fourth! Maybe you have sometimes been in the home of a Mediterranean family, an Italian house, for a Sunday dinner and you know the impossibility of saying "no." You know that somehow the gift of food is linked in an inextricable way with the gift of self—that to reject the food is somehow to reject the giver of the food, and to consume the food is to offer the gift-giver the greatest affirmation. I found myself exactly in such a situation.

I was forcing myself to eat a third cake and to nibble at a fourth. And even then my host began to urge me heartily to a fifth and sixth, and to a seventh. And when my protests became louder and more forceful, the head of the house did something wonderful and something strange! He took one cake after the other of all that were lying before me—all of the bread of his family—and broke each one open, in front of my face! The gesture was unmistakable: he wanted me to know that he had withheld from me *nothing;* he had reserved from me no gift, but had imparted to me everything at his disposal. He wanted me to know that I had been received well, and by this *great* gesture this *extravagant* waste, this *complete* sacrifice, I would be persuaded, convinced, of his kindness. I would be *certain* of his hospitality.

It occurs to me now just how important breaking bread really is in the Near East—just what a significant *sign* it is: the giving of bread by such a gesture. The Bedouins of the desert are the folk heroes of the Semites. Their character is everywhere honored. Courage, skill, self-reliance, nobility, and especially hospitality are the stuff of legend. In villages and cities their nomadic ways are remembered by people who farm, and people who craft, by people who live in different dwellings, and bake in different ovens, but the gesture of the Breaking of Bread remains.

Father Mark Gruber is a Benedictine monk who lives and works in Pennsylvania. He spent a year in Egypt breaking bread and fulfilling requirements for his doctorate. This story was excerpted from his book, Wounded by Love: Intimations of an Outpouring Heart.

*

My mother, a transplanted American, was preparing for her first big dinner party as a young wife, she later told me. Determined to do it in a proper English manner, she starched the linens, polished the silver, and dusted the cut glass. The table was the picture of elegant dining.

Laboring in the kitchen most of the day, she had created dish after dish of artfully arranged vegetables, condiments, and desserts, while keeping an eye on the roast as it cooked to succulent perfection.

Shortly after the guests arrived, my mother ushered them into the dining room. Light conversation and laughter bubbled over the candlelit table, along with compliments on the lavish spread. My mother beamed. Fitting in with finicky English etiquette might not be such a challenge after all.

After a suitable pause, she asked the guests if they would like a second helping. All politely declined. Momentarily disappointed, my mother started to clear the table. What she did not see, however, were the equally disappointed faces of the guests as the buttered vegetables and half-eaten roast slid back through the hatch to the kitchen.

Later she learned her mistake. In some English circles it is customary to ask guests three times if they would like more. To accept the first time might sound overeager, a little too ravenous for English tastes. A second refusal is a simple show of restraint. But the final "Yes!" can burst with genuine desire.

—Susan Llewelyn Leach, "Table Etiquette for the Uninitiated,"
Christian Science Monitor

DAVID YEADON

Bananas

Taken ill in Costa Rica, the author
yearns for a little potassium.

AROUND EIGHT O'CLOCK THE FOLLOWING MORNING I KNEW something had gone decidedly wrong. My mouth was dry and then full of saliva, then dry again. My body sweated like a bilge pump, streams of it, and the day's heat hadn't really hit yet. My simple cabin was still cool.

I had to get to the bathroom—fast. And then again. And again. By midday I'd spent most of my time there and, so far as I could tell, I had nothing more in my body to expunge. But still I sat. Waves of nausea flowed over me, sending hot and cold ripples up my spine. The mirror on the wall showed a deathly face edged in a moldy-green sheen and eyes so tired and egglike that I began to wonder if survival was in the cards at all.

Hour after hour passed. Time twisted in cobra coils; my brain wandered around its confines like an inebriated slug. Crazy thoughts kept popping up—utter free association. I was definitely in the throes of some emerging fever. All energy had long since been dissipated.

I moved to the bed and twisted and turmoiled. Occasional shards of sound came from outside: the surf, gulls, someone passing my cabin. The sounds became a series of symphonic variations, sometimes so distorted that I couldn't recollect what the original sound was as my brain now became a freewheeling bagatelle. The voices of passing children reverberated like Buddhist bells and gongs—booming, peeling, cymbaling into switchbacking roller coasters of sound.

By evening I was far out of the realms of reality. The fading colors played kaleidoscope forms on the walls; shadows became ogreous and then stretched out into landscapes with giant cacti, stunted trees, and shattered mountain ranges.

A butterfly fluttering through my open window became a kite, then a jeweled bracelet freely floating, then a silhouetted hawk, and finally a sinister shadowy presence lurking high in the upper corner of my room. I think a lizard came in for a while or a dragon or just another dream.

I stopped trying to make sense of anything. There was no me left in me—I was no longer fighting back, no longer interpreting and filtering—just letting the tides of images and sounds and smells and colors roll over me in this place where time had long since lost any meaning and I was free of everything.

On the second day—it seemed like the second day anyway—I had a vision. Something so clearly outlined and tangible that I reached out a long sweaty arm to touch...a basket of ripe bananas. Bananas? Something in the recesses of my battered brain was sending a message. Bananas. I had to get some bananas!

Someone was passing the window. I could hear voices. But I couldn't get off the bed. I could hardly lift my head. So I reached out for something hard and found a book I'd been reading before my world collapsed. Gripping a corner as hard as I could I flung it at the window. The noise of the impact was wonderful, the first recognizable noise in almost two days. Swish, thunk, keerplop. Welcome real-world sounds.

The voices stopped and I heard a slither of feet in sand. A face appeared at the window and a young boy peered into my shadowy room. Big black eyes, pink lips, bright teeth.

"Bananas, please. And Coca-Cola." It didn't sound like my voice talking. The boy didn't seem sure what to do. I repeated my request slowly and pointed to my mouth.

A sudden smile and nods. "*Si*—bananas—*si, si,* Coca-Cola." And the face was gone.

More time passed, frozen shapes of time, each one distant, glowing with different colors. An utterly new experience. And bananas were in there too. Curved scimitárs, gleaming, linking blocks of time like golden chains.

A knock.

I said something, but it came out a grunt.

The door opened slowly. I thought I'd locked it, but it opened anyway and in came my little saviour with an old battered tin bucket.

He stood by the bed and smiled.

"Bananas."

He reached into the bucket and pulled out a stem of bananas—a dozen or more beautiful ripe fruits.

"Coca-Cola. And papaya."

There it was—sliced, wet, peach pink. The best papaya I had ever seen!

I pointed to a pile of my usual traveling detritus on the dressing table—pens, notebooks, knife, film, and scrunched-up paper money.

"Take money," I thought I said, but it was another grunt.

"No, I come back—later," he said shyly and left with smile, closing the door quietly behind him.

The next hour (I think it was an hour. Time was still slithering around) was pure joy. Just the sight of the bottle and the fruit made me feel better. And never has Coke tasted so magnificent, that first fizzing gush, listening to it going down, filling all the oh-so empty spaces in this useless lump of wet flesh I assumed was my body.

And the bananas! Such sweetness and softness. I could feel my digestive system eagerly sucking in every molecule of nutrition, every protein, mineral, vitamin, and whatever else that miracle fruit contains. Then the soft sensuality of the pink papaya—if there is such a thing as fruit orgasm I had one as the sloppy pulp ran down my throat, my chin, my chest....

I slept a sleep of utter peace.

Much, much later, deep into the evening, I awoke to find a plate of rice and plantains, some rum, and another full bottle of Coke. The boy must have been back—all the banana and papaya skins had been cleared away. A clean moist cloth covered my forehead.

I was safe. I'd come through the uninvited torment and turned up whole and alive on the other side, hog-happy in banana-papaya-Coke and boiled rice heaven. Who cares about yesterdays and tomorrows? I was here right now and being pampered like a prince in my modest palace, and the sunset was blasting through the window and those wonderful buzzing things outside in the trees were buzzing away again and doubtless more bananas were on the way....

A native of Yorkshire, England, David Yeadon has worked as an author, illustrator, journalist, and photographer for more than twenty-five years. He is the author of numerous books including, The Back of Beyond, Lost Worlds, *and* The Way of the Wanderer: Discover Your True Self through Travel. *He is also a regular travel correspondent for* National Geographic, National Geographic Traveler, The Washington Post, *and* The New York Times. *Currently, he writes the "Hidden America" column for* National Geographic Traveler. *In between travel odysseys he lives with his wife, Anne, in Japan, where she is a Professor in Vision Rehabilitation, and also in a Hudson Valley lakeside house, just far enough north of Manhattan to preserve soul and sanity.*

*

Reminds me of my safari in Africa. Somebody forgot the corkscrew and for several days we had to live on nothing but food and water.

—W. C. Fields

⭐

Slaying the Dragon

The monster Appetite prowls in many guises.

AT SEA, TUESDAY, 20:00 HOURS: BEFORE TURNING IN I CALLED THE Messenger of the Watch on the bridge. "This is Petty Officer Sterling," I said, "in compartment Bravo-37-87. I need a wake-up call at 03:30 tomorrow morning."

"Why so early?" the messenger asked. "You got some early lookout?"

"Yes," I lied.

Then I called Corporal Durum of the ship's Marine detachment. "I need the usual guard at the Special Weapons Office at 04:00 tomorrow."

"Till when?"

"About 04:30."

"And who'll be with you?"

"Seaman Henderson."

"Very well."

Because of still-current security considerations, the name of the ship on which this story took place cannot be revealed, and the names of crew members have been changed.

—RS

The Marines never ask why, they just do. I had made these arrangements because I had to take the Dragon's temperature. Periodically we, in the missile battery, had to measure the temperature and humidity of the nuclear

98

warhead magazine, and it was my turn. We usually did it in the wee hours because the Dragon's presence on board was Top Secret. I was taking Ricky Henderson with me because a nuke magazine is a No Lone Zone, the Two-Man Rule is in effect. No one is supposed to be left alone with the Dragon.

WEDNESDAY, 04:00 HOURS: We arrived at the office door and found the two Marines already posted; their boots, buckles, and weapons gleaming. We showed them our access passes, pinned on our film badges, and signed the log. They passed us through the portal, and the door closed behind us. No one else would enter.

"You really need me to go down with you?" Ricky asked.

"Nah. Stay here and read your skin mag. Just don't answer the phone if it rings. And don't make any noise."

We moved the office desk and exposed the scuttle—a small, circular hatch just wide enough to allow a man to pass through. Pausing to remember, I dialed the combination on the lock, opened the scuttle, and looked down the shaft that sunk three decks to another locked scuttle. Beneath that lay the magazine, three fathoms below the water line, at the very bottom of the ship.

I slipped down the hole, and Ricky closed the scuttle after me. Descending, the hard soles of my safety shoes rang on the flat steel rungs of the ladder, echoing in the shaft. Only the dim shaft light shone from above. By the time I reached the next scuttle, I was in a half-darkness. I noticed that the roll of the ship was reversed now, indicating that I was below its fulcrum, the waterline. The scuttle had been battened down tightly and I had to use a dogging wrench, a lever, to break the closures. Straining, I lifted the heavy portal and eye-squinting light shot through the hole, driving a column of it up the shaft like a fountain. I held my face over the streaming light for a moment, to adjust my eyes, then dropped down inside.

Everything was white: the deck, the bulkheads, the overhead, the lights, the fixtures…and the warheads. All were white, white, white; pure white, cold white, death white. Melville would have known this shade of white. Twenty-four nuclear warheads rested in two rows of six on the port side and two rows of six on the star-

board with a four-foot-wide aisle between them. Each one lying
on its side in a steel cradle frame, strapped in with a steel belt, they
looked like eggs—three-foot-long eggs—Embryos of the
Apocalypse. A few of them had thick, black electrical monitoring
cables snaking out of their aft ends, giving them the look of huge
spermatazoa, perhaps the gametes of Mr. Melville's leviathan.

I stood at one end of the aisle and regarded them for a moment.
Then I listened to the silence. A warship is usually a noisy place.
Engines thrum, chains clank, men shout, machines whir and wind
and wave sing their song or roar in anger. But the magazine was a
quiet place. The only sound was the soft whisper of the water slipping past the hull a fraction of an inch below my feet. And although Death slumbered here, it was not the quiet of the grave.
This was a womb. This was a holy place. The End of the World
slept here. This was Destruction's chapel, and we were his altar
boys. At the other end of the aisle, a shelf jutted out from the wall.
On it lay the open, black-bound log book. Above the shelf, like
two candles mounted on the wall, were the thermometer and the
humidity gauge: a pulpit for this worshipful cure of Nukes.

Walking down the aisle to take my readings, I stopped at warhead number W-18. It was a tactical device, small by nuclear standards, its power in the kiloton range. In it were half, maybe three-
quarters of a million kills. A Nagasaki. I ran my hand over its
perfect, seamless skin. It was smooth like pearl and perfectly symmetrical. The thing was superbly designed to slice through the atmosphere at two and a half times the speed of sound at the tip of
a surface-launched guided missile, one that even I might be called
upon to fire. I admired the magnificent craftsmanship, the skill, the
talent, the care—yes, even the love that had gone into the making
of so perfect an artifact. "Who are the gnomes," I wondered, "that
hammer away in the secret smithies of Bendix and the nuclear
agencies? And what should they be called? Armorers? No, too ar-
chaic and not powerful enough. Nuclear Device Technicians? No,
too clinical. Death Smiths? Yes, that's what they are, Death Smiths."

I took my readings, and as I was writing them in the log I noticed a bit of ash at my feet. I picked it up and smelled. Correli and

Morgan had been smoking dope in here again. I checked the electronics aperture in the rear of a few warheads to see if they had stashed their supply in one. It was, after all, the safest place on board. The only people besides us Missile Men that even knew this place existed were the Captain and a few of his officers, none of whom ever came here.

My search yielded a pack of Salem cigarettes (had to be Arnie's; he was the only one who smoked them), a lighter, and a deck of cards. Some of the guys liked to play cards here. They would place a board across two of the warheads, then sit on the adjacent ones. Arnie always made it a point to fart on the one he sat on. He said it was how he showed his "contempt for war." A. K. Douglas and Ricky Henderson would rub their groins against a couple of Doomsday's Children and then pretend that they "glowed at the gonads." They'd say things like, "Look out wimmen! Nuclear love!" or, "Ooh! A one-hundred-and-twenty kiloton orgasm, comin' at ya. Yahoo! Measure my virility on the Geiger counter."

I pocketed the goods, took one last look at my charges and ascended, out of the light, through the darkness, and up to the light again. Ricky and I closed and locked the scuttle and replaced the desk that covered it. We secured the office and notified the Corporal of the Guard that he could dismiss his two Marines. On Friday we would return. In obedience to the faraway councils of naval command, our ship would rendezvous under cover of darkness with an ammunition ship at some secret point on the map of the South China Sea. There we would haul Death's Cocoons out of their chamber, pack them in individual drums, and send them by the highline across the water to the other ship. A very delicate operation. What a time for me to quit smoking.

WEDNESDAY, 10:00 HOURS: After breakfast we met in the Missile House to confer on the

obacco, I do assert, without fear of contradiction from the Avon Skylark, is the most soothing, sovereign and precious weed that ever our dear old Mother Earth tendered to the use of man!

—Ben Johnson to Sir Walter Raleigh in the Mermaid Tavern

warhead movement. We assigned stations and duties to every man: magazine, ammunition lift, topside, etc. We would prepare the goods for shipment, then turn them over, one at a time, to the Chief Bosun's Mate and his deck crew for highlining.

During a highline operation, two ships, displacing, say, fifteen thousand tons each, steam alongside each other, close enough for the crews to yell out to each other when they see old buddies on the opposite deck. When the ships are in position, a bosun on one vessel fires a shotline to the other. The shotline gun is like a shoulder-held flare gun. It fires a tennis-ball-sized wad of compressed, tightly bound nylon cord trailing a slender, white line. It looks like a big, white tadpole. The men on the other ship dodge the speeding head and grab for its tail. When both crews have a hold on the line, one crew ties a heavy line and a smaller line to it. The other then pulls the two lines back across. The heavy line is wrapped around a pulley on each ship, and ten to twenty men grasp it at each end, as though in a giant tug of war. As the ships roll and pitch, straining or slackening the highline, the men pay it out or haul it in, keeping a constant tension on it. A hook and pulley are hung from the highline, the smaller line is tied to that, and both crews can pull it back and forth like clothes on a line. You can hang anything from the hook: pallets, drums, bags, people, even a flexible pipeline to carry fuel or water; or as the Navy saying goes: "Beans, bullets, and black oil."

Highlining is a complex and delicate dance in which every man and machine has to perform without error. Even the elements have to cooperate. Cross currents, rogue waves, or sudden gusts of wind can carry as much disaster as faulty mechanisms, inattention on deck, or a twitch in the helmsman's arm. Ships that carry bands usually muster them on deck and have them play during highlining. It's a tradition, and it calms nerves.

On one memorable occasion we were alongside a thirty-thousand-ton replenishment ship. She suddenly lost command of her rudder, and it jammed left. The movement ripped apart the highline tackle and threw its handlers to the deck. She bore down on our starboard side like a moving mountain of gray-painted steel.

Many of our men ran like hell for the port side. On the flying bridge, the Captain and his seventeen-year-old phone-talker stood fast as the runaway monster loomed. Relaying orders to helm and engine room through the cherubfaced phone-talker, the Captain masterfully conned the ship out of danger. Everyone on deck cheered. It was a very close call, as the two ships nearly kissed. We liked to say that the plucky young phone-talker's beard grew out the next day.

WEDNESDAY, 21:00 HOURS: That evening I lay out on the main deck near the anchor chains, smoking. The month was July, and we were in tropic seas. The wind was abaft, about the same speed we were making, so the relative air drifted slowly. The clear sky was moonless but dazzling with stars that swung easily back and forth with the slow rolls of the ship. They glistened and twinkled as if alive, inviting me to linger. The ship yawed, and the stars spun on the axis of the zenith, as though changing partners in a cosmic dance. I heard the splash of flying fish as they leaped out of the water and raced ahead of the prow. The warm and fecund smell of the sea bespoke its countless living things. And the ship, as all good ships, felt alive with the low thrum of her engines and her quickening shivers as she met the sea swells. The bitter smoke of my cigarette smelled of ashes and death.

I had been smoking since my early teens, and I was thoroughly addicted to tobacco. I smoked two packs of cigarettes a day while aboard ship and up to three while ashore where I had plenty of beer to cool my burning throat. In the mornings, I lit up before heaving out of my rack, and it was the last thing I did at night before getting into it. I smoked between courses in restaurants, and I smoked before and after sex. I smoked in my dreams.

For the last year my health had been deteriorating. I couldn't walk far without wheezing badly. I often had a cold. Lately my heart had been "fibrillating," as the doctor said. To me, it felt like an engine freezing up for lack of oil, trying to continue but stripping bearings in the effort. I was always tired. I took up cigars and a pipe to wean myself away from cigarettes, but I ended up smok-

In your abuse thereof sin-ning against God, harming yourselves both in persons and goods, and taking also thereby the markes and notes of vanities upon you: by the custome thereof making your selves to be wondered at by all forrain civil Nations, and by all strangers that come among you, to be scorned and contemned. A custome loathsome to the eye, hateful to the Nose, harmeful to the braine, dangerous to the lungs, and the blacke stinking fume thereof, neerest resembling the horrible Stigian smoke of the pit that is bottomlesse.

—King James I, "A Counterblast to Tobacco"

ing those *and* cigarettes. I would smoke a satisfying eight-inch Manila cigar and as soon as it was out I would light up a butt. Like most smokers, I had already quit many times—but only long enough to know what nicotine withdrawal was like. Ricky Henderson would laugh and say "Anybody can quit smoking, but it takes a real man to face up to cancer." I feared I wouldn't live long enough to face cancer.

I knew, I had known, and on this starry night I accepted, that I would die of tobacco if I did not forswear it. I held my cigarette close to my face and gazed at the blushing ember. I didn't want to quit smoking. I loved tobacco. My body demanded it. I loved the mellow tar and honey smell of cured pipe tobacco and cigars. A cigarette in my hand, fiddling with it, rolling it between my fingers, had the same effect for me as worry beads in the hand of an Arab. I loved to take a great lungful from a Marlboro and then let the smoke curl slowly out of my nostrils and form a wispy, gray wreath around my head. After smoking, I often smelled my hands, and they smelled good to me.

Tobacco soothed, like a friend. It was sharp and pungent and masculine and familiar, a constant companion. And sucking on the instrument, whether pipe or cigar or cigarette, was as good as nursing at a breast. A good cigar was better than a kiss. "A woman is only a woman," Kipling wrote, "but a good cigar is a smoke." With the effusive and aromatic stem of a pipe, I could tease the nerve endings of my mouth as well any lover's tongue. And it would never say no. Tobacco was another kind of Dragon, and we had each other by the throat.

But this Lover/Dragon would kill me. It would consume me even as I consumed it. And all the fine nights of dancing stars would be darkened and made void. I reached for the metal, Navy-issue ash receptacle, the kind that looks like a funnel set into the top of a beer can. I looked at my glowing Marlboro one more time. Without taking another puff, I crushed it out against the side of the funnel, smashing its cherry head into tiny sparkles that sifted down into the hole and disappeared. The crinkled butt followed. "That's the last one," I said lowly. I did not feel very good.

I told no one I was quitting. If I did there would always be some asshole who would blow smoke at me and say, "Sure you won't have one?" I went to the berthing compartment, let down my rack, and crawled in. I was hoping I might sleep through the worst of the withdrawal. Since I had already been up since 03:30, I managed to force myself to sleep, but not without my head beginning to buzz for want of nicotine.

THURSDAY, 20:00 HOURS: All day I fought off thoughts of smoking. Every time my hunger for tobacco gnawed, I found something to do, something to read, some one to talk to, something to eat, something to think about. Repeatedly throughout the day I automatically reached into my empty shirt pocket for a cigarette. Several people offered me one, and I made excuses. By evening all my mental energies were occupied with keeping my

ⲚΛΝ icotiana tabacum *and* Nicotania rusticum *are the two most common species of cultivated tobacco. They apparently originated in the Altiplano region of South America, along with such crops as potatoes and chiles. Most commercial smoking and chewing tobaccos are* N. tabacum. *The* N. rusticum *is often used in the making of insecticides.*

—RS

thoughts away from smoking. My eyes began to blink spasmodi-
cally. I had vague, unpleasant contrary feelings, like the cold chills
that accompany a high fever. I felt at once drowsy, as though from
barbituates, and wired awake with amphetamines. I felt no single
discernible physical sensation and yet I felt profound discomfort. I
went wearily to bed, hoping for and dreading my smoky dreams.

FRIDAY, 02:00 HOURS: Typhoon Sally had been running a course
parallel to ours. By midnight she had shifted our way and soon en-
gulfed us. I awoke with the sea change. I assumed the highline operation would be rescheduled due to the rough weather. Just sending a pallet load of groceries over a calm sea is risky enough
business. But to sling a thousand pounds of doomsday under a single line in the midst of a gale would be folly, I thought. I went back
to my feverish sleep, and dreamed of tobacco.

FRIDAY, 04:00 HOURS: A messenger woke me up. I was in a
sweat, both from the weather and from withdrawal. The Brass had
decided to go ahead with the operation. We were keeping to the
edge of the storm where the winds and the seas were lower. The
weather would give us the cover the Brass wanted for what was,
after all, a secret operation. The deck crew boasted some of the
finest practical seamen in the Navy. They wouldn't know what
they were transferring, and they wouldn't ask, but they were confident they could do the job. They respected Howling Sally, but
they did not fear her.

FRIDAY, SUNRISE: The winds and seas were high, the temperature
a steamy 80 degrees when the ammo ship hove into view. She was
coming up from behind us, her fat prow plowing through white
water and rain. The eye of her blinker fluttered on the signal
bridge, telling us to keep steady, and she would come alongside.
She moved gradually through the froth, giving us a coy, wide berth
at first. Our ship drove its prow into a wave, shipped eleven tons of
water and hurled it skyward in a tower of spume.

We and the opposite crew stood on deck and watched each

other through the twilight and flying foam. We watched to gauge the roll and yaw of the two ships to see how closely they would swing toward each other in the sea's churning. The ammo ship yawed and swung her stern teasingly away and then dangerously toward us. We adjusted our courses to put the oncoming sea more closely behind us to even out our keels. Gingerly, rolling, yawing and pitching, the two big ships eased closer together, narrowing the froth between them.

When the two shipmasters judged that they were as close as they dared, they gave the signal. Our bosun stood on the rolling deck and aimed his shotline gun through the spray. The gun recoiled and barked, its report bouncing off the steel flanks of the ammo ship. The shotline sang out. It streaked across the abyss and draped itself over the deck. A perfect shot—the bosun had laid his line right between her stacks. The two ships were coupled. If all went well, they would remain in their tenuous, thrashing embrace until the one had emptied its terrible seed into the other. The deck crew sprang to their tasks. The Marine guards took up their posts. We, the Missile Men, struck below.

We prized open the warhead magazine. We opened up the ammunition lift shaft that ran from topside all the way down to the magazine. A squad of our men took the lift topside and rolled out the specially designed, nondescript-looking drums that would each hold one nuke. Three men handled the lift. Others stood by as runners and relief. Gunner Cassidy, Ricky Henderson, and myself manned the magazine.

The end of a seesaw travels much farther than that part closer to its fulcrum. A rolling, pitching ship is like two seesaws, one across the other, with its fulcrum in the middle at the waterline. The farther from the middle, and the farther from the waterline, the more travel when the ship rolls or pitches. The magazine was as far down from the waterline as it could be. And it wasn't very close to the middle. That day the magazine traveled like some nightmarish amusement park ride. It could have been mocked up as a huge box of dice being shaken and tumbled by a gambling titan: "Come ride the Giant Nuclear Crapshoot!"

Our first task was to attach the warheads' nose cones. Each warhead comes equipped with two, and while in storage, they are bolted to the rear of the cradle. For launch or transit, one is removed and attached to the leading end of the head. In transit the spare is packed along in the drum. The nose cones are extremely sharp and smooth, as they are designed for supersonic flight. If a man were to fall on one it would pierce like a spear. The task of attaching them was simple, but I had a hard time concentrating. My nicotine withdrawal was fast approaching its worst stage.

After the nose cone attachment, we began the warhead movement. To facilitate this, the ceiling of the magazine was crisscrossed with slotted tracks. The central track ran fore and aft down the center of the room. Branching out from the central track ran shorter ones. They each hung over warhead locations. Into the slotted track we fitted a hoist that we could slide to a position over any single warhead. Once the hoist was in position, we could unbolt the steel strap that held the nuke down, lower the hoist, pick up the monster, and slide it over the lift shaft. There we could transfer it to the lift, send it topside and the men there would secure it in its drum. The drum would be rolled out past a cordon of Marines and highlined to the ammo ship, which was named after a volcano—I won't say which one.

Ricky and I took ratchets and began to unbolt the strap of the first warhead. Gunner handled the hoist. A buzzing sound penetrated my ears. It circled counter-clockwise around my brain and made me dizzy. The dizziness moved like a slow current down to my stomach and nausea flickered; the nicotine withdrawal was taking my sea legs.

"How embarrassing," I thought. "They'll razz me for sure." A seasick sailor is like a cowboy afraid of horses. A slow fire burned in my lungs and they demanded nicotine to quench it. I took huge breaths and held them, hoping to fool my lungs into feeling that they were full of smoke. My right hand, of its own accord, rose up to my face and covered my nose. I sniffed hungrily for the aroma of tobacco, but smelled only soap.

We loosened the bolts, and through the buzzing sound in my head the ratchets sent their raspy clicking. The hoist whined when Gunner lowered it. The hooks clattered as we attached them to the warhead. The hoist whined again, and the chain rattled as the little behemoth arose from its resting place. It cleared the cradle, and Gunner stopped the hoist. The inchoate thing hung three feet off the moving deck, smooth and white—its nose cone glistening. Its nose bobbed up and down slightly, like a hound picking up a scent. It began to swing, straining at its chain leash, a dog of war eager to be let slip. But we were taking this one to kennel.

We drew it out to the middle track. In my distraction and dizziness, I failed to note the arc of the warhead's swing. The ship gave a roll. The heavy weapon swung my way. The tip of the nose cone hit me in the right thigh, just below the hip, all one thousand pounds of its terrible weight concentrated behind that one, tiny point. It pierced the skin to an eighth of an inch, and withdrew. Blood seeped from the wound and made a purple stain on blue cotton trouser cloth.

We regained control of the weapon and slid it to the forward bulkhead. We slipped it onto the lift and secured it, then sent it topside. The process took about ten minutes. Twenty-three warheads to go.

Moving on to the next one, Gunner said to me, "Better watch yourself, Dick. Those things are sharp."

"Is that a 'Broken Arrow'?" Ricky joked. That was one of the code words we were to use in the event of an accident. "Broken Arrow," if we dropped a warhead and cracked it open; "Bent Spear," if we just dropped it. Who in blazes thinks up these code words, anyway?

Ricky and Gunner walked easily by me on fluid sea legs, their bodies never deviating from the vertical, as though they were hung from gimbals. I steadied myself by grasping onto protruding nose cones and followed. We worked mechanically for a long time, one weapon following another and another and another. In the process I got stabbed again, this time in the left leg. It was a glancing blow, leaving more bruise than wound, but it tore my trouser leg. I didn't think about it. I couldn't think about anything except standing up straight on a heaving deck and the maddening craving for a smoke. A smoker's longing for tobacco is like thirst—insistent, unceasing, and steadily worse. I swallowed repeatedly, hoping to satisfy the clutching in my throat. I clenched my teeth and bit down hard. I pinched myself. I sweated. My eyes ran. I sucked in air like a man who could get none. I suffered, goddamn it.

As we were setting another warhead into the ammo lift, I heard a loud sophomoric giggle from above. I looked up the shaft to the next deck and saw A. K. Douglas, Ricky Henderson's "nuclear love" mate from Arkansas with a silly grin on his face. He had just opened his fly and was shaking his "glowing gonads" at us. "You want some of this?" he asked with a "Yuck, yuck, yuck." He was inordinately proud of his tool, though I have to admit it could take your breath away seeing it for the first time. It hung in ele-phantine fatness halfway to his knees, and the bulbous crimson head resembled nothing so much as a big meaty strawberry, ready for plucking.

A. K. never referred to his unit as his penis or his tool or any of the many Anglo-Saxon appellations for the male equipment. He called it "The Ol' Arkansas Strawberry." And he never said that he made love to a woman, or fucked a woman, or enjoyed female em-braces. He always said, "I took her to bed, you know, and then I give her the Ol' Arkansas Strawberry. And she liked it real good, too. Yuck, yuck." He always made a sharp jabbing motion with his arm when he said, "I give her the Ol' Arkansas Strawberry," and he ejaculated the words rather than spoke them.

As I stood there looking up the shaft in my misery he repeated, "You want some of the Ol' Arkansas Strawberry there, Petty Officer Dick? It's nukified. Yuck, yuck." Ordinarily I would have made some pat remark, like "Don't point that thing at me when you don't know how to use it." Then he would have proudly holstered his gun having once again demonstrated its mighty caliber and that would have been that. But I had no sense of humor at the moment. And A. K. saw I had no sense of humor. He wagged the Ol' Arkansas

Strawberry at me every time I brought a nuke to the shaft. I knew if I told him to zip up and shut up it would just encourage him.

So I began to think about strawberries. I thought about my grandmother cutting them up to make jam. I thought about the robins and other birds that used to peck at the strawberries we grew at home in Mendocino, California. Their sharp little beaks left deep wounds in the flesh, which turned an unappetizing brown. My frustration with A. K. began to subside. Finally, I thought about piña coladas and margaritas I had seen bartenders make with strawberries—how they whipped and beat them in a blender till they were reduced to a blood-red puree. In my mind, I concocted such a cocktail, and named it An Ol' Arkansas Strawberry. My agitation with A. K. disappeared and he noticed and finally repackaged himself. I was free to go back to being merely miserable.

Smoking is a dying art.
—Observed on a bumper sticker

Halfway through the operation, word came down from topside to hold up for a while. Packing a warhead is not simply a matter of sticking it in a drum and putting a lid on it. Everything has to be done by the book, and it takes time. We were stacking them up, and they didn't want them rolling around on deck.

"Jesus Christ, let's put some hustle on it and get this thing over with," Ricky bitched. Gunner calmly sat down on an empty cradle. I, wobbly at the knees, made my way over to W-18, the small tactical device, sank to the deck next to it and lay my head against its smooth side. I held on to the cradle to steady myself and curled my knees up to my chest.

"You seasick, Dickie?" Gunner asked with some surprise. Still, no one knew.

"Uh huh," I moaned.

"Ha!" Ricky yelped. "What a non-hacker. Ho ho."

I didn't care. I was, indeed, a little queasy, though I wouldn't call it *mal de mer*. I was just plain miserable. A taut string ran inside my skull from the top to the bottom. At one end a screw turned and with each passing minute tightened that strainful cord. It was now so tight it began to sing in a piercing, painful note. The ship kept rolling. The deck rose and fell. I pressed my head against the bulbous Death of a City and hung on.

We had had no breakfast that morning. Because it was so early, we hadn't bothered. Somebody sent down a couple boxes of C-rations to snack on. They were the kind where all the food comes in a can: canned meat, canned vegetables, canned fruit, canned pound cake, canned bread, canned peanut butter and jelly, and canned crackers. Also a pack of instant coffee and sugar, six matches, one stick of gum, a little P-38 can opener, a wad of toilet paper, and a pack of three cigarettes, all packaged in olive drab. "You want anything, Dick?" Gunner asked, as he and Ricky went through the contents.

"Nah, I'm not hungry," I said through a now-snotty nose. I sniffed and thought about those three cigarettes. The string in my head strained to perilously near the breaking point.

"Well, here. Take these then," Gunner said. From one of the boxes he handed me two thick, round soda crackers—the kind you'd see in a cracker barrel.

"Ha!" Ricky yelped again. "Non-hacker!" Nibbling on a soda cracker is a remedy for ordinary seasickness. Gunner was doing me a kindness in giving them to me, but still it was embarrassing. Determined to put my best face forward, I said, "Well, gimme the goddamn peanut butter then, too!" Gunner handed me the flat can of peanut butter, three inches in diameter and three-quarters of an inch high.

With shaky hands I unfolded the can opener and removed the lid. The roasted peanut smell rushed into my nose. The roasted, slightly burned, almost smoky smell filled my nostrils and half-clogged nasal passages with a swirling cloud of relief. To my smoke-starved senses the rich, mellow, sometimes sweet aroma was almost like pipe tobacco. I sucked it in like snuff. I snorted it like cocaine. Like a diver who breaks the surface after too long under water, I gulped in the smell as though it were life-giving air.

With a forefinger, I dug into the peanut butter and scooped out a gob. I scraped it off onto my lower teeth. With my tongue, I maneuvered it to the middle of my mouth and pressed it against my palate, gluing my mouth closed. A buzzing, tingling feeling spread through my lips, as though sensation were returning after a long absence. As I breathed, the air in my windpipe moved past the back of my tongue and picked up the roasty, toasty aroma and channeled it back and forth through my nose. With my

Virtue, however admirable, is frequently dull. Peanut butter needs enlivening.

—Irma S. Rombauer and Marion Rombauer Becker, *The Joy of Cooking*

tongue, I smeared the peanut butter in circles against the roof of my mouth, melting it, dissolving it, driving it into my taste buds, and intensifying the flavor and making my salivary glands gush. The whining string in my head eased ever so slightly.

I used one of the crackers as a knife to scoop out the peanut butter and spread it on the other cracker. I put the two crackers together and made a thick sandwich. I took a crunchy, creamy bite. I held it in my mouth and sucked on it like the end of a good cigar. In time it dissolved into a starchy, sticky paste which I tucked into my cheek like a great pinch of Copenhagen snuff. That one bite lasted several minutes. It didn't satisfy any of my body's craving for nicotine. It didn't quench the fire in my lungs, nor still the buzzing in my ears. But it gave me just enough of a tobacco-like sensory fix to keep the brain string from snapping. It was no substitute for a Marlboro, but I would make it suffice. It would be my Marlboro sandwich; my Nuclear Marlboro Sandwich.

I sat there holding the cradle with one hand and my pacifier with the other. I heard Gunner and Ricky start to work again. They let me sit it out for a while. Finally, they came over my way. Standing over W-18, Gunner said, "It's time for this thing to go." I took another chaw of my plug and stuck the remainder into my shirt pocket. I chomped down hard and pulled myself up. I took a moment to steady myself, then held out an open hand to Ricky who handed me a ratchet. I took a strain on one of the strap bolts and broke it free. We uncradled W-18, hoisted it out and sent it topside. We continued working, and I kept a piece of my Nuclear

Marlboro Sandwich in my mouth at all times, making sure to pass the aroma through my nasal passages often. Sometime during the remaining hour or so of the operation, I got nipped again by the Great White Beast, in the right knee. It hurt and it bled, but I ignored it as best I could.

When we had sent the last of the Dragon's children topside, we unhooked the hoist and put it in the lift to send it to its storage place above. I was about to activate the lift when Gunner said, "Dick, you look like death warmed over. Go ahead and ride up with the hoist. Get those punctures on your legs bandaged. Me and Ricky'll secure."

"Thanks, Gunner," I said, and climbed into the lift and sat down next to the hoist. As I reached for the "Up" button, Ricky got in one last jibe.

"Just a non-hacker," he said grinning. "Just a non-hacker. Ha!"

"Oh yeah?" I challenged him, indicating the three bloody spots on my trousers. "How many guys do you know that have been wounded three times by nuclear weapons and lived to brag about it?" I punched the button and rose up. And I never smoked again.

Richard Sterling is the author of The Fire Never Dies *and* The Fearless Diner, *four books in the Lonely Planet World Food series, and editor of* Food *and* The Adventure of Food. *Since the day of the Nuclear Marlboro Sandwich he has not smoked, but would like to.*

★

From such reflections as these, I was aroused by the order from the officer: "Forward there! Rig the head pump!" I found that no time was allowed for daydreaming, but that we must "turn to" at the first light. Having called up the "idlers," namely, carpenter, cook, and steward, and rigged the pump, we began washing down the decks. This operation, which is performed every morning at sea, takes nearly two hours; and I had hardly strength enough to get through it. After we had finished, swabbed down decks, and coiled up the rigging, I sat on the spars, waiting for seven bells, which was the signal for breakfast. The officer, seeing my lazy posture, ordered me to slush the mainmast, from the royal masthead down. The vessel was then rolling a little, and I had taken no food my lazy posture, ordered me to slush the mainmast, from the royal mast-head down. The vessel was then rolling a little, and I had taken no food for three days, so that I felt tempted to tell him that I had rather wait till after breakfast; but I knew that I must "take the bull by the horns," and that if I showed any sign of want of spirit or backwardness, I should be ruined at once. So I took my bucket of grease and climbed up to the royal masthead. Here the rocking of the vessel, which increases the higher you go from the foot of the mast, which is the fulcrum of the lever, and the smell of the grease, which offended my fastidious senses, upset my stom-ach again, and I was not a little rejoiced when I had finished my job and got upon the comparative terra firma of the deck. In a few minutes seven bells were struck, the log hove, the watch called, and we went to break-fast. Here I cannot but remember the advice of the cook, a simplehearted African. "Now," says he, "my lad, you are well cleaned out; you haven't got a drop of your longshore 'swash' aboard of you. You must begin on a new tack—pitch all your sweetmeats overboard, and turn to upon good hearty salt beef and ship bread, and I'll promise you, you'll have your ribs well sheathed, and be as hearty as any of 'em, afore you are up to the Horn." This would be good advice to give to passengers, when they set their hearts on the little niceties which they have laid in, in case of seasickness.

I cannot describe the change which half a pound of cold salt beef and a biscuit or two produced in me. I was a new being. Having a watch below until noon, so that I had some time to myself, I got a huge piece of strong, cold salt beef from the cook, and kept gnawing upon it until twelve o'clock. When we went on deck, I felt somewhat like a man, and could begin to learn my sea duty with considerable spirit.

—Richard Henry Dana, *Two Years Before the Mast (1840)*

PART TWO

SOME THINGS TO DO

Tomatoes

A mystery is solved in the South of France.

I saw Monsieur Noyer out of the corner of my eye, approaching me. It was a warm day in mid-June. The sun splashed down on the empty square. I was in the midst of loading my car with my hoe, rake, shovel and other tools, getting ready to go to the garden.

"Eh, Richard," Monsieur Noyer said when he reached me. "And the garden? How goes it?"

"It's going very well, Monsieur Noyer," I said. "Very well. I'm working hard."

"And your tomatoes?" he went on. "Do you have any tomatoes yet?"

"No, not yet." I smiled at his little dig. It was much too early to have tomatoes. "No tomatoes *yet*. But the plants look good. And they're growing."

He raised his hand, a thick farmer's paw, and tipped back his hat. This sixty-plus-year-old French farmer was a far better gardener than I probably would ever be, but there *was* a kind of rivalry going on here. Perhaps that is much too presumptuous. But there was something territorial at least. He was, remember, acknowledged to be St. Sébastien's best gardener.

"Have you treated your tomato plants?" he asked.

At the far edge of the big square, and bathed in cool morning shadows, was Monsieur Noyer's pleasant house. Out on the terrace I could see his wife, Madame Noyer, a short, slightly bent woman, busy with something. Every so often she stopped and regarded us, leaning forward and straining, unsuccessfully, to hear what we were saying. Then she would resume her work.

"Uh, no," I answered. "Do I have to?"

He let out a low whistle. Then he cleared his throat. "You haven't treated your tomato plants with sulphur?" he asked.

"Sulphur?"

"Sulphur. Yes."

"What's that for? Insects?"

"No. No. The treatment is for disease."

"Oh."

He examined me. Then he sniffled and rubbed his mouth with the back of his enormous hand. He looked up at the sky.

"Well...to work," he said as a way of saying goodbye. He turned and walked away. After a few steps he paused and looked back.

"You will see, Richard," he said, pointing a low finger. "Gardening is an art. An *art.*"

He walked off. His wife stopped her work and watched him approach the house. I was left standing there, in the empty square, full of doubts. Doubts about my tomato plants.

This wasn't the first time we had talked about my tomatoes. Each time we did, it made me nervous. There was usually something slightly cautionary in Monsieur Noyer's tone. He was never malicious, but he acted as if he knew something I didn't. Of course, since I knew almost nothing, it didn't take much effort to make me feel that way. I think he was just probably suspicious that I, as an American, could be serious about gardening—which to him was indeed a serious matter. I respected that. But whatever the reason, these impromptu meetings we had from time to time always left me anxious. I tried to avoid Monsieur Noyer without seeming rude.

The irony was that when it came to the produce from his own garden, he and his wife were extremely generous. They were always handing us sprawling heads of lettuce and other vegetables, or leaving these delights just outside our door. They even gave us some artichokes once, a lovely treat, since they didn't have many. Still, I have to confess that I wanted to outshine Monsieur Noyer in some small effort—peppers, maybe. I felt competitive, and that was not good, not when it was about a garden. I learned a small, unpleasant truth about myself through Monsieur Noyer.

Tomatoes. I was thinking about tomatoes.

For some reason, everyone in the village saw tomatoes as the benchmark for determining the success of my garden, or any garden. Anyone in St. Sébastien who asked about my garden, and many of them did, inevitably asked me about my tomatoes.

Hey, Richard! How many tomato plants did you plant? Twenty? All hybrids? Ah, well. I don't know. You may get a few.

Richard. How far apart did you plant your tomatoes? Oh? Really? Hmmm.

Richard, just remember. If your tomatoes don't grow, you can have some of ours. We'll have plenty.

Why tomatoes? I suppose because tomatoes are the one thing any serious gardener is expected to grow and one which, ultimately, is not that difficult to grow. And it's emblematic of the south of France. You *must* have tomatoes if you have a summer garden here—fat, nearly obese, crimson things that have a wonderful weight in the hand. Dark, ripe tomatoes that, reeking with the sun, heat and land, are the essence of summer and one of its chief joys. Of course, tomatoes!

Believe me, I watched my tomato plants well. I plucked tiny, errant sprouts from the crotches of the stalks. I attached the vines to my bamboo at regular intervals, careful not to cut off the circulation with too tight a knot in the rag when I did. I dug up the earth around the plants to make it easier for them to breathe and accept water. I even treated them with sulphur as Monsieur Noyer said I should, something I wasn't enthusiastic about doing. (It was, in fact, the only chemical I ever used in my garden. But since *every* gardener in St. Sébastien used it, I did, too.) There was hardly a time when I wasn't thinking about my tomato plants, or tending them.

"*Botanically speaking,*" wrote Supreme Court Associate Justice Horace Gray for the majority in 1893, "*tomatoes are the fruit of a vine, just as are cucumbers, squashes, beans, and peas. But in the common language of the people, whether sellers or consumers of provisions, all these are vegetables which are grown in kitchen gardens, and which, whether eaten cooked or raw, are, like potatoes, carrots, parsnips, turnips, beets, cauliflower, cabbage, celery, and lettuce, usually served at dinner in, with, or after the soup, fish, or meat which constitute the principal part of the repast, and not, like fruits generally, as dessert.*"

The dispute arose because of a tariff imposed at the Port of New York, where a U.S. Customs agent deemed the red globes to be vegetables in spite of the importer's claim that the West Indian tomatoes were fruit. Vegetables were subject to a ten percent tariff; fruits were duty-free.

—Michele Anna Jordan, *The Good Cook's Book of Tomatoes*

Once in a while, I would take a villager to my garden to get his opinion on how I was doing. If he didn't say anything much, why, I assumed I wasn't doing anything radically wrong. No one ever looked at my tomato plants and screamed, Oh, my *God*! What have you done? (Not that that would be their style.) I wanted to show off, too. Over here, I wanted to tell them. Just take a look at these tomato plants. Twenty of them. They're healthy-looking, and they're growing nicely. Not too bad for an American in France. And I believe I will have tomatoes, in August, like you.

In late June, a week or so after my conversation with Monsieur Noyer, I drove my car one morning to the garden to do some weeding and grading. By then I had made the trip scores and scores of times, but I still always enjoyed it. The morning air was sweet and cool. I had my bucket and tools with me, the windows open. I passed by farmers on their way to and from the vineyards. Some ambled slowly by on their tractors, others went by in battered old cars they used for the fields. I waved to them, and they waved back. I honked the horn as I passed by Jules's house. His mother was hanging out the wash. She turned and looked toward the sound slightly mystified, then waved as she recognized my car. I picked up speed as I left the village.

I reached the familiar little bridge and turned off the road onto the lane next to the vineyard. I stopped at my usual place, took out my tools, and walked over the edge of the bank. I walked down the steps Jules had fashioned out of the earth and then over the heavy planks I had placed across the stream and which I had christened *Pont de Jules,* Jules's Bridge. As I did, the sleek frogs that had been sunbathing on the planks fled into the water. I walked over to the rise at the edge of the plateau. I was eager to see what progress my plants had made. I was expectant, as always.

I climbed the second set of steps, reached the garden and blinked my eyes. I blinked again. Then my heart skipped a beat. Each one of my twenty tomato plants had a ripe red tomato there at its base! I couldn't believe it. I had tomatoes! You could see them. It was a miracle!

I shouted "Tomatoes!" in the air. The word resounded into the heavens. Then I put my bucket down and ran over to the far side of the garden where all the tomato plants were. I had tomatoes. *In June!* As I came closer, though, something inside me started doubting. Isn't it a bit odd, a small voice inside me said, that every one of the twenty plants has produced a single ripe tomato? And only *one*? And that each tomato is at exactly the same place?

Suddenly, I realized someone had put them all there.

I laughed. I laughed so hard I nearly fell down. What a trick! I got to the plants, and, yes, it was true. Someone had obviously gone to the store, bought twenty ripe tomatoes—from Spain, no doubt—and placed them neatly one by one at the base of each of my plants. *American needs help. Bad. With his tomatoes.* I looked around quickly to see if the culprit was there, hiding behind a bush, stifling a laugh. I saw there was more to this. That same person had placed tin cans of string beans on each side of my bean plants. I looked at those cans with their labels displaying cut, juicy string beans, and I laughed again. This was amazingly, heroically funny. This was genius.

I had to show Iggy [the author's girlfriend] this masterpiece, this astonishing visual drollness. I didn't touch a thing. I wanted her to see everything exactly as I did. The joke was on me, and I loved it.

I had loosened about three yards of hard-packed earth when I saw a gleam of dirty yellow among the weed roots. Some long-dead farmer had obviously thrown away a pastis bottle one hot afternoon many years ago. But when I cleared away the earth, it wasn't a vintage bottle cap; it was a coin. I rinsed it under the hose, and it shone gold in the sun, the drops of water sliding down a bearded profile.

*It was a 20-franc piece, dated 1857. On one side was the head of Napoléon III with his neat goatee and his position in society—*Empereur—*stamped in heroic type opposite his name. On the reverse, a laurel wreath, crowned with more heroic type proclaiming the* Empire Français. *Around the rim of the coin was the comforting statement that every Frenchman knows is true:* Dieu protège la France.

—Peter Mayle,
Toujours Provence

Who had done this?

I went back to St. Sébastien, thinking about that question the entire way. It mystified me. The joke was so witty, so dry, and that was not typical of the villagers. Or maybe it was. Maybe I had underestimated them, didn't really know them that well at all. I went and found Iggy and told her we had to go to the garden, now. I wouldn't tell her why. When we got there, I made her cover her eyes as I led her up the stairs. Then I showed her. She was just as fooled as I was for a minute. I could tell by her eyes. Then she walked closer and saw the set-up. "*Nou, zeg!*" she said in Dutch. Now, say! She automatically reverted to Dutch when something took her by surprise. Then she laughed. It was still as funny as when I saw it the first time. Tomato, tomato, tomato. *Twenty* ripe tomatoes, all in a row.

We speculated as to who had done it. We could only think of one name.

"Eugéne," we both said at once. Eugéne was Jules's younger brother. He was a habitual and determined trickster.

We drove back to the village and, after a short search, we found Eugéne.

"*Eugéne,* did you do this?" I asked.

"Do what?"

"You know," Iggy said to him.

"I don't know what."

"Come on," we said.

"You're both crazy."

Eugéne denied our accusations so convincingly, we decided it couldn't be him. We told the story to all the villagers we saw and asked them if they knew who had done it. No one knew. But they were amused. Very amused.

We ran into Monsieur Vasquez, who was patrolling the town square as usual, chewing on his small wooden stick and limping slowly along.

"Monsieur Vasquez," I asked, "have you heard anything about the ripe tomatoes in our garden?"

"Tomatoes? Ripe? No."

"Not one word?" Iggy probed.

"No."

"Well, if you do, let us know, will you?" I said.

"Yes." He looked at us oddly.

We ran into Nasim. He knew nothing, but laughed loudly, showing his blackened teeth unreservedly when we explained the situation in our garden. I even asked Albin Polge, the mayor, if he had any ideas about this, but he shook his head, seriously, no. He offered to make an inquiry over the loudspeaker—which was perched atop the town hall—at noon, the customary time for announcements, but I declined. He rubbed his chin with his hand speculatively and said, more to himself, "Ripe tomatoes." Then he produced a slight smile. The mayor had a dry sense of humor.

Did Rémy, who lived next to Marcel Lécot, know? No. Did Monsieur Valcoze? No. But he did want to talk to me about another matter... Did Sully Valcoze know? Why, no, Richard, no. By the way, he asked in his woody voice, how was the garden?

All the people we talked to, and we talked to quite a few in the next two hours, knew nothing. What a mystery!

A little later, still in the dark as to who had done this, I saw Monsieur Noyer. I was in front of the house with Iggy, unloading the car, when I saw him approach. I paused and waited for him to arrive.

"Eh, Richard," he said, tipping his hat back. "And your garden? How goes it?"

"Beautiful, Monsieur Noyer," I said, almost routinely. Then something struck me like a thunderbolt. I waited a beat. "I've got tomatoes," I said to him. "Ripe tomatoes. Now."

He blinked. Then he had such a childlike look of open disappointment, I was almost sorry I'd said it.

"Tomatoes, you say?" he said. "Ripe?"

"Absolutely," I said. "And not just one, *twenty* of them."

"Oh?" he said. "Twenty? Really? Very good."

He couldn't conceal on his face what this information meant to him. Iggy saw this. She nudged me in the ribs.

"*You've got to tell him the truth,*" she whispered forcefully in English. "*Now.* Just look at his face!"

Do I have to? I thought. Oh, what a low character I am!

But of course I told him. I told him it was all a joke someone had played on me. That in fact I didn't have any tomatoes, not even one. When he heard this, he shifted easily and quickly back to his familiar, commanding presence. Everything was all right again. The world was exactly as it should be.

We finally found out who had done it. Laurent Imbert! The most unlikely person in the whole village. A calm, introverted man who, though very pleasant to us, never displayed much of a sense of humor—much less such an elaborate one. But it was he. True, Iggy had worked for him harvesting asparagus, but we hadn't thought to call him till last. I hardly knew him. But we cornered him on the telephone. When he was still at the stage of good-naturedly denying he had placed the tomatoes there, I said to him:

"Well, if you didn't put them there, how *did* they get there?"

He waited a long beat, his timing perfect. "Perhaps," he said deadpan, "they are a new variety."

When I stopped laughing, I had the presence of mind to ask him if he needed any "ripe" tomatoes. No, he said, quite evenly, no, he didn't. I could hear his wife laughing in the background.

I never thought the same way about the villagers again. I certainly learned that some of them could be very funny. Oddly, I never thought to ask Laurent *why* he had done this. It didn't occur to me! I just thought it was funny. I'm sure he thought it was, too. That he didn't know me too well, and still chose my garden to act out his joke, I found endearing. My "ripe" tomatoes went on to become legendary in the village. I was always asked—by men, women and even children in St. Sébastien—if my tomatoes were ripe yet, usually followed immediately by a hand placed to the mouth to stifle laughter. I didn't mind. Why should I? Wasn't teasing a form of affection?

But, oh, Monsieur Noyer, I ask your forgiveness now! Pardon me for taking advantage of you, for seizing what surely was a once-in-a-lifetime moment. Just for the briefest time I had you believing *l'américain* had outdone you. That somehow, I, the American, had pulled off a tomato miracle in St. Sébastien de Caisson!

Richard Goodman is a freelance writer who lives in New York. Raised in Virginia and Michigan, he has lived in many other cities including Detroit, Chicago, Boston, and Paris. He is the author of French Dirt: The Story of a Garden in the South of France, *from which this story was excerpted.*

✳

"*Eki mi gba lenni kpang kpang kpang,*" said Amenan's mother, Akissi Kro—May god give you many, many, many children. I thanked her—this time I was grateful for the wish.

Still, much as I'd been accepted this summer by the villagers of Asagbé, I could never imagine myself as one of them—nor, I was sure, could they imagine me so. There was always some invisible border that prevented me from gaining full citizenship in the Beng circle: my American otherness and my commitment to anthropological distance both asserted themselves, nudging me to question and probe further and above all to avoid the temptation to accept anything as final. Of all that the Beng people had taught me, this stood out: "The spirits will protect you," Aba Louassi told me, "if you believe in them." He, too, understood the relativity of faith, of knowledge.

—Alma Gottlieb and Philip Graham, *Parallel Worlds: An Anthropoligst and a Writer Encounter Africa*

BOB SEHLINGER

⋆ ⋆ ⋆

Etiquette Soup

Make your reservations at Chez Babel.

WHEN I WAS GROWING UP IN THE SOUTH YOU HAD TO LOOK pretty hard to find an ethnic restaurant. Pickings were slim in general if you weren't in the mood for barbecue, fried chicken, or catfish. There were Italian restaurants, of course, and even Greek places down along the Gulf Coast, but we didn't refer to them as "ethnic." The term we used was "foreign." Most rare in the South, and most foreign by a long shot, were Chinese restaurants, although they too had Greek or Italian chefs. In these eateries, Chinese food consisted largely of unidentifiable vegetables, smothered in corn starch, and topped with crispy little noodles.

I'm not sure that I ever saw a real Chinese person until Lyndon Johnson, deciding that I would look spiffy in a uniform, shipped me to San Francisco. Between the Army, the freeways, and the flower children, every day in San Francisco was an adventure that fell somewhere on the continuum between life-changing revelation and anaphylactic shock. In quick succession, and not necessarily in this order, I was introduced to guard duty, Jefferson Airplane, Alice B. Toklas brownies, guided missile repair, incense, cable cars, and real Chinese food.

For me, dining in an authentic Chinese restaurant was like traveling to another planet. Wishing to make a good impression, I approached the experience with diplomatic reserve more in keeping with a Papal audience. I was ever alert for customs and protocols to honor, was exceedingly polite, bowed a lot (because I had seen it done in *The King & I*), and whispered in the manner of people in libraries. I embarked on my exploration of Chinese cuisine cautiously, initially ordering dishes such as Egg Foo Young and Chicken Chow Mein that I remembered from the Chung King brand canned Chinese food days of my youth.

Plodding along thus, I had barely graduated to wonton soup when I lucked into one of the seminal culinary experiences of my life. The precipitant was the arrival of my parents for a visit. My father had college friends in the Bay Area, and consequently my folks and I were included in a group of eight for dinner at a new Chinese restaurant. In addition to being new, the restaurant was different. It was The Mandarin at Ghirardelli Square, the first Chinese restaurant in San Francisco to specialize in dishes from the northern provinces of China.

All of us, including our Oakland hosts (well practiced in Cantonese fare), were dumbfounded by the strange preparations listed by the dozen on our menus. Worse than hopeless, it was like trying to order dinner from the Dead Sea Scrolls. Confused and muddled but nevertheless enthusiastic, we elected to place ourselves in the hands of the chef.

Anyone who has been to a restaurant in Beijing, China or in San Francisco's Chinatown, for that matter, knows that slurping noodles and belching are socially acceptable, even laudatory behaviors that communicate appreciation to the chef. But that sounding off doesn't fall on deaf ears at, say, an Italian restaurant where loud noodle sucking would invite embarrassed whispers. And in Japan, refilling your own cup or glass from a tea pot or sake pitcher would probably elicit the same soupçon of surprise from fellow diners because, at the sushi bar, pouring is the responsibility of your dining companion.

—Sara Hare, "Turning the Tables—Table Manners Around the World"

The chef did not disappoint. For the next two hours we worked our way variously through the Beijing/Hunan/Szechwan equivalent of Marrying Sam's $20 Wedding. Having been lectured all of my life about the "starving people of China," I was amazed, to put it mildly. Here were ingredients, preparations, tastes, consistencies, and aromas never dreamed of. I was in heaven.

As we sat savoring the last morsels, it occurred to me that we had, in essence, eaten our way through four provinces of China without a major *faux pas* or creating an international incident. Though nothing could eclipse the quality of the meal, I nonetheless felt giddy with relief when our tuxedo-clad waiter cleared away the last of the plates and platters.

We remained for some time in quiet, sated repose, and may have languished indefinitely had not our waiter reappeared with a sparkling cut glass bowl filled to the brim with ice water. Large enough to accommodate Esther Williams, the bowl was positioned ceremoniously in the center of our large circular table. After a momentary absence, our waiter returned and distributed to each person a small translucent bowl and two engraved silver spoons, one being slightly larger than the other. This accomplished, he cleared his throat and delivered a short but animated lecture in a tongue known only to Pentecostals. His last words echoing in our uncomprehending ears, he exited the room in reverse, propelled by a staccato series of waist level bows.

For many minutes we studied our bowls and spoons in silence, attempting to fathom both their purpose and their relationship to the tub of ice water in the center of our table. The only thing we understood with certainty, was that something clearly was expected of us.

A sign in a Hong Kong supermarket: For your convenience, we recommend courteous, efficient self-service.

—Nury Vittachi, "Travellers' Tales," *Far Eastern Economic Review*

Wanting desperately to rise to the occasion, we gave the matter serious attention. A spirited discussion ensued wherein a number of philosophical, cultural, religious, and even anthropological constructs were presented to explain the puzzle of the spoons and water. Most of these notions tumbled out breech-birth fashion, generously lubricated with alcohol.

There was consensus among us that there was a ceremonial element associated with the bowls, spoons, and water. Theories incorporating baptism, rebirth, and cleansing, of course, came immediately to mind, followed by a "communion of the waters" hypothesis, as well as some convoluted ideas involving reincarnation and the Ming Dynasty, the Oriental reverence for elders, and metaphors of earth as "the water planet." It was suggested by the wife of the dentist that the melting ice represented the temporary nature of life, and that as the ice melted, its "essence" returned to the "universe of being" (the water). The dentist, being practical, dismissed these theories, declaring that "the whole shootin' match" was simply a "fancy finger bowl."

As might have been expected, discussion ultimately gave way to experimentation, tentatively at first and later with more abandon. Martha (the accountant's wife), dipped the larger of her spoons into the cut glass bowl and ladled a minuscule amount of water into her translucent bowl. This accomplished, she sat stumped staring at her orphaned smaller spoon. The contractor hefted four or five good spoonfuls into his bowl with the large spoon and then proceeded to empty the contents into his mouth with the smaller spoon, advising us mid-slurp that he could perceive nothing out of the ordinary about the water. When my father suggested that the use of bowls and spoons seemed a singularly inefficient way of drinking water, there arose an esoteric debate about the labor intensive methods of Chinese agriculture. Bored, and ready to get on with it, my mother scooped several large spoonfuls of water into her bowl and then placed the bowl directly in front of her on the table. With her large spoon she lifted a spoonful of water and poured it into her left palm. Next, using the smaller spoon, she repeated the process, this time spooning water into her right palm. Variations of this ritual were repeated around the table with varying amounts of water until everybody was at least damp. We then served each other water from the cut glass bowl with our large spoons and splashed a goodly amount onto our hands with the smaller spoons. Before long we had abandoned the spoons altogether and were swirling our fingers in the translucent bowls and splashing gaily with our hands in the now depleted reservoir of the cut glass bowl.

It was this scene, eight American diners flailing like starlings in a fountain, that stopped our waiter more certainly than cardiac arrest as he swooped into the room with a platter of hot, glazed bananas: bananas that under normal circumstances would have been dipped immediately into ice water to harden the glaze before serving. I'll bet they would have been good.

Bob Sehlinger is the creator of the Unofficial Guide travel series, with more than 2,000,000 copies in print. A native Southerner (his name in Cherokee translates to "Man-Afraid-of-His-Grits"), Sehlinger lives in the pine woods near Birmingham, Alabama. You can see him there on his mountain bike, straining mightily to burn all the calories he racks up at the feed trough. He is available for dinner most nights.

★

Now, in our culture, we Ghanaian girls had learned how to eat soup daintily using nothing but our fingers, so the idea of a complex set of rules was a great amusement to us. And complex they were, indeed.

According to our very earnest white instructors, a refined young lady is supposed to sit at the dinner table upright, her feet "elegantly deposited on the ground," with no crossing of the knees or ankles. The proper distance for a body from the dinner table is no more, and no less, than three inches. Her torso should be at a right angle to her thighs, and she is expected to have her hands placed sensibly in her lap. As she prepares to eat her soup, she must lean towards the dinner table at approximately a 30-degree angle, using her right hand to pick up the soup spoon.

Holding the bowl with her left hand, she is to carefully tilt it away from her (approximately 10 to 15 degrees), while the little finger of her right hand rests on the edge of the bowl. Still holding the bowl with her left hand, she releases her right hand from the bowl, turning the spoon so that the soup is facing away from her. Now she fills the spoon until it is one-third to half-full and then slowly, keeping the spoon steady with her thumb, index finger and middle finger, she extends her little finger again as she raises the spoon to her lips, simultaneously lowering the bowl slowly down to its original position. She should then put her left hand back down in her lap and lean her torso (while still holding the spoonful of soup carefully) a further ten degrees forward towards the spoon. Of course, ladies with larger breasts were expected to lean a little bit less forward, so that their bosoms didn't end up in the soup!

Vital to the success of proper soup consumption was the correct puckering of lips—it was recommended that the "O" of the pucker be approximately the size of a shilling. Lifting the spoon to her lips, the lady should slowly tip the contents into her mouth without slurping or spilling, after which she daintily dabs the corners of her mouth with a napkin.

This is all very well if you have Caucasian lips, but when we full-lipped African children puckered up to the size of a shilling to tip our soup in, we'd end up spilling it all over ourselves. Now, if we had been asked to pucker up into two shillings, we might have stood a better chance. Instead, this etiquette lesson turned into a total disaster.

—Dorinda Hafner, *I Was Never Here and This Never Happened: Tasty Bits & Spicy Tales from My Life*

DONALD W. GEORGE

⋆ ⋆ ⋆

The Way of Iced Coffee

Sip slowly and savor the moment.

THREE MONTHS AGO I WAS SITTING IN A TOKYO COFFEE SHOP, lingering over a glass of iced coffee and watching the world go by. I was smiling at everything and nothing, sipping my iced coffee, watching the people passing outside and the people sipping inside, and suddenly it struck me that one reason for my sense of well-being was the little ritual I was enacting—a ritual I had been enacting ever since my first sip of iced coffee ten years before.

As I reflected on this, I realized that I had seen variations of this ritual enacted—unconsciously—in countless Japanese coffee shops by countless people, and that in fact the preparation and drinking of iced coffee had become one of those delightful little rites that unify and enrich Japanese life.

To my knowledge, however, no one had recognized it as such, so I decided to order another iced coffee and to set down my own modest version of *aisu kohido*, "the way of iced coffee."

To enjoy this simple rite, you need first to install yourself in a comfortable coffee shop, then order by saying, "*Aisu kohi, kudasai.*" What follows probably won't reveal any profound truths, but it may make you feel more intimately a part of the mesh of modern

Japan—and it will certainly provide a welcome chance to relax and reflect in the middle of a hard sightseeing day.

When your iced coffee is placed before you, study it for a while: the dark, rich liquid glistens with ice cubes whose curves and cracks hold and reflect and refract the liquid.

Notice the thin silver streaks and peaks in the ice cubes, and the beads of water on the outside of the glass—a cooling sight on a hot day. Then take up the tiny silver pitcher of sugar syrup that has been set just beside the glass and pour it into the part of the glass that is nearest to you. The syrupy stream courses through the coffee like a tiny waterfall, then quickly disperses and dissolves, like the dream of a rain shower on a summer afternoon.

After that, pick up the tiny white pitcher of cream that was placed just beyond the silver pitcher and pour it into the middle of the glass. Watch it disperse into countless cream-colored swirls and whirls and streams, which hang suspended in the middle of the coffee like a frozen breeze. Notice how the cream is pure white in some parts and a thin brownish hue in others. Notice also that a little trace stays on the surface, spiraling down into the middle of the glass.

Then unwrap the straw that has been set beyond the glass and place it in the middle of the glass. This sends out ripples that re-configure the cream's liquid breeze, creating new waves and textures and layers of iced coffee.

Finally, after appreciating this effect to your satisfaction, stir the coffee vigorously with your straw—the ice cubes clinking like wind chimes in a seaside breeze—until the coffee is a uniform sand-colored hue.

Then sip the coffee through the straw, tasting its coolness and complex mix of bitter coffee and sweet sugar and cream.

Now sit back, sip, and watch the world go by—smiling and serene that pleasure can sometimes be savored in such simple things.

For nine years Donald W. George was the award-winning travel editor of the San Francisco Examiner. *His career as a peripatetic scribbler started during*

*his college days in Paris, and has taken him around the world ever since. He
is the editor of* Travelers' Tales Japan *and currently works on the road
for lonelyplanet.com as Traveler-at-large.*

★

You're walking along a street in downtown Tokyo, soaking in the city's famous unlovely architecture—the particularly inhuman high-rise office
buildings, the unending vistas of glass and chrome—when you come
upon a structure that is so out of place you stop short. It's a small building with a thatched roof and wooden shingles dark enough to have ab-
sorbed centuries of urban grit. The style is Japanese—of a traditional sort
that has all but vanished from a city hell-bent on high tech.

Odds are that the holdout against redevelopment is a *nomiya,* one of
the most reactionary of Japanese institutions. A *nomiya* is the classic
Japanese pub, serving sake and tidbits across a rough slab of wood that may
well have held a samurai's refreshments two centuries ago. Like an Irish
pub, a *nomiya* can be an earthy, cheerful spot for a swallow of something
soothing; it can also be a miniature temple to gustatory elegance.

Once there were thousands of *nomiya* around Tokyo. Today there are
only hundreds, thanks to the Western bent of younger Japanese and to
mind-numbing real estate prices. Those that remain, however, are cher-
ished by city residents and knowing visitors.

—Russell Shorto, "Sake on Tap," *Travel & Leisure*

CHRISTOPHER P. BAKER

India on an Empty Stomach

Being derailed doesn't necessarily mean you're off track.

MR. KRISHNA HAD PROMISED ME "EDWARDIAN OPULENCE" IN MY own neat little coupe on the train known as the Palace on Wheels. He wagged his head side-to-side with a Dickensian jollity in the peculiar way Indians signal approval. He made it sound so splendid: silks, ivory, velvet upholstery, gleaming brass fittings, and my own salon captain to press my linens and "prepare breakfast, cool drinks, and snacks at the ring of the bell." There'd be two separate dining cars with "a mouthwatering choosing of Indian or European cuisine," said Krishna. On a more ominous note a "fully equipped first aid centre" was on hand, he added without a pause, as if even on India's showcase train the food couldn't be trusted.

Arriving at Delhi's Cantonment Station, I saw steam rising sibilantly between the giant piston rods of the black hulk of *The Desert Queen* 2-8-2, Y6 class, No. 3438, alias the aptly-named Palace on Wheels. The gleaming carriages had once hosted Maharajahs on their journeys through India. A coterie of tourist-passengers were eyeing the train reverentially while turbaned attendants in traditional blood-red Rajasthani costumes fussed over them.

I sighed, then settled onto a stiff parquet seat of the Upper India Express, an altogether less salubrious affair. I'd been bumped from

137

the Palace on Wheels, victim of a Kafkaesque cock-up caused by faceless factotums of India's infamously maladroit and creaky bureaucratic machine. My rantings had been answered with quizzical looks and shrugged shoulders.

"We are having no Mr. Barkers on our roster."

"It's Baker...as in bread," I replied.

"Ha! This is English humor, isn't it? Nonetheless, you are not on my passenger list."

"Yes, but Mr. Krishna promised me I had been confirmed."

"I do not know Mr. Krishna. Who is this Mr. Krishna to say such a thing?"

"It is not important whether you know him or not. He confirmed it through your Ministry of Tourism here in Delhi."

"This is irrelevant. You are not on our roster. There is no Mr. Bacon."

"It's *Baker*! You know? Butcher, baker, candlestick maker. Listen, the minister himself authorized this," I said. "You're supposed to have a cabin reserved for me."

"Yes, yes yes! But the train is full. And you are not on our roster..."

A scrawny woman emerged from the shadows and approached my window. As a white face I was doomed to a plaintive cry: "*Sahib!... Sahib!* She lifted a pot-bellied child with kohl-rimmed eyes that stared fixedly, and a frail voice that repeated a heartbreaking mantra: "*Rupee...Sahib!*" With a saintly gesture, a middle-aged passenger reached across and passed a biscuit into the hand of the outstretched palm, which withdrew, then reappeared empty a moment later. On the platform, burlap bundles would occasionally stir, roll over, and turn into people, as if a monsoon had flooded the station leaving the human flotsam washed up amid a miasma of filth. Homeless thousands find permanence in this place of passage. Delhi station is a magnet for the macabre. Breughel couldn't have painted a more sordid picture. One willowy destitute was squatting with his rump over the platform edge, leisurely defecating in *flagrante delicto*. He was taking his time, huddled on his haunches, inert as a reptile. He was naked but for a soiled loin-cloth, and his dark skin was made sooty by grime. A mangy dog stood warily in the wings, waiting to lick hungrily at the excrement.

Lacking the Westerner's fastidiousness about their ablutions— not to mention flush toilets—the masses aren't fussy about where they shit. Half of India seems to deposit its turds on the rails. No wonder the curtains were drawn on the *Desert Queen*. Behind them, I imagined my erstwhile fellow-passengers relaxing with a champagne sundowner and nibbling on delicious canapés prepared by a master chef. I was relegated to a bacillary tea proffered by a *chai-wallah* who appeared at my second-class compartment door with a tepid mash served from grubby glasses. My throat was parched, for even this late in the evening the heat was brutal and flooded in through the open window. Earlier, I had seen the wizened crone sipping from the ladle with which she souped out her turbid brew.

Having dropped his calling card by the rails, the wretched ascetic began to shuffle along the platform on his haunches like a mechanical toy, picking at tiny food morsels trodden underfoot by a thousand soiled feet.

Surprisingly, tea is not the all-purpose and all-important drink in India that it is in Iran and Afganistan. What's worse, the Indians, for all the tea they grow, make some of the most hideously over-sweetened, murkily-milky excuses for that fine beverage that you'll ever see. It may go by the name of chai, just like in the rest of Asia, but what a letdown. Still, some people like it and it is cheap.

Better tea can be had if you ask for "tray tea," which gives you the tea, the milk, and the sugar seperately and allows you to combine them as you see fit. Usually tea is "mixed tea" or "milk tea," which means it has been made by putting cold water, milk, sugar, and tea into one pot and bringing the whole concoction to the boil, then letting it stew for a long time. The result can be imagined.

—Hugh Finlay, Geoff Crowther, Bryn Thomas, and Tony Wheeler, *India - a travel survival kit*

It was a miserable sight, though *he* didn't look miserable. Was he resigned stoically to his fate? Had he chosen an appalling abstemious life as some act of contrition? A religious penance, perhaps? I watched him working his way up and down the filthy platform in his duck-like waddle until a long whistle announced our departure and he was swept into insignificance by the mad rush that ensued, as if this were the last train escaping a beleaguered city. The jolt of first motion cocked my stomach, which growled. My thoughts turned to food as the train pulled away amid a gallimaufry of whistles and shouts.

Indians take their food seriously. My fellow passengers had given serious thought to our journey. No sooner were we away than little packages were pulled out and unfolded on laps. Food hampers appeared, and from them emerged deep-fried vegetable *pakoras, samosas,* a three-cornered flour patty with potatoes, *bondas,* made of potatoes and chick pea flour, and desiccated figs. The slow-train to Varanasi metamorphosed in an instant to a veritable fast-food express. My fellow passengers picked at their food with their fingers, eating their tempting tidbits gustily in a great relish of slurps and burps. The calliope set my teeth on edge. As a youth my relationship with my father had been greatly strained and some of our most bellicose feuds were sparked by his noisy munching at dinner. I was sure that he mulched his food as a cow chews its cud for no other purpose than to annoy me. Now, I grimaced in silence while my stomach added strange liquid rumblings to the gastronomic cacophony.

"You are hungry. Please, would you like to be sharing my *papad?*" said a middle-aged lady to my right, tendering a crunchy savory crisp made of roasted rice dough. I eagerly accepted her offer, but as I nibbled, my emptiness worsened. I hadn't eaten in over eight hours. The crumbs seemed to echo in my stomach like water dripping from the roof of a cave. I recalled the advice of *Murray's Handbook for Travellers in India*—a guidebook first published in 1859—that the wise *sahib* should always keep his tiffin-basket well-furnished "with potted meats, biscuits, some good spirit, and soda water." The words fed the taunting self-recrimination I felt for not buying food before boarding.

Mrs. Verma, my neighbor, seemed terribly concerned with her presentation. Perhaps she'd read Murray, too, for she laid out a rippling sky-blue silk napkin and smoothed out the wrinkles as if she were stroking a cat. Onto this she placed a well-washed banana leaf that would serve as her plate.

"No porcelain?" I jibed mischievously.

"Western style is not appropriate," she replied tolerantly in singsong English. "China is fine for tourists on the Maharajas' express," she explained, "but porcelain is not good for orthodox Hindus; it is made of bone ash, isn't it?"

Her forehead was smeared with vermilion *sindur.* Several of our fellow travelling companions, I noticed, were eating their meals from banana leaves, too. Not so a portly Tibetan Buddhist monk en route to the lamasary at Varanasi, which he pronounced with a W like a German. He ate from a packet of digestive biscuits, and sat with his feet tucked under his thighs, studying a book titled *The Macintosh Expansion Guide,* mulling over words like peripheral functioning and evaluation procedure while barren fields flitted by. Cows were lying doggo-style in the blistering heat.

We progressed through villages and towns that seemed as dusty and monumental as the nation itself. When we stopped, hawkers jumped aboard to besiege us. Limbless lepers were in the wings, ready to seize on any hapless tourist who stepped down from the train. They filled the air with their awful murmurings. And beggars with spindly limbs peered into our cell of privilege. At Rampur, a juvenile mother held up a pathetic youngster with bewildered eyes and shocks of bristly ochre-red hair, like a cartoon character portrayed receiving an electric shock. The child's bald patches were a sign of malnourishment. The frail youngster looked like a time-worn Victorian doll. She reached in through the barred window. "*Rupee…Rupeeee!*" she droned. The monk looked beyond her impassively, oblivious to the child's upturned palm, reminding me of a line by the Hindi novelist Premchard: "They became so poor that year that even beggars left their doors empty-handed." The child's echo haunts me still. I turned away, haunted by grief and guilt.

There were stalls at every station. By day they sold food black with flies, and *kanji,* fermented carrot juice and mustard seeds, served from fetid earthenware jars. Now, darkness had descended like a benediction. Coals glimmered on the gloomy platforms where steaming stews were being cooked over smoky fires, and old women cast as harridans by the eerie shadows were kneading *chapattis* that they baked on griddles.

Though ravenous, I remained glued to my seat,...bound by childhood gustatory trepidation. In Yorkshire, we ate unseasoned tripe. Rice I knew only as a sweet pudding. Spaghetti—its squidginess made me gag—was something my mother served on toast. Curry and garlic were familiar to me only through the skin pores of Indians and Pakistanis who began to settle the textile cities of northern England in the 1960s. They smelled foreign and sickly.

My wariness wasn't relieved by memories of a baleful bout of what my mother used to call "the trots," which I had suffered with near-fatal severity in Morocco a few years before. The memory was like yeast to my swollen doubts.

Curries, with their vast partitioned platter of curious condiments to lackey them, speak for themselves. They sting like serpents, stimulate like strychnine; they are subtle, sensual like Chinese courtesans, sublime and sacred, inscrutably inspiring and intelligently illuminating, like Cambodian carvings.

—Aleister Crowley, quoted in *A World of Curries* by Dave DeWitt and Arthur J. Pais

As we progressed down the line the coal embers grew dimmer and eventually faded. Food hampers gave way to bed-rolls. Drowsiness overcame my gnawing hunger...

We were jolted awake at Lucknow, which looked melancholic, aching with age and penury in the steely pre-dawn light. Then the brilliant sun burned through the mists, charging the platform with motion. Cows browsed the station with leisurely sovereignty. Women streamed by in *saris* as red as bright lipstick and blue as the morning sky. Dusty bags and battered suitcases were being thrown from the roof, while others were being tossed up to take their place. The passengers leaped from the train the moment it halted and made a rush for refreshment. The chaos seemed life-threatening, but by now I was famished. Still, I had hesitated too long. As I stepped down from the carriage, the whistle blew and the tide turned. The seething horde squeezed, pushed, and elbowed its way back into the second class compartments. Fearing that I might be left on the platform as the train steamed away, I climbed back aboard. As I ruminated on the madness of India, a young boy appeared and thrust a tattered piece of card between the bars of the window. He had a pockmarked epicene face. Mistaking him for a beggar, I turned away.

"You should take it. Lord Vishnu is working in strange ways," Mrs. Verma said lyrically. Her lips curled cryptically in a Mona Lisa smile.

Good Lord! A menu! It was soiled and hardly inspired confidence. How many filthy hands had it passed through? Reading it, however, made me salivate longingly.

As I read with relish—desire, not condiment—a whistle blew and the carriage shuddered and groaned orgasmically. Now there was no time to ponder. The urchin was running alongside as the train gathered speed. The pathetic parchment had suddenly become a precious treasure. His plaintiff pleas urged my decision. I thrust the menu into his outstretched hand.

"You must please tell him what you are wanting," said Mrs. Verma. "Quickly! Tell him now, for goodness sake!" she chimed, with the exasperation of someone anticipating a grand denouement.

The rattle of the rails had gathered rhythm—*clickety clack, clackety click, clackety clack.* The boy, despairing, stopped running. I thrust my head between the bars and yelled. What I called I can't remember, but I recall clearly how the heat hit me like the searing slap of a jilted Latina. I ducked back inside like a startled turtle.

Now what?

What had I ordered? And where would I be served? As I ruminated on the possibilities—would my water buffalo testicles be crispy like fried calamari, or would they be squishy like marshmallows?—a shower of rice pattered down on my head, spilled by a passenger squatting cross-legged in the luggage rack like the hookah-smoking caterpillar in *Alice in Wonderland.* He looked as if he had been there forever.

The heat built infernally, relieved sporadically by a ceiling fan that shuddered through an elliptical arc. It whined like a hornet and emitted strange groans like a woman approaching climax whenever we rounded a bend.

The train came to a faltering stop. A young boy pushed his way through the mad calliope balancing a large oblong tray. Stretching on tip-toe, he pushed the tin *thali* through the window. My lunch was served.

During the days of the British Raj, when a journey across India took up to a week, it had become established practice to telegraph down the line to the next station for a meal to be put on board, delivered beneath a napkin on a tray. "So immediate was this service that it was as though the man had been awaiting you there all morning, holding his tray; but you had to eat fast, for before you left he would want the plates back, and as the train moved off again, with a creaking of its woodwork and a distant chuffing of its engine, you might see him bowing perfunctorily still as he retreated to the Vegetarian Food Stall for the washing-up," wrote Jan Morris, in *Pax Britannica.* I mused on how McDonald's had been pipped as India's first take-away by the platform lunch. The tradition has lingered, though thankfully I had more time to enjoy my repast.

My meal looked reassuringly delicious and aromatic. Each item was separated in its own tiny *katori,* small metal bowls containing separate items. Potatoes simmered in turmeric. Curried chicken. Lentils. Boiled rice in the center. Sweet mango chutney. *Raita* (yoghurt) mixed with chopped salad vegetables. And a chili relish so searingly hot I feared it might melt the tray and plop into my lap, doing irreparable damage to my sperm count. My meal represented all six *rasas* or flavors—astringent, bitter, pungent, salty, sour, and sweet—that by Hindu prescription must be included in every meal.

Indians eat *thali* meals with their fingers, yet I had been supplied with a grimy aluminum fork. I ate greedily while my cabin companions looked on approvingly. They wagged their heads side-to-side in the inane Indian manner that reminded me of the decorative dogs that Westerners faddishly placed behind the back seats of cars in the 1970s. I found myself parodying the mannerism unconsciously. A fellow passenger would look me in the eye and smile and—*damn it!*—my head would reflexively wag.

At the next station someone took my tray and poured the remains onto the platform. The morass attracted a scrawny dog, which sniffed desultorily until a legless beggar pushed it aside with a crutch, grubbed up the remains onto a broad rounded leaf, and began scooping the food with scabby fingers. I felt a new welling in my stomach. It wasn't hunger.

"In Rome you must do as the Romans do," said Mrs. Verma, enigmatically, pulling out a small brass chest—a *paan dann*—containing condiments representing a potpourri of the savory, the sweet, and the sour. She trilled her Rs, pronouncing Rome amusingly, like Peter Sellers asking the hotel concierge for a "rryoom" in the *Pink Panther* movie.

"No meal is complete without *pann*," she explained, smearing lime paste onto a betel leaf. "It is an essential postprandial pleasure, a good curative for the digestive system," she simpered in her rhythmic Queen Victoria English. Our cabin mates wagged their heads in agreement.

"Postprandial means after-dinner. I just had breakfast," I noted impishly. The heads stopped wagging.

"No matter," she replied, snipping areca nuts with a cutter shaped like a nut-cracker. I watched, fascinated, as she patiently clipped fragrant cardamom, cloves, and other exotic ingredients onto the leaf before folding it into a triangle and piercing a clove through the folds to hold it in place. I thanked her. Mrs. Verma put her fingertips together like a tiny steeple—the Indian gesture of benediction.

The cabin was silent. Eyes followed my every mastication. It tasted delicious. I wagged approvingly. Everyone smiled inanely. As we rumbled into Varanasi, beggars peered in to see a cabinful of nodding plastic dogs.

I was grateful for having been bumped from the Palace on Wheels.

*Christopher P. Baker has famished and foddered from Aachen to Zulueta,
Cuba. He has won multiple awards for travel guidebooks for Moon, Lonely
Planet, Frommer's, and Prentice Hall, and for feature articles in such publi-
cations as* Islands, Elle, Newsweek, *and* GEO. *He is the author of* Mi
Moto Fidel: Motorcycling Through Castro's Cuba. *He lives in
Oakland, California.*

★

My hotel wasn't serving lunch today, sorry. I checked out and lugged my
things to the closest restaurant. It was shabbily posh but overlooked the
sea. I'm like some Bengali vegetarians, who consider fish a "sea vegetable."
Fish sounded good, and would be safe to eat here, fresh from the Bay of
Bengal. The usual line of unshaved waiters in smudged white uniforms
slumped along the wall, which was scabbed with turquoise paint. Five
minutes passed before one of them shambled over with a dog-eared
menu. It was extensive. But I always pick at least two items, since an
Indian menu is a reflection of what's possible to cook, not what is actually on hand.

I asked the waiter what kind of fish they had: "Sorry madame, no fish
today."

No problem. I had my alternative. I asked what they put in their
noodles, knowing perfectly well I'd order them even with the tedious carrots and cabbage. "Sorry madame, no noodles today."

This surprised me. Too hungry to look further, long past the ability to
make a decision, I grasped for the old standby: *biryani*. "Sorry madame, no
biryani."

I gave up. "What do you have, then?"

"Sorry madame, no food today."

—Mary Orr, "India Sketches"

ELIZABETH ROPER MARCUS

Cafe Tacuba

The history of the Americas is
in the history of chocolate.

A FEW SPECIAL RESTAURANTS ARE AS MUCH CULTURAL ARCHIVES
or national metaphors as places to dine. Such is the Cafe Tacuba,
an 84-year-old restaurant in downtown Mexico City. The food,
the people, the decor, together with a curious narrative mural on
the back wall compose a *tableau vivant* that makes it our first stop
whenever my family of four visits Mexico City.

The restaurant is a veritable shrine to *mestizaje,* the fusion of
Indian and Iberian which produced the Mexican culture. As food
writer Raymond Sokolov has pointed out, it is Mexico, with its
complete mixing of cultures and people, that is the true "melting
pot." There is hardly a dish on the menu which does not make use
of New and Old World ingredients, scarcely a person in the room
who does not combine in his genetic make-up something of the
two cultures. This hybridization evokes both tremendous national
pride and persistent denial, and evidence of both are also to be
found in the restaurant.

The Cafe Tacuba is located in the very heart of this Spanish
colonial city built on the ruins of the Aztec capital, the most glorious city in the Western hemisphere at the time of Cortes' arrival.
Although the exterior, like all of downtown, is blackened by pol-

147

lution, the interior vibrates with color and pattern. Entering the
front room we are greeted by a cheerful clatter that bounces off the
high, vaulted ceilings and elaborate yellow and blue tilework. It
doesn't matter what time we arrive; the restaurant, open every day
from morning to night, is always busy. Early in the morning it is
full of people downing coffee and cakes or hearty breakfasts of *enchiladas* or *tamales*. Late at night it is still jammed with people enjoying food which is the very antipode of nouvelle cuisine. The
servers—motherly women, dressed in white with crisp aprons and
huge bows in their hair, like a flock of Victorian nannies—rush
from table to table, struggling to keep up. Alcohol is not served
here and the gaiety is sustained without it. Food is accompanied
by fruit juices, hot chocolate, or coffee in many forms, including a
condensed syrup which sits in a cruet on each table like a condiment and is poured into tall glasses of hot milk. For more than
three-quarters of a century, Mexicans have come here as much to
savor their cultural identity as to eat.

I usually ask to be seated in the darkly paneled back room. We
wend our way through the tables of diverse patrons: romancing
couples of varying ages, trios of elegant women, families with small
children, groups of businessmen, a few foreigners, and bohemian
expatriates. The high-backed wooden chairs are uncomfortable,
but the diners lean forward, gesticulating between bites, as engrossed in one another as in what they are eating. We don't need
to study the menu before ordering. Our first meal here is always
the same: huge flat, corn-husk wrapped *tamales, quesadillas,* and
chicken *mole,* my husband's favorite.

Meanwhile, hanging over this scene, and peculiarly discon-
nected from it, is another gustatory drama—a painted one—
depicted in a life-sized mural on the back wall. The figures in it,
although silent and impassive, are as involved with eating as the real
life diners. The mural is not fine art; it doesn't pretend to be. But
the story it tells and, even more, the stories it avoids telling—
reflects the conflicted feelings Mexicans tend to have about their
hybrid civilization and its legacy.

The painting, a triptych, is a testimonial to cultural fusion; at least, that is its pretense. It recounts the history of chocolate, and, by extension, the Spanish debt to the indigenous people of Mexico. In the left-hand panel, kneeling on the floor of a native hut, a lovely Indian woman is preparing the traditional chocolate drink, rolling the wooden swizzle-stick back and forth between her two palms to bring the liquid to a proper froth. Behind her, two Indian men are drinking, their upturned wooden bowls reverently cupped in their two hands. Framing the bottom of the scene are the twining branches of the cacao tree, the fruit bursting open with ripe seeds. In extreme contrast, in the right-hand panel, two aristocratic young Spanish women, richly attired in 18th century gowns and seated in a baroquely decorated salon, delicately select chocolates from a silver dish. In the large central panel the two worlds come together. Two Spanish women are at table with a bewigged, beribboned gentleman and a bald, rather homely priest to whom one of the women is passing a stemmed glass of chocolate, while the Indian server waits in the background holding an earthenware pitcher of the precious brew on a tray.

Cacao pod

The illustrated story is that of the Spanish appropriation of the Mexican Indian's treasure: chocolate. It was the Mayan ambrosia, literally the gods' food, eaten on ceremonial and religious occasions by mere mortals after the gods had had their fill. Because the Spanish systematically destroyed all scientific as well as religious Mayan writings, little is known about their cultivation of chocolate other than that they roasted the seeds of the cacao pod, ground them, then mixed the resulting powder with water, chili, musk, and honey, whisking the boiling liquid with a wooden implement.

One of the few extant Mayan texts lists chocolate as among the riches paid in tribute to the Aztec king, Moctezuma, who apparently had developed a passion for it. Two thousand jars a day were supposedly consumed in his household. When Cortes arrived in

1519 and was greeted by the benighted king who mistook him for the returning god Quetzalcoatl, he asked for treasure and was shown heaps of ground cacao. So highly valued was the stuff that the seeds, bagged in standard quantities, were used as money until the 18th century. Although at first unimpressed with the bitter brew, Cortes and his men quickly came to appreciate its intoxicating and supposedly aphrodisiac qualities. Perhaps the pomp and ceremony with which it was served helped them to overlook its bitter taste: following an elaborate ceremony celebrating the cacao harvest—complete with human sacrifice, masked dancing, and erotic games—it was offered to them in golden cups by naked virgins.

Freely mixing the exotic chocolate with their own ingredients, the Spanish made something new and original, as they did in all areas of colonial life. The problem of the drink's bitterness was quickly solved in a convent kitchen, as fertile a source of culinary inventions in the New World as in the Old. For the traditional spices, high-born missionary nuns substituted local vanilla and two new imported food items: sugar from the East and cream from European dairy cattle. Chocolate became an overnight sensation as soon as the first cargo reached Spain, and during the 16th and early 17th centuries, it was the most important Mexican export. Spanish ladies developed such a passion for it that they drank it from morning to night, even had it served to them in church. The new and improved version of the Mayan drink of the gods was profitably controlled by the Catholic Church, whose Popes and bishops became embroiled in weighty ecclesiastic debates as to whether drinking it should or shouldn't count as breaking a religious fast. Fortunes were made and souls were sold in the greedy pursuit of profit from a European food fad.

The Cafe Tacuba painting celebrates the cultural benefits of cross-fertilization but presents it as a circumscribed event, avoiding the bigger picture: the complete hybridization of cultures and peoples. The races in the painting lead parallel lives. In effect, the mural depicts the Spanish conquerors' ideal, their original vision of two separate nations—the colonial and the native. But this vision quickly proved to be an untenable fantasy. In fact, with the shortage of women on the first boats, racial mixing began almost as soon as the Spanish soldiers stepped ashore. The supposedly aphrodisiac qualities of chocolate could not have hurt the process either! In contrast to the white population's isolation of native Indians in the USA and Canada, the Spanish continuously interbred with the indigenous population and created a new, mestizo race.

The racial blend was further complicated when, because of the staggering mortality rate of the Indians, the Spanish turned to importing African slaves. The long, brutal voyage and concomitant loss of life made these slaves expensive, in comparison to the freely available, if less hardy Indians and the practice was soon abandoned, but not before over one hundred thousand Africans had joined the Mexican population. Diego Rivera portrays the creation of Mexico's mixed race symbolically in his great stairwell mural in the National Palace: a Spanish soldier raping an Indian girl. The muralist of the Cafe Tacuba, no social revolutionary, keeps his handsome Indians safely in a frame of their own or in the background of the central panel, the suitably meek servant.

The cross-fertilization—readily accepted as enrichment in the kitchen—was thought of quite differently in the sexual arena. As the progeny of these predominantly out-of-wedlock couplings muddled the social and political hierarchy, racial mixing became cause for alarm. Initially these children were treated as a public embarrassment or worse, sometimes abandoned by all the races to roam the streets homeless and pitiable. Later, as their numbers increased, a caste system evolved which defined all aspects of social, political, and economic life. Racial genealogy became a national obsession. Initially the Spanish-born tenaciously maintained their superior position by distinguishing themselves even from Mexican-born Spaniards, known as creoles, contending that the climate and the milk of their Indian nursemaids were sufficient to contaminate the creole character. Between the Spanish-born, "most white," at the top and the Indian at the bottom, the system recognized, in addition to creole, mestizo, and black: mulatto (offspring of black and white), zambo (of Indian and black), morisco (of mulatto and white) and castizo (mestizo and white). Those at the bottom of the social ladder endured dismal lives, deprived of most rights and all opportunity.

In the restaurant's painting, however, there is no suffering. The Indians in the mural, although somber, look like movie stars—the woman shapely, the men muscular and handsome. They are well dressed in costumes that seem to have come straight from the wardrobe room. None of the figures expresses any emotion. If the Indians are feeling angry resentment, they are keeping it under wraps. They are depicted as a proud, noble people (and unbelievably robust in the light of their historic suffering). Moreover, although there is no room for them at the table, the painter has made sure to point out the one place in which they have clearly benefited from the cultural exchange: the kitchen. They have acquired sugar, a large bowl of which sits on the floor of the Indian hut. The Spanish, meanwhile, are depicted as equally handsome and without malevolence. While Diego Rivera and the other muralists generally depicted the ruling class as brutal and vicious, the priests licentious and rapacious, the worst one can say about the Spaniards portrayed in the Cafe Tacuba mural is that they are oblivious to the Indians and to the enormous disparity of wealth and position between their two societies.

In reality, however, when the Spanish conquered Mexico, they began centuries of abuse that, though perhaps no more brutal than that of the blood-obsessed Aztecs, had a much more devastating effect. Enslavement, theft of land, debasement to subhuman status, and exposure to imported disease took an extraordinary toll; in the first one hundred years under the Spanish, the Indian population was reduced by at least 90 percent. Centuries of political change have done little to improve the Indian's plight. Neither the 1810 War of Independence, which freed Mexico from the Spanish and created a creole and mestizo ruling class, nor the 1910 Revolution, which ended the Diaz dictatorship and established the modern Mexican constitution, restored the Indians' land, lifted them from poverty, or freed them from discrimination. The enormous debt owed them—as in the mural's politically correct message—remains unpaid.

The Cafe Tacuba painting is a fiction. Restaurants are frequented only by the relatively wealthy and no doubt the muralist sought to avoid offending them. But, in an attempt to distance the more prickly aspects of his narrative by historicizing his subject, he has ended up white washing the past. He has paid lip service to the long-held goal of restoring the Indian's dignity, but has denied both the reality of the Indian's situation and the hybrid racial identity of the Mexican people. This fiction and its racist underpinnings, the legacy of the Spanish colonial denigration of a conquered people, is as much a part of the country's cultural heritage as its national pride in the Indian's contribution.

Mexico has seen great upheavals since the early years of the Revolution when the Cafe Tacuba opened, but inside the restaurant's double swinging doors—and inside the national psyche as well—not much has changed. How do prosperous Mexicans reconcile their anti-Indian sentiments with the knowledge that the victims are their own genetic relations? Perhaps they rationalize their feelings with the thought that it is class and not ethnicity that is at issue, but can the two really be separated? If the modern diners happened to look up and consider for a moment the figures in the Cafe Tacuba painting, would they think of them, both the Indians and Spaniards, as equally their ancestors?

But no one does look up. No one seems to notice the murals at all. Eventually the server arrives with our order: *tamales* of rough, grainy, New World corn meal wrapped around bits of darkly roasted Old World pork, *quesadillas* of tender, blistered Indian tortillas oozing with molten white cheese from Spanish dairy cattle, and chicken *mole,* an addictive dish invented by an ingenious nun who mixed local chocolate and chilies with imported cinnamon and coriander. We pour the rich, dark coffee syrup into our tall glasses of shimmering hot milk, watching the colors swirl together, mingle and, in a instant, blend, while above us the painted figures float, frozen in their fictitious historic moment.

Elizabeth Roper Marcus, a travel writer, was an architect until she realized she'd rather construct sentences than houses.

★

The conquistador Bernal Diaz reports that the man he always called "The Great Montezuma" liked his cup of hot chocolate flavored with vanilla, sweetened with honey, and spiked with a good dose of red chile. The Spaniards picked up the habit, too, and brought it to Europe and, of course, the rest is culinary and confectionery history. But Diaz and some others stayed in Mexico carving out huge haciendas and quaffing cocoa in the manner of their admired late foe. They kept the original recipe but expanded on it a bit by adding a splash of *"vino de Tequila."* When cattle were introduced to Mexico from Europe they added a little milk or cream. But basically they drank what the emperor had drunk. Only when it had gone through many European hands did the mixture become the confection we know today.

I like to drink what Diaz and Montezuma drank. I've made this drink for years now, adjusting and improving until I've arrived at what I think both the conquistador and the emperor would approve.

—RS

Cacao glyph

THE GREAT MONTEZUMA

12 ounces prepared hot chocolate (not too sweet)	1/2 teaspoon vanilla extract
	2 jiggers pepper vodka
2 tablespoons honey	2 tablespoons heavy cream

Combine the chocolate, honey, vanilla and vodka. Pour into two stemmed glasses or Irish coffee glasses. Float the cream on the tops of the two drinks. Dust with a pinch of cayenne pepper and garnish with cinnamon sticks, or dust with grated chocolate and garnish with dried red chilies. Drink to the Old World and the New.

JULIA DUFFY WARD

One Woman's Spice Route

She travels through her memory on a cloud of spice.

TWICE A YEAR—ONCE IN THE FALL, ONCE IN THE SPRING—I PUT aside my mop, my broom, my Hoover, and my Windex to indulge in a different sort of housekeeping.

This is a restorative act, timed by mood, not moon or calendar. In the autumn my cleaning date falls somewhere between Halloween and Thanksgiving, when memories of the past summer's travel are fading and the coming summer seems too remote to contemplate.

At the elected time I turn my attention to kitchen drawers and cupboards where, alongside useful gadgets—a Turkish lemon squeezer, a German tomato knife, a French tart tin, Brazilian custard cups, a Japanese ginger grater, a Norwegian corkscrew, and a Bulgarian ceramic half-moon that prevents milk from boiling over—I store my seldom-used travel treasures.

To the right of the stove, on the top shelf of a narrow cupboard is a jar with the *salep* I bought ten years ago in Istanbul's spice bazaar. *Salep* is made from wild orchid tubers (*Orchis mascula*), ground to a fine though slightly gritty white powder, something like extra fine cream of wheat. On winter days it is stirred into

155

milk, sweetened with sugar, and boiled till thick, though not too thick to drink.

I wipe the jar, twist off the green lid and rub the grains between thumb and index finger. And I taste all the soothing *saleps* I've drunk at the ferry crossing between Kartal and Yalova, where on blustery mornings *salep* was served from bulky brass urns, reminiscent of samovars. The steamy white liquid was released through a small spigot into cups and then sprinkled with cinnamon.

I dust the corner of this shelf, return the *salep* and then turn my attention to adjacent phials and baby food jars filled with herbs and spices—saffron from Spain, bay leaves from Turkey, *chubritza* and ampoules of yogurt culture from Bulgaria, sumac from Egypt, chilis from Thailand, cinnamon bark from India, and juniper berries from Germany.

Salep

This morning I examine my Uncle Rumen's *chubritza,* a 20-year-old mixture of summer savory, ground walnuts, red pepper, curry, salt, and his secret: sunflower seeds. We were together in the Rhodope Mountains in Bulgaria the first time I tasted the spicy powder spooned from a ceramic bowl onto heavy peasant bread. We were hungry that day, and cold. The surprise was that a simple lodge, with the most unpromising of menus, should serve one of the memorable meals of my life: bowls of tripe soup, hot, delicious, glistening gold with túrmeric, properly sour, accompanied by *chubritza,* bread, and beer.

I sniff the jar's contents and consider the shelf life of walnuts and sunflower seeds. Surely not two decades. But how can I toss out a memory like this? I polish the domed lid, twist it tight, and restore the jar, once again, to its place.

On the middle shelf is a Mason jar filled with *erva,* a South American tea (some say an aphrodisiac) whose color and texture remind me of a cross between henna and sage. After nine years it smells a bit like this too. I have everything I need to make the warming drink, called *ximarão* or *maté* in the south of Brazil. I have the *cuia,* a hollowed gourd covered with suede, and a *bomba,* a stainless steel straw, shaped like an overlong cigarette holder with a perforated ball used to pat the *erva* into place and through which the murky tea is strained and sipped.

Maté is drunk throughout the day in Rio Grande do Sul, where a friendly waiter taught me how to pack *erva* onto one side of the hollowed gourd, leaving a void into which first cold and then boiling water are poured. *Maté* transports me to a *gaucho* supply shop in Santa Angelo, where, in an alcove, a large kettle of water is kept boiling over a gas cylinder and where customers are offered sips of tea from communal *cuias* as they shop for *bombaschas* (baggy *gaucho* trousers), dancing dresses with rows of ruffles and colorful ribbons, ponchos, broad-brimmed, stiff felt hats, bolts of cloth, and equestrian gear—saddles, bridles, spurs, and blankets. *Maté*-sharing is a ritual. Like passing an Indian peace pipe, it's a sign of friendship.

I center the *maté* on the shelf, close the cupboard, and clamber from counter to floor. The kitchen drawers are next, and as I explore the accumulation of little-used treasures, I spot a fold of white flannel beneath my Turkish *oklava* (a narrow wooden dowel used to roll out paper-thin dough). The *coador,* which resembles a small windsock attached to a wooden handle, is used in São Paulo to filter coffee. The grounds are left to steep in a pot of boiling hot water and then the coffee is poured through the white cloth into cups. I bought the filter partly because I loved the rich Brazilian coffee, but mostly because I didn't want to forget the image of three waiters at a green-shuttered corner restaurant in São Carlos who, dressed in black tie and with generous white linen napkins folded over their arms, skillfully-managed pot, filter, cup, saucer,

> *Smells detonate softly in our memory like poignant land mines, hidden under the weedy mass of many years and experiences. Hit a tripwire of smell, and memories explode all at once. A complex vision leaps out of the undergrowth.*
>
> —Diane Ackerman, *A Natural History of the Senses*

and cubes of sugar. I imagined that once home, I would reproduce the taste and aura. I have, but only at moments like this.

Not all my housekeeping evokes such uncomplicated memories. In the lazy susan are jars of preserved sweets from two sides of the Green Line that divides Cyprus. As we were leaving Nicosia five years ago, Rhoula, my Greek-Cypriot friend, gave me a jar of green figs boiled with sugar and known in the south as *glyko;* Aysa, my Turkish-Cypriot friend, gave me a jar of green walnuts, also boiled with sugar, and known in the Turkish north as *macunu.*

Unless the light is very good, I can scarcely distinguish one jar from the other. Both are green and packed tight with small honeyed fruits. They remind me of my friends, each a refugee on the island where she was born, each unable to return to her birthplace.

On the lazy susan, I also keep a tin of powdery green tea from Kyoto, a jar of rose hip jam from Skopje, Macedonia, a can of fiery red pepper paste from Alanya, Turkey, a box with egg yolk marzipan from Madrid and my latest (and freshest) acquisition, a lilac-colored box of Parlsocker, a decorative Scandinavian sugar that looks like particles of very white crushed limestone. I bought it after a stormy Norwegian ferry ride from the Lofoten Islands to Bodo, a trip that only an Akita puppy and perhaps the captain survived with grace.

To regain our land legs and stomachs, my husband and I walked the streets of Bodo until the smell of fresh cinnamon rolls led us into a bakery, where, miraculously, our queasiness was settled by cinnamon rolls topped with Parlsocker.

On dark days like this I imagine the comforting yeast dough, sticky with caramelized nuts, fragrant with cinnamon and sprinkled with chalk-sugar no baker's fire could melt.

Julia Duffy Ward began her gastronomic career simply at a German boarding school, where she subsisted for two years on quark and boiled potatoes. Since then she has lived in eight countries on five continents, expanding her culinary repertoire and love of travel. When she isn't on the road, she is at home in Oxford, Ohio, where she teaches English at Miami University and writes for The New York Times, House Beautiful, *and* New Choices.

Anaïs Nin knew the power of spice, as she wrote in *Little Birds:*

Eventually Albert took her, under the most unusual of circumstances. They were going to give a party for Spanish friends. Although she seldom shopped, Fay went to the city to get a particular saffron for the rice, a very extraordinary brand that had just arrived on a ship from Spain. She enjoyed buying the saffron, freshly unloaded. She had always liked smells, the smells of wharves, and warehouses. When the little packages of saffron were handed to her, she tucked them in her bag, which she carried against her breast, under her arm. The smell was powerful, it seeped into her clothes, her hands, her very body.

When she arrived home Albert was waiting for her. He came towards the car and lifted her out of it, playfully, laughing. As he did so, she brushed with her full weight against him and he exclaimed, "You smell of saffron!"

She saw a curious brilliance in his eyes, as he pressed his face against her breasts smelling her. Then he kissed her. He followed her into her bedroom, where she threw her bag on the bed. The bag opened. The smell of saffron filled the room.

—RS

GINA COMAICH

The Monsoon Cocktail

*On a train dedicated to the pleasures of the senses,
the author happily finds that the senses do not
always have to make sense.*

THERE IS A SOUND THAT MAKES ME HUNGRY. IT PLAYS UPON MY ear and insinuates itself into my memory and then, by the special alchemy of the senses, diffuses itself into my body, fills my nostrils with aromas, my palate with hints of taste, me with a yearning, and I hunger, sweetly. It is a sound that sounds in only one place on Earth, and I will not soon hear it again. But when the rain falls gently and just so, little echoes of the sound resonate in the pattering of the drops, out upon the ear's horizon. Couples may talk of "our song," and perhaps hearing a few bars of it will make them hunger for each other. The sound whose distant refrain I hear in an autumn drizzle is my song.

I had accepted my friend Bryce's invitation to come with him on the Asian sister train to Europe's Simplon Orient Express: the fabulous Eastern & Oriental Express, traveling from Singapore, through the Malay peninsula, to Bangkok. I had a snobbish attitude that the more rigorous the way the more intense the adventure, but it would turn out that the E & O, that benchmark of pleasure and delight, would include its own special twists; the kind that the mischievous muse of travel plans for her devotees.

160

Stepping out of a taxi at Singapore's Keppel Road station, green and gold uniformed porters immediately surrounded us, deftly taking our luggage and quickly ushering us up the carpeted entry way to the special reservations desk set aside for E & O patrons. Here we received our cabin assignments and made our dinner reservations for the following two nights.

Promptly at three a gong sounded, and with great ceremony the gates were thrown back and patrons invited to pass from this ordinary world to the extraordinary one of the Eastern and Oriental Express.

Pana, our congenial Thai porter, led us to our stateroom, richly paneled in rare woods and made comfortable with tapestried chairs and couches. Silk embroidered curtains in delectable shades of green lined the window. I opened the door to the tiny but exquisite bath feeling somehow I'd just released the catch of a fabulous Faberge egg, so rich were its appointments. "Let's just leave our bags here and go exploring," Bryce said.

"The observation car first," I directed. We quickly made our way to the back of the train happily discovering that this car was totally open on three sides. As the train slowly pulled away from the station, ticket collectors from the opposite platform leaned out their windows giving us wide smiles and thumbs up. Even the baggage carriers ran a few yards alongside the train shouting, "Good luck! Good trip!"

The original Orient Express began its life on October 4, 1883 when it departed Paris for Istanbul. Created by George Nagelmakers of the Compagnie International des Wagon-Lits et Grands Express Européens, it was known as the King of Trains and the Train of Kings. It is the most famous train ever to steam through History, Literature, or Film.

—RS

Bryce grabbed my hand as we made our way past groups of enchanted travelers settling themselves into their compartments. He pulled open yet another carriage door and we discovered the library car; an island of calm in our overheated state. From the train corridor its large interior windows resembled a Victorian book store. A whole car devoted to books! The author in Bryce couldn't resist and he was already passing through its oak doors, "This is where I'll stay for a while," he said.

I continued alone, investigating each unique coach until, pulling back one frosted glass door, I found myself in an exquisite dining room worthy of this rolling doll's house. The tables were covered with dazzling white napery spread fan-shaped across plates of fine bone porcelain trimmed in gold. Each setting was flanked by heavy flatware and rested on starched linen tablecloths whose primly folded corners cascaded down toward the elegant green carpet. Tasty yellow orchids in silver vases mirrored the gold embroidery decorating the silk window valances. The windows, their white silk curtains tied back with heavily braided gold cords, allowed sweeping views of the Straits of Jahor we were now cross-ing. All of this was surrounded by intricately parqueted wood in both ceiling and walls. But it was the crystal that intrigued. Large and substantial, the beveled wine and water goblets caught and re-flected the afternoon light to each other and to every part of the car. And then the sound.

Over the rhythmic clacking of the train wheels, I could hear the tinkling of the crystal goblets as they gently vibrated against one another in response to the train's motion. Each goblet a separate crystal tuning fork, each of perfect pitch, yet each ever so slightly different, and all in harmony. A base note hummed out constantly, clearly, callingly, while the subtlest variations played along a tiny scale in a voice that only the spirits can sing. I stood for a moment, caught in a delicious dream. Sensation became hazy. The colors, the sounds of train wheels and the crystal and the fragrance of the orchids all stirred themselves into a riotous symphony and filled the room. This coach, I realized, epitomized the human quest for excellence and exquisite pleasure that is the E & O; not set out in some impersonal way but arranged by caring hands, planned and executed lovingly. And I had touched the heart of this train and its rhythm became part of me. It was singing to me.

We would have a gala dinner here: king prawn *dim sum* as an appetizer, lightly scented with truffles and served with a lotus root salad, a tender entree of lamb medallion with a delicate cumin cream sauce, and assorted petits fours to tempt an already sated appetite. The dinner was served with grace and ease, a signature of the train personnel. Delightful. But it was the memory of that afternoon, and the crystal whisperings of the beautiful things to come that brought the element of magic to that exquisite meal.

The bar car was also a place that would work its own brand of magic on its passengers. Bryce and I had carefully dressed for dinner that first night and entered this coach eager to meet other travelers. As I happily contemplated the brilliant purple and yellow orchids decorating the top of the piano bar, the romantic two-by-two seating, he whispered, "I smell beef jerky!"

Oh well. Nothing to do but follow the scent of what is Bryce's favorite fast food. We nodded and smiled at people as we followed his nose and located the jerky as well as John and Barbara, its owners, at the end of the coach.

"Ah, another aficionado of this perfect food," Bryce intoned by way of introducing ourselves. They laughed, and made room for us at the tiny bar table and we discussed the various types, brands, and just how they prepared it in South Africa, their home. They were here with a group of fellow South Africans who'd earned the trip through their company incentive program. As we talked, the subject of South Africa's recent elections came up and I spoke about how Americans had watched them with a great deal of interest and emotion. "Please don't judge all South Africans by the Boer image that you've seen in the media," explained John.

"Many of us have wanted change in our government policy for a long time," added Barbara, "and were glad it's finally come."

Though their elections had changed their government, they still brought with them their racial legacy. The South Africans were a mixed group of Whites, Blacks, and Indians, and while they all carried the same kind of passport there was a stiffness in the air. People clustered a bit too closely in their own groups. But God bless the piano man, Irving Berlin, and champagne. After a couple of rounds we all began to cluster around the piano, singing old

American tunes that everyone knew, sometimes better than Bryce or I. Then into the car came two Chinese Opera singers in complete makeup and costumes. The car was packed by this time and we were toe to toe with the entertainers and each other. As the train rocked and leaned into the curves we all took turns gently holding onto the edges of their elaborate costumes keeping the couple upright and singing. Smiles all around, eye contact at last, and maybe a chink in the racial armor. Though I could not hear the sounds of the next car, the dining car, I knew that, like the actors, the goblets were singing.

Our last afternoon on the E & O a violent monsoon surrounded the train. Trouble on the tracks ahead had brought it to a standstill, something that rarely happened. Bryce and I decided to watch the storm from the observation coach, picking up a gin and tonic as we passed through the bar car. From there we could see the train stretched around a curve in the roadbed like a cream silk ribbon. Jungle lay thick on all sides; its wild and variegated shades of green dulled by the heavy cloud cover. Forked lightning shot across the sky and thunder rolled and boomed behind. A torrential rain began, pulling a fluid curtain about the train. Lightning flashed once more, this time so near its sharp crack and the thunder's reply were tactile sensations. The wind had picked up and the open sides of the car gave little protection. In a minute both of us were soaked but unwilling to leave this glorious encounter with the elements.

And I heard the sound again. There in the rain. Though it was born of a tempest, it fell upon the roof with a softness, and perfect clarity of tone. A base note, constant. Tiny variations playing up and down the rain scale. And far in the acoustic distance, on the outer reaches of hearing, the crystal sang. We still held our drinks and, on some silent cue, reached out and let the melodious rain fill the glasses to overflowing. Laughing, we toasted and drank the monsoon. Bryce delighted in having "drunk the tempest." But I drank something more. I could feel it still trembling in my glass as I quaffed sense memory. I drank the sound.

Gina Comaich will go anywhere for a free train ride or to shop for vintage clothing. When not on photographic assignments or living in Peru, she teaches school in Oakland, California.

✳

In time, the newborn learns to sort and tame all its sensory impressions, some of which have names, many of which will remain nameless to the end of its days. Things that elude our verbal grasp are hard to pin down and almost impossible to remember. A cozy blur in the nursery vanishes into the rigorous categories of common sense. But for some people, that sensory blending never quits, and they taste baked beans whenever they hear the word "Francis," as one woman reported, or see yellow on touching a matte surface, or smell the passage of time. The stimulation of one sense stimulates another: synesthesia is the technical name, from the Greek *syn* (together) + *aisthanesthai* (to perceive). A thick garment of perception is woven thread by overlapping thread.

—Diane Ackerman, *A Natural History of the Senses*

DANNY CARNAHAN

✦ ✦ ✦

Kenyan Barbeque

It's a hard road to a good meal.

THE CAFE WHERE I ATE MY MOST REMARKABLE KENYAN MEAL cannot be found in any guidebook or on any tourist itinerary. If I had ever set foot in the Third World before or if I'd known another soul in Africa to advise me, I probably wouldn't have gotten within miles of the place. But then I would have missed an experience of a lifetime.

I hadn't even expected to stay overnight in Nairobi. But after being bumped off a flight out of London and missing my only-twice-a-week connection to Madagascar, I found myself alone in a strange and daunting city for four days, with no friends and the limited options afforded by my limited funds. I couldn't afford anything like the Hilton, so the taxi driver took me to a "secure" hotel near River Road that was one-tenth the price. Later, I learned that, according to a popular "survivor's guide" to Nairobi, I ran a 100 percent chance of being mugged if I wandered out at night in that neighborhood. Guess I was lucky.

Determined not to cower in my room for four days, I walked out to see the city. As I was apparently the only white person staying on the "wrong side" of Mboya Street, I immediately attracted every street hustler within blocks, trying to sell me everything from watches to safaris. One hustler named George was particularly charming and kept walking with me after most others had abandoned me as a poor prospect. Eventually, I admitted to myself that I really wouldn't learn anything about this weird place without a guide. George offered to get me a guide and a car and driver for a day trip to the Rift Valley, the coffee and tea plantations, and anything else I'd like to see. Soup to nuts for $100. It took most of my financial cushion, but I agreed.

Fifteen minutes later George drove up in a dilapidated Peugeot. He introduced the driver, Bosko, whose pointed, bony frame was lost in a shiny blue suit and who spoke very little English. The guide Ben, with shaven head, sharp eyes, and a ready guffaw of a laugh, was fluent and charming.

With stops to fuel the car and change money on the black market, we bounced out of town, dodging homicidal *matatu* minibuses and seemingly suicidal pedestrians. We spent hours gazing down from the Rift escarpment, walking through the magically scented tea plantations, driving slowly along the rough roads, talking with villagers, and repeatedly being held up by police demanding that we pay them a cash "road tax" before allowing us to pass. It was well into the afternoon before I realized we hadn't stopped for lunch.

"You want traditional food for lunch?" Ben asked. Sure. "You know *nyama choma?*" The guidebook described it as barbequed goat meat and as close as anything comes to claiming the title "national dish of Kenya." Let's go for it, I said. Ben says Bosko will find the very best in Kiamaiko. I had no idea where Kiamaiko was, but off we went.

The road became rougher. The houses became shacks, and the shacks became hovels. I found it difficult to believe that people could live like this. The only images I could compare it to from my experience were those of Rwandan refugee camps. But people seemed to be happily going about their business as if this was the way of the world. As indeed it was for them.

We turned the car off the dirt road and into a sea of devastation. I wouldn't have believed one could drive into such a place, but people and goats and chickens parted before us and we inched forward past stalls and the milling hawkers selling drinks, vegetables, used clothes, anything.

I just stared and tried to take it all in. This was Kiamaiko, a slum of mammoth proportions just outside Nairobi proper. Nobody knows how many people live there. There is no running water, there are no amenities. The only notice the government takes of Kiamaiko is to periodically bring in bulldozers and level it all. Then, within days, the shacks are rebuilt and life goes on as if nothing happened. Ben explained this to me as we lurched along and the ruts threatened to tear the wheels off the car.

The smells were, well, rich. And when the car had taken the tenth weird turn and then lurched to a stop in a puddle, I knew I'd never find my way out alone. Bosko got out and I asked, in as calm a voice as I could manage, if this was where we were eating lunch. Ben said no. Bosko was going home to get something first. Home. He lived here. Boy, am I glad I kept my mouth shut.

A little while later and another few turns and puddles, we were in an area with nothing but vast herds of goats and meat hanging from the rafters of shacks. We stopped just this side of a large gaggle of goats and Ben announced that we had arrived. This was where we would find *nyama choma.*

The smell was nearly overpowering. As we got out of the car and splashed over to a relatively dry spot, Ben says, "Bosko will find the best meat. We'll go get a drink. If they see you the price will go up." Twin ranks of wood and tin structures, stood—or, rather, staggered—down either side of the irregular pathway, ruts running with animal urine and blood. Each structure sported a large concave chopping block and meat hooks. Men were hanging meat or chopping meat while negotiating heatedly with Somali herdsmen for the price of a live goat.

We picked our way down the lane. I noticed the potholes in the mud were filled with severed goat hooves. I turned to see a butcher cut the throat of a mottled white goat and had to jog to the left to avoid the blood as it streamed steaming into the gutter. "Don't worry," said Ben cheerily, "That's not the one we're eating."

I asked how we could be sure the meat was all right. I couldn't conceive of any quality control being exercised in this waterless chaos. Ben tried to assure me that dozens of meat inspectors roamed Kiamaiko and that not a single animal was slaughtered without an official inspection. I wasn't convinced but I had talked myself into believing that I could probably survive eating anything Ben was willing to eat.

Ben led me through a door I'm not sure I would have identified as a door. I found myself in an actual bar. Beer bottles were stashed behind a locked iron grate. We were the only ones in the place and it was clean and inviting. Shortly after we sat down and ordered Tusker lagers the sound system coughed and began bleating some really bad country and western music. "For my benefit?" I inquired.

"Almost certainly."

Some species are more endangered than others, and, compared, for example, to tracking rhino or elephant, finding stupid-looking white people in Kenya is definitely no problem. We were, for example, sitting in a restaurant where half the clientele were imported white folks, most of them wearing clothes that wouldn't be allowed on a golf course. Right next to us, at a neighboring table, four chatty, happy, tourists sat sucking spaghetti; two men, dressed like Italian waiters, wore tight-fitting shirts left unbuttoned to reveal their hormonal exuberance. One woman wore a native dress and an olive-drab floppy cloth cap bearing the word "Jambo!"—the Swahili word for hello—while the other woman wore a t-shirt across the front of which was emblazoned the legend "Bitch."

—Denis Boyles, *Man Eaters Motel and Other Stops on the Railway to Nowhere: An East African Traveler's Nightbook*

"Well, please ask them for something else!" The music mercifully changed to Kenyan pop.

While around Nairobi most people are of Kikuyu lineage, Ben is a Luo, from Lake Victoria. He told me that he thought he was a good guide because unlike most of his compatriots who were raised in either relative or absolute poverty, he grew up with money. Then he lost it all when his father sided with the losers in the political upheaval in 1978. From private school to hitting the streets at age eleven, he'd seen life from both sides. Now at twenty-eight, he spoke Kiswahili, Luo, Kikuyu, English, Spanish, "enough Japanese to make a deal," and enough French "so that no Frenchman can speak ill of me."

Bosko stopped in, waiting for the designated goat to be dressed out and delivered. He and Ben talked in a matter-of-fact manner about how husbands have the absolute right to beat their wives. They eyed me, waiting for my opinion. I maintained my composure while fishing for just the right response, finally saying something like, "I hope that you exercise this right rarely." This satisfied Bosko. He smiled dismissively, claiming never to have hit his wife, in actual fact, in all their seventeen years together. Ben added seriously that he had done so only once, in order to convince her he was not having affairs. He grinned and said it had worked and now she *understood*. "Now no problem," he said. I kept my California mouth shut tight.

We sat and sipped warm lager and talked for another half an hour. Bosko finally stuck his head in to announce that the *nyama choma* was almost ready. Quite hungry by now, we emerged from the bar and ducked in past one of the innumerable white-hot barbecues into one of the almost-shacks. Ben proudly informed me that this was the very place the former American ambassador had patronized.

Inside stood a dozen wooden tables and a bunch of chairs, all hand-made, all surprisingly clean. There being no water for washing up, the tables were sanded down between patrons. I was amazed at how few flies there were. Ben and I sat while Bosko popped in and out at intervals to assure me the meat was coming. Finally, Bosko delivered the first plate with a broad smile and a flourish. It was plain goat meat—apparently unmarinated, unsauced, unspiced—simply cut up small with the kidneys, accompanied by another plate containing sliced tomato, red onion, cilantro, and whole long, skinny, green chili peppers of a variety strange to me.

Before he allowed me to start eating Ben insisted we step out front first to wash up. Where, I wondered in horror, did the water come from? But next to the barbeque grate was a large copper kettle perched over a low fire. From the spigot ran piping hot water in which we dipped our hands. Hell, I might as well go for it, I thought. There's no turning back now.

Less than an hour after it had breathed its last, we set about chewing on this poor goat. And chewing. And chewing. Never have I ever tried to chew through tougher meat. And boy, was there plenty of it! As I was working away at the first bite the cook came over and plopped a giant wad of green goo on the *nyama choma* plate. Ben identified it as fried mash of potato, maize, and kale. It was delicious. And with the other garnishes, so was the goat. I made the mistake of sampling one of the innocuous-looking peppers. It took a bottle of Tusker to cool a single bite. Even then, my fingers burned all day, and the less said about contact lenses the better.

Conversation ceased as we busied ourselves with stuffing our faces. Bosko finally joined us carrying a third plateful of *nyama choma*. By this time I was full to bursting. My two rail-thin companions agreed that they'd had plenty. I thanked them wholeheartedly and agreed that this meal would stand out as unique among all my dining experiences. We then picked our way back out to the car through the goats and the people and the smells and sounds of Kiamaiko.

I survived my four low-budget days in Nairobi. Most of the rest of my meals I bought from street vendors in Tsavo Road; hot, tasty, and about one-tenth of what the Hilton tourists were paying. And as my plane took off for Madagascar I was still picking *nyama choma* from between my teeth.

Danny Carnahan is a musician and writer based in the San Francisco Bay Area. He's toured the folk and Celtic circuit since 1980, recording nine albums, mostly with his wife and partner Robin Petrie, and performing from Scotland to New Zealand. He teaches recording arts and songwriting at two community colleges while working on his second mystery novel. Danny has traveled widely, most recently to Madagascar, after working with Henry Kaiser on his recent "World Out of Time" CD project.

＊

As impressive as Brazil's *churrascarias* are—and they are impressive—I never dined at one that left quite the impression on me as the legendary gut-busting meat-mad restaurant on the outskirts of Nairobi delicately named The Carnivore. Although a bellyful of bugs I'd ingested in China or Nepal some weeks earlier left me frazzled in Africa, I can vividly recall the barbecue pit that greeted me as I entered the fine establishment, which by coincidence is located only an emu's leap from Nairobi National Park. The "pit" was raised and no larger than a swimming pool. The grill was nothing special—if you're from Australia or you like your horses barbied as God made them—and on it, skewered with Masai spears, were the hugest hunks of sizzling wildebeest and zebra and croc you ever saw. Oh, sure, there were slabs of cow and pig up there too, with spears sticking out of them, and I know I wasn't the only Neanderthal to look upon the sight and think of King Henry VIII. And, sure enough, for the light eater chicken was said to be available, but I don't recall the big black men who brought the spears around and hacked off chunks of Smoking Red Meat until I practically yelled fire, ever bothering with things that weighed less than a Volkswagen. But I do recall eating what some might call a small mixed herd. I wasn't just eating for me; I had hundreds of protozoa to think about. And I remember paying $13 for my forty-pound meal of dripping, practically screaming blood-red meat and thinking, as I waddled out toward my waiting taxi, "Bread and coffee included. Not bad!"

—Scott Doggett, "Where's My Club?"

JOANN MILIVOJEVIC

Crustacean of Love

The mating dance is where you dance it.

MY LEATHER SANDALS ARE LOOSELY BOUND AROUND MY ANKLES, they scrape lazily across the wooden dance floor. Feet don't move much in Caribbean dancing, it's all in the waist. He places his hands on my hips to get me to loosen up. I feel like I'm already grinding my way into white-girl embarrassment. But the heat pulls me deeper, down, to the center of the Earth. I give in willingly— I am an innocent victim. The dominating Soca music pulses from the floor and up through my spine. It claims me.

My indigo batik cotton dress clings, creating a thin transparent layer on my heated skin. Constant dampness is a matter of course on this Caribbean island. And it is not unpleasant; it connects my body to my mind.

Days have passed since the night I met my young dance partner. Sleek, amber-skinned, live-eyes Teh-dey. I wondered if I slowly slid my fingertips across his forearm, would his skin be as soft as it appeared.

I met Teh-dey at Rum Point, a beach bar dance club on the north side of the island where tourists rarely venture. I was doing a TV story on a local band that had reached some acclaim.

I went to Rum Point with Greg-Mahn, the television station's

Jamaican grip. On the way, there were many cars pulled over to the side of the road. People with sacks in hand were milling about the short grasses; they prodded flashlights deep into the fields. As we drove along, we kept running over something that made a crunching sound. Greg-Mahn explained it—crab season.

Later that evening when I talked with Teh-dey, he told me that crabs were quietly gathered at night. They would be sold to small local grocers or simply eaten by family and friends. I have always loved crabmeat and very much wanted to taste this island's creatures.

When Teh-dey finally asked me out for a date, I accepted so long as it was to go crabbing.

His tongue hooks behind his slight overbite as he searches for the right words to apologize for being late on our first date. I later found out the true meaning of "soon come." That sometimes "soon come" could be days later. But I am anxious about this date. I try to convince myself that this nervousness is inappropriate; that this is a date with the island not with Teh-dey. I'm doing this to get a story. He is ridiculously young for me. This date is about crabbing. Besides, I'm wearing DEET bug repellent not Calvin Klein's Obsession. I have a mission: the island experience, the crabbing; Teh-dey is my vehicle.

It's pitch black once we drive out past the downtown lights. But the stars shine down as brightly as the moon here. They light our way in short snaps of light.

Crabs are like anything else in life, when you look for them, they elude you. And when you're not looking, you run right over them unable to miss them no matter how hard you try.

Teh-dey pulls into a cove. We've been searching for the large elusive crabs for almost an hour. The waxing three-quarter moon shines across the water like a search light. Waves lightly lick the shore. "Those are spring waves," Teh-dey tells me. "They roll low and wrap tightly into themselves. They don't loosen up until they finally reach shore." Teh-dey's mouth remains slightly open when he finishes speaking.

The waves look like white softly curling lips that long for the grit of the shore. They grasp for what appears to be stability but end up pulling loose sand back into themselves.

Like the desert, the change of season is subtler here—demanding a closer, more patient look.

We continue our mission. Teh-dey takes me deep into the bush. I question my judgment. I am totally dependent on a boy I don't know. He cuts our path with a machete. His body is long and sleek, his back is slightly sway, his cutting of path sure, sharp, and quick.

Crabs are stunned by light. Place a flashlight into their eyes and they're blinded. Then you just walk right up to them, place your foot on their backs, and pick them up from behind. I keep sweeping my light low across the ground and listen for crab shuffling as Teh-dey taught me.

His dun carapace virtually indistinguishable from the silt in which he hunkered, there was Jimmy, standing guard on tiptoe over his armorless mate, who peered out warily from between his folded chelae, thinking sweet thoughts while awaiting coitus. In a purely reflexive split second, I shot my clam rake into the water at an oblique angle, pulling it back and snaring the lovers even as they whispered sweet nothings into each other's ears. Less than ten minutes later, I stood, still dripping, before the kitchen range, while Romeo and Juliet sizzled in a black iron skillet. Their fatal tryst imparted incomparable sweetness to their flesh, providing unspeakably brutal me with a standard of perfection against which all subsequent sautéed crabs would be measured, to the detriment of the pretenders.

—Jay Jacobs, *A Glutton for Punishment: Confessions of a Mercenary Eater*

We are the crab police, searching for those strays coming home late from the party. They will be taken to our boiling prison.

A flicker of light catches my eye; I rise to meet it. It is Teh-dey. The flashlight glows from his mouth. His arms are outstretched to keep apart the two huge crabs he has captured. Mission accomplished. I eagerly open wide the burlap sack and he swiftly thrusts in the creatures.

We turn to leave and a little way into the bush, right in front where I just was, he spies another crab. He walks off silently and captures it with ease. This is the largest of the three, probably about twice the size of my hand. His claw is so big that unless he pinched you just right, your fingers would be saved within the crescent-moon hole created by his curved claw.

I am sitting on the kitchen counter at Teh-dey's house, banging my feet softly on the shelves below. It is taking much longer to boil the crabs than I had anticipated. Teh-dey holds the crab by his large front claws backside down in the boiling water, their remaining legs scratch the air. Their black bead eyes are so stretched out at the end of their long waving stalks that I expect them to pop any moment.

Teh-dey tells me about his mother. And how in order to sleep at night he has to have a fan on. Not just any fan, but a certain fan with a particular hum. In the middle of the night, if his mother came in to shut off the fan, he would wake immediately. He realizes that he has never told her this. Wonders if he should call her now. He has just moved away from home. This is his second night in his first apartment.

My home is thousands of miles away. I left it in search of paradise and touched down on this Caribbean island two and a half months ago.

I look at Teh-dey and feel an undefined desire. His knowledge of island nature and my thirst for it. He can teach me a great deal about this island and the people. There is an ease with Teh-dey, our conversation is simple, peaceful.

Once shades of blue and green, the crabs are now beige and ready to eat. Teh-dey whacks a knife into a crab claw. He pulls gently and as the meat uncurls from the shell, it is thicker and longer than I thought it would be.

I lay a piece across my tongue, push the smooth meat against the roof of my mouth and let it linger for a moment there. The island creatures need no salt or pepper; they are perfect—salty and succulent. I long to place a morsel of meat into Teh-dey's mouth but I resist. I could like a boy like this and it is dangerous. I am too vulnerable on this island. His olive eyes would quickly blind me. I watch his long calloused fingers as they easily chop open the animal's thin brittle shell.

Days have passed since I have seen Teh-dey. Desire turns to frustration. I recall that he told me that you know something is near the surface of the sea when there is a break in the wave pattern. That this is how sailors find fish. Change brings the new and unexpected.

I go for a swim in the salty sea; the sky is spread open orange and red. The water reflects the sky and is a lightly rippling fiery glow. The water is so clear that I can't judge the depth—it could be 10 feet or 100 feet deep.

As the sun sinks into the horizon, it takes the color with it— slowly—allowing itself to be savored by those who care to absorb fleeting moments.

JoAnn Milivojevic is a Chicago-based freelance travel writer and photographer.

*

"My friend, you never seen crabs making love?"

"Act real horny, they do. Males get way up on their tippy toes."

"Do I think so? I don't think so, I know so!"

"That's right, the Jimmies on their toes and the females rocking side to side, contented like."

"They are talking to each other. It's their way of talking."

The description is reasonably accurate. The male first shows himself by raising his body as high as he can on his walking legs. Interestingly, this is the same posture he must adopt later when he makes a guard cage around the female during her final moult. A forerunner signal, one could say, announcing his protective intentions. Remaining so on "tippy toes," a courting Jimmy next opens and extends his arms in a straight line, surely a good attention-claiming device, and then begins the sensuous waving of his swimming legs, which may be even better. Finally, to make sure he is not ignored, he snaps his body backward and kicks up a storm of sand with both swimming and walking legs. It is a spectacular finish. If all this fails to convince, the Jimmy will patiently repeat his repertoire, as most courting animals commonly do.

—William W. Warner, *Beautiful Swimmers*

That Gnawing Feeling

The author finds too much of nothing in Moscow.

BEFORE I WENT TO MOSCOW TO WRITE FOR MOSFILM STUDIOS, I knew little about the city. I was aware of Moscow's food shortage, but I had, to put it mildly, an inexact understanding of what food shortage meant. When I was advised to take along my own food supplies, I'd cavalierly replied, "I'll eat as the Muscovites eat."

In Moscow, I soon realized that I'd never understand how the Muscovites managed to eat. "Food shortage" was a polite euphemism: there was *no food* in Moscow. There was no food in the Mosfilm Hotel, the tiny hostelry where I was lodged. There was no food in the grocery stores. My first two weeks in Moscow were spent in a jet-lagged, disoriented, and increasingly ravenous stupor. Since I would be living in Moscow another four months, I realized that my survival required a hotel with a restaurant.

My Russian employers were sympathetic. They had noticed that I was literally wasting away, and a dead American writer would be no use to them at all, not to mention the bureaucratic red tape that would ensue should I expire on their premises. After some secret negotiations, they procured a room for me at the Intourist Hotel, which contained not one but *four* restaurants.

I immediately told my friend Natasha my good news.

"The Intourist? Oh, no," Natasha said. "You don't want that. It's full of prostitutes and black marketeers."

Natasha was characteristically pessimistic, so I ignored her comment. Until the next day, when I told an American journalist that I would soon be living at the Intourist.

"The Intourist? Oh, no," he said. "It's crazy there. Full of prostitutes and black marketeers."

A hotel swarming with prostitutes and black marketeers was not exactly what I had in mind. My film studio bosses were again sympathetic, because they knew they would never find another writer foolish enough to come to Moscow, a city with no food. More secret negotiations followed, but after a few days it became clear that Mosfilm could pull strings only at the Intourist.

By then, however, I no longer cared about prostitutes and black marketeers. I cared about restaurants. *Four* restaurants. After three weeks on an anorexic's diet, the Intourist Hotel sounded like Heaven on Earth.

Albeit a strange Heaven, with its own, mysterious logic. When I checked in, a woman behind the front desk asked me who would be paying for my hotel room.

"Mosfilm," I replied.

"You are with the Italian Film Crew?" she asked.

"No, but I work for Mosfilm."

"Then who will be paying for the room?"

"Mosfilm."

"You are with the Italian Film Crew?"

"No, but I work for Mosfilm."

"Then you are with the Italian Film Crew," she said, and directed me to a room on the seventeenth floor.

The room she'd booked me into faced Gorky Street, one of the busiest thoroughfares in Moscow; the traffic noise was unbearably loud. Along one wall, two narrow beds were arranged foot to head. It was perfect, if one were ten feet tall and hearing impaired.

I returned to the lobby. A different clerk, a man, stood behind the front desk. I requested a room away from the street.

"Who will be paying for the room?" he asked.

A man walked into the food store and, seeing the shelves empty, asked the babushka, "Have you no bread?"

"No," she replied. "Here we have no fish. Next door they have no bread."

—Russian joke

"Mosfilm."

"You are with the Italian Film Crew?"

"No, but I work for Mosfilm."

"Then who will be paying for the room?"

"Mosfilm."

"You are with the Italian Film Crew?"

"No, but I work for Mosfilm."

"Then you are with the Italian Film Crew." He handed me another key. "Room 1721."

After settling into my new home, I went downstairs to explore the hotel and its cornucopia of dining possibilities.

The Intourist lobby reminded me of Sheremetyevo Airport: its black-and-white tiled floors, identical to the airport's, were covered with a fine grit, also identical to the airport's. The largest part of the lobby was occupied by the "Spanish Bar," so called because it offered port and espresso. A few potted palms stood among the tables and chairs of the Spanish Bar. Above the bar, two stories up, was a domed, plastic skylight, which was covered with grit.

Located on the lobby floor next to the Spanish Bar, the first restaurant I explored had a ten-by-twenty-foot stage at one end. On the stage, dancers were rehearsing for that night's floor show. The maitre d' told me that the restaurant was booked for the evening. "*Mest nyet*," he said. No seats.

The two restaurants on the second floor were reached by walking up a wide staircase made of copper. It gave you the impression that you were climbing to Valhallah, an impression that the two restaurants on the second floor quickly dispelled. The first had a very loud dinner show already in progress and people waited outside the door. I didn't need to ask; obviously there were no seats. And even if there had been *mests* available, I didn't relish the idea of dining while my ears were accosted by what passed in Moscow for entertainment.

The second restaurant had a row of high-backed, blue velour booths next to windows overlooking Gorky Street. This restaurant did not have a stage, which made it infinitely more desirable than the two I'd already seen. It was empty except for four cigarette-smoking waiters who sat near the entrance and a large orange tomcat who meandered up a blue-carpeted aisle.

I asked to be seated. The waiters looked me over.

"Are you a guest in this hotel?" they asked.

"Yes." I showed them my room key.

"*Mest nyet*," they replied.

"But there's no one here."

I asked to see a menu. This was, clearly, a highly unusual request, and the waiters went on an extended search before they found one for me to peruse. The menu listed a wide variety of foods: red and black caviar, steak, chicken, fish, salads, cheeses, desserts and champagne, vodka, and cognac. Almost a week went by before I understood that the menu had absolutely nothing to do with what was actually in the kitchen, and that the majority of items listed upon it were permanently unavailable; as a piece of printed matter, the menu had about as much bearing on reality as a Tsar's decree. The first night, however, I read it eagerly, salivating at the thought of a hot, four-course dinner.

I asked again to be seated.

The waiters protested. They couldn't serve me, they said. I would have to go to the hard currency restaurant on the third floor. They pointed to a spiral staircase at the back of the restaurant.

I walked up the spiral staircase to the third floor. In the hard currency restaurant, caviar cost twenty-five dollars. Steak was priced at fifteen, a bottle of champagne, twenty. The prices were thirty to fifty times higher than in the second floor ruble restaurant, far higher than my Mosfilm salary allowed.

I trudged back to the second floor and again requested a table. This time the waiters took a different tack.

"We serve only large parties," they said. "We have no tables for one person only."

During a visit to Moscow in 1959, photographer Elliot Erwitt was keeping a respectful distance as Nikita Krushchev and Richard Nixon toured the exhibit of a model American home. When the debate broke out, Erwitt leaped to a rail to stake his spot. "Nixon suddenly poked Khrushchev in the chest," Erwitt says, "and was saying something like: 'We, in America, eat a lot more meat than you do. You eat a lot more cabbage.' And Khrushchev's response was something like, 'You can [expletive] my grandmother.'"

—Picture Caption,
The New York Times (1959)

Well, I had no argument for that, as I was obviously not a large party; I gave up, sorrowfully counted the dollars remaining in my wallet and slinked back to the third floor. After dinner I didn't want to go back to my hotel room; the month spent living in the Mosfilm Hotel, with no company in the evenings except for my novels, notebooks, and typewriter, had left me restless. I was eager to be out among other people and so went to the Spanish Bar for a drink.

As soon as I sat down with my glass of Port, I understood that this would be my first and last visit to the Spanish Bar. It was the scene of many transactions, most involving Asian businessmen and heavily made-up, short-skirted Russian girls. There was something else going on, too, something less overt and perhaps more sinister, which involved a group of five Georgian men who sat at the center table and who kept an eye on the various happenings in the bar.

I could only assume that these men were the Intourist's infamous black marketeers. I don't know exactly what they did, but I do know that for the three months I lived in the Intourist Hotel, these men sat in the Spanish Bar every night and often during the day. It was easy to recognize them since one of the five men was a dwarf.

One night I boarded an empty elevator in the lobby. At the third floor, it stopped and three of the Georgian black marketeers got into the elevator with me.

The one I thought of as their leader, since he was the most handsome, stood to my right and slightly behind me. Another, mammoth and swarthy, who seemed to be the leader's bodyguard, stood to my left. The dwarf stood right of me, in front of his chief.

They didn't say a word. Not to me, and not to each other. All of us looked blankly ahead, as people do in elevators. We rode this way for ten floors.

Then, between floors, the elevator stopped.

Most of the time at least one of the hotel's six elevators was out of service, but I had never been on an elevator that had gotten stuck. I wondered if the Georgians had done something to make the elevator stop.

I glanced at the giant to the left of me, the leader to the right, and the dwarf, down by my right knee.

They glanced at me. They glanced at each other. I waited for one of them to make a move. What would they do first? I wondered. Would the dwarf grab my purse? Would he hold my ankles while the other two raped me, or worse?

I almost burst into an hysterical laughter. Worse? What could be worse than being raped in an Intourist elevator by two swarthy black marketeers and a dwarf?

I stopped breathing. My entire body broke out with a fine sweat. I glanced at the Georgians; they glanced at me. They were silent and stoic. I felt sure that this silence would give rise to some sudden violence against my person.

Then the elevator jerked and we started moving again. When I got out at the seventeenth floor I looked back at them; they were silent and stoic. They looked like wooden Indians or expressionless *matroshkas*, the Russian stacking dolls: one large, one medium and one tiny, unconsciously rocking side to side on his bandy legs.

Although it seemed impossible, I was determined to procure a table in the second-floor ruble restaurant. For the first three nights I lived at the Intourist, the waiters and I went through the same routine. I stood in the entrance of the empty restaurant and asked to be seated. They asked if I was a guest in the hotel; I showed them my room key. When they were finally convinced of my guest status, they would play their trump card; they couldn't seat me, they said, because they only served large parties.

The fourth night, I understood the source of our impasse: the waiters expected a bribe in exchange for a table, something they received regularly from the many prostitutes who worked the hotel. But their assumption of my working girl status and their stubborn refusal to seat me only led to my own stubbornness; I wasn't inclined to offer them any money. After a few rounds of the same argument, which they'd end by announcing their policy of serving "only large parties," I finally thought of a rejoinder that, like magic, instantly produced the desired table.

"I'm with the Italian Film Crew," I said.

Before going to Russia, Christi Phillips was a vegetarian for more than a decade. After less than one week in Moscow, she was standing in a three-block-long line for McDonald's, eagerly anticipating a Big Mac. This story is excerpted from Working for Rubles, *a memoir of a four-month stay in Moscow. She currently lives in Northern California.*

★

From an interview with Shane and Sia Barbi, the models known as the Barbi Twins, who are "recovered bulimics":

Matt: What's the greatest extreme you've ever gone to to lose weight?

Shane: We actually rented an apartment in Austin, Texas. It was like going to a fasting farm, but we wanted to lock ourselves in. We had this idea that we were going to be locked up for forty days and forty nights. We wanted to be spiritual, and in the Bible it says forty days and forty nights.

Sia: I wanted to see visions.

Shane: We had gallons and gallons of water, that's it. Nothing in the refrigerator. We asked this poor guy to lock us in, and we purposely got a third-story apartment so we couldn't get out. I wanted to be skinny.

Matt: How much did you weigh when you went in?

Shane: 145 to 150, which is basically the weight we've been at for almost all our pictures. So there we were, and after the fourth or fifth day you lose desire for everything.

Sia: You lose morals, too. I would have hooked for food at that point.

Shane: We practically killed each other. You can smell everything. I could smell if someone put butter on a potato next door. Then finally we got so crazy—

Matt: After how many days?

Shane: Only ten.

Matt: You lasted ten days?

Sia: I've lasted nineteen days at a fasting hygienic center.

Shane: So we finally had to get out and get to a 7-Eleven.

—Matt Maranian, "Diet Tips from the Barbi Twins," *bOING bOING*

CLAUDIA J. MARTIN

✦ ✦ ✦

Give unto Others

as you would have others give unto you.

IT WAS ONE OF THE COLDEST WINTERS EVER IN PARIS. THE COM-plaints about the government's failure to deal with the homeless were as bitter as the winds that rushed down the Seine, the rue de Rivoli and the Boulevard St-Germain. Government ministers publicly apologized and made all sorts of promises on television in order to appease the furor, as if a few men alone were responsible for the unpleasant sight of hungry people shivering under tatty coats.

In the midst of such cold and misery, I arrived in Paris to study pastry making at the Ecole de Gastronomie Ritz-Escoffier, located in the warm heart of the posh Ritz Hotel. The school provided nearly everything one could require to learn to cook: printed recipes, uniforms, top quality ingredients, translators for those who spoke no French, experienced teachers. But they made no provisions regarding the disposition of the daily supply of pastries, breads, and cakes produced in class. At the end of each session we were expected to package the dozens of croissants, brioches, *gougères,* and tarts we had made into thick white boxes bearing the gleaming blue Ritz insignia, and remove our class assignments from the premises. What we did with the food afterwards was of no concern to the school.

The first day I watched as several fellow students dumped their boxes into trash receptacles along the rue Cambon outside the school, then continue on without another thought to the matter. But I grew up poor, so it was difficult for me to see good food going to waste. I tried eating my own pastries for dinner that night to save money, but it was impossible. After a day of tasting doughs and chocolate creams and nibbling on bits of this and that, I could barely swallow more pastry. The next morning I left the boxes on the desk in my tiny hotel room with a note, *"Pour la bonne, merci."* The maid took the boxes while I was at class, and afterwards I had an abundance of towels, but this did not solve the pastry disposal problem.

The second day of class I left with six neatly tied boxes of lemon tarts, sablés, and almond cream pastries, intending to return to my small hotel room on the other side of Paris. At the entrance to the Tuileries métro stop, a north African woman sat on the stairs, her face towards the wall. A small child lay motionless against her chest, wrapped in a multi-colored shawl. People rushed past her carrying bags like armor, the sharp ends of crusty baguettes poking out like swords.

I knelt close to her face and whispered, *"Voudriez-vous des pâtisseries?"*

She raised her blank eyes and then looked down again. She did not object. I left two boxes on the stair next to her and moved away. She reached for the boxes and opened the top one. Saying nothing, she broke off a piece of tart and pushed it into the child's mouth. Then she ate some. I was several steps below her when I looked back to see her weeping quietly, the child suddenly animated with chewing.

After that, I spent my remaining evenings in Paris giving away whatever I had made in class. I even asked the other students to give me anything that they were going to throw away. I never told them what I was doing with so much pastry, and they never asked.

I would leave the school around 6:30 p.m. and enter the arctic Paris night carrying as many as two dozen boxes of pastries and cakes rigged with string. For the next two or three hours I would ride the métro, randomly exiting, transferring lines, offering the cakes and tarts to anyone who seemed to have taken up residence in some dank and frigid corner.

I was only refused once: a woman with mad black eyes who accused me of trying to poison her. *"Je vous en prie,"* I politely apologized, taking my boxes so I could distribute them elsewhere. As I disappeared down the stairs, her curses flew wildly after me, borne on jets of spit and venom.

On my last night in Paris, it was nearly 8:30 and I still had one last box of éclairs to give away before I could return to the hotel and pack. At the Palais Royal station, two bristly men sat upon the plastic seats wrapped together in a single dirty green blanket. Their heads leaned in towards one another to prop each other up. They seemed to be dozing. I sat down two seats from them and placed the box of eclairs on the seat between us. As the train growled into the station, I got up and walked towards the edge of the platform.

"Madame," one of the men cried, "look, you have forgotten your box."

The doors of the train opened. I walked in and turned to face them. "No, it is for you," I replied and pointed towards the box. I watched them push the string off and lift the lid. They each took out one fat éclair slathered in chocolate. Then they stood simultaneously, and holding a cigar-shaped pastry to their brows, each man gave me that stiff-armed French salute General De Gaulle was so fond of. I responded reflexively by raising my right hand and returning their salute.

The doors of the train closed in front of me. Through the window I could see that they remained in position, holding their salute as my train slid towards the dark tunnel between stations.

Claudia J. Martin is a travel writer and photographer who lives in the San Francisco Bay Area with her traveling dog, Tralfaz. She had her first gallery showing of photographs in 1994, and although she begrudgingly admits to being a trial lawyer, she spends as much time as she can traveling, writing, taking pictures, and working as an itinerant pastry chef.

✱

There is no use trying to be more spiritual than God.
God never meant man to be a purely spiritual creature.
That is why He uses material things like bread and wine to put the
    new life into us.
We may think this rather crude and unspiritual.
God does not:
He invented eating.

—C. S. Lewis

Camaraderie

Join the party.

LAST WINTER I SPENT A MONTH IN RUSSIA, TEACHING AT MOSCOW State University. One weekend, Martha (my teaching partner) and I went with several Russian students to visit St. Petersburg. It was a beautiful train ride through a frozen landscape of thick evergreen forests, occasional fields, and villages of small, dark-brown houses huddled together. The trip was exhausting, lasting about eight hours with music blaring the whole time in the car.

We arrived around 11:00 p.m. Our hosts were a baby-faced medical student and his wife, and they had prepared a Russian banquet for us. There was borscht, thick slabs of dark bread, mounds of butter, salted fish, apples, pastries, cheese, and vodka. By the time we sat down to eat, it was well past midnight. Such a feast at such an hour is not unusual in Russia.

I was tired though, and not particularly hungry. And I remembered that eating late usually makes me feel lethargic and dull in the morning. Like Buddhist monks who do not eat after midday, I prefer to go to bed on an empty stomach.

So when the eating began, I politely explained that I wasn't feeling well and that I would just have some water and apple juice. My hostess, who apparently had not studied the dietary teaching of the Buddha, seemed mortified. She said, "If you don't feel well, the answer is to eat. Yes. Yes. Eat for health." She said this last phrase loudly, as if to convince me by volume alone.

I held to my abstinence, though, with a slight sense of self-righteousness. While everyone else, including Martha, ate, drank, and was merry, I sipped juice and water and waited for the moment when I could politely excuse myself and go to bed. After an hour or so, I did, but the eating, drinking, conversation, and laughter continued long thereafter. One of my last thoughts before sleep was: "Well I, anyway, will be clear and energetic tomorrow when we tour the city."

Alas, such was not the case. I was groggy and out of sorts, and I felt alienated from the others. And they, despite going to bed full of food and vodka, were cheerful and brimming with energy.

I was a bit dismayed by the apparent injustice. I recalled a lesson learned on Thanksgiving 25 years ago. Flushed with my recent discovery of healthful eating, I had gone home and announced that I would not eat turkey (putrefying, hormone-laden flesh), baked potatoes (from a deadly nightshade plant), nor cranberry sauce (sugar-laden), and that I would cook my own (healthful) meal. Thanksgiving dinner turned out to be a dour event with my awestruck family staring at my plate of brown rice, tofu, and seaweed. And on that occasion too, despite my virtuous eating, I had felt poorly afterward.

Soon after my Russian sojourn, I was in Germany. I was visiting a friend in a village near Kassel, and we attended a breakfast marking the end of a local holiday. The meal was served in a huge hall. In the middle was a 30-piece German brass band, playing "oom-pah-pah" music at a mind-numbing volume. Hundreds of men dressed in dark suits and frilled white shirts were sitting at long tables, drinking beer, talking, laughing, and occasionally breaking into song.

As soon as I sat down, a large mug of frothy beer was placed before me, and my immediate

We should look for some one to eat and drink with before looking for something to eat and drink.

—Epicurus

neighbors—red-faced and smiling—raised their mugs in salute. "Beer for breakfast," I thought. "I'll be a space case all day—and will probably lose my passport and shoes." The surrounding mugs were still expectantly suspended in air, though, and it did not seem a time to ask for peppermint tea. I smiled, clicked glasses, toasted "*Zum Wohl*" ("To Health"), and took a sip of my beer. It was thick and delicious. I took another sip and started talking to my neighbor, a policeman from the town. When I finished my mug, another appeared in front of me as if delivered from some celestial brewery by a celestial hand.

Eventually, breakfast was served. It featured a deep-fried pork cutlet about the size of a Frisbee. To one who has eaten little meat and no pork for over two decades, it seemed "The Mother of All Pork Cutlets." Now I thought, "Meat! Pork! I'll have nightmares, just like Gandhi when he ate meat." Breakfast looked inviting though, and what was I to do?—ask our Walkyrie of a waitress to bring my hummus and alfalfa sprout sandwich instead? I dug in, eating the cutlet, potato salad, and everything else on the plate with relish. It was delicious.

When we left, I was relaxed, happy, and so alert that I noticed the floor and other parts of the seemingly solid German building were actually moving. I had a sense of foreboding, though. When will the axe of judgment fall upon my dietary sins? I wondered. But it never did. I felt unusually energetic and ebullient that whole day and for days afterward.

Food is important. The quality and quantity of what we eat certainly affects our physical, emotional, and psychological well-being, immediately and long term. But food is blessed by being shared, by being eaten in fellowship amidst conversation and laughter. In such circumstances, all food is "health" food. In any case, I will never again refuse a midnight banquet, and I look forward to my next breakfast of beer, pork cutlet, and song.

Ronald E. Kotzsch originally wrote this story for Natural Health. *He lives in Fair Oaks, California.*

*

I have a color photograph of myself on my wall in New York that was taken by a friend. I am in our house in St. Sébastien, in the kitchen. The sunlight, even indoors, is intense, rich. I am holding a head of lettuce in my hand. I am holding it before me, and I am looking at it and smiling. It is the lettuce I have grown myself, in my own garden. It is one of those soft, densely packed heads, the leaves of which you find in salads in most bistros in France. We probably ate it with our lunch that day—at least I hope we did—with a little olive oil and perhaps a splash of lemon. And perhaps with it, some slices of tomato, bleeding with summer, also taken from the garden. And since the photograph was taken by a friend, it's certain that he, and maybe some others, shared that meal with us, seated around our long wooden table, the windows thrown open, letting the summer air stream in. Wine, bread, cheese, water, meat, salad before us all.

—Richard Goodman, *French Dirt: The Story of a Garden*
in the South of France

Bush Tucker

*The author discovers more than food
in sampling plants from the land.*

WHEN WE GOT TO THE AIRBOAT, CLOUDS DARKENED THE SKY. MAX Davidson, ex-farmer, longtime bushman, buffalo hunter, and now our guide, fired up the engine and blasted us with water, leaves, and a wide grin. We laughed at his impish delight, then helped get the boat into the water to explore the billabong in this isolated region in northern Australia known as Arnhem Land.

Rain started to fall. By the time we headed up the channel it fell in sheets. We pulled on rain jackets and tied on hats. Already we could see the water was rising; since yesterday it had come up a couple of feet and we had little trouble getting through the stretch that had clutched at us the day before. We hadn't been on the water more than a moment when the storm broke and the rain lashed that silver sheet of billabong. Rain jackets were worthless. We were soaked to the skin. And then Max pulled up under a dense canopy of mangroves and said, "Do you want to hold up for a while?"

"Why?" I laughed.

"Can't get wetter than we are," he said, and off we went, Max's poncho blowing in the wind like a shroud.

It was like flying through a thunderstorm in an open plane. The air was water and we could hardly see. Forward, faster. Birds scat-

194

tered, the boat raced over water, across vegetation. I expected to hit something that would send us flying into the jaws of hungry crocodiles, and once we almost did, sliding on soil and about to stop when the boat shook free to deeper water. Again we were off, running out from beneath the storm.

Eventually the rain stopped. Now we had a chance to look at the land, illuminated in soft, golden light. Max edged the boat aground so we could get out and rest awhile. Soaked as we were, boggy as it was, it was nice to be on land.

Max began digging in the earth with his bare hands to collect some "bush tucker," food the locals have been eating for millennia. Earlier he'd shown us many edible things, plants the Aboriginals and hunters like himself could survive on for weeks at a stretch.

A billygoat plum, a native tree with small fruit, has 50 percent more Vitamin C than an orange. Green ants are lemon flavored (I know, because Max offered me some to sample and I could hardly say no), and Aboriginals take the whole nest, scrunch it up, mix it in water, and drink to treat colds. They eat the bloodwood nut, and use the flaky bark from the paperbark tree to build ground ovens for cooking almost anything. They start with hot rocks in a hole, add a layer of paperbark leaves, some water, more layers of leaves, then fish, wallaby, buffalo, whatever is the day's meal, and cover with paperbark layers. Termite mounds—conical eruptions of the red earth that

The Pintupi were the last "wild tribe" to be brought in out of the Western Desert and introduced to white civilisation. Until the late 1950s, they had continued to hunt and forage, naked in the sandhills, as they had hunted for at least ten thousand years.

They were a carefree and open-minded people, not given to the harsher initiation rites of more sedentary tribes. The men hunted kangaroo and emu. The women gathered seeds and roots and edible grubs. In winter, they sheltered behind windbreaks of spinifex; and even in the searing heat they seldom went without water. They valued a pair of strong legs above everything, and they were always laughing. The few whites who travelled among them were amazed to find their babies fat and healthy.

—Bruce Chatwin,
The Songlines

sometimes reach over six feet tall—are used for medicinal pur-
poses. The pitaradia acts as a decongestant; there's a grasshopper
here that eats this plant and nothing else.

Max was on his knees, digging with his huge hands. I was
amazed at the breadth of his back, the taut muscles of his shoulders, the girth of his arms. He was as broad as he was tall, with a
big belly that must have taken years of effort to acquire, a blondish-
white beard trimmed close. I couldn't tell if he was 55 or 75, but
clearly he was a strong fellow who was completely at home in this
environment.

He was digging for legumes on the roots of grass, busting up the
knotted earth. Clumps of grass flew this way, clots of soil flew that
way. He dug, and dug, fingering the roots, rejecting them as too
scrawny. He kept at it, oblivious of my calls to stop. "It's OK, Max,
we don't need to taste them."

He was obsessed, as if starved, and I began to think he deposited
us here just so he could get some of this bush food. He was up to
his elbows now, hunched over the Earth as if reaching into the
depths of its soul, reaching as if to touch his own soul deep in the
bowels of the land. He was grinning, glowing, completely consumed by this communion.

And then he pulled up some skinny bulbs, knocked the dust off,
put them in his mouth and chewed. He smiled, then looked at me,
eyes bright.

"This one'll be sweet," he said, handing me a dusty clod. It was-
n't. It was dry and starchy, something I wouldn't choose to eat but
maybe could live on if I had to. But to Max it was pure heaven,
God's own repast, and he waited only an instant to make sure I ap-
proved before he dug for more.

Suddenly a wave of melancholy swept over me. Looking around
at this extraordinary land of billabong and flood plain, I felt a deep
emptiness, a loneliness rooted in my sense of having no connection to the land. Where was I from? What did I know of ancestry
and Earth? Was this just a malady of my own, or symbolic of a
malaise shared by all First Worlders? The kind of connection I

lacked you can only get from working the earth, coming from it, knowing it as part of your spirit. The Aboriginals had it. Max had it. But looking at that amazing green land carved in squiggly patterns by rivers and streams and buffalo channels, I knew it was something I would never have, unless I changed my life completely. And maybe even that wouldn't be enough.

On the way back we took it slowly, enjoying the flight of magpie geese, the purple reflections of clouds on the water, the calm after the storm. Suddenly a huge splash erupted to our left and Max stopped the boat immediately. Waves two feet high coursed toward us from the single flick of a crocodile's tail, and the boat rocked as if crossing a wake. There wasn't a sound on the billabong until Max uttered, "Now that was a big crocodile."

The image of that crocodile we didn't see stayed with me. The power of that creature, so ominous, so primeval, so bent on satisfying its hunger and nothing more, reflected the frightening beauty of these wild places. There are things here we cannot conceive, powers that make a mockery of our civilized concerns, hidden creatures with clear meanings. We are at the top of the food chain, yes, but only by a thread.

Larry Habegger is co-editor of the Travelers' Tales *series. He is also co-author of "World Travel Watch," a monthly syndicated column that appears in newspapers throughout the United States.*

✳

Several yards from the elders is a fire circle, about 50 feet in diameter, with rocks outlining the circumference and smoking coals in the center. A large piece of meat—a kangaroo tail—is browning in the fire; the smoke wafts up into the clear blue sky.

"This area is known as the Breakaways because of the way that the rocks break away into the distance," Bill says in standard Australian English. "But to my people it is the Two Dogs Dreaming. The two dogs are those peaks there, one yellow and one white. Do you know about the Dreamings?" Ian asks me.

"Aren't they creation stories?" I respond.

"Yes. From the time of our ancestors," Bill says. "And we're here on our ancestors' footprints."

At the fire circle a woman bends down and brushes the ashes off a mound with a branch, then picks a loaf of bread (called damper) out of the coals. She scrapes the remaining ashes off the blackened crust with her hand, and carries the loaf to the folding table. Following the same procedure, another woman picks several yams out of the ashes, puts them on the table, then returns to the fire and turns the kangaroo tail over. A gust of wind blows smoke up my nostrils; the aroma of roasting kangaroo meat has been etched in my brain so effectively that I'll be able to recognize it wherever I travel in Australia.

"How do you hunt the kangaroos?" I ask Ian.

"Traditionally, with a spear or a hunting boomerang—a long boomerang with a hooked end," he explains. "Today most of the men hunt with rifles."

"Some of the people here are old enough to remember the traditional ways of living - hunting, gathering bush tucker," Bill says. "That man there, for instance, with the long beard. His name is Kungi but no one knows how old he is. Oldest man around here, I'm sure."

I look at the old man, but avoid making eye contact. I've been warned that you shouldn't make eye contact because, according to Aboriginal beliefs, the eyes are the seat of the soul.

—Mark Lamana, "Dinner in the Outback"

DAMPER (AUSTRALIAN BUSH BREAD)

2 cups self-rising flour	3 tablespoons butter
1/2 teaspoon salt	1 cup milk or beer
2 teaspoons sugar	

Sift together flour and salt. Add sugar. Rub in butter. Mix in milk or beer to make a medium soft dough. Knead lightly on a board or tailgate until smooth. Form it into a round shape, about 4 inches thick at the center. Glaze with milk or beer. Place in the hot ashes of a fire and cover it with more ash. Let it cook about 20 minutes, turn it over and re-cover it with more hot ash and cook 10 to 15 minutes more. Remove from the fire, dust it off, and tap it. If it sounds hollow, it is done. The outside will be burned. Break it open and eat the center.

Drinking an 1806
Château Lafite

In vino veritas, ergo bibatum.

CLIMBING, THE ROAD TWISTS BACK AND FORTH ON ITSELF AND then comes up over the escarpment and the village is visible out at the end of its white crag. I get out of the car and gaze across at it for a moment. I haven't been here in a long time. From this distance it looks desolate, jagged-edged. It looks unchanged. The wind is blowing my hair around. The wind always blows in Provence. It is wind that makes the air so clear and the colors as brilliant as they are this afternoon. Les Baux was the site of a singular experience in our lives....

The Michelin guide had awarded the Baumanière restaurant first one, then two, then its highest accolade, three stars. Nowadays there are usually twenty, sometimes more, three-star restaurants in France, but at that time there were four in Paris, only six in the provinces. The Baumanière was the only one even reasonably close to Nice.

We went there because we had been to the bullfight. We knew nothing about the Baumanière's history, had never heard Thuillier's [the owner] name. And when we had taken our places in his vaulted dining room what impressed us most was his wine list, especially the oldest and most expensive bottle on it, an 1806

Château Lafite. We wondered what such a wine would taste like. We wondered who could possibly afford it, for the price was 30,000 francs—$60. We knew little about wine. Hardly anyone did in those days. But though we closed the menu on the 1806 Lafite, ordering I think a beaujolais, we talked about it wistfully. Perhaps someday we would be rich enough to come back and drink it. What would a wine that old taste like?...

I made an appointment to see the editor of *Esquire*.

In France a wine is felt to be alive, I told him. It is born, matures, and later dies. I had conceived the notion of getting his magazine to buy me that bottle of wine. In exchange I would write an article about it. If a wine should hold all or even most of its color, bouquet, and taste for upward of a century or more, I told him, then it became more than a great wine. It would be opened with reverence. It would be lifted to the lips with trembling fingers in a room so hushed as to resemble more a bullring than a restaurant, at the moment before the bull was put to the sword. The comparison was apt, I continued, for the result would be to kill this wine, to destroy this object of veneration.

I looked at the editor, who was peering at his hands. For a moment I thought I had oversold him.

His head rose. "Sounds good to me," he said. "Go ahead and do it."

So I wrote to Thuillier, whom I may have seen but had never met or spoken to. "I think," he wrote back, "that this wine is still perfect enough to appreciate it, judge it, and love it, but you mustn't forget that it was born before Waterloo. However, I don't think the drinking of it will be a defeat, much less a disaster."

I began to research the wine as best I could, and also Thuillier. Who knows what Bordeaux weather was like in 1806? But for the wine to last this long, if in fact it had lasted this long, conditions must have been close to ideal: mild weather during the flowering in spring; sufficient rain all through June and July; little or no rain during August and September, lest the maturing grapes swell up with water; and none at all during the two-week harvest, which would have begun about October 1. We know that fine weather

he Sahara was once a sea-
bottom; and consider the
climate of the Mississippi Valley
today!… But the sun-hardened
rocks of Provence, fretted by neither
rain nor frost, have in the mean-
while changed hardly at all. You
may go back to Les Baux after
forty years and find no changes ei-
ther in the most distant landscape
or the objects nearest you.

—Ford Madox Ford,
Provence: From Minstrels
to the Machine (1935)

existed all across Europe that fall,
enabling Napoleon to crush the
Prussians at Jena.

The 1806 harvest was allowed
to ferment on its husks for two
weeks or more. Nowadays it
would be drained off into casks
after a few days, producing the
"modern" wine esteemed by the
public for its lightness and by
winemakers because it matures
quickly, can be bottled quickly,
and the money banked; whereas
the 1806 Château Laffitte (as it
was then spelled) was for a decade or more so austere as to be un-
drinkable, not to mention unsalable. No wine ever made again
would last such a length of time. Of course it was not certain that
this one had either.

Because the vintage was possibly going to be a great one, a few
bottles were buried in sand in a stone tomb in the château's cellar
for future use. The decades turned into scores of years, and the
wine remained undisturbed. It was unlikely that any of the men
who put it down imagined that the future would extend two-
thirds of the way into the next century. The bottle we would open
would have had three owners: the château, Thuillier, and me.
Thuillier had owned it since 1954 when he got his third Michelin
star. I would own it an hour.

We reached France, drove much of the day across Provence, and
were trembling a little when we presented ourselves to Thuillier.
This was partly fatigue, mostly nervous anticipation. He was 70
years old, thin, energetic, with a quick step and a warm manner. By
now I had read much of what he had written about cooking,
which he considered an art form: "What is art in general if not the
harmonious and subtle expression of all that can be conceived of
the grand, the beautiful, the sublime by the human mind for the

pleasure of the senses? *La cuisine*, par excellence, addresses itself to one of the most delicate and difficult senses to satisfy: taste."

And again: "Relishing a fine dish requires as much attention and culture as appreciating a sonata or painting. To practice the art of fine cuisine requires broad knowledge, real patience, long hours, and a poet's soul, sensitive to beauty. You have to have a feeling for appropriate harmonies and a sense of nuance in order to create a dish and give it life."

I was a bit awed by him. He was an artist, and in his field a superstar. He was twice as old as I was as well, and I sought to reassure him that I knew something about wines and cared about them. I did not want him to think that his only bottle of 1806 Lafite would be drunk by ignoramuses as a kind of gastronomic joke. But he smiled and patted my hand, and I had the impression he understood what I was trying to say. He suggested an aperitif on his terrace, which was surrounded by masses of geraniums and roses. Then perhaps we would want to see the bottle on its shelf in the darkest and quietest part of his cellar.

The trip to the cellar did little to quiet my nerves. The bottle—our bottle—lay alone on its shelf. Nearby were other old bottles, none this old. We stood in a clean, well-lighted corridor lined with raw pine shelving, some of which sagged from the weight of bottles, the way cheap bookcases are sometimes bowed by books. It was a cool, moldless, unvaulted, beamless, unromantic, entirely businesslike wine cellar.

The, well, enormity of what I proposed to do began to build up in me. It felt presumptuous. To be there at all felt presumptuous. This was one of the problems of magazine writing. Subjects were usually glad to see you; the resulting publicity figured to help their businesses, advance their careers, did it not? You were, in effect, an invited guest. Nonetheless the relationship was an artificial one and, ultimately, you hadn't been invited at all; it was you who had invited yourself, and the result sometimes was this feeling of discomfort.

Emerging into the waning sunlight, I told Thuillier that, if he agreed, we would drink the 1806 Lafite at luncheon tomorrow. We

were too tired from the drive to do it justice now. But what I
meant was that this whole idea would take a little more getting
used to.

Thuillier smiled, and again seemed to understand what I was
not saying....

In the morning the maid brought *café au lait*, together with
croissants from Thuillier's kitchen that were as light and flaky as the
tartes the night before, and a morning paper, and she threw back
the shutters to let in the sun.

We had made a date with the sommelier, René Boxberger, to
open the 1806 Château Lafite at eleven-thirty, immediately after
he would have eaten his own lunch with the staff.

Too nervous to wait, we got up to the main building fifteen
minutes early. Boxberger, a friendly, burly man 56 years old, wearing the leather apron of his trade, was pacing back and forth. No,
he hadn't eaten yet. He wasn't hungry, he said. He asked when we
would open the wine. We noted that he had cut himself three or
four times shaving. He was at least as nervous as I was.

He got the bottle up from the cellar. It was hand blown, somewhat lopsided, and the glass was impregnated with air bubbles. Its
shape was one no longer used in Bordeaux, being wider at the
waist than at the base. Thuillier guessed that in its long life its cork
had been changed twice. "I have some other bottles which are almost 100 years old," he said, "and their corks haven't been changed
at all yet." He speculated that the cork was changed for the first
time about 1900, and a label affixed to the bottle. When the cork
was changed again in 1953, a strip bearing this information was affixed below the label and joined to it by the château's stamp.

With the bottle in a silver cradle, Boxberger knocked the wax
off the cork. Inserting his screw, he yanked nervously at the cork,
and half of it came out and the rest stayed in there.

Together with Thuillier, the *maître d'hôtel*, and most of the
waiters, we stood over the bottle watching Boxberger work. We
were all tense. He worked at the remaining segment of cork but
succeeded only in pushing it further into the bottle. He went to

fetch instruments resembling tiny forceps. At last, triumphantly, he got it out.

He held it up for all of us to see. He was ebullient now. He sniffed it. He passed it around. We all had a sniff.

The bouquet it gave off was strong, robust, all the things it should have been....

But what would it taste like?

Boxberger decanted the wine, poured a generous dose into a big, crystal glass. He swirled the wine to air it, then filled his mouth. The rest of us waited for the verdict with our jaws hanging slack. All the while staring into the glass, he gargled the wine, then swallowed it, chewing all the while. He masticated that wine drop by drop it seemed, slowly, all the way down. I had always wanted to see this done by an expert. It was an excellent show.

Boxberger stared thoughtfully into the glass. He frowned, he smiled. Still we waited. "It doesn't quite leave to the palate what it promises to the nose," he said finally.

In truth it was the strangest bottle of wine I have ever drunk. It had the bouquet of a mature, confident wine, and its color had gone off only slightly from its original ruby red. Though not vinegary at all, it tasted thin, almost like a new green vintage that wasn't ready yet. And yet in the background at all times was the robust taste of the great wine which had once been there.

"It's like an old man who's still in pretty good shape," said Boxberger, "though of course he can no longer run the one hundred meters in ten seconds."

I thought of it more in terms of an old baritone whose voice was gone, but who nonetheless could still bring out certain notes that were as beautiful as ever. The former great taste was still in there somewhere; one moment it was on your tongue, the next it was gone.

Luncheon started with *foie gras aux truffes* with hot toast, after which came another of Thuillier's creations, a *poularde à l'éstragon*, chicken boiled in a closed *cocotte* so that it comes to the table with the skin still white and the meat inside very tender. It was served with rice, and over this was spooned a cream sauce tasting principally of tarragon. We had not been allowed to see the menu; Thuillier had decided for us in light of the very old wine we were to drink.

It tasted best with the *foie gras*, its voice coming out in one final absolutely strong, perfectly pitched note, and it seemed to me that I could tell exactly what it had tasted like 100 or so years ago when it was such a great wine, so absolutely sure of itself, that it must have thought, if wines can think, that it would live forever.

All this time people stared at us from neighboring tables, the way film stars get stared at in restaurants. Our waiter stared at us too, so that I said to him, "Would it amuse you to taste this?"

"*Oui, Monsieur,*" he said almost fervently. "A wine like that one tastes once in a lifetime."

"Get a glass," said I.

He took it into the kitchen to sip, and after that our table was surrounded by waiters, as happens in certain poor restaurants where they are hoping for tips. Here it was not tips they wanted but a taste of that wine, and we gave some to most of them. At times the floor was nearly empty; they were all in the kitchen tasting.

Towards the end, though its bouquet was still a pleasure to sniff, the wine began to lose its taste altogether. It got thinner and thinner. It made us think of a feeble old man about to breathe his last, and P. said to a final waiter: "Won't you please have some? It is dying fast and soon it will be too late." We

Think, for a moment, of an almost paper-white glass of liquid, just shot with greeny-gold, just tart on your tongue, full of wild-flower scents and spring-water freshness. And think of a burnt-amber fluid, as smooth as syrup in the glass, as fat as butter to smell and sea-deep with strange flavours. Both are wine. Wine is grape-juice. Every drop of liquid filling so many bottles has been drawn out of the ground by the roots of the vine. All these different drinks have at one time been sap in a stick. It is the first of many strange and some...mysterious circumstances which go to make wine not only the most delicious, but the most fascinating drink in the world.

—Hugh Johnson,
A Cook's Alphabet of Quotations
by Maria Polushkin Robbins

wanted them all to taste it because their curiosity was so great and because it amused us to imagine them impressing patrons for decades to come: "That reminds me of the 1806 Lafite I had the pleasure of drinking once..."

But all day our strain and excitement had been intense, and as we drove away from there, rolling through the villages of Provence in the sun, we both were exhausted. I felt as drained as sometimes after a great football game or a great theatrical performance, and presently I laughed and said to P., "I'm looking forward to the wine we'll drink with dinner tonight. It will be a one-year-old rosé de Provence costing $1.75, and no one will stare at us while we drink it."

And that is what we did.

I wrote my article, which duly appeared, and Thuillier sent a complimentary letter; no one ever suggested he wasn't an excellent businessman. It was one of the few wine articles published in the American press that year, for the boom in wine was not to start until six or seven years later. I took my fee and bought a case of 1959 Château Margaux for under $6 the bottle; and other cases of 1961 second and third growths for $4 the bottle or less.

Once the boom did start, it exploded. Knowing about the great wines, collecting them, serving them became proof of sophistication. Wine-drinking clubs sprang up overnight. Regular wine columns appeared in newspapers and magazines, and wine prices rose exponentially. Ten years after our experience a bottle of 1806 Lafite went on the block at an auction in New Orleans, and an oilman from California paid $14,200 for it. The next year a second bottle, or perhaps the same one, fetched an almost identical price, $14,450, at Christie's in London. At an auction in Chicago in 1979 still another bottle (or was it still the same one?) went for $28,000. Perhaps we shouldn't have drunk ours. Perhaps we should have taken it home. For my article and the accompanying photo I was paid $600.

Gastronomy too became the rage. As the old chefs began to die off they were replaced by younger, more imaginative men who claimed to have invented a *nouvelle cuisine*; men who, as soon as they had acquired their Michelin stars, put their names up over their restaurants in giant letters, left assistants in charge of their kitchens, and set out all over the world making personal appearances, like film stars. In major cities they cooked for groups of so-called gastronomic journalists, or even a single journalist if his paper was important enough, charging no money. More often they cooked for banquets of sixty or more rich people and banked fees. In either case they collected reams of publicity and at home their restaurants filled up with tourists, some of whom were trying to set records—it became chic back home to brag about having dined in ten three-star restaurants in nine days, or the like. The old chefs had been unknown thirty miles from home, sometimes less; the new ones were international celebrities, and the prices on their menus rose exponentially too.

We had planned to stop at Les Baux the following summer but something came up, and the next year was not possible either, and after that we were never in the neighborhood or did not have time. Or perhaps subconsciously we merely wished to preserve a memorable experience by not trying to repeat any part of it. The years passed quickly, and we never came back.

Until today, and I drive across the saddle of the mountain toward the village out on its massive crag of rock and start to turn into the parking lot, which is more vast than I remember, but a man comes out of a booth beside the road and stops me. There is a parking fee of ten francs, it seems, even on a blustery November afternoon like this one when there are no other cars in the lot. So that is the first surprise, though not the last. "Complain to the mayor," says the attendant as he hands back my change. The mayor since 1971 has been Raymond Thuillier.

So I walk through the streets of the village.... I don't recognize any of it.... I walk past one handsome building after another. In most cases the workmen appear to have used the original stones, picked them up off the ground and put them back in place. It's been beautifully, artistically done. It takes a bit of getting used to, however. There are lots of new shops, restaurants, galleries, tea-rooms. They look expensive. In a souvenir store the clerk tells me that the population of the commune has almost doubled since I was here last, from 253 to 433. All this is thanks to the mayor too, or so a shopkeeper tells me. Thuillier was 74 when first elected and he will be 91 in two months' time.

I walk all the way to the end of the village, where the final street used to open onto a stony plateau, where the view, I remember, was one of the most fabulous in France. But I am stopped by a barrier that is new and an obliged to pay twelve francs more before I can get out onto the plateau and walk to the end of it. Well, the view is still there. On a clear day, and today is clear, there is a vast panorama. One can see all the way to the Rhône delta and the Mediterranean about twenty-five miles away.

We drive downhill from the once-ruined village towards the Baumanière.

The place looks much the same, I note when we come to it. The parking lot seems bigger, and there is a boutique now in one corner; you see such boutiques at all the famous restaurants these days. They sell the famous chef's jams and honeys, his *foie gras* and sausages, the cognacs and wines he has lent his name to, and especially his cookbook or books. On sale in Thuillier's boutique is one thing more, his paintings. They are mostly Provencal landscapes somewhat in the Impressionist style, horizontal swaths of rather subtle color, that are quite pleasing. The one in the window, which is of good size, is on sale for about $1,000.

We check in and are shown to our room.

On a table in this room—in all the rooms, I imagine—is a thick and luxuriously printed brochure about the Baumanière and of course Thuillier. There are many beautiful photographs and Thuillier is eulogized on page after page, and the various stages of his career admiringly recalled. Some of the writers extol him as Raymond des Baux, as Raymond l'Accueillant—like one of the medieval lords of Les Baux of hundreds of years ago—as if to say: from them he is descended. He is the man who brought Les Baux back to life. He created his incomparable inn, which not only delights the world but gives employment to 130 people, 18 of them cooks. He owns a second restaurant called Le Cabro d'Or a bit further down the valley; he even made the Vale of Hell come alive. His books are praised, and his paintings, and the table linens he has designed, which are used in the restaurant and can be ordered in the boutique. The various celebrities he has played host to are listed, among them Harry Truman and de Gaulle and various famous French entertainers, even the Queen of England, her husband the Duke, and Prince Charles. Thuillier himself has described the Queen's visit in one of his books, *Les Grandes Heures de Baumanière*. The Queen and her entourage were here two days, ending with a gala banquet for 36 people. The Queen's visit may have been Thuillier's high point.

I did not write ahead to say we were coming because I did not know what kind of shape Thuillier was in and because I was afraid he or someone might suppose we were hoping for a free meal. Now we come into the restaurant to dinner and he is standing near the entrance wearing a white chef's smock as always, though no toque (he was never one of those theatrical chefs), and horn-rimmed glasses, looking frail, and I ask if he remembers the day we opened and drank the 1806 Château Lafite.

He begins to talk about the wines he served the Queen of England. A big smile comes onto his face and he adds: "Ah, but that's another story."

His smile remains in place as I continue to try to talk to him, but he says nothing further, and presently he moves off, taking very small steps.

The Baumanière today is run by Jean-André Charial, the oldest of his grandsons, who was born in 1945 at about the time Thuillier left Paris to start his new life. Charial never intended to become a chef; after secondary school he entered one of France's top commercial colleges and came out and started to make money. But at some point Thuillier must have made a deal with him, because he went back to school, this time in the kitchens of France's greatest chefs: Bocuse, Chapel, Haeberlin, the Troisgros brothers. He also underwent training programs in reception and management at the Plaza in Paris and the Waldorf-Astoria in New York, before coming back to Les Baux permanently fifteen years ago.

I talk to Charial after dinner. He is a tall, solidly built man with a mustache. He says he has heard about that 1806 wine, but has never served anything remotely that old himself. "Somebody ordered a 1900 Lafite one night." I ask about Boxberger. Eight years ago at 70 he retired, Charial tells me; he died just last year. Thuillier has come up in the course of this conversation. He stands listening to us. He smiles throughout, but does not speak.

After shaking hands all around, we go back to our room to bed, and in the morning we drive away.

The oldest wine on the Baumanière wine list today is an 1870 Château Lafite-Rothschild. Other very old vintages are also represented; Lafites from 1877, 1883, 1888, 1890, 1900; and Château Margaux from 1916 and 1918. These wines are listed apart from the others, and no prices are given. I assume they are not really for sale. Although I might have asked Charial what they cost, I did not do so. I chose not to know. Let whatever mystery is left be left.

There was of course no Château Lafite from 1806. To be young and to drink such a wine in a place like this is an experience not to be repeated by us, not to be repeated by anyone. There is nothing more to say.

Robert Daley's work has appeared in numerous prestigious magazines, including Esquire, Playboy, Vogue, Reader's Digest *and* Paris Match. *He has served as a New York City deputy police comissioner and gone hunting for sunken treasure in the Caribbean. This story was excerpted from his book,* Portraits of France. *He lives in Connecticut with his wife and three children.*

✦

Let us not forget the value of rot. All great cuisines use decay and stench as part of the palate. Red wines from Burgundy and the Loire can have a *goût de terre*—an earth taste, like a good garden soil being turned over in the spring—or they can have a *goût de merde*—a shit taste, which has the fragrance of fine cow manure, old, slightly dry, and hay-like on the outside with just enough interior wetness to propel the fragrance outward, and all this nestled in a field of fresh green grass. These tastes, the *goût de terre* and the *goût de merde* are prized by connoissseurs and old bodies like me.

It is a portion of rotten apples that gives good cider its tang and subtlety. I knew a man in Maine who claimed his parents' longevity came from eating a lot of bread with blue penicillin mold on it. *Botrytis cinerea,* the mold that grows on the grapes that make Sauternes, aid the evaporation of water from the grape, making a more concentrated flavor in the wine.

Decay. Pickles are decaying cucumbers. Cheese, yogurt, and buttermilk are decaying milk. Beer is decayed malt and hops. Whiskey is decayed grain (barley, corn, rye). Vodka is decayed potatoes. Sauerkraut is decayed cabbage. Wine is decaying grapes, continuing its decay in the bottle making fine old wine. Some English people like their beef aged to the point where maggots are crawling through it. A good beef stew or red spaghetti sauce should sit on the stove, melding its flavors, for at least a day. I once left a red sauce out for three days and it began to ferment, like wine, and had spritzy little bubbles in it. I was a little leery at first, but I heated it up to kill any strange growths and delicious it was.

—George Vincent Wright, *"Cuisine Sauvage"*

PART THREE

GOING YOUR OWN WAY

FLAVIUS STAN

✦ ✦ ✦

Night of Oranges

A child comes of age.

IT IS CHRISTMAS EVE IN 1989 IN TIMISOARA AND THE ICE IS STILL dirty from the boots of the Romanian revolution. The dictator Nicolae Ceausescu had been deposed a few days before, and on Christmas Day he would be executed by firing squad. I am in the center of the city with my friends, empty now of the crowds that prayed outside the cathedral during the worst of the fighting. My friends and I still hear shots here and there. Our cold hands are gray like the sky above us, and we want to see a movie.

There is a rumor that there will be oranges for sale tonight. Hundreds of people are already waiting in line. We were used to such lines under the former Communist government—lines for bread, lines for meat, lines for everything. Families would wait much of the day for rationed items. As children, we would take turns for an hour or more, holding our family's place in line.

But this line is different. There are children in Romania who don't know what an orange looks like. It is a special treat. Having the chance to eat a single orange will keep a child happy for a week. It will also make him a hero in the eyes of his friends. For the first time, someone is selling oranges by the kilo.

Suddenly I want to do something important: I want to give my brother a big surprise. He is only eight years old, and I want him to celebrate Christmas with lots of oranges at the table. I also want my parents to be proud of me.

So I call home and tell my parents that I'm going to be late. I forget about going to the movie, leave my friends, and join the line.

People aren't silent, upset, frustrated, as they were before the revolution; they are talking to one another about life, politics, and the new situation in the country.

The oranges are sold out of the back doorway of a food shop. The clerk has gone from anonymity to unexpected importance. As he handles the oranges, he acts like a movie star in front of his fans.

He moves his arms in an exaggerated manner as he tells the other workers where to go and what to do. All I can do is stare at the stack of cardboard boxes, piled higher than me. I have never seen so many oranges in my life.

Finally, it is my turn. It is 8 o'clock, and I have been waiting for six hours. It doesn't seem like a long time because my mind has been flying from the oranges in front of me to my brother and then back to the oranges. I hand over the money I was going to spend on the movie and watch each orange being thrown into my bag. I try to count them, but I lose their number.

I am drunk with the idea of oranges. I put the bag inside my coat, as if I want to absorb their warmth. They aren't heavy at all, and I feel that this is going to be the best Christmas of my life. I begin thinking of how I am going to present my gift.

I get home and my father opens the door. He is amazed when he sees the oranges, and we decide to hide them until dinner. At dessert that night, I give my brother the present. Everyone is silent. They can't believe it.

My brother doesn't touch them. He is afraid even to look at them. Maybe they aren't real. Maybe they are an illusion, like everything else these days. We have to tell him he can eat them before he has the courage to touch one of the oranges.

I stare at my brother eating the oranges. They are my oranges. My parents are proud of me.

Flavius Stan was an 18-year-old exchange student from Romania attending the Fieldston School in the Bronx, New York when this was written.

✳

I have often thought about the first time I had ham with pineapple and cherries. This was soon after my arrival in the USA from Nepal where one seldom cooked meat with vegetables—and never with fruits; what one never did was mix sweet and spicy. Thus, in the Nepali household, meat was always curried or spiced; fruits were eaten raw, separate from every other food. One also never drank milk or dairy products with meat during the same meal. These things were simply "not done." That is how I grew up.

So when I first ate a slice of canned ham with a ring of canned pineapple sitting on it, and a bright red canned cherry in the center of the ring, a whole world of possibilities opened up to me. At that instant it became crystal clear to me that, indeed, everything was possible. I was forever going to stop listening to the words: "It's just not done!" There was no need to observe the old mix and match; one could mix the sweet with the spicy, meat with fruits, and that everything was permitted and nothing prohibited. I have taken this food revelation to be the guiding spirit of my years in America. That one should expect the unexpected, ignore the disapproving murmurs of set traditions, and that one should cultivate one's iconoclasm.

A canned lipstick-red cherry in the center of a ring of canned, pale yellow pineapple resting on a thick circle of canned ham—the most liberating moment of my life in America!

—Rajendra S. Khadka, "Mix and Unmatch"

Baking Under the Table

A labor of love is a labor for lucre.

As I rounded the corner of Buchanan and Sauchiehall Streets, the full blast of the Scottish winter afternoon wind hit me in the chest. I dipped my head and pulled my turtleneck sweater over my chin. An unmistakable aroma of chocolate mixed with sweat greeted my nose as I tucked it into the turtleneck. I realized that I'd been wearing the same clothes during baking hours for several days. I jammed my mittened hands deep into my coat pockets. The straining seams gave way. About £30 worth of one pound coins and 50 pence pieces scattered across the damp, gritty sidewalk. My customers rarely paid me with notes. This inconvenient fact of my business life flew in the face of a statement I'd heard from the first cab driver I'd met in Glasgow the previous summer.

When I handed him three one-pound coins to pay my fare, he said, "Ach, dearie, don't do that if you kin help it. Shows you're a tourist."

"Wha…why?" I stammered, crushed that I'd been given away.

"We use pound notes in Sco'land, luv. Pound coins are English."

Sure. I had boxes full of coins at home, all of them given to me by my very Scottish customers.

I knelt to gather my morning's earnings. My fingers were raw from the cold and the strain of having carried fifteen trays of brownies in plastic bags for nearly an hour that morning. A hot bath sounded good right now; I blessed my foresight in remembering to turn on the water heater as I left the flat to make my deliveries a few hours earlier. After four hours, there would be enough hot water in our flat's reservoir for a five-inch-deep bath. I'd use the kettle to boil more as the bath cooled. If I timed it right, I might be able to keep the water warm enough to have a half-hour's soak. Long enough to soak the chill out of my bones, the ache out of my hands, and the chocolate and butter out of my skin and hair. I put the last 50p coin in my bag, straightened up, and set out for home.

Ask travelers who've been to Scotland what they remember about their trip. Most will talk about beautiful, forbidding mountains and moors, ruined castles and abbeys, and damp weather. The honest will admit to remembering tartan shops, bagpipe music, seafood, whiskey, and the friendly, if incomprehensible, natives who welcomed them to their inns, restaurants, museums, homes, and taxis. In contrast, my memories of Scotland can be reduced to one word: brownies.

I baked and sold brownies in the unlikely market of Glasgow, Scotland, and lived off the profits for two years. Ergo, my unorthodox memories of one of the most beautiful countries I've ever seen and some of the friendliest people I've ever had the privilege of knowing. Just say the word "brownies" and I remember hours spent in a tiny kitchen in Glasgow that smelled so strongly of chocolate that the air seemed to be filled with rills of rich brown mist. I remember waiting for assistance in a dark, creepy warehouse that was piled to the ceiling with sofa pillow-sized bags of flour. I remember hundreds of rides into the center of Glasgow on the upper floor of a double-decker bus, coughing in defense against thick clouds of cigarette smoke. I remember sipping espresso on chilly mornings with my favorite customers in my favorite cafés, savoring the warmth and listening to old tapes of Edith Piaf, Sarah Vaughn, and Simple Minds, local boys and local favorites.

I went to Scotland to satisfy my curiosity and stayed to satisfy my heart. I met Brian a month after I graduated from college. I was on a solo backpacking trip through northern Britain, a place I'd never been with my globe-trotting family. Mutual friends had suggested that I look up their college pal Brian if I ever found myself in a place called Glasgow. I found myself there unexpectedly at the end of July, when I was driven out of Edinburgh by the crowds of people associated with the Commonwealth Games. I took the one-hour shuttle train to Glasgow and located my friends' pal Brian. They were right. We did get along. Quite well, in fact. We still do.

When I realized that I'd fallen for Brian and for Scotland, I had to find a way to stay. And so I started my baking business. My under-the-table baking business, that is; it was illegal from start to finish, since I didn't have a residency permit, a business permit, a home-catering permit, a tax identification number, or even a bank account. It was all in the name of love. Brownies for love. And, of course, for money.

The brownies-for-love-and-money idea was born several years earlier when I apprenticed at my friend Sudy's baking business in London. Her business was growing so fast that she could barely keep up with it, and she was short-staffed. Baking was a way to help her out: she'd put me up in her family's guest room for a month, and this was a practical way to thank her. I baked several thousand trays of brownies while carrying on a steady conversation with her employees, Londoners who rarely left the city limits. They told me about the coolest jazz clubs, the cafés where I could get a real cup of coffee, the prettiest parks, the best art galleries, and the antiques markets where the antiques dealers bought the goods that they sold to tourists later at a 200 percent markup.

When Brian asked me to move in with him in Glasgow, I called Sudy in London to see what she thought of my running a much smaller version of her brownie operation out of my flat in Glasgow. After she made me swear, once again, to never, ever reveal the recipe, she sighed, "Baking brownies for love. Do it! Ooh, can I bake your wedding cake?" I laughed and hung up.

If you know how to make them well, brownies are an ideal product for an entrepreneurial baking enterprise. They're easy to bake, they require few ingredients, and, if you wrap them carefully, they refrigerate and travel well. Best of all, they're all but unknown in Britain, which is one of the more sugar-crazy societies I've known.

Scottish cuisine is a mix of the tediously formal—crustless cucumber sandwiches and prissy cakes, which they call *gateaux*—and the alarmingly earthy—sheep's head soup and *haggis*. The Gaelic names of traditional foods are musical and mysterious: cockaleekie is chicken, leek, and barley soup; tatties are potatoes; lights are the guts of an animal, which are the main ingredient in the ubiquitous *haggis; kedgeree* is a Scottish version of fried rice; and *crancachan* is a crunchy mix of oats, cream, Drambuie, and raspberries.

In fact, the Scottish diet is a lot like the Scots themselves. They are exceedingly polite and formal toward strangers, and to their elders. In contrast, most children seem to exist on fried fish fingers and crisps, or potato chips, which are available in a

The so-called national dish of Scotland is haggis, *which is often accompanied by the national drink, malt whiskey. One wit once described this dish as a "castrated bagpipe." It is said that few Scots ever eat this dish, although they present it to tourists as the "national dish." Regardless of what you might be told facetiously,* haggis *is not a bird. Therefore you should turn down invitations—usually offered in pubs—to go on a midnight haggis hunt. Cooked in a sheep's paunch (nowadays more likely a plastic bag), it is made with bits and pieces of the lung, liver, and heart of a sheep served with neeps (turnips) and tatties (potatoes). It is sometimes served with "clapshot," a Scottish version of a dish known south of the border as "bubble and squeak."*

—Darwin Porter and Danforth Prince, *Frommer's Scotland 1996*

huge variety of flavors. An awful lot of people drink gallons of beer and fermented apple cider, not to mention whiskey. Very few people have ever followed any sort of exercise regimen, yet the majority of young people are quite slim, by American standards. Nearly everyone over the age of 15 (and under 60) chain smokes.

Compared to Americans, they're more fit because they don't use cars to get around. They walk, or they take the bus, train, or subway. But mostly they walk.

Brian and I found a one-bedroom flat in a slightly scruffy building on a lovely old rose-filled square near Glasgow University. It had towering ceilings, 14 feet high, and a large sitting room and bedroom, but the kitchen may have been borrowed from the blueprints of the galley for a 25 or 30 foot boat. As for the oven, it was so small that it had only two burners. Only one tray of brownies fit on each of the oven's three shelves. Ach, well, as I was learning to say; under-the-table entrepreneurs can't be choosers. It was a dream flat for a financially strapped young couple. I bought enough ingredients for a dozen trays of brownies, built shelves in the hall to hold my baking supplies, and made a list of restaurants and cafés. I had the materials and the product; now it was time to find my customers.

Armed with a city map, my list, and two bags full of brownies carefully packed in cardboard and cling film, I set off on my first day of cold calls. My first destination was Rogano, an elegant seafood restaurant in the middle of the city. Brian waited tables there sometimes when he needed extra cash. He'd made friends with the manager, Gordon. When Brian told Gordon about my new venture, he'd asked Brian to tell me to stop in with my "brownies."

I'd met Gordon at a cocktail party a few weeks earlier and found him intimidating. A small, thirtyish man, impeccably tailored and groomed, his normal gait was a stride that was enhanced by a theatrically correct posture and a Napoleon complex big enough to silence a kitchen full of sous chefs. Until I got to know him as a friend, his effusive self-confidence and piercing stare intimidated me. I pushed my shaky self-assurance to the back of my mind and straightened up. I was on a mission: the rent was due and I was dangerously close to spending the rest of my savings. This was no time for sissies. I slipped into Rogano's front door, arranged my face into my best friendly, efficient American smile, padded quietly down the carpeted stairs into the basement, and knocked on the door of the office, which was down a low-ceilinged hall from the noisy kitchen.

Rogano was built in the mid-1930s by the people who'd just finished building and decorating the *Queen Mary,* the famous Art Deco-style luxury liner that now rests in Long Beach Harbor. The ship was among the last of the thousands of luxury liners built in Clydebank shipyards, which were for many years the most prolific in the world. In Rogano, the *Queen Mary's* creative team used the same gold-leaf paint and plaster they'd used in the ship to create lovely murals of seascapes full of wistful mermaids and swirling seaweed. They installed banquettes of thick leather and tables of birdseye maple. Rogano's decorative piece de resistance is its carpet, deep red with wave-like figures and thickly padded underneath. The beautiful carpet muffles footfalls throughout the restaurant, adding silent elegance to the smoothly efficient waitstaff.

"Mm, yess, come in." I opened the door and poked my head into the office. Gordon sat behind a large desk. A demitasse of steaming espresso sat beside his left hand.

"Ah, yess, good morning, Kin-et-ti-kit. Brrewnies, I see. Lovely. Pleasse, come in. Come in." I felt heartened; Kinetikit, emphasis on the final "t," was his nickname for Brian. This pronunciation was Glaswegian Gordon's version of the name of our home state. I entered the office and handed him a brownie.

"Right. Let's see here." He took a small bite, then sipped his espresso. "Lovely. Lovely. You make these, yeh? Didn't buy'em from our friends the Italian ice cream makers, didjye?" I pursed my mouth and shook my head. The best bakery in town was run by an Italian family who also ran the city's ice cream concession.

"No, of course not. Just having you on. Let's get Chef in here." He pressed a button on his phone and barked into the receiver. "Yess. Oh, hellew. Dishwasher's answerin' the phone. Ach, well. Miss, tell Chef I need him in the office pleasse." Pause. "Yes now, plisss." He set the phone down, straightened his tie, and smiled at me. I felt nervous all over again.

A moment later, a lanky, mustached man wearing blindingly

white chef's clothes bounded into the office. Gordon introduced us. "Right, this is Bellay, our head chef. Used to run the show at Turnberry."

"I've heard of it," I murmured. "Hello."

I nodded politely, impressed. Chef at Turnberry, eh? The famous golf course and outrageously expensive resort hotel is south of Glasgow, on the Ayrshire coast not far from Robert Burn's birth-place, another mecca for American tourists. For the most part, Turnberry hosts wealthy American and Japanese golfing enthusi-asts. Occasionally it's the site of an international golf tournament. Brian and I had stopped at the main hotel at Turnberry during one of our let's-get-out-of-town-in-a-rental-car day trips. I remem-bered looking toward the sea over the wide greens that were soggy with rain and dotted with determined golfers in foul-weather gear. We'd walked along the beach hand-in-hand.

"Yess, well, he runs the kitchen here now." Gordon's rather shrill voice penetrated my daydream.

"Chef, this is Miss Kelly, from America." Kail-ey from Ameddica. "From Kinetikit. She makes these brewnies. She wants us to sell them. Whatd'ye thenk?"

He handed one to Chef, who ate it in one bite, widened his big eyes, and grabbed my hands.

"Fabulous darlin!" He gulped the rest of Gordon's espresso. "I knew it, fabbydoo with coffee. Right, let's put them on the menu. Serve them with coffees."

We discussed prices and delivery schedules. My timing was perfect; they were about to change the menu, and they would put the brownies on the coffee list, alongside the millionaire's short-bread, the traditional cookie covered with caramel and dipped in chocolate, and tablet, a delightful, wickedly sweet concoction of brown sugar mixed with heavy cream, then cooled and cut into tiny cubes.

After we agreed on prices and an initial delivery schedule, I ex-plained that I had to have their promise that they wouldn't tell any-one who was making the brownies. I wasn't sure what would hap-pen if anyone discovered me, I said, but I didn't want to find out.

"No problem, Tex," Chef reassured me. "We wouldn't want anyone to know that we've got something on the menu that's not made in our own kitchen." I hadn't thought about that part. I felt relieved. They wouldn't tell. And I had a customer.

Bellay meant Billy, I knew, but out of respect, I never called him anything other than Chef. Throughout our two-year friendship, Chef called me Tex. He said that he didn't care where I said I came from, all Americans were from Dallas. When he saw that this bugged me, he did it even more. He was a cheerful guy who pretended to be a bit of a hick. He was no hick, however. He'd been trained on the Continent and had won several British cooking awards. During the frantic pace of the dinner service at Rogano, he snapped orders to his sous chefs at a mad pace. He inspected every plate before it went to the wait staff. I saw him turn back plates all the time—not enough sauce or too much, poorly carved vegetables, or the seafood platter arrangement wasn't to his satisfaction. Chef was tough, but he wasn't too tough to ignore the teaching part of his job. Any proper chef spends a good deal of time instructing sous chefs. I often saw him teaching one of them how to make a particular sauce, or how to slice an unfamiliar cut of fish. Every movement he made was lightning fast, deft, and absolutely necessary.

When he saw me walking into the steamy heat of the kitchen, he began bellowing in a fake Texan accent. "Rustle us up a langoustine, cowboy," he'd shout to one of the sous chefs. "That's one langoustine lobster, and be quick about it. Giddyup, pardner," and he'd hand three inspected plates over to a sweating waitress. "Now y'awl hustle up them stayars quick-like or I'll git my cattle after ya." He'd beam at me, then clap his huge hands suddenly. None of the kitchen staff dared smile when Chef could see them, but they all shot quick glances at me from under their tall hats to see if I reacted to his banter.

During my first week of marketing my product, I relied on my American accent to get me in to see the manager, then let the brownies do the rest. My success rate was staggering: I ended up selling brownies to 80 percent of the restaurants and cafés whose

managers I approached. My customers ran the gamut—from traditional Scottish coffee shops to expensive, glamorous restaurants like
Rogano, to comfortable pub-like places that served meals during
the day and presented live music at night to their lager-drinking
young crowds. I sold several trays a week to a supper club at the
Tron Theatre, a popular repertory group in a lovely old theatre
building near the River Clyde, and to Babbity Bowster's, a tiny,
comfortable restaurant on the first floor of a small hotel. I sold
brownies to several delicatessens in my own neighborhood, where
they displayed my goods in baskets on top of the refrigerated cabinet that held tins of caviar, rounds of Lanark blue cheese, and
bowls of Scotch eggs, olives, and artichoke hearts. My brownies
became the favored after-lunch sweet at a dingy old pub near a
large city office building. Lawyers, chartered accountants, civil service workers, and secretaries washed down their steak and kidney
pie with pints of lager, then ordered espresso and brownies.

British people who haven't taken the time to experience the
city's cultural and architectural treasures laugh at the translation of
the city's name, which means "the dear green place" in Gaelic.
Glasgow has a reputation among non-Glaswegians as a depressed
city that's full of old and young unemployed steelworkers who
beat each other up at soccer matches. This image is so far off
the mark, it's laughable. In 1991, Glasgow was voted "European
City of Culture." Its cultural scene is incredibly active: this
city of less than a million people is home to Scottish Opera,
Scottish Ballet, the Scottish National Orchestra, the Royal
Scottish Academy of Music, and the BBC Scottish Symphony
Orchestra. Within the city limits

*I find Glasgow, a tidy city
of steeples and sandstone
buildings, to have a certain subdued charm. Glasgow is considered
by some as the greatest surviving
example of a Victorian city.
Glasgow has ancient roots and is
much older than Edinburgh.
Many of the city's sedate buildings
wear bright aprons of dark green or
burgundy red—the colorful first
floor storefronts that are pubs,
banks, post offices, and small shops.
Their windows flash with gold-
leaf lettering.*

—Reed Glenn,
"A Scottish Food Primer"

are the world-renowned Burrell Collection, the Hunterian Art Gallery, Glasgow University, and several buildings designed by hometown boy Charles Rennie Mackintosh. In fact, Glaswegians are so proud of their city's cultural sophistication that they're not afraid to joke about its false gritty reputation. A few years ago a well-known local entrepreneur who runs a chain of glamorous hotels told a journalist that "Glasgow is no longer a place where Englishmen go to get knifed," then showed the reporter into one of his stylish hotels.

I managed to confine my baking to two days a week and arranged my deliveries so that they were all on the same two or three days, depending on the week. Since the temperature in our flat rarely topped the 60 degree mark, I wasn't worried about the brownies getting stale from sitting for a day or two. When a heat wave hit Glasgow that summer, and we had three days of 75-degree weather, I put the brownies in the refrigerator. This wasn't a convenient option, since the fridge was smaller than the oven, and the dozens of one-pound blocks of butter had first dibs on fridge space. I had to limit our milk purchases to a pint at a time, and we never refrigerated eggs, vegetables, or fruit. I even banished my bricks of black-and-white film to the coolest, darkest closet in the flat. Nothing was more important than those stacks of brownies, tightly wrapped in cling film, carefully labeled as to customer, delivery day, and price.

Since we had to limit our fresh produce to food that could be stored at room temperature, I quickly took on the efficient European habit of buying only one or two day's worth of groceries at a time. The closest fruit-and-veg shop was a tiny place at the end of our street run by three generations of a strikingly beautiful Pakistani family. The grandfather was nearly blind, apparently from a nasty long-ago fall, or a more sinister cause. His left eye was swollen closed and surrounded by dark purple permanent bruises. In two years I never heard him speak a word of English. A young grandson, a skittish six- or seven-year-old, was devoted to the old man. The boy conducted the translation part of his family's business with charm, grace, and perhaps some wiliness; his sly smile often made me wonder whether he altered his grandfather's prices in his favor during the translation from Urdu to English.

On Christmas Eve, when I went to the shop to buy provisions for the feast we were planning for the next afternoon, I brought a small ribbon-wrapped package of brownies with me. "Please tell your grandfather that I baked these for him and for your family. These are called brownies. They are a delicacy in America, where I come from. I sell them here in Glasgow." The boy looked at me through huge black eyes. He said nothing. "I know that you don't celebrate Christmas, but I wanted to give this gift to you anyway." He smiled slightly and glanced at the package. His smile broadened when he saw that chocolate was involved. "Oh, yes, I tell him, miss. Thank you." I doubt that any other member of the family saw those brownies, but I don't really care.

Kelly Spencer is no longer an illegal alien. She now lives with her husband in the USA. She still bakes brownies, but she shares them rather than sells them.

★

The first known published recipe for brownies appears in the 1897 Sears, Roebuck catalogue. Probably created when a careless cook failed to add baking powder to a chocolate cake batter, the dense, fudgy squares have been made for some time by housewives who received their recipe by word of mouth.

—James Trager, *The Food Chronology: A Food Lover's Compendium of Events and Anecdotes, from Prehistory to the Present*

1897 BROWNIES

2 squares unsweetened chocolate
   or 6 tablespoons cocoa melted
   with 2 tablespoons butter,
2 eggs, beaten light
1 cup sugar

1 cup flour
1 teaspoon baking powder
1/2 cup chopped walnuts
1 teaspoon vanilla
1/4 teaspoon salt

Combine chocolate, eggs, and sugar and beat thoroughly. Add baking powder, flour, walnuts, vanilla, and salt and stir until combined. Pour into a greased eight inch square pan and bake in a 350 degree oven for 35 minutes. Cool and cut into squares to serve.

LOIS MACLEAN

The Huntress

Our ancient ancestors sleep lightly under our skins.

AFTER FIVE MINUTES ON THE ROCKY TRAIL, MY LEGS WERE SHAK-
ing from the weight of my pack. It had been twenty years, and
twenty pounds, since I had carried two weeks' rations on my back.
The jagged track cascaded deep into the tall conifers. I was out of
shape, and out of sorts.

We had much-needed vacation time to use, but we were broke,
and too burned out to consider a full-scale backpacking trip. John,
my companion, had unearthed a cabin in the Northern California
woods where we could rusticate.

This was a new relationship. We were still discovering unexpected talents in each other.

"It belongs to friends of friends, back-to-the-landers. They built
a place on the Trinity River, then moved back to town when their
kids needed schooling. We'll have to hike in, but it's less than two
miles, downhill all the way, and we'll have the place to ourselves,"
he told me with a grin.

I was as delighted with him as he was with himself. A cabin by
a river suited my fantasies exactly. I imagined hiking for maybe ten
minutes, then stretching out in the shade with a stack of paper-
backs. I might not move again for a week.

We loaded up the car with freeze-dried tofu, ramen soup mix, powdered spaghetti sauce, and took the backroads to unwind. The first night, we camped beside my station wagon in a state park, the sparks from our campfire evoking images of family vacations from our childhoods. Lying on our backs, listening to the wind whistle in the treetops above us, we told each other the stories: being awakened by our parents in the starry dark of the morning to get an early start, ourselves and our siblings a tangle of pajamas and arms and legs in the back of the Chevy; the strange-tasting water and restaurant food; highway games counting blue cars or train cars or songs with the names of states; campgrounds and teepee-shaped curio shops along the way.

Rising at dawn for no particular reason, our shared histories a newly woven bond, we breakfasted on foraged blackberries, then drove slowly along a dusty logging road to the designated turn-out.

We crammed our books and packaged provisions into our packs, and found the entry to the trail.

How far could a mile and a half be? John was sort of jogging down the hill, but I couldn't feel at all sure-footed on the stony grade with my thigh muscles trembling so. I fretted about twisting an ankle, and tried to reassure myself that my pack would be a lot lighter, hiking back up in a couple of weeks.

Abandoned objects began to appear among the trees: discarded appliances, a lame wheelbarrow, an overturned potter's wheel. We looked at each other in dismay as we passed the sorrowful litter, the scrap lumber, and scattered plumbing pipe. Perhaps a free place to stay wasn't such a great deal after all.

But all at once the trail poured us into a wide golden meadow, and the debris, hidden in the murmuring foliage, fell far behind. To our right, in a corner of the sunny clearing, an ample house of honey-colored logs watched serenely over apple, pear, and peach trees. Three broad steps led up to a windowed porch, whose railings embraced a rocking chair, a swing. River sounds rippled in the firs just behind, and big, puffy thunderheads billowed beyond the forest-filigreed rim of the sky. Deer grazed beneath an older, scragglier orchard at the boundary of the glade, their untroubled foot-steps whispering legends of the early homesteaders.

A flock of doves fluttered in, settled in the treetops, suddenly swooped away. We had re-entered the dream we'd both pursued, then regretfully forsaken in the '70s: a piece of land, a garden, a quiet life far from the city.

We sat for awhile, abandoning ourselves to our individual memories. I opened the heavy front door into a bright country kitchen; braided rugs and muslin curtains, patchwork potholders, cast-iron skillets hanging against the wall.

The bulletin board, covered with children's art work, postcards from exotic places, and photographs, told the saga: a young, bearded long-haired man, a soft-faced woman in flowered calico, ground-breaking and house-building gatherings, a newborn baby, another, the growing children, Christmas. Bedecking the frame were dozens of rosetted red and blue ribbons from the county fair, embossed in gold: first prize for preserves and pies and pickles, second prize for quilting, grand prize for woodworking.

We wandered through the house, touching the hand-hewn bedsteads, the embroidered pillow shams and quilts, conjuring the stories. Everything was neat, organized; the family could return whenever they wished to take up the life once more.

Soon the mid-day heat drove us outdoors to explore the shady river. I stripped down, striding the shallows in only my flip-flops, much to John's amusement. I was gazing into a deep eddy, considering a dip in the icy water, when a flash of red caught my eye. A crawfish, propelling backward with its big claws, flicked past me, heading for the swirling pool. I dove after it.

I emerged, dripping, breathless, my shoes washed away, the creature wriggling in my hand. My exhaustion, my longing for languor, had vanished. Shouting to John for a bucket, I spied another crimson streak. I dove, spotted another, dove anew.

All afternoon I stalked the rocky shoals, my eyes alert for the darting blood-colored pincers. A primitive, unexplored relationship had awakened: the huntress and her prey.

Heedless of the cold, of the sharp pebbles under my feet and the serrated pincers, I plunged again and again into the deepest caves, thrusting my fingers into crevices, retrieving the squirming, spiny bodies. A shiny black crow cawed at me from an overhanging branch. Tendrils of my hair curled around my face under the green water. Drops sparkled on my shoulders; the sun dappled my legs. In my nostrils mingled the scents of the river, of moss and mineral and dripping wood, and another more primal perfume emanating from my own skin.

All of my senses quickened. I felt strong, agile, fearless. I knew just where and when to look, as though my mind had merged with the cunning of the crustacean, or the river's song, as though sunlight and clear water pulsed through my veins. A crawfish beckoned; it belonged to me. Nothing else was of interest. Each one was a prize, a triumph. I held it aloft to admire, then tossed it into the cool bucket with its brothers, and hunted on.

To the ancient Greeks, Artemis the Huntress was Apollo's sister. She went armed with bow and arrows and, like her brother, had the power to send plagues or death to mortal creatures, and to heal them. She is the protectress of little children and of all sucking animals, but she loves the chase. She is often depicted in a ritual bath.

—RS

I caught three dozen, while John read in his sun hat, and watched bemused from the shore. We cooked them for supper, in a big pot on the huge black woodstove, after gathering volunteer greens from the garden for a salad. Each snowy sweet morsel of meat, when released from its shell, was no larger than my thumb. In a lavender twilight, we wandered through the old, lichen-crusted orchard, searching for remnants of the original homestead, plucking an apple for dessert.

I wouldn't have guessed it then, but that summer evening turned out to be a twilight of a different kind for John and me. After a while, we became chapters from each other's history, the history we walked into that day. I often think of him, and of the family I had never met, whose generosity allowed me to roam through time, back through the longings of my early twenties and the hopeful journeys of my childhood, back even further to imagine the sturdy pilgrimage of my great-grandmother, who traveled from Europe across the West to build a life in a rough mining town. But the memory I'm most grateful to have recaptured is far more ancient, and far more compelling. That afternoon I became my own ancestor: the primeval huntress, who doesn't plan or build or even think. Untamed, wordless, vibrantly female, she lives by her instincts and her vigor; leaping on bare feet across rocks with all her senses alive to the elements, responding to signals written in wind and water and moonlight. Sometimes, I dream her dreams: of silver fishes and flickering flames, of leaping deer and sweet berries, and white clouds, dancing across the sky.

Lois MacLean is a social worker, painter, and writer who lives and works in Mill Valley, California. She is a regular contributor to The Pacific Sun, *and her work has appeared in* The San Francisco Chronicle, Veggie Life Magazine, The Eclectic Gourmet Guide to the Bay Area, *and* Traveler's Tales: San Francisco. *She has been eating for many years.*

✳

It was late in the afternoon of a hot dry day in the eastern Cascades when I staggered, bleary-eyed, from the shack. A loud hissing broke my reverie, and I looked up to see a Serpent of Yore not five feet away. I seized a stick and set about to slay him only to have the Serpent bounce, coil, and hiss again. I progressed from stick to rocks and boulders until our struggle had taken on a Biblical cast (I, Cain, slaying Abel), though I suspect this was only the case in my own mind. By the time I had lofted a boulder worthy of Conan, my adversary had slithered away into a maze of brambles.

The next day, out for a stroll with wife and daughters, the Serpent was spotted in a bed of pine needles not far from the shack. He looked like a Gary Larson snake with a crooked neck—so I had good reason to believe he was the same one I had injured the day before. I set upon him with a stick and rocks, and finally lopped his head off with an ax. Headless, he wriggled toward the girls, who were understandably concerned at his approach. We buried the head, which has been known to confer a bite hours after death.

We took the body home, lamenting the fact that our friend Richard hadn't sent us his recipe for Rattlesnake Piccata. My mother-in-law then deftly showed us how to dissect *Crotalus viridis oreganus* and how to preserve the skin. He was just over three feet long, with twelve rattles, which in this climate meant he was anywhere from six to ten years old. His skin, I thought, will make an excellent hat band or picture frame.

I marinated him in lemon juice, white wine, soy sauce, and tomatoes from the garden, pan-fried him for a few minutes, and then baked him for an hour. I served him coiled on a plate with a wedge of lemon and a sprig of parsley.

How did he taste? To paraphrase another friend, "Taste is a function of hunger"—and we were not overwhelmingly hungry. I would characterize rattlesnake as a Poor Man's calamari. Long strings of chewy meat embedded in an amazing architecture of bones.

Fortunately for all at the table, there was also Chicken.

—James O'Reilly, "Encounters with the Serpent"

COLIN THUBRON

* * *

Then I Slept

Boozing and feasting on the caravan trail.

TOWARDS DUSK IN THE DEAD CITY OF MERV I REACHED A SEVenth-century citadel crumbling on its mound. Its battlements resembled a rectangle of vast clay logs upended side by side, and I wondered why this petrified stockade had not been manned against the Mongols. But perhaps the human heart, in the old man's words, had not been right, and now the crenelations had worn away and the entrance-ramp was blurred in the sand.

I waded across stagnant ditches, and skirted a seasonal pond where a flock of black-winged stilts was tiptoeing through the shallows. Ahead of me, a giant mausoleum reared out of nothing above the littered plain. For 40 feet into the air its cube of walls loomed blank. It had been heavily restored, and only a pair of high doors broke its austerity. But near its summit it opened on an ornamental portico, and above its drum, from which all decoration had gone, a great dome hovered.

This was the tomb of the much-loved Seljuk Sultan Sanjar, grandson of Alp Arslan, whose rule vacillated for 50 years across the eastern provinces of the disintegrating empire. At first his triumphs over Turkic enemies shored up his delicate realm, but in Middle Age disasters made his name a byword for humiliation. In

1156, at the age of 70, he died in a half-ruined city and was entombed in the mausoleum which he had built himself, and called "The Abode of Eternity."

He was succeeded by chaos, in which his memory glittered. The form of his tomb—its walls closed against the earth but open to heaven—signalled to his people that he was perhaps alive and might return to resurrect his empire. But inside I found an echoing emptiness. The whitewashed walls lifted to an octagon from whose pendentives floated a cavernous inner dome. It moaned with the beat of pigeon wings. Decorative strapwork, still painted blue, radiated over its surface and meshed at its apex in an eight-pointed star. But vertically beneath it, in the centre of the floor, a plain grave, protected by a sheet against pigeon droppings, subverted the glory of the ruler with the platitude of death.

"You watch out in those ruins," said Murad the lorry-driver. "They're haunted."

"Who by?"

"I don't know. People have been heard crying there." He was trying to dissuade me from returning. He was jaunty and impetuous, and wanted me to join him on a picnic in the desert. "And that castle you saw," he went on, "there's gold buried all round, but nobody can find any. Its sultan kept a harem of forty women there and a tunnel leads from it underground to the other end of the city. It's dangerous."

The region now called Turkmenistan was, in ancient times, a part of Sogdiana, where Alexander the Great met and married Roxanne. The city of Merv was established in 327 B.C. as a fortress town by Alexander's general Craterus. Its original name was Alexandria.

—RS

These fables of gold and tunnels attend ruins all across the Islamic world, so I agreed to the picnic instead, and the next moment we were crashing through the side-alleys of Mari recruiting his friends. He blasted his horn and bawled his invitation beneath half a dozen tenement-blocks, until a flock of grizzled heads sprouted from rotting oriels and balconies, to bellow down their assent or refusal. Then he would march inside to harry them, yelling for me to follow. We bounded up stairwells fetid and awash with recent rain, where bottles and cigarette stubs and sometimes broken condoms floated. We were joined by a big, hirsute man with violent eyebrows and a lax, cruel mouth. Then came a wizened old Mongoloid clutching a lute in a velvet case. And soon we were careening across the desert in a gust of anticipation, while over the hummocks around us the goosefoot and artemisia thinned, and all signs of habitation vanished.

After an hour Murad's face—a quivering profile of high bones—quickened into expectation. "We're here!"

He veered over virgin sand and we settled in a dip between the dunes. A weft of yellow and mauve vetch shone all over the savannah, and poppies turned the ridges scarlet. He had forgotten nothing. A felt carpet, such as once covered Turkoman yurts, was unraveled over the sands. Bags of spiced mutton appeared, with two charred samovars, an outsize stewing-pot, a basket of raw vegetables, sheafs of kebab skewers and some fire-blackened bricks. As we scavenged for dead saxaul—the wind-blown plant whose pallid stems litter the whole country—a familiar euphoria broke out. Their voices were light and bantering. Their bodies seemed balanced only precariously on their bow-legs, as if they longed to leap on horseback. Soon we had a triple blaze of fires going. The samovars were cremated in a nest of flaming branches, the *shashlik* oozed and spat over charcoal heaps, and the stewing pot—into which Murad had tossed a calf's head—simmered balefully on a brick hob. The men's faces lit up in sybaritic grins. The bitterness left the big man's mouth and the Mongoloid's face dimpled into glee.

"Isn't this better than home?" he cried, as we settled ceremoniously on the carpet. "Nothing compares with this!"

Soon the *shashlik* was being thrust triumphantly from hand to hand. Dribbling blood and fat, it was tough as rope. But the three men swallowed each morsel wholesale, or clamped it between their teeth like mastiffs and worried it to and fro, until it separated with a noise like tearing sheets. They celebrated every mouthful with a carnivorous burp, and dipped gluttonously into mountains

of radishes and olives. The brief respites between skewers resounded with an anticipatory grinding of gold and ivory molars
and the smack of oily lips. They looked artless and timeless. At any
moment, I thought, they might break into shamanistic chant or
propose a raid. The time was not long past when their ancestors
had cantered 80 miles a day to harvest Persian slaves—the
Mongoloid's father might just have known it—and the desert still
seemed subtly to nourish them. Their earthquake-stricken country
gave no confidence in building, or perhaps in any permanence at
all. Better the open sky!

Assiduously they plied me with the tenderest chunks of *shashlik*, but my teeth recoiled even from these. I smuggled them out of
my mouth and secreted them wherever I could: in the bush behind me, under the sand between my knees, in my shirt pockets.
Murad kept thrusting more at me, the point of his skewer threatening my chest. But he was grinning with hospitality. They all
were. The big man detached the most succulent nuggets to press
on me, with the crispest onions. But soon my pockets sagged with
the telltale meat, and a betraying stain of fat was spreading across
my shirt-front.

As I masticated despairingly on another hunk, I bit on something hard, and assumed it was mutton-bone. Then I realized that
it was one of my own bones I was chewing on. I had lost a tooth.
Neurotically I ran my tongue back and forth over the gap. Nobody
else noticed. I longed to inspect it in a mirror, but I could picture
it well enough: the double rank of ivory now breached by a
slovenly void, as obvious as a fainted guardsman. Viewed from the
right, I might pass muster. But seen from the left, I thought, I must
show a Dracula-like unreliability. Would I be refused permits, visas,
even hotel bedrooms, I wondered, on account of this lost incisor?
Would conversations dry up the moment I grinned?

These broodings were halted by the arrival of soup. Murad el-
evated the caldron above his head as if at a pagan Eucharist, while
the calf's head bobbed obscenely to the surface. The big man
skimmed off the fat and threw it on the sand. Then we drank, and
it was delicious. Fumbling in my rucksack, I found a packet of

English cheese biscuits and passed them round complacently. They nibbled them without comment. Later I noticed Murad dropping his into the sand.

Little by little the party's spirit mellowed. The men's quick, guttural language was mysterious to me, but they translated their jokes into a babbling Russian, and finally Murad conjured up three bottles of vodka. "This is the whole point!" He slopped it into shallow glasses, and we flung them back in one gulp, Russian fashion, at every toast. Only the old Mongol refused to drink at first. It suborned his stomach, he said. "He's an *ishan*, a holy one!" roared the big man, mocking.

"They drink most of all!" retorted the Mongol, and they were rolling in the flowers with laughter.

Some charred pots of green tea created a moment's hiatus. Then the vodka-drinking went on. Sometimes, secretly, I spilled mine into the sand, but Murad replenished my glass at every toast, and fatally I lost count of them. Meanwhile they absolved themselves with blessings, and peppered their talk with "If God wills!" or "Thanks be to God!" while pouring out the forbidden spirit. Then they expatiated on remedies for hangover, and confided the medicinal properties of saxaul root or green tea (sovereign against headaches if you inhaled the aroma between cupped hands).

> *Merchants from this country travel to all parts of the world; but in truth they are a covetous, sordid race, eating badly and drinking worse.*
>
> —Marco Polo,
> *The Travels of Marco Polo*

"Try it! Try it!" But it was too late. The vodka had already detached me, and I was seeing them all from far away. Sitting cross-legged on their carpet among the flowers, they seemed to have regressed into a Persian miniature. Yet squatting amongst them was this outlandish foreigner, with a black stain advancing over his shirt...

The big man turned to me with inebriate slowness and asked: "*Where* are you from then?" All countries, I think, lay in mist to him beyond the oasis of his own. "London? That's in America!"

"No, no!" yelled Murad. "Great Britain!"

The giant looked bewildered, but said: "Aah."

"Margaret Thatcher!" mused the Mongol. "She is very beautiful. I did not think that such an old woman could be so beautiful. So slender!" He shook his own hands in congratulation. "Who is president of Great Britain now then? Does she have a son?"

By now the shadows of the shrubs were wavering long over the dunes, and the sand grew more deeply golden, the sun descending. The men picked their teeth and let out soft whistles of contentment. For a while the Mongoloid had been plucking the poppies round him, and munching them. But now he took out his *dutah*—the frail-looking Turkoman lute shaped like a long teardrop—and started to play. From this coarse instrument he conjured tiny, plangent sounds on two wire strings, to which he sometimes sang, or half-spoke—but the words, he said, were untranslatable—about love, longing, and the passing of everything. His voice was a husky shadow. His shaven head, furred over by a gray and white *chiaroscuro*, bent close over the strings, as if striving to hear. He had never been taught to play, he said, but had learnt by listening to the old bards in his youth. Yet his gnarled fingers fluttered along the wires, and long after this right hand had plucked one, his left darted up and down the lute's stem, while the notes faded.

Far away on the horizon, billowing back into the sky, an enormous column of smoke was ascending, where some oil installation had gone up in flames.

The sun dropped into the dunes. The last of the *shashlik,* ignored, had charred to a line of basalt pebbles, and a postprandial weariness descended. The last song left the old man's lips, and he eased the *dutah* back into its velvet sheath. Our picnic had shrunk to husks and rinds. Flies were glued to every abandoned scrap. We groped to our feet and began to clear up. The old man was slapping his head against the flies. He cleaned the skewers by stabbing them into the sand, as the Romans had cleaned their armor. Nobody seemed to notice the long rail of dung-beetles on a gastronomic pilgrimage to the bush behind me.

The vodka had vanished too, and all the way back to Mari my head was separating from my body. I glimpsed it swaying in the lorry's mirror. Whenever I opened my mouth my missing tooth struck me with a seedy shock. It had not so much dropped out as disintegrated, and had left a stunted fang dangling above the gap like a yellow stalactite. But by the time we reached Murad's house in a village on Mari's outskirts, I had ceased to care. My legs dropped from the lorry independently, and embarked on a wavering half-life of their own.

I remember his home only as a series of vodka-sickened lantern-slides which light up in my memory even now with a tinge of shame. Two women in native dresses are standing near the doorway. They are Murad's wife and eldest sister. His wife comforts her small son over something as he sobs against her breast. I greet them feebly. The half-light from the door, or an overhanging vine, seems to turn them biblical. I imagine I am back in Syria. The starlight shows a private vegetable patch, and two cows standing under a byre. A puppy wags a disfigured rump. To save it from being mauled by other dogs, its ears and tail have been sliced off with a razor.

My legs carried me weightlessly into the bare interior. In its reception room a dresser shone with cheap ornaments, and a television stood mute. Murad was drunk too, strutting and shouting. The women looked at us with the indulgence accorded to hopeless children.

The drink-haze lifted a little on a mild-faced schoolmaster who was invited in to speak English with me. He did so in a doggered monologue of Dickensian sentences, once or twice beginning "It is painful to reflect…" or "As is my wont…" Meanwhile I propped myself on a cushion like an indolent sultan, and tried not to sink into catalepsy. A young musician, too, was summoned from the village to amuse me. In the middle of his improvised concert, I watched through dulled eyes as he slapped two batteries into his *dutah*—"It makes a bigger noise like this!"—before launching into new arpeggios.

The music tinkled far away. A great tide of blackness was lapping up behind my eyes. I remember hoping, as they thudded shut, that this would be construed as ecstasy at the *dutah* music rather than a bursting headache. Whatever happens, I thought, I mustn't sleep.

Then I slept.

Colin Thubron has written much about the lands east of Suez, from Damascus to the hinterlands of China. He is the recipient of the Silver Pen Award for his novel A Cruel Madness, *and is the author of* Among the Russians, In Siberia, The Silk Road, *and* The Lost Heart of Asia, *from which this story was excerpted. He lives in England.*

★

The fifth of the heirs in succession to Genghis Kahn was the Sultan Oljeitu, who came to this forbidding plateau in Persia to build a great new capital city, Sultaniyeh. What remains is his own mausoleum which later was a model for much Muslim architecture. Oljeitu was a liberal monarch, who brought here men from all parts of the world. He himself was a Christian, at another time a Buddhist, and finally a Muslim, and he did—at this court—attempt really to establish a world court. It was the one thing that the nomad could contribute to civilisation: he gathered from the four corners of the world the cultures, mixed them together, and sent them out again to fertilise the earth.

—Jacob Bronowski, *The Ascent of Man*

Caller of Dolphins

Is it all a dream?

HOW DO YOU SAY "NO" TO FOOD? IN MANY PLACES, IT IS SIMPLY the most important gift possible. To refuse it, is to refuse the embodiment of place. It is like going to church, but when communion time comes around, peering suspiciously at the wafer and saying, "No thanks, I…uh…just ate." To travel is to taste life and, sometimes, it tastes awful.

I have grinned through gritted teeth while choking down whole garlic cloves laced with pickled octopus tentacles in the Yaeyama Islands. I smilingly pretended the Okinawan raw horse meat I chewed, for what seemed like several weeks, was actually (very) rare roast beef. I graciously plunged my hands up to the wrists in a congealing brownish glop that my Malian host assured me had been, at one time, goat and muttered "yum yum" as I sucked on the sinewy chunk that had snagged my fingernail. You do what has to be done.

However hard it was for me, the giving is, often, more difficult than the receiving. Who knows how many precious chickens were throttled in my name; how many winter stocks I have inadvertently pillaged. Procuring food takes its toll. Which is why I want to tell you this story. It's not my story. It belongs to Winnie Powell, the indomitable medicine woman of Butaritari Island. It belongs to her and to her island, which isn't really an island but rather an atoll in the central Pacific. Butaritari belongs to a country no one has ever heard of called Kiribati. It is a real country and this is a real story.

I only know it because I was sick. I went to visit Winnie, and within 36 hours, was curled up on a *pandanus* mat, shivering with fever and suffering from what Winnie knowingly called "the flu with a touch of 'epatitis." She mixed me some medicine out of twigs, roots, and rainwater (which doesn't actually qualify as "food" so I will pass over them as quickly as they passed through me), and initiated a regime of massages designed to lower my temperature and channel the flu into my stomach. This didn't seem like such a good idea, as my stomach seemed to already have its fair share of the flu. Which brings me closer to The Story.

What with my stomach filling up with flu and all, I wasn't very hungry. Winnie insisted I eat and offered me the full range of local dishes: bananas, fish, *paw paw,* coconut, and swamp taro. That was it. The full range. Oh, granted there is a world of difference between roasted swamp taro and grated swamp taro but being deathly ill allows you certain privileges and it gets to the point where you grab those privileges by the throat and scream into their collective face "NO MORE SWAMP TARO OR I WILL PUKE."

And that was when Winnie told me The Story. It started, as all good stories do, once upon a time, not so very long ago....

The dolphins and the humans lived in separate but equal worlds. The dolphins kept watch over the sea and the humans oversaw the land. There was mutual respect and liking but they rarely got together for a chat. In fact, there were only two families on Butaritari Island who had the knowledge that allowed them to Call the dolphins.

Calling the dolphins was difficult and dangerous and would only be undertaken in times of hunger. It started when the Caller was asleep. She (or he) would guide her dreams towards the land where dolphins dream. There, unhindered by physical considerations like incompatible vocal chords, she could speak directly to the dreams of the sleeping dolphins.

The Caller of dolphins was invariably well received. The dolphins loved company. Once introductory pleasantries were over ("Thanks for returning that lost sailor." "No problem, glad to do it. He had a lovely way of caressing my blowhole."), the Caller stated the real reason for the visit. "I have been sent to invite the dolphins to a dance in our lagoon. Can you come?"

That always thrilled the dolphins. They would get excited and the shades of their subconscious would glimmer a bit brighter. "Oh yes! Yes, of course, we would be happy to come. How many of us would you like? Just the big ones or the small ones too? The usual place?" The Caller would say of course the same place and add how many were invited and of what age. Then, politely excusing herself, she would quietly fade back into consciousness.

The next day, just before high tide, the whole village would go down to the lagoon and watch the sea channel expectantly. Soon the dolphins would start to arrive. The teenagers and young adults of the village took off their clothes and hung them on The Tree Upon Which You Hang Your Clothes, then they dove into the lagoon and paired off with the dolphins. The humans, gently holding onto their hosts, would murmur sweet nothings into where they imagined dolphin ears to be. As parents and siblings watched from the shore, singing and dancing encouragingly, the human/dolphin couples frolicked in the crystal aquamarine waters. Occasionally, a mischievously adventurous pair would even go out into the darker blue waters of the open sea, returning only hours later.

Eventually, the tide would fal-

> *They sing with a certain lustiness and Bacchic glee; the volume of sound and the articulate melody fall unexpected from the tree-top, whence we anticipate the chattering of fowls. And yet in a sense these songs also are but chatters; the words are ancient, obsolete and sacred; few comprehend them, perhaps no one perfectly.*
>
> —Robert Louis Stevenson on Butaritari, *In the South Seas: A Footnote to History*

ter and the time would come to end the dance. The dolphins knew what to do next. One by one, they would beach themselves, always in the same spot and always facing the same direction. The swimmers quietly got their clothes from The Tree and stood watching. Emotions crackled in the air. Sorrow, pain, gratitude, love and, darting about like an embarrassed streaker, hunger.

Some of the stronger men picked up the hatchets that had been lying on the cool grass since the morning and, caressing the lean and still wet dolphins with one hand, hacked them to death with the other. As soon as they beached, they were butchered. The meat was quickly and equitably distributed all throughout the island.

Everyone got a piece. Everyone except the Caller of dolphins. She had known the dolphins as friends, she had spoken with them. It would be unacceptable for her to eat them.

There was also another price she would be expected to pay. The Caller of the dolphins always died young and when she died, she could not be buried on the island. Just off the coast of Butaritari there was a dark blot on the turquoise ocean, a bottomless hole in the sea floor that, it was believed, led down into the home of the dolphins. The body of the Caller of the dolphins was brought to this spot and placed in the water. Other bodies would have just floated away, but hers sunk, down, down, reuniting her again and forever with the dolphins, who were always happy to have company.

And that sacrifice, dying young, forever being separated from her family, the Caller of the dolphins was willing to make for the honour of being able to provide food for her hungry Island.

And that was the end of Winnie's story.

She looked rather pointedly at the now cold dish of roasted swamp taro.

"Boy," I said, "that swamp taro looks delicious." Brushing away the flies that weren't already imbedded and struggling in the beige mass, I started munching away dutifully. "Yum yum."

"But Winnie, is that true? Do they still Call the dolphins?"

"The last time the dolphins were Called was about thirty years ago. I had just had my first child so I couldn't swim with them. I watched though…. You know, my husband's family is one of the two who can Call. I ask my sister-in-law why she won't do it. She says she doesn't want to die young. I told her it's unlikely, since she is already in her sixties but she still won't do it. I guess she prefers the safer honour of buying the whole island tins of corned beef. Oh well, youth today, don't know the value of a good meal."

Girl Reporter (BBC, CBC, The Economist) Cleo Paskal exists exclusively on airline meals. She highly recommends the herring on Icelandair. Otherwise, she always orders a special meal, if only to annoy the people sitting next to her.

★

Balinese dogs, being reincarnations of thieves from Java, are treated with scant honor. They are, however, regarded useful in two ways. First, they frighten away those destined to be dogs in the next lifetime. Their second use is…well, let me tell you a story.

The two dogs in our compound led a charmed life by Balinese standards. Djarum, also known as Anjing Turis or Tourist Dog, attached himself to the household's long-term guests, exchanging watchdog services for food and affection. Opah was big and tough enough to bully his way into a fair share of the scraps. People hardly ever kicked them.

One day I noticed Opah dragging himself around the porch.

"What's wrong with Opah?" I asked our landlady.

Wayan's smile was compassionate. "Very sick."

"Will you take him to a doctor?"

Giving me an incredulous look, she turned to watch the dog, whose path was marked by a smeared trail of blood. The look turned thoughtful. "Some people say I should make *saté*."

How kind, I thought. Then I realized the matter needed clarifying. "You mean, you want to make *saté* for Opah to eat?"

Wayan turned back to me with a smile that pitied this naive foreigner. Very gently she said, "No…"

—Meredith Moraine, "Alas, Poor Opah"

BRETT ALLAN KING

✷ ✶ ✷

Spanish Guts

A vegetarian voyeur learns what it means
to eat with his eyes.

TEN TO MIDNIGHT AT THE TEMPLE OF INTESTINAL LOVE—AND NOT enough bread. Our waitress-madam-priestess blushes at denying us an Iberian sacrament, but we are famished and forgiving. We have dodged icy Castilian winds and a "closed" sign to consume the air-conditioned, grease-laden Muzak of Freiduria Nely. Unaccompanied entrails it shall be.

Nine years in Spain will put hair on the chest of any vegetarian. In a land where dusty pig legs hang in bars and carrion means window decor, my stomach and I were forced into manhood.

Those first months in public markets meant a straight shot for the vegetables and a "get thee behind me, Satan!" whenever meat marred my peripheral vision. Gradually, though, I'd venture in with the dead things. Emboldened, I could soon bear the spectacle of untamed, middle-aged senoras shoving and sparring over prime cow heads, dead piglets, tongues, eyeballs, and snouts. Though still the recalcitrant herbivore, I began to discover repressed ocular passions in spectatorial strolls through the *carniceria,* where inevitably some old butcher would be hacking away at a hunk of flesh, splashing blood and bile all over postcards of the Virgin Mary.

Then I saw the light. In the bars and backstreet restaurants of Madrid, I finally came to understand Dr. Freud's connection between sustenance and sexuality. Through years of gastronomic intercourse with Latin lovers of food, I gradually learned that mastication is nothing short of sensual, and that those who eat merely for nourishment are little better than culinary eunuchs.

Anxiously awaiting Nely's oral pleasures, Rolando gloats to Luis about a luscious *bocadillo* he once conquered. His kiss-and-tell look turns to lust when the waitress finally brings out the plate of guts. *Gallinejas, entresijos, finas, negras.* So many names and so few clues as to what fried things lie before us.

"They're from down about here on the sheep," says the plump, middle-aged server, caressing her hips and smacking her lips, "and are they ever tasty!"

"I don't know about this," mutters Luis, nervously. "I was up for some tripe, but...I'm gonna need some bread."

Rolando plucks an intestine from the common plate and sticks it in his mouth. "Kinda crunchy on the outside...soft inside," he ponders. "Greasy but delicious. Mmmmm. The crunchy part's the best."

"Claire wouldn't forgive me if she knew what I was eating," he laughs. His English girlfriend has threatened to leave him if he doesn't diet.

Luis' original inhibition appears to evaporate as he slurps up a greasy gut like an unwieldy strand of spaghetti. Juice dribbles from his chin. This is not a time for intellectualizing taste sensations, but for living them.

Susana, his vegetarian girlfriend and my ally in flesh rejection, looks on in disgust as the two men finish their foreplay with the food chain and reach for a second alimentary tract. Luis pokes one of these plumper intestines with his fork, and a white pus oozes out.

"Only a girl from Madrid would let her boyfriend eat these things," he declares.

"Mmmm. It comes with its own sauce," jokes Rolando.

"Heavy," shrieks Luis. "It's the soul of the animal coming out to greet you, saying 'Hi, I want you to eat me.'"

Rolando gobbles down another gut and repeatedly nods in approval. Words are useless. At the next table, a dapper young man and his blond date get closer and closer. They ignore the sole small intestine remaining on their platter and look playfully into each others' eyes.

Amidst subtle munching and moaning, our discussion quickly turns to eros—and the sexual connotations of a Spanish verb.

"As usual, food brings us to sex," muses a ruminant Rolando, "I have to tell you this.... Some things are delicious and some are exquisite. This was delicious, but not orgasmic."

"I don't know...I almost came with the sheep," retorts Luis. Just as Rolando sops the grease off his plate with the last precious chunk of semi-stale bread, there is a tap on the window. Jose and Rocio are outside, late as usual. The two join us and we all stand to exchange kisses. Enough with pleasantries—Luis is insatiable and they are starving.

> *To the table or to bed, you must come when you are bid.*
>
> —Laura Esquivel,
> *Like Water for Chocolate,*
> translated by Carol Christensen
> and Thomas Christensen

In minutes, we are foraging for delicacies amidst the copper glow of Lavapies, brick streets trapped between ochre walls and decaying, balconied walk-ups. An ancient, dingy wisp of a man glares at us and feeds chopped liver to an alley cat. The neighborhood is a militant testimony to the Madrid that was. The only MacDonald's to open here was closed by apathy. What self-respecting Lavapiecero would trade blood sausage for Big Macs?

Susana and Rocio talk food.

"Pig fetuses?!" shrieks Rocio, "that's gross. A good pig's ear—now that's good eatin'."

Jose and Rocio stand shattered before a closed Bar Castilla. He's been boasting about their *callos a la madrilena* (boiled tripe) for weeks. "Maybe we can find an Extremaduran bar around here—they dish up a mean lizard." We recall the indigent Extremaduran who was fined for eating a near-extinct reptile, smothered in onions. Spaniards outraged by the injustice done him raised the money to pay off his fine.

Fluorescent and neon lights beckon our migratory *menage-a*-six to window shop the open bars of Tirso de Molina Plaza. One, with chopped octopus in the window, is virtually empty. But Bar Mariano (with a soccer ball for the 'o') is blessed with noisy diners and a window display teeming with culinary delights. Guts on a stick? No, we've done that. Brains? Maybe. We are intrigued by the neatly arranged row of raw sheep heads, cut lengthwise into perfectly symmetrical halves.

As a student in Madrid I experienced a temporary surfeit of Hemingway. Not his works, but his eateries. It seemed every other restaurant in town bore a proud notice proclaiming that "Hemingway ate here." If the signs were to be believed, Hemingway ate in more places than George Washington slept. I avoided any establishment that made any reference to Hemingway. Except for one little hole-in-the-wall with a small sign on the door quietly reassuring me that, "Hemingway never ate here."

—RS

"Alright, now," announces Jose, "who's game for half a sheep's head?"

Rolando looks eager. Luis is reluctant.

"Sheep's head for three?"

The two nod.

"Sheep's head for four," Rocio grins.

"ARTICLES CONSUMED AT THE TABLES MUST HAVE BEEN SERVED BY THE WAITER," warns a sign on the wall.

"One ear!" the waiter bellows toward the grill, writing our order on the back of a cigarette carton, "Half a sheep's head!"

We see *pajarito* (little bird) on the menu. "Probably sparrow," whispers Susana.

"One *pajarito*," I say, with a straight face, as though I habitually munch on bite-sized Tweety birds.

"Oh, no. We can't serve that anymore," laments our pudgy, white-haired waiter. "It's completely forbidden. The police came in here and looked absolutely everywhere—even the cellars. It's sad, because many people ask for it. Would some chicken wings do it for you?"

Well-dressed couples and frumpy old *taxistas* stand amidst the used napkins and cigarette butts tossed to the floor. Intense fluorescent lighting douses *tapas* lining the stainless steel bar. "GOOOOOOOOOOOAAAAAALLLLLLL!!!" The soccer match blares from the TV set mounted on the wall, in direct competition with the incessant bleating of the slot machine. Macho waiters toss plates and bluster over the din of clanking silverware and a boisterous clientele. A tiny soul with sportcoat and tennis shoes parades silently up and down the bar, a toothpick jutting from beneath his bushy growth of a moustache.

We eavesdrop on nearby diners as they speak of roast lamb, but our hearing is intercepted by an ear. The gigantic pig ear has been grilled, chopped, and doused in hot sauce. Rocio is ecstatic. Carnivores clutch forks and jab into a mouthful of porcine appendage.

"It's like it's alive," ejaculates Rolando. "It's great, I mean the cartilage. You bite into it, you think you've broken through it—and then it bounces back at you…this is what you call exquisite." He sighs with eyes rolled upward, half-talking and half-savoring his greasy bliss. *"Me corro viva!"* he yells, feigning female orgasmic frenzy.

A tall brunette in spiked heels, heavy mascara, and black leather short shorts traipses into the bar. She is accompanied by a pock-marked man with greased-back, shoulder-length hair. They

He was twenty-five and he treated me like a little girl. I was in love with him. Sitting next to him in a car when he took us all for long rides, I was ecstatic just feeling his legs alongside mine. At night I would get into bed and, after turning out the light, take out a can of condensed milk into which I had punctured a little hole. I would sit in the dark sucking at the sweet milk with a voluptuous feeling all over my body that I could not explain. I thought then that being in love and sucking at the sweet milk were related.

—Anaïs Nin,
The Delta of Venus

hold hands and French kiss as a waiter slices them some ham and cheese to go. It is 1:38 a.m. and she is wearing sunglasses. Brandishing a sword-like loaf of flour-caked bread, they duck into the night.

The man with the toothpick devours an egg sandwich as an equally silent friend joins him for a *café con leche*. "Real Madrid won!" rise hysterical cheers at match's end. The two are oblivious to the news, gesticulating with all the fury of deaf-mute Mediterraneans.

The sheep's head has been bathed in scathing oil before reaching our table. Admiring its intrinsic beauty and sensuous curves, Jose squeezes a lemon and bathes the crispy cranium in its juice. He yanks the crooked incisors out of the animal's jaw and attacks with his own, chomping into its jowls as if they were the inner thighs of Aphrodite. He squints his eyes at me, nods his head and puts his forefinger against his thumb to indicate ecstasy.

"With those teeth, it makes you wonder who's eating whom," says Luis.

"Jose, you look like a cannibal!" cries Susana.

"You're supposed to suck on it," he assures them.

"What's this?" asks Rocio, grabbing a fork. "The brain?" With an easy flip of the utensil, she plucks out the entire cerebral hemisphere. "Not the whole brain?!"

With the grace of one well-versed in European table manners, she daintily isolates a chunk of golden grey matter, slices it off with her knife, and pops it into her mouth with overturned fork. She grimaces. "Oh, yuck! It's horrible!"

"It's really soft, yet dense, with the same texture throughout," adds Jose with the objective, authoritative voice of cerebral connoisseurship.

He stabs his fork at yet another ovine morsel.

"The eye, the eye!" come the cackles, almost in unison. Any takers? He almost puts it in his mouth, but the mind is stronger than the palate. There are no objections when he returns it to the platter.

Rowdy soccer fans down beers and crash into one another as a Chinese woman wanders through the bar with roses for sale. The frenetic counterside companions continue to scream in their earnest silence.

"I'm full," declares Rolando, smiling. "I'm fulfilled. I'm realized."

Susana puts her arm around him and gives him a peck on the cheek.

The rest of us kick back in the greasy afterglow of their feeding frenzy, staring at the plateful of gnawed bones and oily napkins before us. Only one eye—the sheep's—stares back. Rocio begins to yawn off as Jose reaches over and kisses her. She lights up a cigarette.

The younger, puritanical me would have shuddered at the sight. But years in Spain have transformed me. This herbivore was party to sexual bonding over body parts—if only in a voyeuristic sense— and savored every minute of it. The new me savors the *tortilla española* with sensual twists of the tongue and finds his *petite mort* in a plate of *patatas bravas*. I still don't need a sheep's brain to keep me warm at night, but maybe it's only a matter of time.

I ask Susana if she'll be able to kiss Luis after all this.

"I'll have to think twice about it," she warns.

I remind her of the tiny ceramic sign at Nely's: "Neither in bed nor at the table is there room for shame."

As the twisted offspring of hippies and Seventh-day Adventists, Brett Allan King has been condemned to life-long vegetarianism. Even as an integrated American-Spaniard, he has never seen a bullfight or snacked on a pig's ear.

*

"I could eat these things all night." "These things" were ordinary commercial potato chips. The setting was a raffish tavern in Carthage, Missouri, where I was maladroitly attempting to romance an Ozark mountain girl over a few late-evening beers.

I should have known better when my inamorata bet me I couldn't finish two family-size sacks of chips in ten minutes. As an occasional ingester of glass and razor blades (talents she would display after a pleasant sufficiency of 3.2 brews), Kate had made herself privy to certain masticatory arcana of which I was altogether ignorant. (Another of her wee-hour specialties was traversing a lengthy railroad trestle in the semi-nude while hanging by her hands from its underside, a hundred feet or so above a boulder-strewn gulley.) Hell, I reasoned, two large sacks of chips don't add up to a pound of provender. How could I lose? "What do you bet?" I demanded. "You do it, and you can feel my tits," she replied. I don't remember what I'd have forfeited had I failed. Perhaps just the chance to fondle the flesh.

The upshot of the story is that I felt Kate's tits that night. I also felt as though a troupe of Cossacks had performed a saber dance in my mouth and rubbed the contents of a salt mine into my myriad wounds. What I'd failed to take into account was that potato chips snaffled up in inordinate quantity and inordinate haste have the same effect on human tissue as so many improperly masticated razor blades or drinking glasses. Exquisite as it might have been in other circumstances, the first real feel I'd ever copped didn't seem worth a week of painful convalescence.

—Jay Jacobs, *A Glutton for Punishment: Confessions of a Mercenary Eater*

MARIANNE DRESSER

* * *

Momos at Tashi's

Not every girl is material.

FOR MOST WESTERN TRAVELERS, BODH GAYA, BIHAR STATE, northeastern India, is pretty well off the beaten track. Little more than a string of houses and shops along a dirt road, this small village has had electricity, which falters regularly or fails outright, for only a couple of decades. But the town and its central landmark, the Mahabodhi Temple, is one of the world's true holy places. Renowned as the site of the Buddha's enlightenment, Bodh Gaya is a spiritual magnet for Buddhists from all over Asia; temples and monasteries punctuate the surrounding rice fields. Besides the shifting populations of pilgrims who gather here at different times throughout the year for various *pujas,* the town is home to Hindus, Muslims, Sikhs, and a sizable population of Tibetans. While the rest of India regularly tears itself apart in bloody sectarian strife, various expressions of faith seem to coexist peacefully in Bodh Gaya.

I'm here as part of a group of 25 American students on a semester-long Religious Studies program. My fellow students are college kids from all over the United States, most of whom have never been out of the country before, most of whom regard the study of Eastern religions as a strictly academic pursuit. As a college "resumer" in my thirties, and a Buddhist practitioner with a fair amount of travel in Asia already under my belt, I'm rather a rough fit to the "study abroad" profile. Armed with native shyness, a lack of enthusiasm for the group ethos, and an overdeveloped sense of my own difference, I do little to close the gap between the sometimes raucous adolescent community of my young co-travelers and myself. I cherish my solitude and my time here as an extended retreat, and occasional loneliness seems a small price to pay for four months of uninterrupted study and reflection.

Our group is housed at the Burmese Vihar, a pilgrim's lodge on the far end of town, where we attend morning and early afternoon classes in philosophy, history, anthropology, and Tibetan or Hindi language. The Vihar provides the group two meals a day, served at an open pavilion in the courtyard. The menu is limited, but the food is hearty and plentiful—eggs in various guises, *nan, chapati,* and *puri,* vegetable curries, *dal,* rice, freshly-made yogurt, fruit, and bottomless urns of *chai*—strong, sweet, milky Indian tea. Every few days, Devi, the Vihar's cheerful, matronly Indian cook, gives us a treat: a Western meal of spaghetti or pizza. The students look forward to this with a degree of longing all out of proportion to the actual food, which usually barely approximates the form, taste, or texture of the "original." But familiarity and nostalgia are powerful condiments.

Besides providing guest lodging, the Burmese Vihar is a working monastery and temple. So, in accordance with Theravada Buddhist custom, no food is served after the second and main meal of the day at noon. The monks in residence, fortified by their monastic training and vows, take this in stride. But middle-class Americans, conditioned to three meals a day, packed refrigerators, and immediate gratification, haven't cultivated such spiritual sustenance. By four or five o'clock, most of the students are heeding their appetites and heading off for snacks and long discussions over endless cups of *chai* or watery Indian beer in a village café.

Lately, Tashi's, one of the Tibetan restaurants, has become a favorite hangout. Tashi's has especially tasty *momos,* dumplings stuffed with spiced meat or vegetables which are either fried or steamed. *Momos* are savory and filling, and you can get a big plate of them for just a few rupees. By general consensus, after weeks of sampling Bodh Gaya's culinary offerings, the *momos* at Tashi's have become the preferred surrogate supper. Though I generally avoid the mass exodus to town in the evening, I like Tashi's, too. I've taken to going there during the slow afternoon hours when I can sit quietly with my open journal or a half-written aerogramme and a pot of tea before me.

Tsering, a stout woman of indeterminate middle age, single-handedly runs the makeshift restaurant with one young helper, the girl called Tashi. Tsering seems weathered beyond her years—a hard life in exile—but exudes the unassailable good cheer and sturdy energy that all the Tibetan refugees in the village—especially the women—seem to have. Even in the Indian heat, she wears traditional Himalayan clothing: a heavy, dark wool robe embroidered with red, blue, and gold thread, and thick yakskin boots. Her long black hair streaked with grey is bundled in a thick braid that rests on her wide back. Wild wisps of escaped hair frame a handsome face animated by warm brown eyes.

The delta of wrinkles creasing off to her temples deepens whenever Tsering laughs—and she laughs often, an easy laugh that hints at depths of wisdom and experience. I imagine her as one of those fierce female Tantric Buddhist deities who specialize in messing with the egos of pompous practitioners. A terrific *dakini* disguised as a decrepit old woman who, in order to test his attachment to his own spiritual attainment, delights in offering some overly pious monk a slab of meat dragged through the dust, or herself for an amorous tryst in the charnel grounds.

Tashi's is in a big rectangular tent with reinforced walls. Several long wooden tables flanked by benches take up most of the space. Extending into the room is a wall formed of planks on which are draped colorful Tibetan rugs. Woven from coarse wool that still smells faintly of highland sheep, the rugs are available for purchase, as Tsering will casually inform you when she delivers the requisite pot of dark barley tea to your table.

This woolen wall separates the main eating room from the cramped, smoky kitchen, a closet-sized area in which a cast-iron woodstove holds pride of place, next to a banked brick cooking fire. A dented, smoke-blackened pot, bubbling over merrily with rice, is suspended at flame height from a hook–and–chain attached to a ceiling beam. There is a wooden table where chopping and other food prep is done, next to a large plastic tub full of washwater balanced on two metal industrial drums. On the earthen floor, glossy-black with countless footfalls, are several plastic buckets of water in varying shades of cleanliness. Today when I arrive, I see a passel of *momos*—the fried variety, greasy but delicious—sizzling in a good inch of highly suspect amber oil in a pan on the stovetop.

A small freestanding shelf facing the dining area has been made into an altar that bears a picture of the Dalai Lama, a smiling, kind-faced monk on a brocade-draped throne. In front of the faded photo postcard sits a small bronze statue of Shakyamuni Buddha draped in a white lama scarf, and an incense urn with a stick of Nag Champa always burning, its familiar cloying scent mingling with the steam, woodsmoke, and cooking smells oozing out of the kitchen. Along the other side of the tent runs a raised packed-earth platform layered with thick wool rugs and dusty cushions. I've occasionally been lucky enough to have been here when a group of Tibetan women informally convenes at Tashi's for a chat. Ignoring the tables, they lounge casually on the cushions, threading occasional peals of laughter through the bright tapestry of their conversation.

Bodh Gaya is one of several places around the world with a large community of Tibetan exiles who comprise what has become a Tibetan diaspora. The Chinese invaded Tibet in 1950, and the Dalai Lama fled in 1959, taking many of his people with him. Since that time, thousands have followed suit.

—RS

In a corner of the platform, close to the table nearest the back wall where I like to sit, is a battered old Chinese tape player. Sometimes it's straining Hindi pop through its tiny speakers, more often traditional Tibetan or Nepali folk music. When a Western student or tourist comes in, though, Tsering usually sends her young helper to put in one of the Western music tapes they have on hand. True to form, as I settle myself at my favorite table, Tashi runs over to the tape player right away, without Tsering's prompting. She puts in a tape, turns to me, and smiles proudly as Madonna's voice, unremarkable in the best of circumstances, begins to warble unsteadily through the room. The murky, third-generation bootleg tape is badly warped, the sound tinny and distorted. "Holida-ay…" sings the Virgin-Whore icon of American pop culture, "it would be so-o nice…"

All travelers must at some point encounter a cracked-mirror version of their own culture abroad. My travels had held their share of odd moments—hearing the reedy, soulful voice of Mississippi bluesman Robert Johnson in a Yogyakarta café, being treated to broad smiles of delight on the faces of two Indonesian boys who conjured up a Creedence Clearwater Revival cassette with which to repeatedly serenade me, the lone foreigner, on a torturous eight-hour bus ride across the mountainous spine of Flores. I had deciphered enough fractured English on Japanese t-shirts, Bangkok menus, and New Delhi shop signs to fill a warped dictionary.

But today, as I sit waiting for my order of steamed *momos,* I begin to gnaw at the bones of the culture clash unfolding here in this dark, cool tent: the Dalai Lama and Madonna, the sacred and the self-consciously profane. In the West, the original meaning of "holy day"—a day dedicated to honoring the sacred—had long since been watered down into the notion of "vacation," an absence. I think about what has been lost in the translation, and uneasily digest the extravagant irony of hearing Madonna's paean to holiday leisure in the company of Tsering and Tashi, a people living in a diaspora. A creeping sense of complicity lodges in my gut as I trace my link to the machinery delivering this trite message—manufactured in China, Tibet's oppressor, a country aided in its economic development by the "most-favored nation" status granted by *my* country. And yet, here my good-natured Tibetan hosts, not without a savvy sense of good business, wish to make me, a privileged Westerner, feel comfortable in their humble restaurant by playing the familiar music of my world.

Collapsing under the mental weight of these thoughts, I feel sadness and a profound sense of isolation. Perhaps my self-seeking wanderings in Asia, my presence here in India, even my adopted Buddhist identity, are themselves evidence of a particularly insidious form of Ugly Americanism.

I sip my warm tea, musty with the taste of dust and poverty, so caught up in my own internal meanderings that it takes me a few seconds to notice that Tashi has come and sat down next to me on the bench. She stares at me, resting her head on her hand, brown eyes alight with a child's unashamed curiosity. She says something to me, inflected as a question. "What did you say?" I ask back, hoping the tone of my voice conveys the gratitude I feel for having been pulled back into the present, into reality. So begins a half-gestured, half-spoken, completely fractured and delightful exchange.

Tashi keeps repeating some words to me, *"oo-laà,"* while pointing to herself, and then *"a-caà,"* pointing to me. I go along with the lesson, repeat *"a-caà"* and point to myself, *"oo-laà"* at Tashi, back and forth. I've no idea what this signifies, but she seems happy with the game, and I marvel at the unexpected, and unexpectedly welcome, contact. (Later, I discover that these words are the familial terms for "younger sister" and "older sister." Tashi had named me her sister, and I—dedicated loner, confirmed renunciant—had in turn claimed her as mine.)

Meanwhile, Madonna drones on, until suddenly the tape breaks and sputters to a stop, mangling the last strains of "Material Girl." Fitting end, I think. My companion laughs as I exaggeratedly wince and cover my ears. Tsering leans out from the kitchen and calls out to Tashi, who leaps up and goes over to the wooden shelf that supports the shrine. She motions me to follow her, and kneels on the floor in front of the shrine. I wonder if I'm about to be initiated into some esoteric rite, or allowed to offer incense to the image of the Dalai Lama—for Tibetans, the incarnation of Chenrezi, the Bodhisattva of Compassion. Instead, Tashi lifts the thick, burgundy cloth draping the shrine and points underneath to a cardboard box that holds a bunch of cassette tapes. Another sort of honor: I'm being invited to select the next tape.

I rummage through the pile of cassettes, many trailing twisted, frayed strips of magnetic tape. In India, nothing is thrown away; these plastic carcasses might yet find some use. I finally choose one bearing Hindi characters; whatever it is—an exquisite *raga* or more of the ubiquitous brash Indian pop music like the stuff that comes over the wall from the compound next door during morning meditation at the Vihar—it surely won't be American pop music. Tashi seems to find my choice funny and calls out to Tsering, who pokes her head out again and adds her laughter to Tashi's and mine. It *is* funny, and tender. Like the varicolored streamers ship passengers toss to well-wishers on the dock, our shared laughter is a connecting thread thrown across borders of culture and language.

The place begins to fill with the sound of South Indian folk music. Tashi and I return to the table just as Tsering emerges from the kitchen with a plate of hot, wonderfully aromatic *momos* and a fresh pot of tea. I thank her in English, sketching an *anjali,* that graceful, commonplace Indian gesture made by joining one's hands at heart level and bowing slightly, in greeting or gratitude. She smiles and nods, gesturing to Tashi to follow her, to leave me alone to eat. I demur politely, motioning for Tashi to stay, and she does, chattering happily while I apply myself in earnest to the savory dumplings. These *momos* are especially delicious—the best I've ever had. Mingling with the spices is the taste of newfound connection, the rich flavor of hospitality.

Looking up from my empty plate, I see Tsering approaching with a small dish of two unordered *gulab jamen.* I'm momentarily nonplused and sit blankly, trying to recall if perhaps I mistakenly indicated that I wanted some of the sticky, dense Indian sweets. Tsering's back disappears around the wall into the kitchen. Well, no matter, it's only a few rupees more. I pick up one of the *gulab jamen,* and push the dish gently toward Tashi as I tip back my head slightly and slowly place the sweet in my mouth. I watch her from the corner of my eyes. She grins shyly and reaches for the other one. We chew together companionably.

Washing down the gritty, sugary traces of the *gulab jamen* with a last cup of tea, I realize the afternoon has slipped away. It's nearly time for evening meditation back at the Vihar, and I must say goodbye to Tashi's for today. I pick up my unopened notebook and walk toward the turned-back canvas flap that serves as a doorway. Tashi skips along with me as far as the table near the front where Tsering is relaxing with a glass of tea, smoking a *bidi*. I ask her the amount I owe; she holds up both hands: ten rupees. But that can't be right, I protest, it just covers the *momos*, not the dessert…. I hand her fifteen rupees.

Tsering shakes her head, no, and hands me back five rupees, saying in halting English, "Please, you welcome." She smiles that luminous smile that sends the wrinkles scurrying from her eyes, and with one arm draped around Tashi's shoulders, waves me off casually, the way one does an old friend. I walk back on the narrow path that winds through the fields flanking the village, enjoying the various rich smells from the cooking fires in the houses along the way, and the fading light glinting off the flowering tips of the rice plants. It's nearly harvest time. I'm perfectly content. Nourished. Wanting for nothing.

By the time the red-brick wall of the Vihar comes into view, I find myself humming a tune. *Celebrate…just one day out of life….*

Writer and editor Marianne Dresser has edited Buddhist Women on the Edge: Contemporary Perspectives from the Western Frontier. *She lives in San Francisco and wanders off to Asia every few years for a different taste of life.*

★

Tell the cook, thanks for the meal.
—Buddha, his last words

MARGO TRUE

Backstage at Cafe Annie

The journey is not through a time zone,
but through a kitchen door.

ONCE A WEEK FOR FIVE MONTHS, I LEFT ALL THAT WAS FAMILIAR TO journey to a world few people have ever seen. This place to which I traveled was not far by measures of distance, but was, at least in the beginning, as foreign to me as Timbuktu. It was behind the scenes at one of the most elegant shows in Houston—Cafe Annie. I thought its kitchen would mirror the dining room's subtlety and polished reserve. What I found was a different story.

Happily eating in the warm, luscious, mahogany-paneled dining room at Cafe Annie, you'd never guess what really goes on in the kitchen. Behind that beautiful copper-lined window at the back of what is arguably the best Southwestern restaurant in the country, a kind of orchestrated madness prevails, with cooks scuttling in front of a bank of stoves and griddles, preparing a half-dozen orders simultaneously in a breathless sort of dance. Where you sit, all is calm, gracious, dignified; but in the kitchen, adrenaline flows, the flames from the grill practically boil the blood, and searing hunks of meat and fish fly from oven to broiler to plate. And every once in a while, the cooks will stop and peer through the window out at you, the customer, serene in your enjoyment of the food.

The first time I ate at Cafe Annie, I knew, from the initial bite of cream biscuit with spicy shrimp filling to the last crumb of buttery, chewy almond cake, that I was having a rare meal. Each course seemed connected to the next by an underlying concept; the layers and sequences of tastes, though distinct as notes in a piece of music, had an integrity of style and flavor. Hoping to find out how this gustatory symphony had been produced, I called the kitchen manager and asked if I could work as an apprentice. He agreed, but it was a calculated risk: the restaurant would be getting an extra pair of hands, for free—albeit an inexperienced pair, since I'd never worked in a professional kitchen. But they knew I was a food writer, too; what if I found a hair in the mashed potatoes or slimy lettuce in the salad? As the months went by, I began to look forward to my weekly sessions at Cafe Annie not just for the lessons in food preparation and technique, but also because of the people who work there. My Saturday night sojurns became eight-hour immersions not just in a world of gastronomy, but in a kind of human comedy.

JUNE 6: At 4:30 p.m., I go around to the back entrance and climb a beat-up set of stairs—black scuff marks trailing down the wall, peeling paint near the baseboards—to the office, where the walls are plastered with receipts, memos, awards Cafe Annie has won, and framed articles about the restaurant. Greg Martin, sous-chef and kitchen manager, sits at an IBM clone, cursing WordPerfect for Windows as he struggles to print the specials menu for dinner. He's tall—nearly six feet—and broad-shouldered, with bright round blue eyes and a shiny crewcut the color of wheat in the sun. He has the face of a cherub.

Greg hands me a side-buttoning cook's jacket made of heavy white polyester. Down we go into the kitchen, passing executive chef and part-owner Robert Del Grande, who looks a lot like a young Rock Hudson, on his way up. Though his face is boyish and soft, he wears a slightly worried expression that I soon learn is nearly constant. His artfully tousled hair is threaded with gray and he carries about him the aura of a rock musician; maybe it's the sloping shoulders, or the way his upper body leans back, relaxed, like it's waiting to hold a guitar. (In fact, he does play one—he and Dean Fearing, executive chef at Dallas's The Mansion, have an occasional two-man band called The Barbwires.) When he talks, his voice stays down deep in his throat.

The air in the kitchen is sharp with the aroma of roasting poblano peppers. Though the restaurant won't open for another hour and a half, the room hums with activity. The dozen or so cooks rush to and fro, throwing herbs into blenders, chopping, whipping up sauces, and tasting, constantly tasting—the mark of all good cooking. Greg strides through the clean, spacious prep area, bellowing, "Put your aprons on! Where are your aprons?" Next to the prep area in a long narrow room of its own is the service line, where the food is cooked and set on the stainless-steel pickup counter for the waiters. Four small printers spaced along this counter churn out the orders, which waiters have punched into one of the IBM-clone terminals out in the restaurant. The equipment in the kitchen—including a 15-gallon steam-powered stockpot, a 10-gallon tilt braiser, a 4-foot grill and a special smoking oven—is state-of-the-art, and cost more than $150,000.

Though Robert is clearly the driving force and inspiration behind Cafe Annie, and San Hemwattakit, his head chef from Thailand, develops many of the recipes, Greg is Big Daddy in the kitchen. He's everywhere at once, solving problems, culinary and interpersonal, with good humor and directness. Like Robert, he is always teaching. "Why is dairy equipment lined with copper?" he asks me. I have no idea. "It's to give Americans the trace element of copper in their diets."

6 p.m.: Cissy Yin, a sweet-faced Chinese-American with short, shiny black hair, is the only woman here tonight other than me. Her spine is ramrod-straight, her motions rapid and precise; she looks incredibly alert and with-it. She gives me my first job— stripping thyme leaves from the stem. I'm all thumbs. The little leaves refuse to detach neatly and the stems break up in my hands. Cissy is moving at warp speed. Hell, they all are: I feel like I'm watching a Julia Child video on fast-forward.

I start to peel and chop a pile of big, firm shrimp. Greg watches as I hack away, then asks gently, "Do you know how to use a knife?"

"Er, only in my own kitchen."

"You don't know how to use a knife. I'll show you."

He hands me a wicked-looking cleaver he's just sharpened. He grasps the food with his left hand, tucking his fingertips under his knuckles; he holds the knife in his right hand, and touches the blade to the knuckles of the left hand. "That way you always know where the knife is," says Greg. Then he slices through the food with a fluid, fast, rocking motion. My God, I'm afraid I'll lose a finger. All around me, blades are flashing through tomatoes, onions, and peppers. An everyday utility knife at Cafe Annie has a short life—maybe two months.

Greg, who started eight years ago at Cafe Annie as a butcher, gives me a crash course in cutting meat. "It's just anatomy," he says, carving up a rack of lamb. "Animals are made to be taken apart." He heaves his cleaver aloft. THWACK! A chop is born.

Now he's butterflying salmon steaks. "You know, dreams are being sold here tonight. Nobody in their right mind would pay $25 for a piece of fish. It's all image…That's what they pay for: dreams," he says, hefting a firm, perfect steak in his hand. This restaurant, he says, is about so much more than food. "It's a big production. It's entertainment. It's showbiz."

6:15 p.m.: "Come watch the sharks," says Greg. Milling around the pickup counter, which separates the kitchen from the restaurant, are about a dozen black-jacketed waiters, gobbling from several plates of food and firing off questions. "How is this made?" "Is there thyme in this?" "Man, these potatoes are good." Waiters here can earn more than $50,000 a year. Line cooks start at $7 an hour, plus a monthly bonus of $175.

8 p.m.: I'm watching Bernardo Orozco, one of the three sous chefs; he's in charge of appetizers. Originally from Michoacan, Mexico, Bernardo started ten years ago as a pot-washer and is now considered one of the best cooks in the kitchen. He's small and

round-cheeked and can cook what looks like six things at once, banging the oven door shut with a well-placed kick, hurling skillets and plates from stovetop to oven to broiler with tongs and a towel. Every now and then he flips a plate in the air just for fun.

Without warning, he starts howling like a wolf. No one pays the slightest bit of attention; I'm told he does it all the time.

Before the night is over, Bernardo has prepared for us a slice of spicy black-bean terrine with a round of smooth white goat cheese embedded in the middle, and smoked chicken enchiladas in a rich, dark, complex *mole* of roasted almonds, chocolate, and pasilla chilies.

*M*ostly chefs are maniacs. High-strung. I think most of them take it very seriously, no matter how bad the food may be. They think this art thing is going on.

—Michael Salmons, quoted in *The Chefs, the Cooks, and the Churlish* by Bruce Griffin Henderson

Tommy Child, the pastry chef, gives me a slice of his intense chocolate pecan pie. It starts to melt as soon as it hits my tongue, and I feel like I've just driven fast over a rise in the road and am momentarily suspended in space. I also manage to eat half a biscuit grilled with butter and honey. Thank God I'd been standing up and moving around a lot or I think all this eating would've felled me.

8:45 p.m.: Our aprons are stained and the towels tucked into them are grimy. Food litters the floor. Mimi Del Grande, Robert's tiny, energetic wife and the restaurant's general manager, dashes through the kitchen in a backless blouse, miniskirt, and high heels, navigating shreds of lettuce and blobs of sauce. The front of the house is her province; she's the one who orchestrates seating and oversees the wait staff. "Work, work, work!" she yells cheerily, hands waving in the air, and disappears into the dining room.

9 p.m.: The kitchen goes into overdrive. I'm standing in front of a bank of stoves and griddles, sandwiched between the line cooks, trying to stay out of the way as they fling hunks of meat onto the grill. All of us are scarlet-faced and bug-eyed from the

heat. Gary Miller, a big redhaired jokester who is wearing a t-shirt with a tongue on it under his cook's whites, is absolutely pouring sweat. Later he tells me that if he ever writes an autobiography, he's going to call it *Hangover in the Heat*. Greg yanks the meat orders sputtering from his station's printer: "Order an antelope medium rare. Order two rack, both medium. Pick up a chick, a tuna, a sword, a snap." I can't hear much over the whirring of the fans and the thunderous roar of the dishwasher.

Down the line, Bernardo howls. The line looks like a MASH unit in triage; sizzling hot iron skillets full of fish and chicken fly through the air, tongs flash, plates vanish into the arms of waiters. Sam Saddemi, a small cook with mournful brown eyes who resembles Al Pacino, cuts his hand on the jagged edge of a can and runs over to the first-aid station to doctor himself.

Suddenly, through the narrow window that opens onto the restaurant, I glimpse a customer who's come up to the kitchen to watch for a moment. All I can see is a low-cut, black velvet sheath, tanned smooth skin, and on the perfect, tapering arm, a diamond bracelet. I imagine how clean and cool she is, how good she must smell. The ends of her shiny black bob are just visible. She's a visitor from another world.

10 p.m.: Tommy plates desserts. On his counter sit a bewildering array of sauces: cold ones (vanilla, caramel, orange, espresso, raspberry, and creme fraiche) and hot ones (chocolate and caramel), plus berries, nuts, grated chocolate, and powdered sugar. Each dessert is finished with a different combination of sauces, and each is garnished in a different pattern. Tommy finishes off a slab of chocolate cake with sauces and powdered sugar in 30 seconds flat. Somehow, he can spin a lacy ribbon of hot caramel from a blunt ladle. When I try, I get thick glops.

Midnight: Though the restaurant closes at 10:30, people are still eating. My feet are killing me. Not just my feet—I hurt from my strained hip bones to the tips of my toes. I've never stood up for eight solid hours before. Tommy confides that he wears orthopedic shoes.

JUNE 13: I'm standing right in front of the mesquite grill, the hottest four square feet in the kitchen, trying to learn to cook meat. After ten minutes I'm slick with sweat inside my polyester jacket. At the lip of the grill rises a sheet of ferocious hot wind, sucked straight up by the fan's intake valve. Every time I lean in to turn a steak, my eyeballs broil. I wonder if my bangs will suddenly combust. "You gotta go like this," says John Moore, the third sous-chef, darting his tongs in and out of the heat curtain like he's jousting with an invisible enemy. It helps, but not enough. I run to the walk-in freezer and stand in the cold air while fish on ice stare silently up at me.

JULY 11: Bernardo is one of those lucky people who has found his life's mission. When he gets home after cooking all day, he says, "My mind is tired, but my body still wants to cook. I get excited. I love to cook."

It's slow tonight. Bernardo hates it when it's like this. "The white boys, they like it," he jokes. "But when it's fast, you just cook, and you forget about your problems."

From the celebrated Monsieur Auguste Escoffier down to the palest and most anonymous aide de cuisine, the roof-top photograph presents in microcosm the rigid hierarchy of what the cooks themselves called le métier. The fiery underworld to which the brigade returned, once the photographer had folded up his tripod and put away his black cloth, was another of its unquestioned elements. The kitchens, however, were a region almost totally unknown to the vast majority of the Carlton's clients. Few ever expressed any desire to see them, and there were long-standing historical reasons for this. For centuries kitchens had been shunned as places of blood, dirt, grease, and undesirable smells, animated by the shouting and swearing of uncouth, uneducated and obscene cooks. They were also well-recognized sources of flooding and fire. Even in the 1850s, French domestic handbooks advised the mistress of the house never to set foot in her own kitchen lest she be tainted, physically and morally, by its polluted atmosphere; whenever it became necessary to communicate directly with the cook, the interview should take place in the more salubrious atmosphere of the drawing-room.

—Timothy Shaw, *The World of Auguste Escoffier*

10 p.m.: Robert bends over some *chilaquiles* (tortillas with soft-scrambled eggs) he's frying on the stove. When he cooks, he leans in close to the food and frowns at it as though willing it to tell him how to improve the flavor. After plating the food, he rummages through a container of cilantro, looking for the perfect sprig to decorate the plate.

Often, when a dish isn't quite right, he'll poke through raw ingredients, looking for inspiration. I ask him if he can taste the missing flavors in his imagination. "Yes. It's like a hole that needs to be filled. It's harder when it's already good, when it just needs a little something." He adds a few drops of maple syrup to tomatillo guacamole, tastes, ponders. Flavor, for him, should be dynamic, like the tension in a work of art. "It's like Kant's theory of the imagination versus understanding. Jalapenos and sugar—wow! The brain can't process it."

11:15 p.m.: Cleanup. The big black rubber mats are hauled outside to be sprayed, and the floor is slick with food. Hurrying to finish and go home, everyone walks with short, waddling steps to avoid slipping. We look like a bunch of racing penguins. Each cook returns food to the walk-ins and scours his station with soapy water; the griddles are still so hot that the soap cooks into little balls and rolls away. The kitchen is spotless.

AUGUST 7: Greg is in an experimental mood. He hands me packages of Japanese miso and tempeh from Whole Foods Market, and tells me to get creative. So I use the recipes on the backs of the packages as a starting point, throwing minced jalapeno and lime juice into the miso to make tempeh marinade. Greg adds vinegar, brown sugar, julienned lemon zest, and tamari. The taste is zingy. Unfortunately the tempeh, even when marinated, skewered, and grilled with onion and portobello mushroom, still tastes like sour pressed beans. What to do? This is supposed to be the night's special appetizer. Greg quickly replaces the tempeh with butterflied shrimp, and salvages the dish.

Gary comes up to Robert, clutching his chest and moaning, "I'm going to pass out." (He's ready to head to Live Bait, his favorite bar.) Robert gives him an appraising look. "You know, Gary, I really admire a line cook who passes out on the job, and still keeps turning steaks with two fingers. But the best line cook is the one who says, after he goes down, 'Use my body for firewood.'" Gary shuffles back to the grill.

Midnight: Robert and Greg and I go up to the cool wine room to taste buyer's samples. I'm a novice in the complex world of wine, so I keep my mouth shut while they talk about vintages and structures and the curious burgundy nose of a certain pinot noir. Robert launches into a treatise about the proper way to cook chicken. He holds a Ph.D. in biochemistry, and it pervades his cooking technique: When a sauce breaks (separates), he once told a reporter for *Elle,* "the scientist in me knows how to save it." When he dots his fiery "voodoo sauce" over quesadillas, he knows it will lose some of its heat, because the oil molecules trap the chili.

Rusty Sanjana, the dapper, charming Pakistani floor manager (Greg likes to call him the "ringmaster"; in other restaurants, he'd be called the maitre d'), ushers in a garish couple. She's heavily made up and already grinning; her suit is a bilious lime-green. He's wearing a loud Op-art shirt and a thick Rolex studded with diamonds. The woman squeezes Robert's shoulder as if he were her pet dog. "Oh—was this a good year?" she says, lifting a bottle of wine. Her date talks about his vendor in New York and a particular wine that he just loves, but damnit, can't remember the name of. Robert just nods, courteously noncommittal. They are the guests.

AUGUST 15: I'm mincing onions for a sauce. Though I've been chopping for weeks now, my entire upper torso seizes up with tension. Greg tells me I'm gripping the knife like a beginning driver grips the wheel, and shows me what to do: cut the bitter core off the onion first. Then choke up on the knife so that your fingers are resting on the blade, cut the onion in half, slice easily down in 1/4-inch increments, saw it twice horizontally, turn it, and then chop it vertically again. Beautiful.

✳

AUGUST 29: Greg beams with excitement. "I'm making the special apps tonight. HOMEMADE FLOUR TORTILLAS AND FAJITAS!!" He gives a little leap of joy.

Using packaged *masa,* Greg forms a ball of dough and rolls it out into circles. Bernardo, a man from the land of tortillas, clearly thinks Greg is nuts. There are bundles of perfect La Espiga de Oro tortillas in the walk-in. "He thinks they're beautiful—but I don't think so. People, they like to dream," says Bernardo.

8:45 p.m.: Mimi bursts in, harried. "I need glasses upstairs," she barks to the dishwasher. "Pronto move move please please run run." Fifteen minutes later, she's crouched in a chair in the office upstairs, glistening and panting, spritzing her face with water, her neck with perfume. On busy nights—and nearly every Saturday is frantic—she really gets a workout. When she was pregnant two years ago, she tells me, she sometimes ate two steaks a day. "I need meat. It has to do with my aggressive personality."

Midnight: Greg and I are standing in the walk-in freezer, taking the nightly produce inventory. Greg checks through the boxes and crates while I tick off the amounts needed for the next day; when we're finished, Greg calls the order in to Kalil Fruit and Vegetable, Inc., which also supplies Tony's and Carrabba's. Cafe Annie uses dozens of purveyors, though some supply just one item.

We taste wine again tonight. Before we leave, Robert wanders around his wine room, talking to the dark, gleaming bottles, touching a few. "Hi, sweeties, how are you?" It took him and a few selected staff members years to build this collection, and it heavily reflects his personal taste—lots of red Burgundy and Bordeaux. We walk downstairs into the cavernous, dim, empty dining room, the whole place fragrant with mesquite from the grill. "This restaurant has a soul," says Greg. "It's like a freight train."

SEPTEMBER 5: In the big, spotless prep room behind the line, Greg peruses his new *Cocina Prehispanica* cookbook, his eyes bright. An idea for the night's special appetizer begins to form in his head. With Greg directing, I make pre-Hispanic guacamole, approximating the quantities: serrano chilies, white onions, a shallot, garlic, and tomatillos, diced and boiled together until soft. I blend them with avocados, salt, cilantro, and lime. The Aztecs, the cookbook tells us, called the avocado tree the "tree of testicles." With a zest born of creativity and very little time, Greg positions a curly radicchio leaf in the center of a plate, blobs egg salad on top, and curves a shrimp around it. A squiggle of the manly guacamole on the left, mahogany-brown "buckaroo sauce" on the right and fiery red voodoo sauce on top, and the dish is complete. "Robert will LOVE this idea. He LOVES egg salad," crows Greg.

The earliest written references to chile con carne date to the 1830s in Texas. It was composed of beef fat, dried beef, and crushed chile pepper, pressed and formed into the shape of a brick. It was compact, could be easily carried in saddle bags and it kept well. It could be eaten plain or cooked with beans. Some people call it the original MRE.

—Dave DeWitt, *Chile Pepper*

Robert approaches, stares at the plate, and fiddles. "This should be just a little bite, an amusement." Silently, he chops up some shrimp into the egg salad, tastes, and tells me to add a bit of minced serrano. He slices the radicchio leaf down to a small flag—"Ah! An accent!" murmurs Greg—piles a mound of the salad at one end and pushes a shrimp tail underneath the mound so it curves up like a pink sail on a small red boat. Instead of squiggling the sauces, he uses a big dot of each, and finishes by scattering chopped cilantro and grated *cotija* cheese over the plate. "Tight, focused, and centered," he says. "It shouldn't look like it's sprawling."

The line cook who was to be plating these appetizers goes home sick, so suddenly I'm in charge. Pressure! Tension flows from my neck to my hands, turning them into clumsy, fingerless blocks. Greg rushes by on the way to the grill and sprinkles fried sweet-potato shavings over the plates for texture. One of the line cooks bellows, "Four special apps!" and I'm on my way.

Several orders later, just when I think I've got it, Robert appears near my elbow and two of my carefully placed shrimp tails promptly fall over. I've cut them too short. And the radicchio leaves aren't centered. I feel like I've got bees in my head.

After 30 orders, my hands move more surely, and I'm finally able to follow the design I see in my mind. Like sports, this requires kinetic skill; you can't learn by watching alone.

8:30 p.m.: Mimi flounces through in a tiered, ruffly white eyelet dress. She looks like a cream puff.

SEPTEMBER 13: It's 6 p.m., and three of us are squeezing roasted garlic pulp from the crackly-skinned cloves for tonight's special appetizer—a melba-toast, goat cheese and marinated bean concoction. The pungent odor fills the air. Preparing the garnish, Greg wraps minced parsley in a dishtowel, runs water through it and squeezes; the towel turns vivid emerald, soaking up chlorophyll. Typically, wet parsley clumps when you sprinkle it, but now it's as easy to scatter over the plates as confetti. We anchor each little toast with a blob of goat cheese so it won't slide off-center when the waiter carries it away. Mashed potatoes under steaks work the same way, as does a walnut half under a scoop of ice cream.

10:15 p.m.: Robert and San return from catering a private dinner. San's hair spills in ringlets to his shoulders, and he wears thick-rimmed black glasses. Cooking has grown old for him, he admits. An avid hunter, he'd rather work for Texas Parks

> *The longest-running restaurant in the world, Ma Yu Ching's Bucket Chicken House, opened for business in A.D. 1153 in the Chinese city of Kaifeng. Despite several changes of dynasty and two revolutions it still serves up cheap and nourishing food to a vast throng of customers.*
>
> *Ma Yu Ching's establishment is a remarkable survival from the Sung Dynasty (A.D. 960–1279), when restaurants of all kinds blossomed in the country's capitals. They were already flourishing under the previous Tang Dynasty (A.D. 618–906): texts from that era describe the streets of main cities as being full of restaurants "to wait upon wayfarers with food and wine."*
>
> —Peter James and Nick Thorpe,
> *Ancient Inventions*

and Wildlife. San talks in rapid bursts, in a heavy Thai accent. "You have good ideas, bad ideas, and stupid ideas," he tells me. A stupid idea, he says, is when you copy a dish everyone else within a 200-mile radius is doing. Pointing to the containers of salt, pepper, and sugar, which are always used in combination to season steaks, he says, "Most people only use salt and pepper. But we use all three. In Thailand, we always have to have the sweet too." An architecture major in college, San has drawn almost every dish Cafe Annie serves; the sketches help him explain his concepts to the staff.

SEPTEMBER 26: The stars must be crossed tonight. Greg is at home, nursing the toe he broke on his kitchen wall while trying to step around his dog. Yesenia Miranda, the new pastry assistant, nearly fainted at the dessert station yesterday and was rushed to the hospital for a burst ovarian cyst. And Kip Cox, one of the line cooks, collapsed from insulin shock while driving last week and was hauled off by a police officer who presumed him drunk; he revived the next morning, behind bars. Everyone is urging him to wear a medical bracelet. Gary whips up pesto for the swordfish, tamping herbs and lemon juice and roasted pumpkin seeds into the blender with a rubber spatula. He tamps too deeply and there's a horrible grinding sound. The spatula emerges, chewed. "Adds depth," he says, grinning.

On the counter in the prep room sits a steel bowl of impossibly thin julienned leeks, carrots, and bell peppers. Robert tosses a bit of the julienne onto a plate and studies it for a moment. Then he adds lemon juice, walnut oil, and salt. More staring. Off he goes to the salad station to poke among ingredients lining the counter there. Back he comes, a thin pink sheet of smoked salmon in hand, saying, "I've got it!" He rolls the julienned vegetables up in the salmon so that the multicolored tips wave out at one end like blades of grass, and squeezes the other end into a point. "There. It looks like a squid." Moments later, he's concocted a frothy, gentle mustard-cream sauce, which he drips in dots across his "squid." Chopped chives and fried shallot-rings form a little belt across the creature to finish the plate. Food art. My job is to recreate these appetizers for the night.

9 p.m.: I've started tweaking the "tails" slightly to the side to increase the movement in the design. Robert, passing by, looks at two of my plates and murmurs, "Nice. Very nice." And Carolyn Farb, sending word back to the kitchen through her waiter, says her salmon appetizer "looks like art and poetry together." I can't help but be thrilled.

11:30 p.m.: The orders are still coming in. Robert steps away from the grill, face flushed, eyes red. "You just gotta keep going, gotta rock and roll."

Currently an editor at Gourmet *magazine, Margo True grew up traveling around the world as the daughter of a foreign service officer. Her earliest memories are of eating (rice, beans, and bananas in Brazil). She loves to cook, and, though living in New York now, still dreams about the chicken enchiladas at Cafe Annie. This excerpt is from her story of Cafe Annie which received the James Beard Foundation's M. F. K. Fisher Distinguished Writing Award in 1994.*

★

"Always have a Chinese cook," said the woman who had followed her sailor seven times round the globe, and settled at last inside the Golden Gate. "Yes, always have a Chinese cook—and never go into the kitchen!"

Is this foul slander, or the cool tongue of wisdom? When on the bottom of a casserole doth grimed grease hiss, is ignorance bliss? Probably.

Surely I have eaten many a tart that felt the floor before it felt my plate, and more than a hundred bowls of soup whose temperature was tested, consciously or not, by a fat thumb. I have even pushed dead flies to one side of an omelette or ragoût, and eaten to the last bit undaunted. I have not really minded, inside of me, because what I ate was good, and I do not think that good food can come from a bad kitchen.

It can come from a cluttered kitchen piled with used dishes, redolent with the escaped smells of garlic, vanilla, and wine-vinegar, a kitchen steamy and full of rattle and clash.

Madame Rigagnier's is like that—a dark cabinet not nine feet square, its walls banked with copper pots and pans, and a pump for water outside the door. And from that little hole, which would make an American shudder with disgust, she turns out daily two of the finest meals I've yet eaten.

Or good food can come from a gigantic factory of fine dishes, such as Arnold Bennett describes so well in a book he wrote about grand hotels.

But good food can never come from a bad kitchen. A bad kitchen is what it is for two reasons: either nobody cares whether it produces decent victuals, or it is filthy.

—M.F.K. Fisher, *The Art of Eating*

✱ ✱ ✱

Si, Simpatica

The dinner table is a bridge between cultures and sexes.

WE CAME INTO FLORENCE ON A SUNDAY EVENING, SO HUNGRY that we just dropped our packs off at the hostel and immediately started wandering around, looking for a trattoria whose smell would call us to dinner. The hostel was on the other side of the Ponte Vecchio, in an old working-class neighborhood. I was glad to stay in a less touristy area than the one we had just left in Venice. Venice had reminded me of going on Disneyland's "Pirates of the Caribbean" ride while listening to Beethoven's "Moonlight Sonata," absurdly commercial and yet…somehow sublime. After the silence and dark alley romance of Venice, Florence was a madhouse, a true city. I quickly learned that for every serene gondola in Venice, there are three sputtering Peugeot scooters in Florence.

Five minutes into our food hunt, I got my first impression of the neighborhood. We saw an angry young man sitting behind the wheel of a shiny white little puddle hopper of a car that was in an impossibly tight parallel parking spot, caught between a mini-delivery truck and yet another battered Peugeot scooter. After two attempts to maneuver his way out, he pounded the steering wheel with his fist and yelled something obscene out his window—at whom, I don't know; we were the only ones on the street. Then, he gunned his engine, and backed right over the scooter. I stood and gaped while the scooter got dragged into the street. The driver shook it off his car's fender like a person kicking a scrap of toilet paper from the bottom of his shoe and drove away.

A few minutes later, still amazed by this demonstration of local etiquette, we were drawn to a little basement place that exuded the blessed aroma of roasted chicken. The entrance was swarming with locals. We took this as a good sign of a decent meal that we could afford, for once. The Florentines were looking extremely stylish though, so before we entered we briefly debated whether or not our clothes—the backpacker's requisite unwashed sweater, jeans, and tennis shoes—would pose an aesthetic problem for the management. It had been an issue the night before in Venice. But hunger brought us to a quick decision and we hurried down the stairs to the main dining room, a rather nondescript, low ceilinged room with a large Italian flag and a framed painting of the benevolent Virgin Mary hanging on the back wall.

Inside, it appeared that every seat was taken. A few small groups, young and old, stood around the tables, talking loudly to each other and to friends across the room. Jokingly, some made encouraging gestures with their hands and faces to get other diners to hurry up and leave. So, we felt discouraged by our prospects until Anna noticed that there was one table in the back corner that had empty seats. No one else seemed interested in joining the big woman who sat alone at a six-person table, so Anna and Leonore—the friendly, multi-lingual Portuguese girls my friend and I had the good fortune to travel with since we met on the train to Venice three days before—led the way to the table where the woman graciously waved us a welcome.

Our new dinner companion's voice was startlingly deep when she greeted us, but I didn't take a good look until I was seated beside her. "Her?" My mind stumbled over the pronoun. My first coherent thought was, "Oh God, do all transsexuals have such bad fashion sense?" I knew I was gaping again, but I grew up in Sacramento, for God's sake. I had only seen transsexuals on talk shows before, like the ex-James Bond girl who admitted on

Donahue that she was once a boy. With this image in my head, I found myself immediately disappointed with our dinner companion—she was hardly glamorous, and she was not beautiful.

The features of her face were swarthy and strongly masculine. They didn't translate well into a woman's face. She winged her dark eyes heavily with black liquid liner, smudged a little at the inner corners. The rest of her makeup was done in garish crimson and green, and the layer of pasty pancake base didn't cover her stubble convincingly. She wore a silver lamé blouse, unbuttoned and tied at the midriff. It flopped open when she leaned forward to greet the others and I saw her bare breasts which were real but even smaller than mine. Undeniably, she was proud of them. The skirt she wore was a bold jungle floral print, the wraparound kind that showed the entire length of her bare, muscular legs. Her perfume, too, was floral; I remember it was a little sour on her. During dinner, I leaned back in my seat and caught a glimpse of the large tennis shoes she wore. She had badly permed hair, dyed a conspicuous shade of red. Her hair hung over shoulders that were as broad and powerful looking as a construction worker's. Her arms, too, were large and covered with dark curling hair.

When I saw her arms, I self-consciously glanced at my own. After two months of non-stop backpacking around Europe, I hadn't had a chance to bleach my arm hair, and I felt a pang of anxiety as I noted the black outgrowth. As an Arab-American girl growing up in an upper-middle class "white" neighborhood in California, I had been an easy target for cruel classmates. Surprisingly, my ethnicity was rarely the cause of direct attack, so it was my body that determined the nicknames: Mustache girl, Gorilla girl, Afro queen, Groucho Marx, Paul Bunyan. Learning quickly, I developed a sarcastic wit, and I was ready to turn it against everyone, including myself, so long as it kept the others away.

At eighteen, I had given up on fighting back by dressing and acting as androgynous as possible—I used to think, "If they're going to stare, I'll give them something to really wonder about"— and was well into what I now call my "femme" stage. Still, I couldn't get the insults out of my head, though years of electrolysis, bleach, tweezers, and razors more or less successfully fought off those "unsightly hairs." With the help of mass quantities of hair products, my curly black hair now touched my shoulders. But nothing could tame my tall, broad bone structure. I just stayed as thin as possible, and wore form-fitting clothes so that clerks in stores wouldn't come up from behind and ask me, "Can I help you with something, sir?"

My ex-boyfriend used to tell me that I was beautiful, that he got jealous when men stared as I entered a room. But I only noticed that they were staring, and I came to resent people who seemed so fond of calling me "exotic." In frustration, I once said to one of these complimentary friends, "Look, I want to be a rose, not a bird of paradise," some strange-looking flower that couldn't stop drawing attention to itself. I didn't want to admit it, but this person next to me looked like a reflection of my worst self-image. Part of me felt the urge to lean towards her and whisper confidentially, like a bad joke, "You know, you look as bad as I feel." I wanted to be rational, sensitive and non-judgmental, but instead, I became highly self-conscious of my reactions. I didn't want to stare, but I did, and she knew it.

Apparently, she had ordered before we arrived and our waiter suddenly appeared with her meal, abruptly placing it on the edge of the table without a word or glance. Either she was on as tight a budget as us or, like me, she was very conscious of her figure because she only had one small salad, a few slices of bread, and a half carafe of white wine for dinner. I looked at her dinner as curiously as I looked at her. She noticed this, too, and had the Portuguese girls ask me if I had ever tried the salad, made from fresh buffalo mozzarella, ripe Roma tomatoes, and young basil leaves. I answered that I'd never even seen mozzarella like that—could you make cheese out of buffalo milk?—I was used to the rubbery stuff we put on pizzas at home.

She expertly took the flasks of olive oil and balsamic vinegar in her massive hands, delicately holding aloft her long flame red nails, and poured it over the sliced tomatoes and cheese. Then, she sprinkled a little salt and fresh black pepper over the whole plate and

immediately offered it to me. I was impatiently waiting to order
my own meal and the salad looked incredibly appetizing, all white,
red, and green—I thought, "They must love this dish, it's the colors of their flag." For a moment, I felt afraid that she would entreat
me to use her own fork or something, but she generously waited
until I speared a piece before she took her first bite. It was gorgeous. The light, spongy soft texture of the mozzarella was set off
by the tomato's firm freshness, and bits of basil stuck in my back
teeth, aromatic and warm. The olive oil lent just the right touch of
mellowness to the tangy sweet balsamic while crunching on the
pepper made sparks of hot flavor in my mouth. I wanted another
bite, but was too shy to ask.

I don't remember much of the girls' conversation with our dinner companion. I spent most of the evening waiting for the girls
to translate bits of the conversation for me while I did the "smile
and nod" thing, trying not to
smile too broadly at her theatrical flamboyance. Like most
Italians I've met, almost everything she said was not just spo-
ken, but delivered with great passion. Her voice and laugh drew
gawks and mutters from the diners around us. I was embarrassed
for both of us, so I kept my wine glass in motion while she spoke.
Once, she laughed with the girls, leaned over, and filled my glass
from her own carafe. I understood the gentle, mocking generosity
of the gesture. A minute later, she reached out to touch my hair. I
let her, noting to myself (rather cruelly) that all Italian men seemed
to love my curls.

*To the hungry soul, every
bitter thing is sweet.*
—*Proverbs 27:7*

She was a Neapolitan, she said, but left Naples because "life was
not so fun there." Florence was better because the Tuscans "knew
how to live." She was deeply (and loudly) patriotic. She proudly
listed places we tourists had to experience while we were visiting
her beautiful country: Had we been to Venice? she demanded. One
phrase, emphatically repeated while she sat with us, stuck with me,
even in Italian: *"Vivi nel momento, come se l'ultimo."* Finally, she
turned towards me and struggled to translate it herself, gesticulat-

ing as if she wanted to pull the right words out of the air: "You have to live your life, you know…every moment like—the last!" When we were halfway through our meal, she paid her bill, wished us a good end to our trip, and left the restaurant. I was fascinated—and exhausted—by her. At that moment, I was relieved to see her go.

We slowly finished off our small plates of pasta and bread, drank the red house wine, and talked until the restaurant emptied out and closed around us. We talked about our lives, the next day's plans, and the transsexual whose name, we acknowledged then, we never did ask. The fettuccine alfredo I had for my dinner was very good, but I wish I had ordered that salad. It has been a favorite of mine since that night, but it's never been the same. Maybe the mozzarella was particularly fresh, or maybe I was just starving and the beauty of that bite was unnaturally enhanced by delirium. Maybe I need a local to help me put all the ingredients in the right balance.

The Portuguese girls chatted with the waiter while we pooled together money for our dinner and I caught the bitter tone in his voice. Profanity is the first thing any traveler learns in a new country, along with "hello," "thanks," and "where's the bathroom?" so when I heard him say *"puttana"* more than once, I understood. While Anna argued with him, Leonore translated. The waiter said our dinner companion was a "local whore, a freak with the worst hygiene, who would sell himself to anyone on the street." He'd even dared to approach the waiter, "just once." He also hoped that none of us had eaten off her plate because "he had all kinds of diseases." I blushed violently at that—"I used my own fork, if that's any consolation." The violence of the waiter's reaction angered me and the girls warmly defended our companion. *"Simpatica,"* they said.

"Simpatica o simpatico?" the waiter demanded.

I'M NOT REALLY CRYING

> it's just
> the sheer
> number
> of chopped
> onions
> in the world

—Francisco X. Alarcón, *Snake Poems: An Aztec Invocation*

"*Si, si—simpatica*," they answered, resolutely determined to say that the person who sat with us at the table had been a nice woman, not a nice man. The waiter, thoroughly disgusted with all of us now, called us fools, slammed his starchy white apron down on the table and left.

I wonder at how lonely the life of this transsexual prostitute must have been. Obviously, the rest of the community ostracized her, but she was making a living somehow. And she was so determined, even extravagantly so, to "live her life." Considering the waiter's violently disgusted response to us for even eating at the same table with her, I realized that what she said about living every moment "like the last" went beyond simple dramatic bravado, and it frightened me. Her career choice wasn't one for me to emulate. But even so, I knew that she had summed up the lesson I needed to learn from my journey.

Tanya Monier was born and raised in Sacramento, California. She prides herself for living by the maxim, "All roads lead to Sacramento; fortunately, they also lead away." Currently, she is a graduate student of English at Columbia University in New York.

★

A word of warning is in order. For some years now, Florentine psychiatrists have recognized a peculiar local malady to which foreign tourists are particularly susceptible. It's called "Stendhal's Syndrome," after the 19th century French novelist, who was the first to describe it in print. The symptoms can be severe: confusion, dizziness, disorientation, depression and sometimes persecution anxiety and loss of the sense of identity. Some victims immediately suspect food poisoning, but the true diagnosis is far more outlandish. They are suffering from art poisoning, brought on by over-exposure to so-called Important Works of High Culture. Consciously or unconsciously, they seem to view Florentine art as an exam (Aesthetics 101, 10 hours per day, self-taught, pass/fail), and they are terrified of flunking.

                                                    —*Fodor's Guide to Italy*

SHERDYL (CHARLIE) MOTZ

Eating up the Mekong

In the midst of war, the author learns that the hearth
is where you make it.

THE LUSH GREEN JUNGLE ON THE BANKS OF THE MEKONG RIVER Delta moved languidly by our patrol boat. The muddy water sloshed past our bow. A soft sea breeze gentled the sun. No one was shooting at us. It should have been a marvelous day. Then I looked down at the can in my hand and the day was ruined.

For our dining pleasure on our interminable fourteen hour river patrols, the Navy issued us the much maligned C-rations. Rumor had it that the ones issued to us in Vietnam were left over from World War II.

At first we ate them cold. The congealed grease mixed with the unpalatable food in their ugly little olive drab cans did nothing to whet our appetites. We put the main canned "entree" on the manifold of the boat engine and they got lukewarm. It wasn't much of an improvement.

Two of the C-rations were passable. The spiced beef tasted okay, and came with a bone-dry, ossified, totally tasteless cracker and some Velveeta cheese that claimed to be hickory-smoked cheese. The lima beans with ham were good, too, although I couldn't really tell the difference between the flinty ham chunks and granite pebbles. We haggled, bartered, and wrangled endlessly over these two prize selections.

Near the other end of the spectrum was the alleged spaghetti and meatballs. It made Franco-American canned spaghetti look like French cuisine. No aromatic Italian herbs *ever* graced the cauldron it was bubbled in and the meatballs were mushy. The turkey loaf looked like caked bog from the Great Grippen Mire and tasted like sawdust sweepings mixed with used motor oil.

But the worst on *Le C-ration Menu* was the scrambled eggs and diced ham. It was just plain unfit for human consumption. Self-respecting pigs would have turned their noses up at it. It looked disgusting and smelled like a week-old cat box. If you held your nose while eating it, and had a truly strong cast iron stomach, you could just keep it down. Boiled monkey might have tasted better.

One C-ration came with a canned dessert that masqueraded as fruit cake. The rumor went that it was collected in the petrified forest. Sometimes I got the little can of peanut butter and jelly. The jelly was crystallized and the peanut butter hard as a brick. The dessert purporting to be pound cake was palatable but incredibly dry. We used to skip them off the water like flat stones.

A little packet came with each C-ration box. It contained a plastic spoon and fork, a salt packet, a piece of petrified chewing gum, a tooth pick, some toilet paper that felt more like sandpaper when used, and four incredibly stale cigarettes, probably rolled by Sir Walter Raleigh himself. The instant coffee, however, did make my eyeballs snap to attention.

There was case upon case of something labeled candy bars. They were supposed to give you a quick energy burst. Actually, they looked like squashed dogshit or a health food experiment that flunked. They tasted like horse-hoof glue. I always had some in each pocket to give away to the Vietnamese kids who flocked around us. They loved them.

Yes, it's bad to get wounded or maimed or killed in war, but a prolonged diet of C-ration cuisine was a subtle and exquisite form of torture in its own right. They did, on the other hand, provide us with endless hours of entertainment, dreaming up stories about their derivation, vintage, and composition. Yes, Uncle Sam procured nothing but the very finest for his boys at the front.

Thank God these rations were lovingly supplemented by care packages from home. Anyone who received one had an instant flock of friends. Month-old, stale

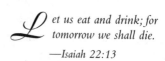

Let us eat and drink; for tomorrow we shall die.
—*Isaiah 22:13*

cookies were mouthwatering. A mouthful of crushed cake was a banquet. My mom sent me a package once. I never found out what was in it because some sleazy jerks broke into the mailroom, tore the package open, and absconded with its contents. All that was left was those little styrofoam things Dad packed the packages with. In retaliation I put them in my pocket and slipped them unobtrusively into the food and coffee cups of other unsuspecting sailors. Some guys ate them and never knew the difference. One scurvy old bosun's mate said, "I love 'em. They're nice'n crunchy, almost as good as fried dog!" I always suspected that bosun's mates weren't playing with a full deck.

The skipper of our cover boat scrounged up a coffee pot and got it to run off the boat generator. A hot cup of coffee was very welcome at two in the morning when we were trying to stay awake and alert for another six hours. It was potent stuff and we drank it gratefully, since it was an unaccustomed luxury while on patrol. It is a well-known fact that the U.S. Navy *could not run* without gallons of high octane coffee on hand at all times.

When we got a liberty in Saigon, we went to the main exchange and loaded up on canned goods. I remember thinking how strange it was that you could never find a bottle of aspirin there, but there were always hundreds of cases of Midol! We used Midol for hangovers. Anyway, back on the boat we had this coffee pot rigged up and we would dump these cans of stuff into it and warm it up. None of us could cook and the combinations we made were pretty horrific. We made one particularly repelling mess consisting of leftover coffee grounds, tomato soup, tamales and baked beans. But for all of that, those meals were still infinitely preferable to C-rations.

The chow at the base mess hall was nothing to brag about either. There was little in the way of fresh fruit or vegetables, just canned or dehydrated stuff. It wasn't the cooks' fault. We were a small base at the tail end of the supply line. The worst thing, though, was no fresh milk. Instead, we had to use canned, evaporated milk in our coffee and on our stale cereal. We called it *castrated* milk. I would have killed for a glass of cold, fresh milk. We became increasingly desperate for palatable cuisine.

Soon we got a little more sophisticated. On day patrol we cruised the two-mile wide Soirap River that teemed with thousands of junks and sampans. We inspected hundreds of them every day for contraband. Many of larger junks and fishing boats had food on board. We would buy rice and fish or meat and fresh fruit. We didn't care a whit about health concerns and often

> *Heaven punishes, Heaven reprimands, but Heaven does not punish people when they are eating.*
>
> —Vietnamese proverb

got the runs. We hoped we weren't eating dog or monkey meat. We bartered for their food with cigarettes, the sawdust candy bars or, even better, with our C-rations. Both parties thought that was a good deal.

But at night no junks were out on the river and our quest for food became an obsession. One day our interpreter Vinh said, "Vietnamese Army not pay much. Sometimes forget to pay us for months. My wife Mai and our four children go hungry. Very bad. Maybe we catch fish, then Mai fix for us. OK?"

We didn't fish in the normal way, however. Our technique was to drop a concussion grenade into the water and speed away. The grenade would explode underwater and when we circled back there would be a pile of fish floating on the surface. We scooped them up and headed for home and the feast was on. Mai made a delicious rice and fish soup with simply delightful, tangy spices. Sometimes she grilled them on a little hibachi and basted them with *Nuoc Mam*. We supplied the beer and the sounds of our gratefully smacking lips and contented burps could be heard from a mile away.

Nuoc Mam was a kind of Vietnamese fish sauce. There was a large concrete vat at the north end of the village that this stuff was fermented in. The vat reeked. One day I saw some fishermen dump fish heads into it so God only knows what else was in it. Maybe they used monkey carcasses too. It was kind of sharp tasting, like vinegar, and quite spicy. It sure made the fish and rice taste good, though. I was quite addicted to it.

The beer we drank on liberty was a local brew called Ba Mui Ba, or Thirty-Three in Vietnamese. The brewers used formaldehyde as a preservative. It gave it a weird flavor, but so did a lot of Vietnamese food and drink, and we soon got used to it. Our little village offered a "liquor" they called gin. I tried it a couple of times, but it tasted suspiciously like kerosene and made me sick as a dog, so I went back to Ba Mui Ba.

About half the year I was there, the two-mile wide lower Soirap River was covered with ducks. The Mekong Delta is a major stopping-off place for migratory waterfowl. The river would be covered with ducks, as far as the eye could see. There were billions of them within a few miles of our lower patrol station. One day Vinh mentioned that Mai loved to cook duck.

Our eyes lit up and we looked around at this mother lode of delectable chow floating around us. My buddy Brian, always a world class chow hound, mentioned it to both boat skippers and soon we were chasing ducks all over the river. At first the ducks would let us get close enough to use the M-79 grenade launcher and, boom! presto, seven or eight dead or dazed ducks, waiting to be plucked and devoured.

Soon the ducks got wise, however. When our little brown patrol boats got too close, they would fly away. We then adopted the strategy of approaching them at cruising speed, with all guns at the ready. When we got too near, the ducks would get real nervous, start quacking and prepare to fly off. Then we'd ram the throttles home and swoop down on them at flank speed with all guns blazing. It was a bad day when we didn't come back with at least a dozen or so ducks. It wasn't very sporting of us, but then hunger and the search for variety at any cost made us merciless. And, duck hunting relieved the tedium of endless patrolling.

We even used the .50 caliber machine guns on ducks. Of course, a duck hit square amidships with one of those huge rounds became instant duck burger and quite useless for eating. Only a few feathers floated down. But some of them were grazed and would land, wounded but alive. When we approached a wounded one, the wily quacker would duck under water and emerge elsewhere. It took some pretty sharp shooting to bag one with a head shot when it surfaced for air. But our long quest was about to be rewarded.

I remember well the sumptuous duck feasts at Vinh's hut. We would clean them and take them home and Vinh's wife would roast them with *Nuoc Mam* and some other Vietnamese spices. Sliced duck in soup with rice or noodles and mint leaves was also great. We drank cases of Ba Mui Ba beer and stuffed ourselves with fresh duck. No niceties here. Amy Vanderbilt would have been appalled as we snarled gleefully and tore savagely at the duck meat like starving barbarians. Globules of rich, fragrant duck fat covered our shirts, hands, and faces, but we didn't care. Soon mounds of naked duck bones covered the table and littered the floor, competing for space with legions of empty Ba Mui Ba bottles. There were moans and groans and signs of contentment. Long into the night, we made fowl toasts to the ducks that gave up their lives for our culinary pleasure. After months of C-ration cuisine, it was a lavish repast indeed.

I often ruminated on how many zillions of dollars of government money we wasted on grenade fishing and duck hunting. We used up ammunition at a prodigious rate. We told the officers it was target practice! They never knew the difference. All I know is we got a desperately-needed respite from the wretched C-rations, had some super feasts, and fed several Vietnamese families and orphans to boot. We rationalized that we could chalk it off to good will and foreign aid.

We often ate in the village where the food was standard rural Vietnamese fare. There was always lots of rice. The Mekong Delta is one of the mega-rice producing areas of the world. You could always get a large bowl of steaming rice or rice soup or rice cakes anywhere you went. It was often spiced with the ubiquitous *Nuoc Mam* or mint leaves or other strange spices. Sometimes it came with vegetables or meat. There was always plenty of fresh fruit available, such as succulent mangos.

A few village establishments tried to make hamburgers but they didn't resemble any hamburger I ever ate. I think they used tough old water buffalo (or something worse) instead of beef. A running debate raged amongst my shipmates as to the true origin of these hamburgers and what they called steaks. The scurvy old bosun's mate snarled, "You guys are all pussies! I *prefer* monkey and dog-burger to beef. You can't tell the difference no how!" A Vietnamese hamburger flavored with *Nuoc Mam* was a real olfactory experience, I can assure you. Ditto with the ersatz French fries.

There were several places in the village that served food, but we had to expend so much energy fighting off the insistent solicitations of the night ladies, it ruined our appetites. I would be taking a bite of something and all of a sudden one of them would grab my private parts and screech something obscene. It was not only disconcerting but it wasn't all

The best Nuoc Mam *comes from Phu Quoc, a tear-shaped island with beautiful palm-fringed beaches and rich marine life off the coast of Vietnam near the Cambodian border. In commercial factories located along the coast, the sauce is made by layering tiny fresh anchovies with salt in huge wooden barrels and allowing them to ferment. After about three months the liquid which drips from the barrel is poured back over the top, and after a further three months it is drained off and bottled. This is the first pressing, producing a rich, dark sauce, which is reserved for table use.*

—Annabel Doling,
Vietnam on a Plate

that good for mindful digestion! And neither was the stench emanating from the canal only ten yards away.

I always went on liberty with my buddy Brian. When we wanted to eat or talk and not be disturbed by the legions of whores, we would go to Nga's laundry, which was right outside the main gate of our base. Nga was a cheerful, 50-ish woman with a toothless smile who ran a laundry and sold food, beer, and cokes. She didn't allow any women of questionable virtue in her establishment. Like most of the village, it was a ramshackle place made out of a rickety frame of two-by-fours covered with surplus tin from America with beer can ads on it. Straw mats covered the earthen floor. Nga's warmth lit up the place and made it a mellow sanctuary.

She did a good job of cleaning our clothes, although we found out she used potatoes for starch. We loved the place, and Nga's joyful smile and her three cute, bubbly daughters made the war seem far, far away for a few precious moments. This peaceful place of refuge in the combat zone was something we treasured.

I loved to entertain Nga's daughters. They gave us a little plate of peanuts when they served our drinks. After we gobbled them up, I went through this elaborate pantomime over the empty plate rather than simply ask for more. I would hold it upside down, shake it, examine it ruefully, show its emptiness to Brian, feel it, and tap it, and so on. They would watch me and laugh and giggle. It was a lot of fun for all of us and became a standard part of our routine.

We always had the beef mint leaf noodle soup at Nga's and it was always steamy, rich, and very aromatic and fragrant. I must have eaten hundreds of bowls of it during my year tour in Nga Be.

About a month before the end of my tour, I was sitting with Brian at Nga's having the soup as usual. I remember that it was exceptionally delectable that day. There was a large piece of beef in the bottom of the bowl and I saved it until near the last in order to savor it. Finally, I fished it out with my spoon and, lo and behold, peeking out from amongst the noodles and mint leaves was a hairy paw!

I showed it to Brian, and asked, "What do ya think? Dog?!"

"No," he replied firmly. "Definitely monkey!"

I screeched and Nga and her daughters came over. She took a look at the paw and said, "Whatsa matter! You long-time friend so I saved the best part special for you!"

Sherdyl (Charlie) Motz wrote this story in participation with the Veteran's Writing Program, developed and conducted by author Maxine Hong Kingston and funded by the Lila Wallace Readers' Digest Fund. Sherdyl is a 53-year-old poet and writer, currently working on his war memoirs. When not doing digital art and graphic design on his home computer in El Cerrito, California, he does penance for the murder of numerous Vietnamese ducks.

✳

I spent the next four days walking through the jungle and hiding in trees and rice paddies from the Viet-Cong patrols that seemed to be everywhere. By the end of the fifth day I was hungry, dehydrated, and ready to give up. As I stopped to rest, my nose picked up the smell of smoke in the distance. I followed my nose and found a small village nestled back in a remote area off the regular paths. Knowing that I had to find food and water soon, or die, I straightened my green beret and walked boldly into the village.

The chief of the village told a young woman to bring me some food. By that time, I told myself, I would eat anything and have the good sense not to ask what it was until later. As I waited for the food I admired the beautiful people around me. They were the first Montinyards I had encountered since arriving in Vietnam.

A young girl brought me a wooden bowl of stew that smelled like heaven and a big bowl of rice. The meat of the stew tasted much like corned beef and cabbage and the broth was thick and creamy and very rich. It tasted a lot like the stew that I had eaten at the Markee Hotel in Denmark. I had always hated rice as a child, but the rice I had that day changed my mind forever. It was light and had a hot spicy taste that left me wanting more. The best part of the meal was the small loaves that looked like French bread that had been shrunk, and tasted almost as sweet as cake.

After finishing my fourth bowl of stew I finally worked up the courage to ask my host what I had been eating with such relish. An old woman about 70 years old, grinned at me flashing a mouth full of black teeth and motioned me to follow. At the edge of the village I was shown a skeleton of a small elephant. The elephant had been captured from the VC and had been used as fresh meat by the people of the village. I later learned that the Viet-Cong sometimes used elephants to pull artillery pieces through the jungle and there was a bounty paid by the U.S. government for killing them.

During the next week I was fed and hidden from the Viet-Cong by the villagers at great risk to themselves. I finally found in the kindness of these simple people a worthwhile reason to be in Vietnam.

—Thomas J. Lakey, "Jungle Stew"

⋆ ⋆ ⋆

Morocco Blue

The fundamental things apply.

HAVING JUST COMPLETED A TOUR PLAYING JAZZ IN SPAIN, I WAS offered—last minute—five days of work in Morocco with a Spanish avant garde group. The pay was awful and the music even worse; what's more, the Gulf War (sic) had just taken place—perhaps not the best of times to visit an Islamic country. But there are few gigs for American jazz trombonists in Morocco, so I couldn't refuse what might be my only chance to sample all my favorite dishes in their native habitat.

We set out early one morning from Madrid (wedges of silky potato omelet), our van heading south through the plains of Castillia (tender fried calamaris) and into Andalusia (hearty stewed wild boar), finally breaking through the mountains at the southern coast (pizza, hot dogs, bad soft-serve ice cream). Across a shockingly puny strip of water lurked, shrouded in mist, Africa. The Rock of Gibraltar is just some rock, but Africa's got serious ambiance.

We crossed over by ferry, and, while waiting for the road manager to pay off The People Who Get Paid Off, I quietly noodled "As Time Goes By" on my trombone (I think I caught a Berber wincing; sentimental *gringos* must do this all the time). Eventually we passed through customs, and suddenly everyone was palming little balls of sticky, skunky blonde hash.

Some pull into a town looking for booze. Others seek shopping bargains, still others museums or romance. Me? I want to eat something unbelievably great. But my traveling companions, not just Españoles but Madrileños, for crying out loud, had their priorities. So hash it was, defiled with tobacco so as to corrupt the heady aroma and thwart any potential cannabic epiphanies.

I was Spanish, too. I had to be. Many in the Islamic world were railing against the demonic Americans, so I adopted a Castilian alter ego, Jaime Izquierda. I was so in character that even the ubiquitous pesky guides, normally carny-perceptive at guessing nationalities, flipped through Spanish and French before trying English as my sulky non-comprehension remained unbroken.

The following day we were to play in El Centro Cultural Española de Tangiers (there are no jazz clubs in Morocco; we were hired by the Spanish Government to do a sort of Bob Hope-meets-Sun Ra for the troops of resident Spanish bureaucrats). Things were going badly; the band was becoming mildly annoyed by my constant food-associating. These guys live to smoke. *To live,* they drink. Eating is simply not a part of the equation. I, by contrast, had been dreaming of fluffy mounds of couscous topped with ultra-complex lemony *tagine;* and *bastila,* the is-it-meat? is-it-dessert? specialty of ground pigeon with sweet spices in pastry topped with powdered sugar and cinnamon. Flame-singed *koftas* bursting with juice and spiked with heady spices. While I had managed to feed admirably in more familiar Spain, here in Morocco it would be much, much more difficult.

Sizzling sounds and intoxicating aromas pummeled me as I walked the streets, but they always led tantalizingly out of reach, leaking from under closed doors or spilling forth from second-story windows. For restaurants I could find only McMaghreb tourist joints. All my chowhound instincts were useless in this profoundly foreign world; try as I might, I could not find a "real" place to eat. The authentic and the touristic chase each other's tails in a city whose very existence seems geared toward scamming visitors (this is only the case in the north where the ambitious gear up for their final move into Europe). Everyone has an agenda; multitudinous winds blow you in various directions, few of them in your own interest. Thin sincerity coats a desperate avarice driving essentially good people in tough straits. You're woozily unsure of what the system *is*, much less how to beat it. Senses are overstimulated until you're left saturated and unable to resist, yet the resultant liberation is not cathartic because you realize that in this whirlwind (my native New York City is a provincial backwater compared to the frenzied street pace of North Morocco) to fully let go is just not at all advisable.

What's more, try as I might, I was unable to blend in for even a moment. You can't know a place until you put yourself into it, but Tangiers was rejecting me like a slug in a Swiss stamp machine. I was Tourist, and the slightest attempt to deviate from the well-worn path (eat bad food, buy phony carpet, tip obnoxious guide) would require megawatts of energy and savvy and carry uncertain risks.

Hustlers try to insinuate themselves into what they imagine your world to be—for their own ends—but their friendliness rings false. Our music was also fake; I was a ghost travelling with a band of ghosts, trying to find my way to the vast depths that teased from the corners of my perceptions.

Culinary end result: a bunch of overpriced skewers (quite good actually) and, everywhere, blessed mint tea, entire hedges of mint crammed into a juice glass full of boiling sweeter-than-sugar-itself water. The handleless glasses burn fingertips; you are somehow refreshed in the hot afternoon by a hot, cloying drink…and blistered as part of the deal. No experience is without ironic complexity here.

After the gig, the band was invited for Spanish food at the cultural center. Too frazzled to resist, I joined them for *entrecot con patatas* tasting but exactly like Restaurante Sanchez in the Madrid plaza where we'd eaten our Last Supper the day before.

The next day, on the road to Tetuan, we ate at a highway rest stop. Once again, kebabs, french fries, and sweetly burning, treacly sating tea. Not bad, but my thoughts drifted dreamily to aromatic stews dotted with slices of salty preserved lemon, pastry flutes stuffed with spicy ground meat, peppery lamb sausages. A fake street musician wandered in while we ate, hustling us for tips with his faux flute playing. One of our (Spanish) musicians was actually a master of Moroccan flute, but he wouldn't take out his instrument and embarrass the man. He instead offered some money and clapped his hands in time to the "music."

Dinner the next night: Italian. We're sorry, Jim, but there's just no time for anything else. We're here to *work*, not to eat, after all. So I choked down my pizza, bereft of even a mitigating *merguez*, eyes welling with tears. I'd leave Morocco in a day and a half, with perhaps only some kebabs and junky Eurofood to show for it. The music was ponderous and the musicians had no sensitivity; they played bad pizza. They played road stop kebabs. They played *entrecot con* goddamn *patatas*.

> *D*on't ever let them tell you that goats don't grow on trees.
>
> *Argan trees are related to olive trees. Moroccan goats climb them and graze on the leaves and the fruit. Argan oil, which is extracted from the excrement of the goats, is a prized traditional seasoning. We would bring some back, but it doesn't keep well. This may account for why you do not find it on your supermarket shelves. It is really quite tasty stuff, very piquant. We particularly liked it in almond butter.*
>
> —Annette Bonnell,
> "More Spices from
> Off the Beaten Path"

In the Tetuan *medina*, I saw toothless old men selling mysterious snacks (the road manager was too busy to translate, but instructed me not to try anything, as it's "all dirty") and marvelled at the new and the old coming together seamlessly as they do only in the Third World: Levis amidst Egyptian cotton, Bob Marley tapes stacked next to 14th century Sufi music, briefcases piled under *djellabahs*.

Strolling through that *medina*, I experienced the single most romantic moment of my life when, having gone four days without seeing a woman's face (one gets to the point where the other sex is largely forgotten), I laughed at a companion's remark, and one of two young women walking in front of us pivoted her head back—simultaneously laughing at *her* friend's remark—and caught my eye. She was mostly unveiled, actual (deeply beautiful) *features* exposed, and I was not at all prepared to meet, much less return, her unfathomably hip gaze. My face sliding in twelve directions, composure totally lost, I saw things in her eyes that I'd never seen anywhere before. Mysteries solved and still greater mysteries alluded to. All my puny ideas about this society (especially of the subjugation of women) turned upside-down, whatever wisdom I'd thought I had reduced to a discarded over-chewed Chiclet in the light of what was revealed to me and me alone through this unimaginably exciting woman's glance.

I was completely shaken, yet I realized that a branch in my path had opened—if I could but only seize it. But no. She had for some reason sensed a presence behind her, and turned, with great intentions, to be presented with the spectacle of me falling apart: my mouth cringing to the right, my brow furrowing, my general demeanor one of abject wide-eyed discomposed shock. I stumbled and stuttered and started, and with the same smooth motion she pivoted back to animated conversation with her friend—the entire encounter having lasted a nanosecond—and they turned right and were gone. No more branch. No more "other road." It would be Route 66 (sans kicks) from there on in. Yet another trap door to the seductive Moroccan soul had slammed shut in my pining face. But a long drive to Casablanca lay ahead, temporal fodder for endless wistful yearning.

Africa's only superhighway runs a few dozen miles from nowhere to nowhere, but we veered out of our way to take it. Fat old women walked across the roadway, chickens and children following. Along the shoulders were strewn several newly flipped over buses. I was feeling pretty flipped over as well. We Spaniards were floating through, not eating, not even really playing music. We were still in Madrid, like TV weathermen standing in front of the blue screen while the audience at home thinks we're in Morocco.

My companions never looked out the van's window; instead, they were running through a long litany of bandleaders who owed them money. And smoking. And above all, determinedly not eating anything special.

Casablanca The City has far less charm than *Casablanca* The Movie; chow prospects were grim, and I was in A Mood. We played our last gig, ending far too late to find open any interesting eats. The road manager came over, aglow with the delightful offer he had for me. "Jim! *Wonderful* news!! Did you know that Casablanca has a *superb* Chinese restaurant?!?" Flushing with anger, I suggested—in my fluent, utterly ungrammatical Spanish—an anatomical juxtaposition for the egg rolls and stomped out. Sputtering to myself and walking fast, trombone on my back, I made my way through midnight Casablanca—it might as well have been Europe for the weighty grimy architecture and bad late night Snack Shops. Finally I returned to Pension Abdul and literally begged our desk clerk to recommend a *real* restaurant, a place for homeboys, not tourists. A place where I could eat something delicious and purely Moroccan. The clerk tried to sum up my needs "Ah, monsieur would like an *inexpensive* restaurant?"

"No!" My mental state, frantic before, turned almost psychotic: "That's not it!! I want *good* food! *Real* food! The food *you* would eat if you were moving away and could enjoy only one last meal in your beloved homeland!"

I was handed a card for a Restaurant Abdul down the street (apparently, the entire block was a wholly-owned subsidiary of Abdul Enterprises),

The hustler and the hassler will pursue the visitor in Meknes endlessly, while the shopkeeper in Taroudant will barely pay you attention. There are perhaps more important visual distinctions, and they remind me of Fouad Ajami's caution that there is nothing self-evident behind the shrouding veil and the forbidding door. Don't assume anything: a hovel entrance may lead you to unimagined magnificence or to garbage.

—Martin Peretz, "Morocco Diarist: Hide and Souk," *The New Republic* which I threw back in the poor fellow's face. Now I was furious. The next day I'd spend eight hours traveling back to the ferry, odds of eating something great with those clowns, asymptotic to zilch. I might never return to Morocco; this was perhaps my only chance, my last *harissa*. Late night in the downtown streets lurked scary characters, but I was scarier still, stalking about in my dark cloud of determined rage. My trombone case, I realized, appeared to locals to carry some sort of armament, and for a flickering moment I considered using this to my advantage: perhaps I'd waylay someone and force him to take me home, wake his mother, and have her cook me a meal.

Pizza, pizza, burgers, kebabs, pizza. It was not looking good. Then, in the distance, I spotted chickens; beautiful, spinning chickens. As I got closer, I smelled the wood smoke and the tangy marinade. They were perfect; naturally plump (foods are always more wholesome in areas without high-tech agriculture and the attendent artificial shortcuts). I looked in, but despite my desperation and general chowhound fearlessness, I just couldn't bring myself to enter. A few of the many eaters crammed into the…space (I can't call it a restaurant) returned my glance, sensing in that intuitive Moroccan way my trepidation and whole-heartedly encouraging its consummation. "No," I thought, "I'd better not." I walked on, but I'd covered the main drag and it was turning residential. I found myself inexorably pulled back, as if by tractor beam, to what might quite possibly have been a private poultry party.

As I entered, all conversation stopped (it seems corny in the telling, but wasn't at the time—Morocco is like that). People were standing—for there were no chairs—in the woody, dimly-lit interior, ripping chicken savagely apart by (right) hand—for there was no silverware—drinking Coke and chain smoking. I approached the counter, such as it was, and weakly assumed the Jaime Izquierda persona. Voice trembling, I asked someone who seemed in a position of authority whether he spoke Spanish. He roared a response, clearly negative, and walked away. I shouted after him—with pleading urgency—four of my seven words of French: *"Poulet!!*

Poulet, s'il vous plait!!!" He didn't turn but gestured cursorily at me
with his finger as he receded from view. Wait there? We're all out?
Be gone by the time I return with my pistol? I could not tell.
Conversation was subdued. All eyes were on me though few faces
pointed my way. It was unbearably crowded, so I retreated to a corner where I hugged trombone to chest and shrank to occupy as little space as humanly possible. Suddenly, a simple white plate with
a big hunk of chicken careened my way, coming to a spinning halt
in front of me on the counter. It was the most beautiful thing I'd
ever seen: bright yellow from herbs, the skin as unblemished as a
fine Cuban cigar.

I eat rather like a hunger-crazed Berber even in the most refined dining rooms, so I felt utterly at ease *ripping* off a hunk of
chicken flesh and *jamming* it into my mouth, good pungent golden
grease clinging to lips and cheeks. I was so immersed in my bird
and its yellowness that I failed to notice that conversation had returned to normal; I hadn't realized it yet, but my feeling of well-
being stemmed not only from At Last Real Food, but also from the
cresting comradeship of my fellow fressers. Some were watching
and smiling. One came over and slapped my back, greeting me
with his one word of Spanish: *"Amigo!"*

They liked how I was eating.

And I liked *what* I was eating. The flesh was meltingly tender;
none of that wet sawdusty graininess in the white meat you find
in American chickens. It was all relentlessly marinated to a flavor
stasis of imponderable complexity; rational thought kept breaking
down as I tried to identify components. Eyes shut while waves of
bliss crashed, all of space and time converging on the interface of
mouth and chicken. Trying to analyze was like attempting to speak
seriously on the phone while someone is tickling you.

Alongside: a hefty mound of rice, each corpulent grain glistening, lots of yellow chicken sludge seeping in—its color not at all
diluted by fraternization with the snowy starch. My baguette was
good: chewy and wheaty, completely pure of flavor. They'd *like* to
give you crummy processed bread, but for that you need factories

and chemicals and stuff, and they simply can't afford them. So there's no choice; you get *good* bread everywhere. The Coke was in the kind of old fashioned thick-glass bottle you can't find in America anymore, and I was *jabbing* things into my face, practically barking with primal Cro-Magnon approval of my repast. I'd entered the realm of the experiential. I was in Morocco at last.

I paid the check (three dollars) and took my leave amidst chicken-scarfing grunts of universal "take it easy; have a good night, now" intent, and strutted—grinning ear to ear, higher than hash could take me, and completely "In The Picture"—back to Pension Abdul, where the others were just returning (thirty five dollars poorer) from their Maghrebian *moo shu* and *poo poo* platters. "It was *delicious*, Jim. You should have come!" I smiled kindly at the infidels, wiped a smidge of gravy from my lip, and retired to a long sleep rich with profound Moroccan dreams.

Jim Leff is a New York–based jazz trombonist and food and beer writer. Spain's national newspaper, El Pais, *has dubbed him "The Iron Lung," which supposedly is a compliment in Spanish.*

✳

The bus stopped at the crest of a hill. It was market day in Morocco, and a single skinned goat hung upside down from a leafless stunted tree. "Excuse me," the *djelaba*-clad man said in his halting French, exiting the bus, walking over to the goat. The blood-stained butcher ran his hand over the carcass, brushed away the flies and whacked off several ribs and wrapped them in newspaper. The man returned to the bus, and put the chunk of goat overhead on the luggage rack, on top of my backpack. The package leaked, blood dripping down the window, bisecting the landscape. Another fifty miles of silence, the two of us occasionally smiling or nodding. Then, shyly, he made an eating motion, pointing at me, the goat, then at himself. "With my family," he said.

"Thanks. Thanks, but I can't," I said, pointing to my watch, then my Michelin map. "Melilla," I said. "Got to be there there by tonight."

The man nodded gravely.

When we reached the outskirts of Melilla, he suddenly stood, reached up, took down his package, opened it. With a small pen-knife he divided the piece of goat in two, wrapped each half, and handed me one. "For your family. Use salt, oil, herbs," he said, trying to describe the Moroccan way with goat. The man ran his tongue over his lips. We both laughed. I stepped off the bus, my bloody backpack in hand, the fine taste of travel on my tongue.

—Bob Burton M.D., "Morocco Diary"

SIMON LOFTUS

Fried Eggs and *Chapatis*

The author finds that his morning meals in Pakistan
provide serenity as well as sustenance.

EDIBLE HISTORY IS THE MOST VIVID TESTIMONY TO VANISHED EM-
pires. The last steam locomotive from the railway works at Crewe
will eventually grind to a halt in the subcontinent, irreparable even
by the standards of Indian ingenuity, and there may come a day
when it will no longer be possible to recognize a Scottish face behind the counter of National Grindlays Bank in Karachi. Artefacts
and institutions disappear, but the gastronomic archaeologist will
still be able to trace the influence of India in the English addiction
to curry and to find, as I did, that the most poignant evidence of
our former glory is the survival of porridge in Pakistan.

The discovery was made in a small village of mud houses on the
edge of the desert, where I arrived late at night in a sandstorm. We
had been travelling all day from Zahedan, in southeast Persia, a
monotonous journey through a landscape of dirty shale, rattling
over the corrugations and potholes of an unsurfaced road. By early
afternoon we found ourselves in a vast empty space, dun-coloured
and featureless, across which the road meandered to the horizon.
In the middle of this desert was a large military tent and a white
awning, under which a few Pakistani officials were drinking tea.
This was the border and someone had begun to draw the line on

the ground, marking the boundary with white painted stones, but had abandoned the effort after a few yards. A chain across the road formed a token barrier.

Curiously enough, the flies recognized the political geography. I had hardly noticed them in Persia but as soon as we crossed to Pakistan we were assailed by a dense cloud, black and biting, and from this point onwards they never left us.

It was dark and nearly midnight when we came to the village of Dalbandin. Sand filled the air and the *dak* bungalow was locked, but eventually we found the old *chokidar* who let us in. I never ceased to be amazed by these government Rest Houses, built for visiting officials in the days of the Raj and maintained thereafter to serve the needs of occasional visitors. Havens of the thirties, we found them in the most unexpected places, furnished with decent beds, chintz-covered armchairs and solid English plumbing. The service, too, seemed a survival of another age. That night we asked, with due diffidence, whether it would be possible to have something to eat. Fifteen minutes later the old man reappeared with two boys bearing trays of supper—tea, fried eggs, potatoes and tomatoes, brown bread and butter. Memories of Yorkshire.

The night was intensely cold and my rest was disturbed by loud snorts from below my bedroom window, but it was too dark to make out what sort of beast or rascal had taken shelter there. I eventually drifted into sleep and dreamt of the Raj. Dream became reality as bearers woke us, bringing logs. They lit fires in every room and placed jugs of hot water on the washstands. Shaved, refreshed, and wrapped against the chilly morning, I went to explore.

Two grumpy camels, the nocturnal snorers, were kneeling in the sand behind the bungalow, together with a couple of boys, twelve or fourteen years old. They had evidently taken shelter there from the sandstorm and were now preparing to be off. The boys had the mischievous air of joyriders, swaggering like adults, and there was no sign of any baggage. Perhaps they were camel thieves.

Breakfast was announced at eight by the arrival of the *chokidar*, followed by three or four bearers carrying trays. The meal was an intriguing mixture of traditions: the fried eggs were served with *chapatis* and preceded by porridge. We seemed, indeed, to be living in an earlier time than the rest of the impoverished village, cosseted in our Rest House, lapped by sand dunes. The lawn was green, the flagpole white, the palm trees grew in straight lines and there were enormous goldfish in the pond. Five servants waited on us, including one who did nothing but sweep the steps as soon as we trod on them. The bill came to four shillings a head.

As we were leaving, the *chokidar* asked sadly, "When are the British coming back?"

Breakfast on an equally imperial scale was served me a few days later at the railway station in Lahore. In the confusion of the arrival of the overnight train from Karachi, with passengers trying to climb through the windows and competing with red-turbanned porters for their baggage, my wallet was stolen. I lost all my money, lists of useful addresses, my driving license, and a permit to study in the Print Room of the British Museum. So I went to the Railway Police. "Well, my dear sir," said the courteous officer, "you must understand that there are many poor people here and they are tempted to theft. It will be quite impossible to apprehend the criminal but I shall take down the particulars for the record. Would you like some breakfast?" He clapped his hands and a few minutes later I was tucking into tea, eggs, toast, and marmalade. My momentary panic at being marooned and penniless, thousands of miles from home, was entirely forgotten. Fortified by the breakfast, I was able to ignore the condescension of the British High Commission ("Terribly sorry old boy, we haven't got any lolly. I believe the usual procedure is to sell something"), and to relish the fact that I was finally rescued by the Salvation Army, who gave me a bed and a few rupees to tide me over.

A week later, having sold my camera, I went to the races and wagered my subsistence on a series of elegant horses ridden by incompetent jockeys. It was a lovely place, with perfectly green grass, perfectly white railings and a spreading tree under which dignitaries of the Lahore Race Club sat behind a table laden with silver trophies. After losing steadily all afternoon I spotted a promising horse in the ring before the final race and bet my shirt on it, emptying my pockets of every last rupee. It was a foolhardy move but the horse had the sense to ignore its rider, paced itself well and stormed home to a sensational finish, half a length ahead of its nearest rival. I lived for a month on the proceeds.

This balmy day at the races, just before the turn of the year, was my last in Lahore. It was suffused, even at the time, with a sense of nostalgia which has grown stronger in the memory. Glimpses of an unknown but familiar past, images of pre-war England, were mingled with the jostling, crowded reality of provincial Pakistan.

Lahore itself is a particularly bizarre blend of indigenous tradition and colonial extravagance. The old city contains a tremendous fort, a huge mosque and a wonderfully noisy, smelly, colourful and chaotic bazaar. The buildings of the Raj, by contrast, provide an extravagant summary of English architectural history and imperial fantasy. The parish churches, naturally enough, are Victorian Gothic, and the administrative offices are housed in the decent order of neo-classicism, but the rest is a riot. In the middle of a splendidly English park beside The Mall I fell asleep after Christmas lunch and awoke to a cricket ball in the ribs as a ten-year-old batsman hit a six. I gazed with a confused sense of dislocation at a large building on the boundary, a stucco chunk of Carlton House Terrace, labelled MONTGOMERY in giant capitals on the cornice. The railway station attempts to recreate Windsor Castle in red brick and then there is the High Court of Justice, most fantastic of all. I think it's one of those cases where the drawings got muddled up, something that happened frequently in Victorian England (churches were built as public baths, and vice versa). The High Court obviously started life as a cricket pavilion, designed by a schoolmaster whose heart belonged to Gothic but who was prepared to make concessions to Islamic taste. Horrendously magnified in red brick and grey stone, its effect is startling, especially as I first saw it on Christmas night, picked out in red, blue, white and green by batteries of coloured floodlights, with the scales of justice outlined in flickering neon like an advertisement at Piccadilly Circus.

These architectural incongruities may not have resulted in anything as beautiful as the creations of the Mogul emperors at Agra and Fatehpur Sikri, but they are immensely enjoyable. Lahore is a good place to arrive but the most eccentric and delightful expression of Englishness is Simla, product of a colonial nostalgia strong enough to build a Victorian country town on a steep ridge in the Himalayas. Above the half-timbered almshouses, the lending library, and the Puginesque parish church with its stained glass windows, monkeys chase parakeets through the rhododendrons and a signpost points north to the snow-capped peaks: "Tibet 30 miles." The Empire left behind it a rag-bag of legacies. Some survived in incongruous circumstances, like this town in the hills, and others have taken on a surreal, Dadaist character, transformed by haphazard displacements.

Indian English is imprinted with historical curiosities; it preserves the formal written phraseology of the nineteenth century administrators, sprinkled with upper class Edwardian slang, rather than the common, spoken idioms of any epoch. Notices in the railway stations, political speeches and leading articles in the English language press share this imperial tongue. It confirms my childhood suspicion that only provincial officials, with heavily accented self-importance, ever spoke in the measured cadences of Cicero; the Romans rattled along with more verve and less grammar.

As the Roman empire disintegrated, language, customs, and symbols evolved in unexpected ways. The finely modelled image of a charioteer on a Roman coin, for example, was eventually transformed into an abstract pattern, quite unrecognizable but somehow more vital than the original. Much the same process was at work on the legacy of the Raj. I saw a couple of camels harnessed to an ancient English plough and two hump-backed cows pulling a lawnmower across a well-watered lawn. Unplayed bagpipes were flourished by the village bands in a Sikh procession which included elephants and spear-wielding cavalry. A 1930s

Morris con-rod, the solitary spare part in a repair shop at Ambala, was optimistically produced as the answer to a serious breakdown.

They lifted the damaged engine out with a block and tackle suspended from a convenient tree and agreed to make the replacement parts on a pre-war lathe. We stayed at the Rest House and played bridge every night in an effort to live up to the expectations of the *chokidar*, an amiable man with an enormous mustache who tolerated a late breakfast (more porridge and marmalade) but served high tea promptly at six. We basked on the roof, read ancient thrillers in the drawing-room or wandered past the potted palms on the veranda to a luxuriant garden, full of chipmunks, parakeets, and cockatoos. Our peace was only once disturbed, by the arrival of a government minister (in black limousine, with machine-gun-toting bodyguard) to confer for a couple of hours with an important Sikh.

They met each other in the neutral grounds of the Rest House and discussed their differences while sitting in chintz-covered armchairs around the bridge table. These scraps of our imperial past, I increasingly felt, were what gave a sense of unity to a fractured subcontinent. It seemed like a map made of mud, cracking as it baked in the sun. Fissures appeared after Independence, splitting a vast country into three, but other cracks have continued to divide and subdivide. There was a move to replace English with Hindi as the official language of India. "We demand equality for all fourteen national languages," responded the graffiti.

Such arguments expressed what I found invigorating, the rich diversity of cultures, peoples and languages. Travelling across Pakistan, meandering through India, down to Ceylon and back, I was constantly struck by the scale and the dramatic variety. What has gradually surfaced in the memory is an even stronger awareness of the vast underlying unity, the land itself.

All the more impressive, against the massive inertia of so huge a place, are the lasting effects of British Imperial rule. In many curious ways, English culture was revitalized in India, as it was by the Irish. There are entertaining parallels. "Have another slice of toast," said the policeman, as he interrupted for a moment our leisurely conversation about Shakespeare. It could have been Dublin; it was actually Lahore.

Simon Loftus is a wine merchant by trade, and and a lot of other things by inclination, including musician, cook, writer, and bon vivant. *He is the author of* Anatomy of the Wine Trade *and* A Pike in the Basement: Tales of a Hungry Traveler, *from which this story was excerpted.*

★

Government Rest Houses, also called Circuit Houses, Inspection Bungaloes or Dak Bungaloes (*dak* means a stage of travel), these are usually two or three unit guest houses run by government agencies for staff on business, and are available to tourists if nobody else is using them.

To some you may need to bring your own bedding. Rates for tourists are mid-range, and there are both very good and very bad bargains. Each has a *Chowkidar* (caretaker) living nearby who can, by arrangement, prepare at-cost meals from whatever is available.

Most rest houses in the north are run by NWFP Communications and Works Department (C&W), Northern Areas Public Works Department (NAPWD) or Forestry Districts. A booking—just a chit from the regional office to show the *Chowkidar*—is a good idea, or you can drop by and take your chances. The Azad Jammu & Kashmir Tourist Department has its own "Tourist Resthouses" which are very good value.

John King and David St.Vincent, *Pakistan - a travel survival kit*

LAWRENCE OSBORNE

Gastronome's Dream

In which the human mind mirrors the layered scum
of the large intestine.

SUMMER HAS ARRIVED AT LAST WITH A WHIFF OF PLAGUE AND
pollen and the peasant, with his implacable and unreasonable snob-
bery, has withdrawn like a snail into a small dark shell which is entirely mental. What disgusts him most about this unbearable season, aside from its blatant flirtation with the aromas of decay, is the
deliberate conversion of the nucleus of his beloved City into a
kind of dry aquarium for the benefit of thirty-five million visitors
whose rollicking, inebriated, plastic faces fill him with the most
dandyish and unjustifiable of moral paroxysms. The streets fill with
grotesque human curiosities carving peripatetic careers on the
pavements of the tourist capital of the Western world. On the first
hot nights he roams through Les Halles out of morbid curiosity,
not of course to disport himself in the chic terraces of the Café
Costes or the Bon Pêcheur, but simply to get a glimpse of the odd
knife fight by the Fontaine des Innocents, especially if the resident
CRS get to beat up the offender in complete privacy between two
parked meat wagons, or to judge the *artistes* executing their bold
and hallucinatory performances: a fire eater in front of the
Pêcheur, his skinny chest slimy with petrol, the flares of fire arching like ignited vomit over the spectator's heads; the imitation

Popeye with a smashed-up little face crunched over a pipe, a tin can in one hand, who moves with dreamlike slowness through space while a fat man in a straw boater plays an accordion. The tourist zones are heaving and unstable stomachs ingesting vast amounts of pulped material, sharks' bellies filled with human tyres and bones and capable at any minute of reacting violently against their own rapacious *gourmandise,* spitting up bile, burping, rumbling, throwing up or wallowing in hedonistic contentment. The warm atmosphere of early summer brings crowds on to the streets for most of the night. The City at least has none of the morguish dullness of London or Milan. Millions of excitable and blind corpuscles course through its arteries along with the diseases peculiar to human blood, the parasitisms, alcoholisms and intoxications.

While the peasant enters this flowing of blood willingly, it causes him physical anguish to enter the tourist *arrondissements,* the sixth or the second, for example, which—although their indigenous inhabitants might pretend otherwise—are slowly disintegrating under a bacterial wave, a miasmal tide, of virile vulgarity that will not be stopped by little things such as superior sneers and graceful retirement from the scene. No, the tribes of vicious gnomes (the hordes of ululating, tattooed atavars in Viking gear) are here to stay. They deeply appreciate the Coca-Cola sunshades on the rue de Buci and the stench of processed flesh by St Michel. The intestinal streets between Boulevard St Michel and the rue St Jacques have lost forever their medieval or even their Flaubertian overtones. Rue de la Harpe has dissolved the ghosts of *L'Education sentimentale* and opened its heart to the urban Disneyland, whose paying guests expect much more than facile nostalgia and literary regrets. It is surprising that the entire area has not yet been enveloped in a gigantic film of high-tech plastic like a sealed sandwich in a motorway café and placed under permanent spotlights and electronic surveillance. Just as there has been a "Disneyland of the Revolution" in the Tuileries for the Bicentennial celebrations, a cardboard leisure park of such phantasmal vulgarity and pointlessness that upper zones of sublimity are unconsciously attained, so the rest of Paris should logically submit to the same treatment.

Those ineffable geniuses Hennin and Normier, grandiose archi-
tects of the Park of Spectacles designed to commemorate
ephemerally the Revolution (everything will be dismantled the
following November!), have set the pace for the imperialism of
kitsch in the next century. History lives again, neatly telescoped, in
these fake guillotines, orators in fancy dress, fluffy "street girls"
showing us the wiles of revolutionary seduction, *papier mâché san-
sculottes,* androids delivering fiery jeremiads against monarchy and
slavery, period barrel organs, 1789 boxer shorts and videoed de-
capitations. Why should the same thing not be done everywhere?
The principle should at least remain inviolable, whatever variations
there are in the application. The only problem is that it cannot be
summer all the time, and it is summer that breeds kitsch as a dead
body produces ptomaine. As Europeans become voyeurs of their
own history, it is only natural that they should become voyeurs of
their own cities.

As spring and then summer bring warmer days, the giant belly
which is the City—and not just that bohemian part of it formerly
located at Les Halles—becomes acidic and bilious with kitsch, so
that even crimes take on a hallucinatory quality which mark them
off for crimes committed in more temperate times of the year. The
pepsins and rennins of this digestive organ—we mean the police,
the judiciary and the arbiters of good taste—become somnolent
and ineffective against the onset of festival barbarity. In the Bois de
Boulogne, transvestites are found shot in the head—first
"Francine," assassinated on April 5th and then one Pierre Saboni,
or "Clémentine," found with a bullet through the temple at dawn.
On the rue de Budapest a tenement is set on fire by underground
arsonists and a client, edging his way to safety along a third-floor
windowsill after interrupting proceedings with one of the
"Ghanaians," slips and falls to an uncomfortable death, thus en-
gendering a spate of black jokes among the whores. At the same
time the Grand Rabbi of France, Joseph Sitruk, sends a telegram
of condolence to Father Armogathe, curé of the church of St
Pierre de Chaillot after he is wounded by a bomb planted by a
mysterious commando group called Gracchus Babeuf Section,

sworn enemies of "Islam, Christianity and Judaism" and all other sects actively engaged in implanting "fascism" in the heads of the masses. Meanwhile on the rue Dunois in the thirteenth, a seventeen-year-old is defenestrated in his own apartment block by two thugs of the same age for having refused to hand over his scarf and 200 francs at exactly the same moment as a hotel on the rue Bailly in the third bursts into flames and carbonizes two immigrant workers asleep in their beds. The same Section Gracchus Babeuf running amok in honour of the summer solstice? Incredible bacilli stirred up by the heat, by the release of the fumes of decomposing food and the gases of indigestion? The churning stomach of the City of Food, the Temple of Gastronomy, is certainly capable of releasing a whole gamut of noxious odours into the atmosphere and rising to the head, infiltrating the nervous system and causing assorted migraines, flatulences and attacks of dyspepsia. The peasant who treads so daintily and distastefully through the streets of the summer capital of Europe, who feels his own stomach turning nauseously on its axis and whose malignant nose picks up every tiniest malodour emanating from the bacteriological combustions of the mountains of food that surround him on all sides, is aware—in his morbid and over-sensitive way— of the fraudulence of metaphors. For him the City is not a metaphoric stomach but a real one. The function of eating, the ritual of refined gorging, the processing of millions of tons of produce fills him simultaneously with awe and derision. Of all the

We see only when there is light enough, taste only when we put things into our mouths, touch only when we make contact with someone or something, hear only sounds that are loud enough. But we smell always with every breath. Cover your eyes and you will stop seeing, cover your ears and you will stop hearing, but if you cover your nose and try to stop smelling, you will die. Etymologically speaking, a breath is not neutral or bland—it's cooked air; we live in a constant simmering. There is a furnace in our cells, and when we breathe we pass the world through our bodies, brew it lightly, and turn it loose again, gently altered for having known us.

—Diane Ackerman,
A Natural History of the Senses

cities he has known Paris is the one where the human nose is the most elongated and refined. It is the mouth, lips, tongue, belly and anus of its continent. It is the pearl of gastronomic Shangri Las, boiling in its food lust, barely ceasing to wipe its lips, clean its teeth or inspect its own stools. It is the capital of devouring and the metropolis of sauces. Its secret life is one long, sweetly convulsive bowel movement. It is the great intestine that connects the mouth of a whole civilization to its lightly perfumed rectum. It is the guts and liver of Europe, alive with enzymes and chemical chains. We no longer have the right to talk about the belly of Paris; from now on we will refer to the Paris-belly, the urban liver, the Urinal Tract of Light, the Great Stomach of the White Shark: that which eats and spits out everything under the sun.

The peasant is a dreamer, this is his record. According to our doctors, dreaming is no longer necessary, it can be replaced by waking activities such as bicycling, writing, water-colour painting, callisthenics, cooking or group sex in dimmed and carefully warmed swimming pools. But nevertheless there is one thing he cannot prevent himself from dreaming about, and that is the endless, terrifying fluxion of food.

It's not that he likes gastronomic idylls, expert effusions about *foie gras* and Iranian caviar, or any kind of food journalism for that matter. On the contrary.

To protest the plethora of dog droppings desecrating Paris streets, twelve French professors and artists circled each steaming mess with chalk to form a plate and then added real spaghetti, salad flatware and glasses. They hoped to disgust Fidos' owners into curbing their dogs. While 650 Parisian pedestrians landed in city hospitals last year after slipping on dangerous dog dung, this art ploy is likely to have little success. "Telling the French not to do something doesn't do a bit of good," sighs an organizer.

—Fred Dodsworth, "Poop Art,"
au Juice

Along with his *bête noire*, travel writing *(Enlightening Train Odysseys to Ulan Bator and Back, My Favourite Transylvanian Vineyard Reappraised by Donkey),* he hates all forms of peripatetic drooling over exotic places, gorgeous food and new-colonial hotels. The poetic eye of the experienced and eloquent traveller throws him into spasms of disgust, just as the slippery expertise of scribbling epicureans brings out the forlorn ascetic in him. He would willingly subject all of them to excruciating and ingenious Oriental tortures in order to turn them back into ordinary people. In fact, it is merely sufficient for him now to see an insouciant but perfectly evoked tropical décor in the background, a whiff of Technicolor Third Worldism or off-the-beaten-track parading, for him to fall to his knees foaming at the mouth and begin mashing the carpet with his teeth. The dancing paradises of other worlds leave him stone cold and, worse, terminally suspicious. His dreams of food are not sensual or touristic, they are pathological and inevitable. They are part of the immediate and fascistic reality that subdues and controls him and from which he regards it as pointless to escape. Nor can it be theorized about, for there is nothing to attach thought to and there is nothing to which anything as playful or trivial as an idea could be relative. The matter that presses against his bowels or his ribs is too primitive to be appropriated by any conceivable academicism. It impinges, lightly and mysteriously, presses in upon him and causes him to collapse inwards without the benefit of any kind of compensating idea. He is simply alone with his guts and his toilet bowl. When he imagines dying he imagines it above all as a loss of control over the processing of food, a ludicrous and anti-tragic ataxy of the bowels resulting in embarrassing noises, foul stenches and an inner fluidity, a liquefying of the works.

The structure of the human being, its dignity and godlikeness, lies in the firmness and order of the digestive organs. It lies in control over matter. We are brainwashed into accepting the moralism that nature must never be dominated, but as food is the part of nature we know best and which most intimately affects us, it will have to be admitted once and for all that loss of dominance in the area where human and nature interact with the greatest continuity—that is, in the intestine—is tantamount to reduction in the order of things, to an obliteration of significance. Or do you think that the farcical loss of a specific dignity—as specific to the human genus as an atomic weight is to all the elements—can be suffered with impunity? What if Hamlet farted on stage? What if Adam, father of the race, developed unmistakable symptoms of diarrhoea? What if Medea came down with dysentery? What is disease but the absolutely serene course of nature sodomizing her creations? What is diarrhoea but the cheerful revenge of food upon our so-called gastronomes? Believe us, fellow peasants, food is not an innocent and sweet trifle to be played with, even though it appears to waltz so benignly upon our plates and tables. It is nature herself, stupid, cruel and ruthless. Everything is food, including yourselves, even if it is only bacteria which eat you now. Nature, over which you naturally and melodiously coo and rub your hands, that plump and fertile part-time goddess who manures your unconscious and whose backside you would so dearly like to kiss, that fat cow of a deity whom you vaguely imagine as some tinkling ethnic icon or as a smiling dairymaid covered in gossamer and tentacles of ivy, is no other than the mindless sadist who has commanded all living things to eat all other living things with a perpetual and inane violence, that lobotomized designer who casually exterminates dinosaurs and dodos, sabre-toothed tigers and hairy mammoths, and whose supposed capacity to maintain harmonious order is merely the effect of the relentless whip that ensures continual discontinuity, the stick which flagellates every beast on its path to consumption. Nature, as all true peasants are fully aware, is the greatest advocate of vulgar consumerism the universe has so far produced.

Armed with this foreknowledge the peasant dreams about the things he eats, a dreaming which is incessant, infantile and pseudosexual. There is nothing profound in his dreaming. There is nothing witty or perceptive about it, it lurches through his sleeping or waking head with the insolence of all cerebral masturbation. If he wasn't dreaming about food, after all, he would be writing sub-scientific Marxist pamphlets or measuring the flights of birds. He would be as abstracted, self-deluding and irrelevant to the world as any human being could be. He is salvaged by his persistent and frequently dirty oneiric habit.

He opens his dreaming eye, then, and in one glimpse he sees the City laid below him like an Edwardian banquet table laden down with innumerable heart-burning courses separated here and there by bitter sorbets and plates of fruit. The City is a pyramid of food with tiny human insects attached to it, nibbling away at its edges. And immediately, without the slightest prompting from the unconscious, he dreams that he is floating down the rue de Montorgueil equipped with a magical oesophagus and stomach capable of ingesting without limit, a monstrous digestive apparatus appropriate only to dream figures of the order of Pantagruel and Cyrano.

What is it that draws him to the street that winds its way from Les Halles to the rue Réaumur, last diluted fragment of that legendary belly which survives only in the betrayal of literature? Why, of course, the smell of caramelized apples emanating from Stohrer the *pâtissier*. What, in fact, could be more complementary to the aforementioned oneiric habit than the blue and white striped awning, navy blue facade in carved wood and multi-coloured ice-cream trolley posted outside at Stohrer, Parisian *pâtissiers* since 1730? While odour-hunting down the sprawling, noisy, hedonistic rue Montorgueil he cannot stop halting himself on the pavement under the dainty awning and the two windows filled with geraniums above it and peering through the small shop windows into the fantastic turquoise interior that reduces him to the blind and adoring consumerism of his childhood. His eyes go round and glazed.

It is a curious fact that no man likes to call himself a glutton, and yet each of us has in him a trace of gluttony, potential or actual. I cannot believe that there exists a single coherent human being who will not confess, at least to himself, that once or twice he has stuffed himself to the bursting point, on anything from quail financière to flapjacks, for no other reason than the beastlike satisfaction of his belly. In fact I pity anyone who has not permitted himself this sensual experience, if only to determine what his own private limitations are, and where, for himself alone, gourmandism ends and gluttony begins.

—M. F. K. Fisher,
The Art of Eating

The smell of apples and butter comes out in solid gusts, knocking pedestrians off balance. The windows themselves are divided into sweets and savouries, the former on the left, the latter on the right-hand side of the door. The right-hand side filled with trays of *gigots d'agneau glacés, bavarois de crevettes* and tubs of hare terrine does not interest him. This goes for the right-hand side of the interior as well, despite the opulence of its *feuilletés* and flans. The left-hand side, however, is the proper focus of his sleep-walking: here, there is a delirious display of pendant plastic parrots perched on wire seats surrounded by boxes of Stohrer chocolates bearing the same incomprehensible motif. Below them, ranged like their savoury counterparts on plain trays that reveal a charming smack of honest provincialism sit the dreamy pastries, tarts and geometrically severe *gâteaux* whose edges are razor sharp and whose colours are simple and pure. Next to these stratified confections constructed like sections of Jurassic soil, with layers of *pâte macaron, mousse praliné* and caramelized nuts packed into dense and formidable cubes with all the gravity of a Japanese picnic, lie casual assortments of macaroons. But it is necessary to venture inside, into the pale Pompeian-First Empire décor of large wall mirrors and delicately painted mouldings, of life-sized frescoes of sweet-eating nereids in fluttering chitons and recumbent bowls of summer fruit set within gold garlands, in order to submit to the narcotic profusion of Stohrer's fantasies.

Here there is nothing of the slick modernism of Peltier or Christian Constant, no lamina of arty professionalism laid over the childish indulgence of stuffing your face with sweets. Stohrer is the house of Hansel and Gretel, the chocolate cottage of the fairytale. Its frills are modest and rooted in the tolerance of other ages. The mirrors produce sparkling but subdued reflections. Above, a turquoise oval ceiling, which should be filled with *trompe l'oeil* scenes of angelic turbulence. Under the glass counters, submerged in the blues, creams and golds that surround them on all sides, sleep the rows of Ali-Babas, *royal menthes, nouméas, noisettines* and *tartes bourdaloues*, along with the *croissants, pains au chocolat* and *napolitains*. A notice outside the shop confronts the casual stroller with a highly scientific graph in which most of the famous bakers of Paris appear acidulously appraised in relation to each other in the matter of making *croissants*, and by means of which we learn that while the *croissants* of Le Fournil de Pierre are grossly shaped, over sugared and in all ways ambiguous, and those of Réné St Ouen thick, supine, mushy and floury in taste, those of Stohrer are perfectly crusty, imbued with a pleasing classical crab form, ungreasy, sufficiently firm in texture and shot through with the correctly light taste of butter. This is indeed a rarity in the heretical City of today. The *pains aux raisins,* too, although the notice does not boast about them, are filled with just the right amount of custard and are cooked to the perfect degree of semi-resistant hardness around the rims. But at this point, as he is perhaps letting his greedy infantile eyes roam lustfully over the arched chocolate back of an Alhambra decorated with brown and cream leaves and truffle berries or the caramelized top of a *puits d'amour* set off against a background of paper lace, and dreaming of rum punch and layers of cream in either, he is rudely not to say catastrophically awakened from his wallowing in the turquoise boudoir of pastry by the incestuous cackling of food dandies all around him, for suddenly he is surrounded and there is no getting away from them. Professors, experts, self-taught men, culinary aesthetes, little Neros of the taste buds, gastronomic pedants, pastriologists, Professors of Higher *Pâtisserie*, dons of the world of flans, PhDs in strawberry tarts, lecturers in *forêts noires*. They have appeared out of nowhere in a swarm, their notebooks are out and already they are arguing, analysing, discoursing, holding forth upon this and that aspect of the sweet tooth's art, a mad circus of bearded gastronomes with moist lips and honeycombed, elongated noses! What a dream it's become, and in the middle of the rue Montorgueil! The peasant holds his hands to his ears but nothing can stop the deluge of masterful comments and observations, of argument and counter-argument, from overwhelming his simple, rustic brain.

"Too insolent, the *royale menthes,* and too prejudiced against the *mousseline de chocolat.* Seven out of ten."

"Rubbish! Blatant racism!"

"We will have to wait until your notes are published in full. However, we can say with some certainty, not to say…well, in short, you're forgetting the origins of the *royale menthe*. The essence, sir, is mint. *Menthe fraîche, si je peux dire*…as fresh as possible *et tutti frutti!*"

> *My family's story of the Steak and Dye Incident reinforced for me at an early age the value of the serendipitous and unexpected in dining. My parents were preparing a steak at my grandmother's beach cottage on Fire Island when they unexpectedly dropped the steak in a pail of blue dye. Screaming disaster, they rushed the steak into the ocean and gave it a good washing. Much to their surprise it was the tastiest steak ever.*
>
> —George Vincent Wright,
> *"Cuisine Sauvage"*

"*Tutti frutti!* The analysis holds!"

"What you say, sir, about the *menthe fraîche* in the *royale menthes* may be true, but how can you explain the overbearing arrogance, the injudicious injudiciousness, the tone…*pimpante et rageuse, que puis-je dire?*…of the *punché au rhum léger* in the Alhambra, not to mention the sheer iconoclasm of the *chocolat amer* in the Criollo? Do we not detect a note of false values? Six out of ten for the Criollo and five for the Alhambra!"

"Liberal fags!"

"*A priori! In grosso modo!*"

"Honorary election for the *mousse de fruits cassis!*"

"An evident and inexcusable bias towards pears…*tutti frutti* revisionism…dignity for *charlottes*…a re-examination of *péchés mignons*…a radical and uncompromising re-evaluation of the entire hierarchial system of *bonbons,* tarts and *crèmes caramels*…absence of ethnocentricity in the matter of the three Pyramids…"

"The Pyramids are African!"

"*A posteriori* and QED…"

"Honorary election for the Three Pyramids!"

Yes, it's true, Stohrer manufactures three different types of pyramidal confection, one of dark brown chocolate (*le Kheops*), one white (*le Khephren*) and one coffee (*le Mykerinos*). The City's pseudo-Masonic, revolutionary Egyptian imagery lives on even here, perpetuating the charming but fraudulent fantasies of Nilotic omniscience. And since our academics are mesmerized by questions of ethnic and cultural displacement, they go into paroxysms over the Three Pyramids (not to mention, of course, the Ali-Baba, the *nouméa* and the *criollo*), so much so that the peasant, momentarily drowned in their lecherous discourses, finds himself drifting away from them, sucked back into the rue Montorgueil and away from the blue and cream shimmer of Stohrer. But it is not only his old-fashioned and reactionary tastes that expel him from their company, it is also the pungent smell of fish coming from the other side of the street. The tumult of this artery, given over almost entirely to the delirium of food, sacks and pillages his frontal lobes, rendering them entirely subjective. He waddles past the butchers' shops at the end of the street where it debouches by St Eustache and the alien reflective pavilions of the Forum des Halles (the glittering eggs of some pterodactyl of the unpleasant future) and goes in and out of the aisles of hanging rabbits, their livers dangling from carved-up underbellies by tiny webs of fat, the thickets of pheasants, capons and moorhens, the enslaved piles of trussed-up-ducklings and corn-fed chickens, the bowls of trips and *boudin noir*, *tournedos* and blanched tongues, arrays of nutty brains and under-estimated ears, trotters and jellies, horse steaks and sides of boar. He is an omnivorous customer. Like the shoppers of the neighborhood he flinches before nothing, and this can be liberally interpreted, as it always is, as a calm and wholesome acceptance of the diversity of nature, a refusal to be squeamishly selective when confronted with its awful riches. The proletarian opulence of the Montorgueil butchers is reflected in the tumbling crushed-ice displays of the two major fishmongers, especially the bigger of two at no. 62. The smells from here have dragged him away from the Stohrer boudoir, after all, causing him to ignore in passing the honourable Enard next door, and that in spite of their superbly vulgar enamelled chandeliers. The *poissonnière*, on the other hand, reminds him of the cascading crustaceans of the rue Lepic which he visits scrupulously every day, if only to "window-lick" and which successfully populate his waking dreams with impossibly armoured

submarine edibles, green and morose sea snails and the tragic lobsters whose enigmatic and incessantly active pincers denote the
value they place upon their own lives.

The Montorgueil shop, on the other hand, surpasses even those
delectable emporia of living gastronomic corpses of the deep. It is
deeper inside, or at least seems so due to the size and seriousness
of its theatrical displays: the banks of ice containing hundreds of
marine species swirled around decorative boulders, fishermen's
baskets, palm fronds, clusters of enormous fresh irises, fir twigs,
lemons and bales of rosemary. Through this artificial but convinc-
ing sea-landscape in which the "water" has been arrested in the
form of that fine and granular ice that so elicits our admiration, the
confused eye, scrambling among the diverse medley of mineral and
animal forms, comes across arched red snappers in the act of jump-
ing, whorled skinned eels roped around rocks, salmon sliced into
steaks and reconstituted into their original languid shapes while
their mouths protrude into the street. John Dorys, rainbow trout
and fleshy whitings mate against a dazzling backdrop of crystals
while sea slugs, crayfish and scallops slide in and out of nooks and
crevices, pile themselves up like mounds of heads under the powerful lamps that make them glitter. Shoals of macherel and sprat
weaving through the exotically unmarine vegetation, ambushes of
squid and fillets of shark, pike and sword fish, grey shrimps and
sombre colonies of sleeping crabs, everything edible in the oceans
dredged up from the sea floors and brought into the cruel and
crystalline light of the store where electricity and ice combust together to recreate the palatial interiors of the Snow Queen. The
bodies of these prostrate organisms, given a paradoxical and titil-
lating glory by their exposure among these miniature symbolic
landscapes, are cold and diamantine: the cold they give off hits the
lungs and makes the peasant recoil at the thought of graves.

The store is organized as a refined and sensual bordello of marine food. Unlike the Spartan and ludicrously plain emptiness of
English fishmongers, where it is a struggle to see anything interesting and which deliberately militates against the immoral enjoyment of carnivorous activities and aesthetic stimulations (it is sur-

prising that the dour trays of limited produce aren't covered with mourning shrouds), the Parisian fish shop exults in visual whorishness, flourishes its catholicity of taste and deliberately takes upon itself the glory of biological diversity. Even the little tubs of seaweed cavort with the consumer. Even the cashier, enthroned at the back of the shop in an open kiosk bedecked with herbs and citrus fruits, flirts with the unsatisfied and salacious hunger of the eaters of fish. She could be a mermaid for all the awed shoppers know—sympathetic sister of the cavalcades of oceanic animals that surround her. She wears a knowing and lascivious smile. Her eyes are green and correspond in unforeseen ways with the speckled and mucal spines, glazed black eyes, tinted underbellies and motionless fins. The galoshes and blue overalls of the men do not concern or in any way compliment her. She is the Alice Ozy of the aquatic cornucopia, inspirer of delicate fish soups, haughty *soles Bercys* and *fatal bouillabaisses*. In her eyes are printed the boredom and spiralling sensuality of the trade in flesh.

She reminds the peasant of the magnificent woman who stands behind the counter at the Compagnie Coloniale du Thé on the rue Lepic, in her two-tone tan shoes, transparent specs, Walkyrie chignon and perfect red mouth, majestic and hyper-sexual guardian of the orange and strawberry teas, lime infusions and tin Lipton boxes emblazoned with courtly Chinese scenes. The two women are identical in their relation to their produce. Like the cashier at no. 62, the busy *patronne* of the Compagnie Coloniale is surrounded—if you peer in at her from the outside—by verdant clumps of bamboo and bric-à-brac symbolically or practically related to the purveying of tea and coffee: percolators, odd little grinders and other esoteric appurtenances, the lovely round green boxes of Yunnan tea, packets of cinnamon and lemon grass, pepper pots and wicker filters. Like the mermaid her lower half is often not revealed and she floats seductively and maternally among her fragrant charges, a Renoir bar-girl in front of a mirror—no, how revolting!—a *diva* of tea whose hair you imagine as being lightly scented with bergamot, whose unparalleled, mature cleavage, if you were so lucky as to be able to bury your childish face in it, you find to be musky, smoky, pungent with the dry perfume of Lapsang Suchong.

French women may have the aura of modesty and coyness about them, but they are unerring about when to drop their veils or their drawers. One can well imagine the erotic effects of amorous adventures in a venue that relays the atmosphere of secret, clandestine, and unexpected locations. Few healthy men would be likely to resist such an epicurean orgy. Surely an American man who grew up with puritanical sexual values would be easy prey for such a scene, and probably float out of the restaurant feeling as if he had visited another world hitherto unknown to him. A visit that would make pale all previous dining encounters. Thus some inklings into the term "femme fatale," as these women are fatal to men who have been in the hands of unsophisticated or careless women.

—Edith Kunz,
"French Food Fantasies"

Why is it always women who fill these dangerous and ambivalent posts, who act as the agents of the elective affinities that draw us to the eating of food? It is best, or worst, in the *crèmeries*. Yes, in the intense cheese and dairy produce shops—those specialist stores of genius which are the paramount glory of Paris—you will find the presence of women behind the counter most volcanic, deranging and intoxicating. There is something in the textures of curdled and processed milk that reacts alchemically with their flesh and their hormones to turn them into minor cheesy goddesses fully equipped with atavistic charms and bodily attributes which in turn make their *chèvres, vacherins, crèmes fraîches* and St Aulbrays insidiously and alarmingly irresistible. They know they do it, too. They are never the first to wipe those knowing smiles off their faces. Their cheeks are pale and waxy, chilled along with everything else, but out of the background of pale yellows, creams and lactic whites their lips stand out brilliantly, as do the chocolate and cyan centres of their eyes. As the peasant makes his way up the rue de Montorgueil in the direction of the rue des Petits Carreaux, the rue Réaumur and the green lattice gate that announces the realm of food, he is more and more distracted by these tutelary deities ensconced in their altars of titbits. And not only the dairymaids, but the Rubensesque women who thrive in the moist darkness and secrecy of the *charcuteries,* whose secondary sexual features derive potency from the proliferation all around them of mounds of *oeufs en gelée, coquilles au crabe, bouchées à la reine,* puffy gnocchi, gelled rabbits surmounted by glazed nuts, heavily minted *tabbouleh,* Baltic herrings, *foie gras de canard, croustades au thon, pamplemousses exotiques in a sauce cocktail,* bundles of asparagus in *sauce mousseline,* artichokes with *crevettes, grenadin de veau* in pineapple and eclectic bales of *blinis, mille feuilles,* stuffed mussels, *brioches au roquefort* and chestnut flans. In the unreal interior of the *traiteur,* buried in the most highly organized and rarefied chemistries of food on earth, all human beings take on the look of the clients and "servers" of the near-by rue St Denis, and we would even go so far as to claim this as a compliment.

The peasant, ambling in his primitive way up the rue Montorgueil, stopping for a marc at La Grappe d'Orgueil, avoiding scrupulously the rundown offices of the Parti Socialiste in case he is accidentally recognized by someone, feeling, it is true, tempestuous inflations afflict him in his reproductive zones, appears to be convinced only that women are essentially treated in the same way as food, consumed, tasted, ingested, swallowed, burped up, expelled in the form of faeces—but suddenly interrupting his dream in order to recoil with revulsion from such crude, pseduo-liberal, sub-feminist meditations (which are truly not worthy of the complexity of the subject and which, to speak frankly, he considers not without a certain amount of sadistic intrigue), he finds himself before he knows it standing aimlessly, like a stranded gastronomic angel, on the pavement of the rue Réaumur with a taste of cheese in his mouth. Let's face it, he thinks to himself literally dreamily, we live not in the City of Food but in the City of Women. The supermarket will divorce cheese from plunging *décolletés,* plastic wrapping will keep bananas and erections apart, people will see through all this childish and anachronistic erotic-flim-flam, they will think about vitamin value, fibre content, waistlines and love handles, iron levels and quotas of trace elements. The presence of selenium or zinc will weigh more with the conscientious consumer than the corny poetry of dairymaids and cherry-like nipples. You will serve yourself without the inconvenient intermediary of winks, half-smiles, flirtatious games or the possibility of secret rendezvous with food nymphs smelling, even in the back row of the cinema, of fresh artichokes, smoked cheeses and *saucisson sec*. The desensualization of food is perfectly inevitable. The English example will be universally followed. The rue Montorgueil will have to go, of course...for one thing, it's unhygienic, it swarms with microbes and lethal doses of listeria. The dream of food ends with nostalgic onanism in the dark. It is time to pinch yourselves and assure a speedy and healthy return to reality. The glory and exhilaration of the sexless supermarket awaits you, and it is even a curious fact that the peasant himself has no hesitation in looking forward to it. But before he goes shopping at the gigantic temple of functional food at the Carrefour shopping centre, he is resolved to indulge himself in another dream altogether: the dream of the City of Women, for this City at least has an endless and verifiable future. The City of Women is all around us and recently, quite independently from the metaphors of food and consumption, it has made an impressive transformation from slave state to monarchy to fledgling republic. The City of Women is the only part of the present that will exist in the future without uncertainty. It is the seed of future meteoric storms.

Thus confronted with the imminent end of his dream, the gastronome-peasant decides to pinch himself hard and, taking his nose between his index finger and his thumb, proceeds to do so in order to wake up. For a moment he blacks out and then, as always happens, he blinks his eyes as he emerges from his state of sleep. Yes, the severe pinch makes him wake up. But what is his surprise when he finds that, instead of cosily ensconced in a warm bed surrounded by a pleasantly aired and darkened room, he is still standing lost and disappointed, at the corner of the rue Réaumur and the rue Montorgueil, at the miserable edge of his own banished dream?

Lawrence Osborne is the author of The Angelic Game, Ania Malina, *and* Paris Dreambook: An Unconventional Guide to the Splendor and Squalor of the City *from which this story was excerpted. He lives in Paris.*

✳

Thanks to the eyewitness accounts provided by Hans Städen, a German sailor who was shipwrecked on the coast of Brazil early in the sixteenth century, we have a vivid idea of how one group, the Tupinamba, combined ritual sacrifice with cannibalism.

On the day of the sacrifice the prisoner of war, trussed around the waist, was dragged into the plaza. He was surrounded by women who insulted and abused him, but he was allowed to give vent to his feelings by throwing fruits or broken pieces of pottery at them. Meanwhile old women painted black and red and wearing necklaces of human teeth brought out ornamented vases in which the victim's blood and entrails would be cooked. The ceremonial club that would be used to kill him was passed back and forth among the men in order to "acquire the power to catch a prisoner in the future." The actual executioner wore a long feather cloak and was followed by relatives singing and beating drums. The executioner and the prisoner derided each other. Enough liberty was allowed the prisoner so that he could dodge the blows, and sometimes a club was put in his hands for protecting himself without being able to strike back. When at last his skull was shattered, everyone "shouted and whistled." If the prisoner had been given a wife during his period of captivity, she was expected to shed tears over his body before joining in the feast that followed. Now the old women "rushed to drink the warm blood," and children dipped their hands into it. "Mothers would smear their nipples with blood so that even babies could have a taste of it." The body was cut into quarters and barbecued while "the old women who were the most eager for human flesh" licked the grease dripping from the sticks that formed the grill.

—Marvin Harris, *Cannibals and Kings: The Origins of Cultures*

PAULA MCDONALD

✦ ✦ ✦

Waltz at the End of Earth

Amazing things happen when you journey
to the edge of the map.

THERE ARE MOMENTS WHEN A SUDDEN, UNEXPECTED CONNEC-
tion is made somewhere in the world, powerful and undeniable.
When the energy is exactly right, it doesn't seem to matter where
you are. Things just happen as they should. My experience in a tiny
hovel on a far-distant Chinese island was one of those moments.

Two of us were on our way to "End of Earth," the most remote
beach on remote Hainan Island, the furthest south in a string of
Chinese islands in the South China Sea. A ridiculous place to want
to go; there's nothing there. But the ancient Chinese believed the
earth ended at the southern tip of this largest of China's islands.
Thus, to journey to "End of Earth" was to show great "strength
and courage," qualities of utmost importance to the Chinese. To
journey to "End of Earth" was to bring great good fortune to
yourself. In such a strange way, my journey did.

Getting to Hainan Island from Guangzhou isn't easy. Eighteen-
hour village-bus rides through the mountains with the inevitable
breakdowns in the middle of the night are followed by tedious ferries, incomprehensible transfers, and more tedious ferries. To even
attempt Hainan Island without speaking fluent Cantonese requires

a strong belief in personal luck, guardian angels, and good fairies. To this day, I can vividly remember every moment of that journey; for the life of me I can't figure out how we arranged it or what compelled us so completely at the time.

But, the journey itself is another tale. Suffice it to say that we found our way to "End of Earth" eventually, a peaceful, serene place with an aura of great continuity. Beyond, with quiet waves lapping at our feet, the sea seemed to stretch forever. Like the ancient Chinese, who could know what was out there? Or what would come next? What came next was one of the most important gifts of my life.

In a tiny village nearby, we stopped for lunch at a small roadside house, a hovel actually, one of those one-room shacks that serve as home, restaurant, and mini-zoo, a combination so common in rural China.

Joanne Turner, my fellow traveler, and I had eaten in many similar places in the few weeks since we'd met and completed a stint together as volunteers on a scientific project meant to catalog China's southern rainforests. We'd camped on remote mountaintops, sea kayaked the uninhabited Outer Islands, trekked through leech-filled jungles, and eaten, standing up, in every street market in Southern China it seemed.

Along the way, we'd become expert pantomimists, ready smilers, and absolute gourmands on the street-food scene. The shabbiness of the shack didn't bother us. The luxury of eating from an actual table instead of a rock seemed rather civilized, in fact.

This particular shack was poor even by Chinese standards though. It held only the bare wooden table, a rope bed, and several cages full of eight- and ten-foot snakes. The dirt floor was swept clean, and an old bicycle hung on the wall. Nothing more adorned the place. Cooking, as is customary in the countryside, was done out back on an empty oil drum with a wood fire below.

The 80-year-old owner and her granddaughter immediately began to display their snakes. Out they came from their cages and were handed to us, one by one. Which did we want for lunch? We tried to pantomime that it was very hot, that we weren't very hungry after all, and that the snakes were very large. There would be so much waste.

Perhaps rabbit would be better, suggested our hosts. Or so we assumed as they took us to a shed in back where three rabbits were caged. Unable to look any bunny in the eye and then eat it, we politely tried to say that the rabbits were also too big. The only other choice seemed to be an old chicken pecking at the edge of the dirt lane, so we opted for him. Least of all possible sins, or so we thought.

*T*he southern Chinese, as any northerner will tell you with distaste, will eat almost anything. I have heard Southerners themselves tell the story about the Indian and the Cantonese confronted by a creature from outer space: the Indian falls to his knees and begins to worship it, while the Chinese searches his memory for a suitable recipe.

—Paul Levy, *Out to Lunch*

Twenty minutes later, the food began arriving: the usual Chinese mystery soup, followed by several courses of vegetables, rice, and endless pots of steaming tea in the 100-degree heat. Finally the meat arrived.

It was unmistakably rabbit! Oh, lordy, where had we gone wrong? Perhaps we should have drawn pictures instead of doing charades. We ate it, of course. With grace and a good deal of hard swallowing. Not to would have caused a loss of face for the two gracious women whose humble hospitality we shared.

The heat was oppressive that day, as it is all over southern China in May, and even to sit still was to sit and drip. During lunch, the old woman kept smiling at me as if to say, "I forgive you for sweating in my house. There is no loss of face in this," and fanning me with a marvelously ingenious fan made completely of feathers. I had never seen anything like it.

Since there was literally nothing else in the one-room house, not even a change of clothes, and the fan seemed to be her only possession besides an old watch, I was careful not to admire it openly. Chinese custom demands the giving to guests of whatever they admire. But despite my intentional disregard of the fan, I was immensely grateful for the momentary illusion of coolness each whoosh brought.

Perhaps because I was trying so hard to ignore the feather fan, what happened next caught me completely by surprise.

Suddenly, for no apparent reason, the old woman broke into a great grin, hugged me hard, handed me the fan, and then hugged me again. I was stunned. It was obviously a gift, but her generosity, under the circumstances, was astonishing. What had prompted the act? What could I, a lanky, perspiring stranger with a sunburned nose, in her life for so short a time, have possibly done to deserve the gift of one of her few possessions? Nothing that I could conceive of, but something had changed dramatically in the little room. The old woman now sat smiling beatifically as though I had pleased her more than I could ever imagine. But I couldn't, for the life of me figure out how.

Despite the baking heat inside the house, we lingered awhile after lunch and drank more tea just to stay and not seem to rush away. And then, to our amazement, when her granddaughter finally left to take care of other chores, the old woman began to speak in halting English, obviously a language she had not used for decades. Bit by bit, straining to understand the stumbling words, we learned her story.

Her husband had been imprisoned under Mao for being a follower of Chiang Kai-Shek and had died a prisoner. She had watched as he was led away. She never saw him again.

Before the Cultural Revolution the woman had been a teacher, the daughter of educated diplomats, one of the new regime's despised intellectuals. After the Communist victory in China, she had been exiled from Shanghai to the remote island village for the double sins of being educated and being the wife of a political enemy. She had lived in the isolated village for more than 30 years, surviving as best she could by cooking and selling the snakes and rabbits she and her granddaughter were able to trap.

Her story, told with no rancor, captured our hearts, and despite the need to get on, we stayed. The long-forgotten English words seemed to get easier for her as we asked questions about her life and encouraged her to reminisce. She told us of her childhood, of traveling and learning English at embassies as a youngster. Memories of another, so very different life. Yet, for all her losses, she truly seemed to have no bitterness. With one strange exception. When I asked her directly if she had regrets, she could think of only one: that she had never learned to waltz.

One of her most vivid childhood memories was of being taken, as a young girl, to a grand ball in Hong Kong where there were many English guests in attendance. The music was international that night, the first time she had heard anything besides the harsh, sharp cacophony of China's music, and suddenly the ballroom was filled with swirling skirts and the sweetest sounds she had ever heard. Couples were waltzing, and, to the young Chinese girl, it was the most beautiful sight in the world. Someday she would grow up to become one of those graceful waltzing women.

She grew up, but China changed. There were no more waltzes. And now there were no more illusions in her life.

In the silence that followed the story, I took her hand across the table. Then I quietly asked if she would still like to learn to waltz. Here. Now.

The slow smile that spread across her face was my answer. We stood and moved together toward our ballroom floor, an open space of five feet of hard-packed dirt between the table and the bed. "Please, God," I prayed, "let me remember a waltz. Any waltz. And let me remember how to lead."

We started shakily, me humming Strauss, stepping on her toes. But soon we got smoother, bolder, louder. "The Blue Danube" swelled and filled the room. Her baggy Mao pajama pants became a swirling skirt, she became young and beautiful again, and I became a handsome foreigner, tall, sure, strong...perhaps a prince who carried her away. Away from her destiny at "End of Earth."

The feather fan hangs on my office wall today, next to her picture. Next to our picture. The two of us, hands clasped, smiling strangers from such different worlds, waltzing around a steaming hut in a forsaken spot I visited by chance that day. That day I met strength and courage at "End of Earth."

Paula McDonald lives on the beach in Rosarito, Mexico. On the clearest of days, if she squints, she can almost see China's "End of Earth." When the waves are quiet, she can certainly hear Strauss.

＊

Dear Sister,

After you went, a low wind warbled through the house like a spacious bird, making it high but lonely. When you had gone the love came. I supposed it would. The supper of the heart is when the guest is gone.

—Emily Dickinson

PART FOUR

IN THE SHADOWS

Pass on the Primate

The author finds some tough things to chew
in the cultural stew.

AT TWILIGHT, IT WAS DIFFICULT TO TELL THE SIMPLE DWELLINGS from the workshops, the brothels, the restaurants, the stores. In this quarter of San Pedro, a large, dirty port town in the Ivory Coast, the buildings were all single-room huts—thrown together directly on top of the hard dirt floors by nailing pieces of wood of various lengths and states of rot into a vague square—topped off with tin or palm leaves. At this time of the evening the women sat out front of the huts braiding each other's hair, and the men gathered on certain corners, squatting over a brazier to prepare the heavily-sugared tea, smoking cigarettes, and watching.

No one was too busy to look up as I passed. Groups of children followed me at a distance, calling out *"Toubab"* (their word for white person) to announce my approach. I was looking for a restaurant, for something to eat.

"Vous avez un restaurant ici?" I asked a woman who sat in front of a hut through whose door great billows of gray smoke were ejected. As she smiled and stood up, the bravest in my entourage of children rushed to touch my skin and hair. Others hung back, fingers in mouths, staring at the white stranger. At first I'd found them amusing, but after two months in West Africa they were no longer.

Guiltily, I considered them as annoying as the constant buzzing of flies and the mosquitoes who had given me malaria in Guinea.

The woman beckoned me inside the hut where the orange flicker of fire danced under a great iron pot. She lifted the lid and pointed inside. "There is this," she told me, stirring the stew, bringing up its contents for my inspection. The white, triangular skull of a goat emerged: eye sockets, jawbone, teeth, ear holes...I looked around. There were no furnishings in the room. Another woman slept in one corner on the bare ground swathed in her robes, in the other corner slept a pet monkey.

"If you wait an hour there will be something better," the woman whispered, conspiratorially, and she turned her eyes upon me in the smoky hut. With her gaze came the now familiar sense of oppression settling upon me, along with alternating waves of sorrow, irritation, and guilt.

I hadn't wanted to eat in a hut again. I was finally in a real city, and I wanted a restaurant. I thought she'd send a child to take me to a restaurant, but by eating here, I would be doing a great favor to this woman and her family. My 200 CFA, less than an American dollar, could be used to buy rice, manioc root, and other staples. More likely, though, she would buy lipstick or nail polish...another wave of guilt at my disparaging thought.

I told myself that I couldn't always be concerned with how the family would spend the money. It's like giving a quarter to a beggar on the corner, knowing it will be spent on food or rot-gut, whichever is the priority at the moment. An adult may thoughtlessly spend money needed to feed the children on tea, cigarettes, or cosmetics. And tonight I didn't want to be faced with the welfare of a family or a village. I didn't want to watch the women pounding grain and manioc for my dinner, to see the calluses on their hands, to see their skinny children, to eat seated on a packed earth floor or to be given the only chair and watched by dozens of hungry eyes while I was given the choicest bits, knowing that when I walked away they would fall upon it, sucking the last drops of nutrition from among the bones I so casually discarded.

After two months in West Africa I needed a break. This was a big town. I wanted to find an established restaurant where I could sit at a table, have a beer, and not be obliged to become emotionally involved in a family's personal life. Just by sitting at someone's hut I would be face-to-face with the woman and the children whose economy I was so directly affecting, face-to-face with the unbelievable hand-to-mouth existence of these people as they stared at me, not as a person but as a piece of incredible luck that had brought them 200 CFA, and more, if they were clever.

Of course the boy would escort me to my hotel that night, and another child, probably the girl, would be outside in the morning, waiting to bring me back for breakfast. They would lead me through the streets of this dirty port town, over the sturdiest planks that lay over stinking open sewers from the quarter of my hotel to the quarter of their family. If I ate here, I would be their patroness, and for the duration of my stay I wouldn't be able to forget them. Indeed, I would be pressed to take photos, to send money from America, or Walkmans or jeans. I would have to give them my address, promise to be a correspondent. Already I had dozens.

They knew about the material things because this was a large town, unlike others where my only option was to call upon the chief to ask his permission to stay and eat, and where I paid for my meal and my night's lodging

Appetite, necessity, and therapeutic ideas had dietary consequences which disconcerted foreign observers. Cavazzi has mentioned the consumption of caterpillars, insects, savannah rats, snakes, etc.; craving for meat, but also refinements of taste, explain this custom. The mediocre flour derived from the kernel of the palm nut, which Pigafetta mentions, was used by villagers only "in time of famine," as the compiler of the Historia *remarks. Geophagy—the soil of termites' nests being the only dirt consumed—was a way of outwitting hunger; but under certain circumstances it was prescribed for pregnant women; it also answered the needs of gourmets who wished to "drive away the taste of fat" after too heavy a meal.*

—Georges Balandier, *Daily Life in the Kingdom of the Kongo: From the Sixteenth to the Eighteenth Century* in trade for cigarettes, sugar, candy, tea leaves, Nescafe, or maybe my t-shirt. Money is practically useless when one must walk 100 miles to a store. In the villages there is no stench. In the bush, villagers are innocent of education, of cash, of technology, and of medicine. The food supply determines the size of the village. A malnourished mother will lose her child. The village will shrink or grow according to the abundance of the forest. It is clean, it is healthy, it is subject to laws of nature that little affect Westerners or these impoverished ghetto-dwellers.

Surveying the litter of San Pedro, inhaling the stench, avoiding the beggars with their oozing wounds and missing limbs, it is impossible not to feel shame for my culture, for the entire Western world, for pressing civilization upon these people. And it is impossible to reconcile myself to my guilt at feeling that the villagers who live in the bush—away from any modernity and subject to the laws of nature, and the cruel reality that only the fittest will survive—are better off.

Because here in a city a family needs money. There is no jungle in which to hunt. No forest where papayas and bananas grow wild, no clearing where one can plant manioc and grains. Garbage is inorganic. In bush villages, goats and chickens eat discarded fruit peelings and inedible grain. Teeth, bones, and hooves are recycled into weapons and jewelry. Skins are used as floor coverings, blankets. The toilet is a hole in the ground which will eventually be composted.

In the city, goats cannot eat all the cigarette and candy wrappers, oatmeal tins, and other manufactured garbage imported from the West. The presence of goats in a city cause an additional health hazard. In the city, early in the morning, one is confronted with the sight of men, women, and children squatting over the sewers, or emptying buckets of sewage in the street. No, the Western world has not done a big favor to Africa, by bringing it civilization.

Eating alone while being watched by a mother, her children, and all the neighbors in a city influenced by America and Western Europe is nervewracking. There is perhaps one metal spoon in the neighborhood, which is brought for me, because of course I cannot use my hands as they do (I can, but it is expected that I use the spoon). They watch my fingers handle the tool, bring the food to my mouth, chew, smile, swallow. In their eyes is respect, admiration, hatred, curiosity, jealousy, wanting, and greed.

Electricity runs from a pole to a TV where 50 people gather, mesmerized by *Baywatch* and *Dallas,* which they vehemently believe to be documentary programs of daily American life. I try to tell them that these "realities" are missing something—if they could only see the evening news that shows the poverty, the violence, the deviations from their dream world. But they would, I am sure, believe our evening news to be fiction.

Perhaps they need to believe in this dream world, the static-ridden blue-hued flickering dream world dragged as far as its umbilical cord will allow into a dusty street. I cannot convince them that this is not my country, this world where on every street jostle blond, bikini-clad lifeguards who live in mansions off the riches of oil wells with views of sparkling oceans and go shopping daily for cars, jeans, and cowboy boots. Confronted with such scenes I cannot get my mind to stop its turning round with reasons for such clear desperation.

My eyes became used to the dimness of the hut in the twilight. The smoke floated past me in a stream out the front door. I looked around. A back door. The woman stirring the stew and the one sleeping in the corner. The front door. The monkey sleeping in the other corner. Really funny, considering the nervous skittering traits of monkeys, that this one still slept as the woman chattered on to me about dinner in French and Mandinke.

I looked closer. Instead of being curled up in a sleeping position the monkey's limbs were spread out, and its head, which I thought was resting on its side, was actually turned all the way round so that its chin rested on its back.

I looked even closer, unwilling to come to the obvious conclusion. Its pointy teeth glittered white and its eyes were open, dark and soulless. The woman followed my gaze, and pointed to it. "In an hour, I will cook the monkey for you," she announced proudly.

I looked at her closer, shocked, but she was proud. "In an hour…" she repeated. The stews I had so far eaten in West African huts numbered around 50, I reckoned, as I nodded, comprehending the meaning of this.

While in military survival training I was taught that the jungle can harbor many flora and fauna that are poisonous to humans. But if there are monkeys present, I was told, observe them. You, the human, can eat anything the monkey eats. Then, of course, you can eat the monkey. He is said to taste like chicken.

—RS

And I fled, mumbling polite excuses that must have left her confused. The meat in these stews, I had assumed, was one of the hundreds of sheep or goats that roamed cities and villages sharing in the garbage piles with the slinky yellow dogs and vermin. Or it was dik-dik, a small deer often hunted in the forest, or wild pig, or even bush-rat, an elusive night creature that a Peace Corps worker had assured me was a rare and delicious treat—a large, sleek animal, she told me, that fed not on garbage but on leaves and grubs in the jungle.

I even laughed once, upon the realization that the tough pieces of skin in my stew was porcupine hide. The woman who cooked it had shown me its quills.

Not being cognizant of the words for these creatures in Mandinke or Woloof, and the women, largely being uneducated and unschooled in French, I would never know what had been in those stews. Most likely, for the white stranger, a special guest with money, an entertainer in villages with no TV, who shuffled cards and carried a battery-operated lamp, a self-inflating air mattress and other magical wonders of the Western world, I was probably served the prestigious delicacy of monkey stew quite often—unrecognizable to my palate from the gamey tastes of bush-rat, porcupine, goat, and pig, especially among the standard pungent mixture of manioc chunks, yams, peppers, onions, and garlic.

The night I fled the hut I wandered around town, my hunger staved off by the horror of dead tangled limbs, until I stumbled into the French quarter, where there was a restaurant with electric light bulbs hanging from wooden ceilings that sheltered tables and Adirondak chairs, and refrigerators filled with beer and soda. I wished I was already in Abidjan, but this would do.

Civilization, I thought, relieved, until the panicked bleating of a goat caught my attention and I turned. It was bound by the feet and hung upside-down on a hook in front of a hut, writhing in the firelight. Before I could look away a hand appeared and its throat was severed with a large knife, its glint dulled with blood that shone black in the faded light. The animal, a strong animal, kicked and bucked and its back arched and writhed, even as it hung there upside-down. Its nerves reacted automatically to what its brain could no longer control—the severance of its sum parts. I had seen it all before—why was it different now? I had done this myself, having grown up in the country, no stranger to the wrung necks of rabbits and chickens, no stranger to the bleatings of lambs and calves being led to slaughter.

I will be a vegetarian, I thought as the butcher gripped the animal by a front leg, which still kicked, and opened its stomach. The shadow of a surly yellow dog—it moved like a jungle cat—hovered just out of range of the light of the cooking fire where a man squatted to pick up a small pot of boiling tea. He lifted it out of the fire using a crushed cigarette pack as a potholder, and poured the frothing liquid into three tiny cups as goat intestines slowly unraveled into a neat pile onto the dirt.

In the restaurant, I collapsed into a low wooden chair, leaning into its hard, cool, slatted back, varnished white with paint that bubbled and peeled. My beer came immediately, the cold brown bottle coating my hand with its cold sweat in the dark equatorial evening swelter. Willie Nelson sang "Georgia on My Mind," followed by John Denver's "Rocky Mountain High."

No, I wasn't ready for dinner yet. Just let me sit here awhile, *s'il te plaît*. The patron bowed and left me to contemplation.

All the tables and chairs had been sponged clean, the white paint only beginning to wrinkle and chip. I believe it never quite dried, being so humid.

The dirt floor had been pounded down hard and level, swept

clean of bottle caps, cigarette butts, and street gravel. I peeled the label off the beer bottle. It depicted a man, not black, not white, holding a bottle of the beer, a Bock Solibra: *la biere de l'homme fort.* The beer of the strong man.

The only other customers, three African men dressed in Western suits, were seated nearby. They appeared to be of different nationalities, on a business trip, perhaps. The Woloof was distinguished by his purple-black skin and his height. The Mandinkes, who predominate in this area, were shorter, lighter-skinned, and rounder. Perhaps they were entertaining their Senegalese business partner.

I'd seen men like these in Dakar. They'd been to Paris. Their accents were clear when they spoke to me, the dialects nonexistent. They knew life on the other continent. I watched them eat, speak, do business. They laughed loud, these men, and ordered, not requested, but ordered more beer with curt voices and the quick snap of fingers. The beer came quickly. Was served unobtrusively. These men, how did they feel about San Pedro, about Dakar, about Abidjan?

Children peeked over the whitewashed half-fence that separated the tables and chairs from the street. I must have looked an apparition in the light of the bare bulbs that illuminated the dining area. One of the suited Mandinkes took it upon himself to reprimand the children who gathered to stare. He spoke sharply to them in the native language, startling them so that they jumped and ran away. The Mandinke laughed. He was polite, used to Westerners, and did not ask me my business, or to join them. *"Mange, mange,"* he urged, heartily. *"C'est bien, ce soir."* Men of the world.

His companions smiled and raised their beers. The dishes from which they ate did look tempting. A big pile of rice on one, chunks of meat on another, sauce on yet another. The Mandinke gathered a small amount of rice into his palm, added a chunk of meat and with a quick flick of the wrist shook the mixture into his closed fingertips. Then he rubbed the compacted mass into the sauce and popped it into his mouth. *"C'est bien,"* he repeated.

Loretta Lynn's "Stand by Your Man" played next. I raised my brown bottle in the air without looking round, and another beer arrived. I drank deeply, the liquid cooling my throat and emptying my head of the inherent violence caused by my order for dinner.

Had vegetarianism been a possibility, I would have entertained it. But however rich the soil and moist the air, the Africans are either unwilling or unable to tend vegetable gardens, and only in small areas in the Ivory Coast did I see lettuce, beans, and tomatoes. Perhaps there are bugs and animals that eat them. Manioc grows everywhere, but is merely a filler, with no nutritional value. Yams and rice do not take up the slack. Therefore, I would be a carnivore. Soon, I would probably be eating that freshly butchered goat.

During my travels I had seen sheep and goats transported in vans racing down potted, single-lane highways at 60 miles-per-hour. They munched hay under the fishnet with which they were secured. I had seen motorcyclists drive by holding half-a-dozen live chickens in their hands. On the beach I'd passed piles of dead fish smoking between layers of dry wood smoldering directly on the sand, and in markets pounds of fresh meat were displayed for hours on fly-infested tables in direct sunlight.

I didn't mind porcupine, bush rat, or even venison from dik-dik, an endearing little creature. I even enjoyed goat, mutton, chicken, pig, and the rare cut of beef, if I was sure it was cooked well. By the sea and near rivers I ate fish and crustaceans. But I draw the line at monkey. At least, knowingly, I draw the line at monkey.

I planned to have another beer, and to see what they could cook-up for dinner. Country music hour was over and now it seemed to be disco-hour. I called over the proprietor. What was for dinner? He turned down a strange rendition of "Stayin' Alive" that I was sure wasn't produced by the Bee Gees, and came over to recite the possibilities.

He could get many kinds of meats tonight. It had been market day, and he would send a boy for dik-dik, pig, or fish, as I liked. My dish would be accompanied by rice or manioc root. They had a special, too, it seemed. For an extra 100 CFA, he knew it was expensive, of course, but he knew of a place nearby where—and this was a rare treat in a city—and if I hadn't tried it, as a Westerner he was sure I might not have tried it—but he could provide me with the rare treat because he knew where he could even buy a monkey, freshly killed, and just brought today from the jungle.

Carla King lives in San Francisco with her two motorcycles, a bicycle, and a portable computer. Her work has appeared in numerous travel anthologies and magazines, including Travelers' Tales France *and* Pacific Rim Travel. *Her first guidebook,* Cycling the French Riviera, *has just been released. She is currently working on a travelogue based on her dispatches published on America Online's GNN Travel Center, about her solo circumnavigation of United States borders on a Russian sidecar motorcycle.*

⋆

Once the fire is to his liking, Gabriel lobs the meat into the blaze, and a horrid smell of burning flesh and hair gags me. Innocent holds his nostrils, but the others inhale the smoke as if it's precious incense. Gabriel waves everyone back. He's cooking tonight and doesn't want any interference. He uses his machete like a spatula to spread the salt and tend the meat. The body fat dripping into the flames sizzles and pops; the monkey skin tightens, and the body parts look more and more human. Grease spits at us, and Raymond sucks the oily stains out of his shirt. Gabriel flips the meat after a few minutes. More than five minutes a side is too much, I'm told. "You want it chewy," Gabriel says.

He lifts the cooked meat onto a bed of leaves, where Ange quarters it and hands us each a piece. The meat has been blistered to charcoal on the outside, but it's pink, bloody, and nearly raw on the inside. I throw my piece back on the fire until it's well done. It has a gamey, sour taste, but I manage to eat most of the thing.

—Rory Nugent, *Drums Along the Congo: On the Trail of Mokele-Mbembe, the Last Living Dinosaur*

ZHANG XIANLIANG

TRANSLATED BY MARTHA AVERY

* * *

Even Their Eyes Are Hungry

It was the author's misfortune to be trusted.

MY ENTRY FOR 25 AUGUST NOTES THE WEATHER, OUT OF HABIT: clear with occasional clouds. The entry had no special significance, yet it was this kind of clear sky with occasional clouds that seduced me into wanting to stay alive in the damned world that I was living in. From what I wrote in the diary during this period, the reader can tell that I was still relatively stable—both in terms of my emotional state and in terms of my living conditions. I did not plan to escape again nor did I think of committing suicide. After all, I was still alive, still eating grass soup, and every few days I could get hold of a luxury item such as some salt, a gourd, some tobacco. I even managed to find time to write a few so-called poems. Only one thing kept bothering me, and it was the sky.

Few people on earth can have been so painfully aware of how beauty can torment a man. Yes, even beauty can torment. In the sky, in the interplay between evening light and clouds, in every

> *Zhang Xianliang spent 22 years in Chinese prison and labor camps, a Maoist Gulag, until he was declared "rehabilitated" in 1979. In this prison world of death, trust was a curse and only food had value.*
>
> —RS

351

blade of grass and every branch of a tree, in the course of the growing and final maturity of the crops, in the thawing and once again
the freezing of the ground, in every shovelful of the earth I
dug…in all of these was hidden an inescapable fascination, a temptation. They made it hard for a man to leave this earth lightly.
There were no springs here, no tripping brooks, no exotic mountains or fantastic rockeries. Nothing bloomed here except weeds.
Even the grasses were plants with absolutely no aesthetic value—
dog-tail sedge, reeds and that sort of thing.

And yet, this place had unique spaciousness, boundless reaches,
an emptiness which shook a man to the core. The line between
heaven and earth was so distinct—the sky was sky, the earth was
earth, with only wind passing back and forth between.

At early dawn, the wooden gate of the compound would scrape
open against the ground, and we convicts would emerge from the
barracks where we had been locked up all night. In those moments, I could barely endure the sudden contrast between the filth
inside and the fresh purity of the world outside. We were like travellers who have flown half-way around the world overnight, and
find it hard, so suddenly, to adapt.

We would look out over the summer landscape, and see every
weed, every grass, every plant absorbing nutrition, growing, thriv-
ing. It seemed that man alone was suffering from hunger.

Why was that?

Why?

There was another matter that tormented me, and that was the
dividing of things. Striving to be as fair and honest as possible
could make one suffer even more.

The diary often notes that on a particular day certain things
were allocated: salt, tobacco, watermelon, musk-melon, cucumbers,
and so on. Why should such trivialities be included in my record?
These items were worth a few cents, or a few tenths of a cent.

Yet the divvying-up and allocating of these things constituted
the most important event in our daily lives. After work, on the way
home, if we saw a cart parked in front of the camp compound, we
would become amazingly cheerful. Bodies that had toiled all day

would suddenly liven up. Eyes that gazed out from faces already bearing traces of the "death mask" would begin to glow with a certain kind of greedy cunning. Hands and feet would begin to shake uncontrollably. Like disturbed ant-hills, the barracks would erupt into action—the only difference was that ants would not call out like the convicts:

"Dividing melons! Dividing melons!…"

The man on duty from each group would race to get the group's hemp bag. This was considered one of the group's great treasures. Normally it would be folded neatly and tucked safely under the Group Leader's bedding. Now it was shaken out, clamped under an armpit and hurriedly rushed to the line forming by the cart. The Troop Leader or a freed convict (like the middle-school teacher who was in charge of watching over the vegetable cellar) would already be waiting there. Once the man on duty from each group was present, the divvying-up would begin, according to the number of men in each group.

At the cart, the measuring was done with a balance. Once the food was taken back to the small group, however, where was one supposed to find a balance? Eighteen pairs of eyes would be staring at this pile of sustenance, watching to see how fair the division was.

From the time I entered the camps, the responsibility for dividing things up always fell to me. I don't know why. No matter which group I was reassigned to, I was asked to be responsible for the division of food. Convicts in a group never trusted their Group Leader, nor did he ever trust the other convicts. Seventeen pairs of eyes therefore would stare at my pair of hands; some of the men would squat on the ground, some would stand to one side looking sideways through cold eyes. Every motion I made was watched with attention; people vied with one another to give suggestions on how to make the split.

Among the eighteen men there were eighteen different standards of measurement. Splitting up a pile of food was infinitely more difficult than writing a poem. Let us say, for example, that the group had been allocated thirty-six *jin* of cucumbers. Each man was to get two *jin,* but without a scale how was it possible to get eighteen identical portions? There are always large cucumbers, small ones, good ones, bad ones, fresh ones and others that are not so fresh. You must take all of these various factors into account. Until you have it worked out so that the entire group nods in approval, you are not allowed to stop. The men are all hungry, their eyes are hungry. I divvy out the portions until my head is spinning and my eyes are blurred, until the sky and earth seem to be floating in cucumbers, like stars, until the Group Leader finally demands of everyone: "How about it?! Speak up!"

And what does everyone say? Certainly no one says a word of agreement. Ultimately one man makes a small move to grab a cucumber and immediately all are struggling to get their share. In a moment, seventeen small piles of cucumbers are snatched away. Just one, mine, is left there—the one nobody else wanted. An important principle has been agreed upon before the process: the man responsible for splitting the food into equal portions takes his portion last.

Personally I feel that I need a larger portion than anyone. A death mask has already made its appearance on my face, and yet I have to let myself get the worst of the deal. I silently pick up the pile of cucumbers remaining on the ground, one by one, and when I eat them the flavour is often mixed with my tears.

Why was such an important event not specifically described in the diary?

Starting from July 1960, the division of food in the manner described above was not a daily event, and this is reflected in the journal. But from November 1958 until October 1959, I had to endure this torment three times every day.

During that period, when convicts went to get their meals they didn't line up neatly by the kitchen window in their own groups. The cooks did not ladle food directly into each convict's basin. Instead, the men on duty from each small group (for it was always two men, in order to prevent anyone from stealing mouthfuls on the way) would take the food bucket and the water bucket to the kitchen and bring back food and water for everyone. After returning to the barracks, the food would be divided by the convict most trusted by all the rest. The lives of all the groups were tied to the ladle of the cook; and the lives of the men in each group were tied directly to the ladle of the man, namely me, serving out the food.

Whether or not a man kept on living, or whether he was able to live one more day or two, appeared to depend on whether he was given two extra or two fewer grains of rice. One's survival did *not* depend on the vitamins or protein in one or two grains of rice—but it did depend on the spiritual sustenance, the encouragement those grains gave a man. After every convict had received his portion, he would stir it around in his basin a long time, glancing at everybody else's basin and comparing their amounts to his own. If he had received one grain of rice too few—or what he, anyway, regarded as less than others—he would quickly develop the syndrome mentioned above: the wilting sickness.

"I'm getting less than the others! I'm getting less than the others!" How can a man who has this refrain inside him from morning till night not collapse?

The wooden bucket in which the small group hauled its food was another of its treasures. Every man in the group regarded it with love and affection. Never mind that it reeked, that it was sour and filthy from previous meals; never mind that the rope attached to it was slimy with countless watery soups. When the convicts went out to work, or when they switched fields during a workday, the first thing they thought of was making sure to bring the bucket along. It was as though the bucket was more important to them than a child. Yes, for without it you were unable to eat. And if you did not eat you would die.

The man on food duty from each small group had major responsibilities. Among other things, he had to calculate the best time to go to the kitchen to get his group's food. When the cook made a meal, he would pour finished soup from great cooking pots into a wooden keg that was as tall as a man. From this vessel he would then distribute the soup to the small groups, ladling it into their buckets. Groups who arrived at the beginning of this process would naturally get the thinner soup floating on top; those who came later would get the benefit of thicker material that had sunk to the bottom. If you got it just right, you might even find some undissolved lumps of flour.

Each Station, however, had over one thousand men, and so the kitchen needed at least a dozen large wooden kegs for each meal. The small groups did not pick up their food according to any specific order—whichever group's man arrived at any given time got served. The trick was to work it so that you came just at the time when a large keg was reaching the bottom. You certainly wanted to be there before the next keg was started. How to do it? This depended on the talent of the man on food duty.

Relying on this man alone was sometimes not enough—you had to send out one or two scouts to reconnoitre the situation. If it happened to be a particularly good meal, then the entire group would be mobilized. Men would take turns keeping surreptitious watch at the kitchen window. The Group Leader would sit inside the barracks and direct the action. A man who could hold back and not jump the gun, like that graduate of the Whampoa Military Academy, managed it best. He would appear calm, as though he held the security of a million soldiers hidden in his back pocket—convicts would rush in and out, giving him reports, while he sat back looking very much like a figure in a Peking opera. The man on duty, holding the bucket, would wait beside him, ready at any time to make the assault.

When a convict came in to report to the Group Leader that the large keg was just at the right stage, he would, with one word, order the charge and the man on duty would dash out like the wind. Group Leaders who could not restrain themselves, who became even more nervous and agitated than the man on duty would plunge in and out of the action themselves. They would be mortally afraid of bringing the ultimate misfortune upon their group. These pitiful men generally had the worst luck—the food that came back to their barracks was often the thinnest gruel. The old convict named Group Leader Wang was one of these.

As a result, every time the small groups were reorganized, convicts would enquire carefully into the qualifications of the Group

Leader. Did he have this unique talent? If he did, then they would be satisfied, even if he was more severe than the others.

As the convicts put it: "Follow a wolf and you eat meat; follow a dog and you eat shit."

Unfortunately, no matter what group I was assigned to, the others always trusted me. After the man on duty had brought in the food, it was always I who was handed the ladle to divvy it up. The ladle had a fixed capacity, which made it easier—each man got one ladle or one ladle and a half. But how many bits of vegetable were there in the soup bucket? How many clumps of rice? There were slight distinctions between each ladle of gruel—some were a bit thicker, some thinner.

I say I was trusted—in fact, this was purely relative. No convict would completely trust any other person. As a result, the men studied every possible means of dividing the food fairly. One method was to have one convict turn his face away and not watch me divide it. Eighteen bowls would be set down on the ground. After I had filled them, dividing as evenly as I could into eighteen portions, he would close his eyes and randomly assign each bowl to a person. "So-and-so takes bowl number such-and-such," he would call out, until all the bowls were taken.

People complained about this method, however, since they weren't able to use their own bowls to eat. Another method we tried was as follows: I would very carefully fill a ladle full of soup or rice, and I would hold it there in my hand. Then a convict, whose back was turned to me, would shout out who this ladle was for. That man would bring forward his bowl and get the food. There was a third, and a fourth way—the ingenuity was endless. Among the hundred-odd small groups in the labour reform camp, at least ninety different methods were probably being practised at any given time. Some groups even made themselves their own unique weighing and measuring devices.

When not working, convicts were most interested in exchanging information on these different ways of measuring food. I have seen many different balances and scales made for the purpose. A small branch would be polished until it was a glossy as jade, then fine measuring lines would be carved on it with great mastery. Each mark shone—the thing was so exquisite that a person holding it wouldn't want to put it down. Seeing it, one could believe that these men, scraped clean of everything including freedom, could have made an aeroplane with their own bare hands.

Zhang Xianliang is widely regarded as China's greatest living writer. Since his release from prison he has written numerous books, including Getting Used to Dying, Half of Man is Woman, *and* Grass Soup, *from which this story was excerpted.*

★

How well I remember any change of diet on the long road from Pinsk to Northern Siberia. I struggle sometimes to remember in sharp detail some of my experiences, but small incidents concerning food come back to me clearly and unbidden. There was never enough of it and the thought of it nagged at us always. Men would have given a handful of diamonds for an extra slice of bread in these circumstances and counted themselves the most fortunate of beings, because only food had value. It was beyond price.

—Slavomir Rawicz, *The Long Walk*

GARRETT CULHANE

The Laughter of Rul

Feeling lucky?

LATER, IT WOULD BE EASY TO LAUGH ABOUT THE YOUNG VENDORS who sold plates of dysentery sticks, or brochettes, each with half a dozen flies nestled in the crevices of overcooked meat. But those I had avoided. In fact, the meal of my demise I locate at the road-side lunch with lots of rice and little pieces of chicken in a light red sauce.

The restaurant seemed decent enough: slabs of wood on cinder blocks for tables, stools on a concrete floor, bars for windows, no screens. A large woman wrapped in a flowing garment greeted me, said things I could not understand, coaxed me to the back door, and pointed to the skinny chickens scratching in the sand.

"Yes," I nodded. She responded with a big smile revealing her teeth stained yellow and brown.

"Fanta?" she asked, to which I again nodded yes.

That was two days ago.

Today, I am violently ill. Since early this afternoon I've oscil-lated between chills and a delirious fever. In delirium I am assigned Sisyphean tasks of sorting order from chaos. It is a numbers game like counting patterns in sand. Inevitably, I cannot keep order in

359

my mind. The measures I'm using for a semblance of control and familiarity unravel. From behind comes darkness followed by an aperture of diminishing light. My dream comes to an end. I awake and reestablish my bearings.

My bed roll is sprawled out on thick sand. I look out in all directions and see the drab and parched skyline of dust and particles of Sahelian topsoil all carried seasonally by the *harmattan* winds. Thomas Carlyle likened the *harmattan* winds to a breath of doubt, others have viewed them as sheer revenge.

I am in Niamey, the capital of Niger. I arrived yesterday afternoon. First stop—the Grand Hotel where beer is pulled from a refrigerator, the first cold beer I've encountered in over a month. Outside the window is the Niger River. Down below, on the shoreline, fishermen toss nets into the passing waters while women clean clothes, slapping the wet garments onto the rocks to dry. "This is it," I kept saying to myself, the sub-Saharan Africa I'd been wanting to see since old enough to spin a globe. And there is the Great Brown God, as it is known, the river the Scottish explorer Mungo Park traversed while trying to confirm his hunch—that the Niger ultimately flowed into the Atlantic, and not the great body of water now known as Lake Chad, as European mapmakers had long fancied. But the world would wait for this contribution of geographic accuracy until Richard and John Lander reached the coast in 1830. For little did Park know he was floating toward doom with his whittled down party of listless and malarious soldiers, all of whom drowned not far from here in 1805 while trying to avoid a fusillade of lances, pikes, arrows, and stones.

After two beers, I felt an illness coming on. So far I'd been lucky: two months of crisscrossing the Atlas Mountains of Morocco, traveling along the Mediterranean to Algeria, then through the Sahara to Niger. Perhaps that was the problem. Feeling lucky, that is. I was growing reckless (hell-bent for leather, as they say). I'd shown little restraint, indeed thought my desire to expose myself, in a strange way to become the Sahara, made it necessary to share *couscous* with Tuaregs and drink from the ass of the Guerba, the sewn waterbag made from the full skin of a goat so often seen hanging from the sides of vehicles crossing the desert. After all, eating and drinking is a gateway to culture, and not something I was planning to govern too strictly for reasons of bodily integrity.

There is no way of knowing for sure if it was the "skinny chicken in red sauce" meal. For that matter, it could have been my meal yesterday morning. I'd decided to cook breakfast. I began searching the stalls in the marketplace for the basics: cooking oil, lamb, three eggs, and bread. I prepared a small fire. I filled the billy with water for a cup of Arab coffee, cooked the lamb, sliced the bread I would toast over the fire, then slowly reheated the oiled pan to an optimal temperature in preparation for my eggs. I was very excited. I grabbed my first egg, cracked the shell on the pan, and pulled on the edges. Out came a half formed, rotting chick with quills in lieu of feathers. I froze, starring at its eye, its beak, its skin, a thin membrane, resembled a gross and tangled web of varicose

Having survived the perils of astonishingly huge rapids on the Zambezi River below Victoria Falls, and having found places to sleep where we would not be devoured by crocodiles, we looked forward to dinner.

Darkness fell in the great wildness of the canyon, blanketing our eyes as the roar of water did our ears, and so we were heartened by a roaring blaze and the intoxicating smells of roasting chicken—"Zambian chicken" our competent boatmen said proudly.

When we were finally summoned, it took all our will not to fall like jackals on the golden-skinned birds being removed from the spit. We settled ourselves on choice boulders and sank fangs into the perfectly prepared meat. But they hit the merest patina of flesh, could gain no purchase on the leathery covering on the bones. The aroma drove us mad, for in fact there was nothing to eat, nothing to chew, and nothing to swallow. To call it boot leather would have been a high compliment. Cruelly disappointed, we licked the carcasses like wistful curs and turned to our beans and potatoes.

—James O'Reilly and Larry Habegger, "Zambian Chicken and Other Stories"

veins. It, along with my idea of a delicious meal, began to sizzle
away in the heated oil.

The second egg was the same. Again, I scooped out another rotting chick and cleaned the pan. The third egg was good. I had the
meal I'd planned, just a scaled back version.

There are no shadows to be seen on account of the *harmattan*
winds. The sun is obscured, leaving only a halo to the West. I am
in a campground on the margins of Niamey alongside a sandy
road marked by a cinder block entrance where a few sparse
patches of grass designate the choice campsites. I do not have a
choice campsite.

I was warned there would be a number of "adjustments" when
traveling through Africa. You will see things you have never seen
before, and learn to accommodate what in the beginning will test
every threshold of discomfort. While crossing the Sahara there will
be sand and flies served with every meal. The former will grind
against your molars as if a staple ingredient. The latter, as much as
you try to keep them away, invariably will squat in your food. And
flies are inclined to bowel movements while eating. Flies feed by
vomiting onto their food, then sucking back their vomit. Flies
alight on rotting flesh and filth of every kind, quite possibly even
that "anchovy sauce" you left behind on the distant parameters of
camp. And finally, flies are couriers for typhoid, cholera, trachoma,
and dysentery (to list a few), which is just one of the many reasons
why, in the Sahara, you will begin to measure time in showers and
baths and rolls of toilet paper.

I am again faced with my illness, faced with the immediate
cause at hand—a sickness I cannot contain.

I repeat the path I have traveled too often this day. I tilt my head
in the general direction of the loo, get up from my sleeping bag,
hover on all fours and pause—this is not what I envisioned a year
ago staring at a large map of Africa, full of awe and excitement. I
stand and totter—my upper body poorly coordinated with the legs
below. With an awkward gait, I make my way to the loo, the hole
in the ground, framed by a rim of cement, circled in dust, and shel-

tered from the sky by corrugated steel and a cinder block wall. I squat down and lean forward, resting my elbows on my thighs, to visit a particularly gruesome trio: vomit, diarrhea, and urine—all at once. I have considerable difficulties aiming such a mess. By the looks of things, so have others before me. There is no running water to wash anything down, nor breeze to upset the vile and offending odors. The cement surrounding the hole in the ground is less than a foot in diameter. What doesn't hit the cement splatters onto the powdered mixture, leaving craters of various excrement. Flies race in tight circles, falling quiet only to alight on the newest contributions.

I return to my bed roll now, having completed the same grueling ritual three times on this long afternoon. I feel better for the moment, but exhausted. I stare into the tawny Niger sky. I sense my throat has been raked by a metal scraper. My entrails have been scoured. My ass feels like a ragged sleeve. It is now 5:00 p.m. I recall stories, images, and moments that come with uncanny clarity. Having my passport seized for two days for, as I would find out later, not saluting an Algerian customs official as we passed one another near a narrow entrance to a bathroom. Listening to the bad angel of strayed travelers known as the laughter of Rul: the strange snoring noise of trembling sand; rocks that loudly shatter when graced by morning light; and beautiful formations that gnaw and grate as the vast desert warms by day and cools by night. A jaded expat in Agadez who delighted in telling stories of entire caravans having departed but never arrived, the carcasses of men and camels alike dried-out somewhere on the sandy waste. Other unfortunate souls found half-mummified by the dry desert air in the featureless landscape of the Tanezrouft, literally the "Land of Terror." And how dehydration can paralyze the mind first with headaches, then a general irritability, leading to small mistakes that collectively add up to disaster and slow death by thirst accompanied, as the story goes, with visions of four-horse chariots at flying gallop racing through what was once a generous savannah home to giraffes, gazelles, even hippos and crocodiles.

I turn on my side, writhing to place my body atop a small mattress. I stare at a strip of duct tape covering the seared nylon skin of my sleeping bag after an ember popped from the fire like a meteor, coursing through the black night. That was over a month ago, I think. The tape, now frayed and curling, is a sticky magnet of the various types of sand I've managed to sleep on: the *reg,* pebbles from a gravelly surface that makes up most of the sublime Sahara. And sand from the *erg oriental,* the tiny grains that recall both the beauty of shifting dunes and the difficult time spent bogged down to the rear axle shoveling to free the sunken wheels of a Bedford truck.

I returned to the marketplace yesterday for a much-sought-after refund. I tried to explain by pointing to the caged hatchlings then back to the eggs. The trader, an elderly man, stared at me blankly with the slight interruption, a nod, as if to say "yes, there is a connection." I realized the idiocy of my efforts and left to find an interpreter. We returned. Alas, our entreaties were to no avail. The trader claimed I had not bought the eggs from him. My interpreter told me there was no recourse. Though he did show how to avoid such occasions in the future—make an okay sign with your hand. Place the egg in your hand and look to the sun.

I see an enlarged wafer, dispersed in dust. Down the west falls day. I need water.

Upon returning from Africa, Garrett Culhane had a large African moth removed from his ear and finally had his malaria properly diagnosed (vivax) and treated while traveling through WaKeeney, Kansas. He is a freelance writer based in San Francisco.

★

In the Bangkok emergency room I explained my symptoms to the Thai doctor. Peering into my eye, he felt for the hard lump above my right eyebrow that had become my recent traveling companion. "You have gnasthosomiasis," he announced. "It's a worm that grows under the skin, and yours is quite big so you must have had it for some time. We'll do a blood test, but there's only a fifty percent chance that it will show positive, as it only comes up at certain times, for feeding."

"Feeding!? Feeding on what?"

"Well, it lives in your soft tissues and feeds on nutrients in your blood. The usual remedy is to surgically remove it, although if you decide not to, the average life span of these worms is only about ten years."

He went on to explain that one gets this worm from eating under-cooked shellfish here in Thailand. I had expected a sinus infection. Maybe even a brain tumor. But a worm living in my head? Why did I come here?

I shuffled out to the waiting room to await the results of my blood test. Two nurses were settled in front of a video screen holding hands and giggling. Miserably, I settled into a chair next to them. Sigourney Weaver flashed on the screen, screaming. I realized, as a huge worm-like monster ripped its ugly head through the stomach of her spaceship-mate, that it was the movie *Alien*. I was mesmerized by the messy birthing of this plasmic alien being tearing, screaming, and viciously cracking through the body of its host.

"Good news," relayed the doctor as he interrupted my viewing from the doorway. I returned his gaze with a crazed glint in my eye. "Now we know for sure," the doctor smiled. "The test is positive."

—Alison Wright, "Don't Eat the Shellfish"

★ ★ ★

There Was a Train

And the dining car was the author's prism.

THERE WAS A TRAIN, NOT A PARTICULARLY GOOD ONE, THAT stopped at Vevey about ten in the morning on the way to Italy. Chexbres and I used to take it to Milano.

It had a restaurant car, an old-fashioned one with the agreeable austerity of a third-class station café about it: brown wooden walls and seats, bare tables unless you ordered the highest-priced lunch, and a few faded advertisements for Aspirina Bayer and "*Visitez le Maroc*" permanently crooked about the windows.

There was one table, next to the galley, where the cooks and waiters sat. In the morning they would be talking and sorting greens for salad and cutting the tops off radishes for the *hors d'oeuvres*, and in the early afternoon they would eat enormously of some things that had been on the menu and some that certainly had not. There was always a big straw-wrapped flask of red wine with them.

M ary Fisher's lover, Chexbres, was diagnosed in the late 1930s with a debilitating illness that wasted away his body limb by limb. As World War II and her lover's death approached, they raced across Europe, tasting as much of life as they could in the time they had remaining.

—RS

Sometimes the head chef smoked while he drank, or read parts of a newspaper aloud, but usually he worked with his helpers. And if one of the two waiters sat there, he worked too.

We liked to go into the restaurant partly because of the cooks, who after a polite salute ignored us, and partly because of the waiters, who were always the same ones.

Of course, it is impossible that they were on every train that went to Milano through Vevey at ten in the morning. But they were on that train every time we took it, so that very soon they knew us and laughed and even patted Chexbres' shoulder delightedly when we appeared.

We always went into their car a few minutes after we started…after we had been seen by the conductor and what few travelers there were on the unfashionable train. The restaurant would be empty at that hour, of course, except for the table of amiably chattering cooks.

We would order a large bottle of Asti Spumante. That delighted the waiters, whether it was the young smooth one or the old sour withered one. We would sit drinking it, slightly warm, from the thick train-goblets, talking and watching the flat floor of the Valais grow narrower and wilder, waiting as always with a kind of excited dread for the first plunge in to the Simplon.

The champagne would stay us, in that familiar ordeal. We'd drink gratefully, feeling the train sway, knowing a small taste of death and rebirth, as all men do in swift passage through a tunnel.

When we came out finally, into the light again and the high mountains, we'd lift our glasses silently to each other, and feel less foolish to see that the cooks too had known the same nameless stress as we.

Then people would begin to come in for lunch, and we'd go back to our compartment. The younger waiter would always call us when there were only a few more people to serve, in an hour or so.

Usually both waiters took care of us; they seemed to find us strange, and interesting enough to crack their cosmic ennui, and in some way fragile, so that they protected us. They would come swaying down the aisle as we ate, crying to us, "There will be a few bumps! Hold tight! Hold tight!, M'sieu'-'dame! I will help you!"

Then they would grasp the wine, and usually my arm, and we would, it is true, make a few mild grating noises over some repairs in the road. Then they would gasp with relief, and scuttle away…one more crisis safely past.

It made us feel a little silly, as if we were imbeciles of royal blood, or perhaps children who only *thought* they had gray hairs and knew how to survive train trips alone. It was fun, too; almost everyone likes to feel pampered by public servants.

The young waiter with the smooth almond face was more given to the protective gestures, equally lavished on Chexbres or me to avoid any sexual misunderstandings, but the older one, whose body was bent and whose face was truly the most cynical I have ever seen, was the one who watched our eating.

He hovered like an evil-visaged hawk while we ordered, and we soon found that instead of advising changes then, he would simply substitute in the kitchen what he preferred to have us enjoy that day. After the first surprise it was fun, but we always kept up the bluff of looking at the menu and then watching him pretend to memorize our order.

One thing he permitted us: simplicity. The people who traveled on that train were the kind who liked plain food and plenty of it. The menu might or might not list meat or fish, but it always had *pasti* of some kind, and lentils or beans cooked with herbs, and of course fine honest garden salad. Then there would be one or two *antipasti:* the radishes we had watched being fixed, and butter for them in rather limp and sooty curls, and hard-boiled eggs and sliced salami. There would be cheese for dessert, with fruit…fat cherries or peaches or grapes or oranges, according to the season, and always green almonds in the spring.

The people ate well, and even if they were very poor, and brought their own bread and wine into the restaurant, they ordered a plate of beans or a one-egg omelet with dignity which was no rebuke to the comparative prodigality around them. The two waiters served them with nonchalant skill, and everyone seemed to agree that Chexbres and I should be watched and fed and smiled at with extra care.

"Why are they like that? Why are they so good to us, all the people?" we would ask each other. I knew reasons for him, and he knew some for me, but for the two of us it was probably because we had a sort of palpable trust in each other.

Simple people are especially conscious of that. Sometimes it is called love, or good will. Whatever it was in us, the result was mysterious and warming, and we felt it very strongly in places like the restaurant car to Milano, always until the last time.

That was in the summer of 1939.

We were two ghosts, then. Our lives as normal living humans had ended in the winter, in Delaware, with Chexbres' illness. And when we got word that we should go back to our old home in Switzerland and save what we could before war started, we went not so much for salvage, because possessions had no meaning any more to us, but because we were helpless to do anything else. We returned to the life that had been so real like fog, or smoke, caught in a current of air.

We were very live ghosts, and drank and ate and saw and felt and made love better than ever before, with an intensity that seemed to detach us utterly from life.

Everywhere there was a little of that feeling; the only difference was that we were safely dead, and all the other people, that summer, were laughing and singing and drinking wine in a kind of catalepsy, or like cancerous patients made happy with a magic combination of opiate be-

𝒢ive strong drink unto him that is ready to perish, and wine unto those that be of heavy hearts. Let him drink, and forget his poverty, and remember his misery no more.

—Proverbs 31:6–7

fore going into the operating theatre. We had finished with all that business, and they had it still to go through.

They looked at us with a kind of envious respect, knowing that

war was coming to them, but that we were past it; and everywhere
we went, except the one time on the Milano train, we moved
beautifully incommunicado, archangels on leave. None could
touch us, just as none could be harmed by our knowledge of pain
yet to be felt.

The train was the same. By then we had grown almost used to
miracles, and when the young almond-faced waiter stood in the
door of the compartment and gaped helplessly at us, we laughed at
him. He stammered and sputtered, all the time shaking our hands
and laughing too, and it was plain that he had buried us long since.

When he saw what had happened to Chexbres, he turned very
red, and then said quickly, trying not to stare, "But the Asti! At
once! It will be very chic to drink it here!"

And before we could tell him how much we wanted to drink
it in the old restaurant car, and look once more at the faded aspirin
signs and listen to the cooks, he was gone. It was necessary for him
to disappear; we were used by then to having people do impetuous things when they first saw us, ghosts come back so far....We
sighed, and laughed, because even that seemed funny.

The boy brought the champagne, wrapped elegantly in a red-
checked napkin for the first time. He was suave and mischievous
again, and it was plain that he felt like something in a paper-bound
novel, serving fair wine that way at eleven in the morning in a
first-class compartment. He swayed with exaggerated grace to the
rocking of the car, and flicked soot from the little wall table like
the headwaiter at the Café de la Paix, at least, with his flat black
eyes dancing.

We saluted him with our first taste, hiding our regret at having
to be "gentry" and drink where it was chic. The wine was the
same, warm and almost sickish, and we looked quietly at each
other, with delight…one more miracle.

But at Sion, before the tunnel, three Strength-through-Joyers
got on, bulbous with knapsacks and a kind of sweaty health that
had nothing to do with us. We huddled against the windows, not
invisible enough, and I wondered how we could ever get past all
those strong brown hairy legs to the corridor.

But there in the doorway, almost before the train started again, stood the little waiter. His face was impassive, but his eyes twinkled and yet were motherly.

"*Pardon, pardon*," he murmured. "*Entschuldigen Sie, bitte…bitte…*"

And before we knew it the German tourists were standing, trying to squeeze themselves small, and the boy was whisking us expertly, nonchalantly, out of the compartment, down the rocking aisle, and into our familiar hard brown seats in the restaurant.

It was all the same. We looked about us with a kind of wonder.

The old waiter saw us from the end of the car. His face did not change, but he put down his glass of wine and came to our table. The boy started to say something to him in an Italian dialect…it was like Niçois…but the old man motioned him bruskly aside.

His face was still the most cynical I had ever seen, but his eyes were over-full of tears. They ran slowly down his cheeks for a few minutes, into the evil old wrinkles, and he did not wipe them away. He stood by the table, flicking his napkin and asking crankily if we had made a good trip and if we planned to stay long in Milano. We answered the same way…things about traveling and the weather.

We were not embarrassed, any more than he was, by his tears; like all ghosts, I suppose, we had grown used to seeing them in other people's eyes, and along with them we saw almost always a kind of gratitude, as if people were thanking us for coming back and for being so trustful together. We seemed to reassure them, in a mysterious way…that summer more than ever.

While the old man was standing there, talking with his own gruff eagerness about crops and storms, flicking the table, he had to step in behind my chair for a minute while three men walked quickly through the car.

Two were big, not in uniform but with black shirts under their hot mussy coats, and stubble on their faces. The man between them was thinner and younger, and although they went single file and close together, we saw that he was handcuffed to each of them.

Before that summer such a thing would have shocked us, so that our faces would be paler and our eyes wider, but now we only looked up at the old waiter. He nodded, and his own eyes got very hot and dried all the tears.

"Political prisoner," he said, flicking the table, and his face was no more bitter than usual. "Escaped. They are bringing him back to Italy."

Then the chef with the highest bonnet saw us, and beamed and raised his glass, and the others turned around from their leafy table and saluted us too, and the door slammed behind the three dark men.

We got through the tunnel, that time, without feeling our palms grow sticky. It was the only difference: the train was the same, the people were the same. We were past the pain and travail, that was all. We were inviolate.

We drank the rest of the Asti, and as people began to come in to lunch, we made the signal to the suddenly active boy that we would be back later.

Just then there were shouts and thuds, and the sound of shattering glass. A kind of silence fell all about us, in spite of the steady rattle of the train. The old waiter ran down the car, not bumping a single table, and the door at the end closed sharply behind him. People looked strangely at one another.

Gradually the air settled, as if the motors inside all the travelers had started to hum again, and the young waiter took orders for lunch. When he got to us he said without looking at us, in his bad French, "I suggest that M'sieu'-'dame attend a moment...the restaurant is not crowded today."

As a suggestion it had the icy command of a policeman or a guardian angel about it, and we sat meekly. There was no more champagne. It did not really bother us.

Finally the old man came hurriedly back into the car. His face was furious, and he clutched his shoulder. The travelers stared at him, still chewing. He stopped for a minute by our table. He was panting, and his voice was very low.

"He tried to jump through the window," he said, and we knew he was talking about the refugee. "The bastards! They tore my coat! My only coat! The dirty bastards...look at that!"

He flapped the ripped shoulder of his greasy old black jacket at us, and then went madly down to the galley, muttering and trembling.

We stood up to go, and the smooth almond-faced waiter hurried toward us, swaying with the downhill rush of the train under a big tray of hot vegetables. "I am bringing M'sieu'-'dame's order at once," he called.

We sat down obediently. We were being bullied, but it was because he was trying to protect us, and it was kind of him. He brought two glasses of a dark vermouth, and as he put them in front of us he said confiding, "A special bottle we carry for the chef…very appetizing. There is a little muss on the platform. It will be swept up when M'sieu'-'dame have finished. *Santé!*"

As we lifted our glasses, willy-nilly, he cleared his throat, and then said in English, "Cheerio!" He smiled at us encouragingly, like an over-attentive nurse, and went back to serving the other people. The vermouth was bitterer than any we had ever tasted, almost like a Swiss gentian-drink, but it tasted good after the insipid wine.

When we went through to our compartment, there was indeed a neat pile of broken glass on the platform between the cars, and the window of the door that opened when the train stopped was only half filled: the top part of the pane was gone, and the edge of the rest curved like ice in a smooth fine line, almost invisible.

The Strength-through-Joyers leaped politely to attention when we got back to our compartment, and subsided in a series of small waves of questions in English…did smoke bother me, did we mind the door open, did we feel a draft…

I forget the name of the town now where the train stops and the passport men come on. Is it Domodossola? How strange, not to know! It is as if I have deliberately wiped from my mind a great many names. Some of them I thought would stay there forever, whether I wanted them or not, like old telephone numbers that suddenly come between you and the sound of a new love's voice. I never thought to disremember this town, that man, such and such a river. Was it Domodossola?

That day we were there a long time. There seemed more po-
licemen than usual, but it was always that way in Italy. We got the

questions of visas and money
straightened out; that used to
upset me, and I'd feel like a blushing diamond-smuggler when the
hard-eyed customs man would
look at me. This time it was easy,
unimportant.

I kept thinking it would be a
good idea to walk back to the restaurant car while the train was
quiet, but Chexbres said no, we should wait for the boy to call us.

Finally we started, very slowly. We went past a lot of roadwork.
Men were building beds for new tracks with great blocks of gray
stone, and the Germans looked at them with a grudging fascination, leaning over us to see better and exclaiming softly.

We were glad when the young waiter came to the door. "Your
table is ready, M'sieu'-'dame," he announced loftily, and the men
stood up hastily to let us out.

When we got to the end of the car, the boy turned back. "Take
care, please," he said to Chexbres. "There is a little humidity on the
platform."

And the place was wet, right enough. The curved piece of glass
was still in the window, but it and the walls and the floor were literally dripping with water. We went carefully through it, and into
the almost empty restaurant.

The chef rested at the end, reading a paper, but got up and went
back to the galley as we came in. Our table was nicely laid, with
fresh linen, and there were two or three little square dishes of pickled onions and salami and butter. We felt very hungry, and quite gay.

The boy brought us some good wine, a fairly expensive red
Chianti we always drank on that train, and we began to eat bread
and salami with it. I remember there were some of those big
white beans, the kind Italians peel and eat with salt when they are
fresh and tender in the early summer. They tasted delicious, so
fresh and cold…

It was good to be eating and drinking there on that train, free forever from the trouble of life, surrounded with a kind of insulation of love...

The old waiter came through the car. He was going to pass our table without looking at us. Chexbres spoke to him. "Stop a minute," he said. "Your coat...how is it?"

The man turned without answering, so that we could see the neat stitches that held his sleeve in place. I said something banal about the sewing...how good it was...and Chexbres asked quietly, "The man...the prisoner...did he get away?"

The old man suddenly looked at us, and his eyes were hateful, as if he loathed us. He said something foul, and then spat, "It's none of my business!" He hurried away, and we could not turn to watch him.

It was so shocking that we sat without any movement for quite a time. I could feel my heart beat heavily, and my throat was as if an iron collar hung around it, the way it used to be when Chexbres was first ill. Finally I looked at the few people still eating and it seemed to me as if they met my eyes with a kind of hatred too, not as awful as the old man's but still crouching there. There was fear in it, and fear all around me.

Chexbres' face was full of pain. It was the first time it had come through for weeks, the first time since we started to drift like two happy ghosts along the old current of our lives together. The iron collar tightened to see it there. I tried to drink some wine, but I couldn't swallow more than once.

The young waiter hurried past us without looking, and Chexbres stopped him firmly. "Please," he said. "What is wrong? What happened?"

The boy looked impassively at us, and for a minute I thought he was going to be rude. Then he whispered, still protecting us, "Eat, M'sieu'-'dame. I will tell you in a minute." And he hurried off to the galley, bending supply under the last great tray of emptied plates.

"Yes, you'd better eat something," Chexbres said coldly to me. "You've drunk rather a lot, you know." He picked up his fork, and

I did too. The spaghetti was like ashes, because I felt myself coming to life again, and knew he did.

When we were the only ones left in the car, the boy came back. He stood leaning against the table across the aisle, still swaying with the motion of the train but now as if he were terribly tired, and talked to us so softly that we could hardly hear him. There was no friendliness in his voice, but not any hatred.

He said that when the train stopped at Domodossola, or wherever the border was, the political prisoner was being taken off, and suddenly he laughed and pressed his throat down on the edge of broken windowpane. The old waiter saw it.

"That was probably the plan in the first place," the boy said. "The poor bastard was chained to the cops. There was no escaping. It was a good job," he said. "The border police helped clean up the platform. That was why the train stopped so long.

"We're making up time now all right," the boy said, looking admiringly at the rocky valleys flash past us. "The old man keeps fussing about his coat. He's nuts anyway."

By the time we got to Milano everything was almost all right again, but for a few minutes the shell cracked. The world seeped in. We were not two ghosts, safe in our own immunity from the pain of living. Chexbres was a man with one leg gone, the other and the two arms soon to go...a small wracked man with snowy hair and eyes large with suffering. And I was a woman condemned, plucked at by demons, watching her true love die too slowly.

There in the train, hurrying across the ripe fields, feeling the tranced waiting of the people everywhere, we knew for a few minutes that we had not escaped. We knew no knife of glass, no distillate of hatred, could keep the pain of war outside.

I felt illimitably old, there in the train, knowing that escape was not peace, ever.

Mary Frances Kennedy (M. F. K.) Fisher was widely regarded in the middle of this century as the finest writer of prose in America. She said that her chief responsibility as a writer was, "To write the good and pleasing sentence." She was good, and she pleased multitudes. Of her many works some of her most well known are: How to Cook a Wolf; Consider the Oyster; The Gastronomical Me; Sister Age; An Alphabet for Gourmets; *and* Serve it Forth. *This story, originally titled "The Flaw," is found in her book,* The Art of Eating. *Mary Frances died in 1992.*

✳

The six most important necessities which the Creator imposed on mankind are to be born, to move about, to eat, to sleep, to procreate, and to die.

—Jean Anthelme Brillat-Savarin, *The Physiology of Taste,*
translated by M. F. K. Fisher

HARRY ROLNICK

* * *

To Serve Man

"On our list of specials today…"

WHEN LUNCHING WITH FIJIANS, YOU MUST UNDERSTAND THAT telling cannibal jokes is a serious breach of etiquette. The Fijians are faithful Methodists, loyal members of the British Commonwealth, and wonderful rugby players. But they shy away from their people-eating past.

Until recently ("recently" being a relative word, as you will see), Fijians were the most feared cannibals in the South Seas. First, they were feared for their well-deserved ferocity. (Fijians win international rugby tournaments through that same ferocious character.)

But this ferocity was teamed up with enthusiasm. For, amongst the international cannibal community, Fijians were unique. They are…sorry, they *were* the only people who actually loved the *taste* of good man-meat.

The wimps of the cannibal world—Nigeria, Colombia, Brazil, New Guinea—"ingested the spirit" or "pleased the gods" or "punished their enemies" by eating them. Like the Chinese, who get embarrassed by talking about good banquets and insist their dishes have "medical properties," the cannibal-wimps can't accept human flesh on its own terms.

The Fijians aren't cannibal-wimps. They are…sorry again, *were* gourmets.

One rarely learns this from the Fijians themselves, certainly not in the main towns. They have been taught by gaggles of Anglican and Methodist missionaries that eating people was a Very Bad Thing. Today's Fijians, who go to church and sing and play football and pay obessiance

> *There shall be no sin imputed to those who believe and do good works for what they may have eaten in the past.*
>
> —*Koran*

to the British Crown, don't talk about their history. They'd rather tell you how they are the only people in the world who celebrate Prince Charles's birthday as a national holiday.

"And talking about the Prince of Wales," I told an Australian hotel manager near the crazy sailor-ridden capital, Suva, "Herman Melville used to sail around here. This is the home of Moby Dick. I'll bet I can find quite a few prints of whales in the archives."

"Not in Suva," he said. "This place is new. For tourists and golfers. For history, you go to Levuka island. Levuka was the old capital until about 1880. That's where the whales were and still are. That's where the archives are. And the cannibals too."

"But that was a century ago, right?"

I had been avoiding the subject of cannibals, since my assignment was doing non-controversial travel pieces for middle-class homes. But the Aussie assured me that the Levuka people weren't so reticent about their past.

"You can start with the Mayor of Levuka," he said. "He's half-American. But his feelings are Fijian. He'll tell you stories…."

Two days later, I was on the motorboat to Levuka. And yes, on the way through the sprays, was a pod of whales. So rare today, so plentiful when the seas were crowded with harpooning ships from around the world.

Melville isn't buried in Levuka, but the headstones in the cemetery tell many a tale about unfortunate whalers of the time. One had been "slaughtered in the Great Massacre," others had died "unfortunate deaths and their bodies never recovered."

Levuka has a single beach side street, with a Japanese cannery on one side, the aforementioned cemetery, a few clapboard houses, a few unlit shops, and an eerie quiet. Above the town lie some foreboding hills, behind which came the Great Massacre people.

Basically it is a ghost town, but the 75-year-old mayor was an ebullient sort. His grandfather had come from Michigan during the Civil War, when Fiji went into the cotton trade.

"He was planting cotton here, right on this spot," said the Mayor. "Then the natives killed him. "

"And ate him," I suppose.

"Yes," he sighed. "My grandmother tried to save him by burying him on one of the outlying islands. But they loved white meat and they came after him. They dug up his body and devoured him."

Toward the back of Levuka was an old barn with the "archives." The place is filled with hornets and probably rats. All I heard was the scurrying. I wanted to read about the death of Charlie Savage, a typical 19th-century brigand. An old newspaper told his history. How he had come off a ship in 1808, introducing firearms to the Levukans. He also killed anybody he wanted, apparently hundreds. He gathered twenty companions who were "reckless, cruel, profligate, with muskets, their depravity amazing even to the Fijian natives." He was massacred finally, but the Mayor told me the real story.

"They loved the meat, they did. Usually, when Fijians killed, they waited patiently until the bodies were clubbed to death. Then they would patiently take the meat and throw it into the fire and wait until it was roasted.

"But Charles Savage was different. He was seized and made to dig his own roasting hole. His veins were cut, the blood ran down, and the Fijians lapped up his blood. Fishhooks were put into his tongue, his arms and legs were torn off and roasted. The meat was scorched over a fire, the hair and skin were scraped off with shells. These bivalve shells here on the beach.

"The bones were put to use as well. You know how we drink *kava*? Well, they ground up his bones, and mixed that with the *kava* root. From behind the hills, where they came from, younger people still say that *kava* doesn't taste really delicious until you have bones mixed in with it. But I don't know.

"Oh," he finished, "Savage had taught them how to make fishing nets. As a sign of...I don't know, maybe respect...they used his finger bones as needles. I've never seen them, but I've heard they were used."

Fiji was of course once known as the Cannibal Islands. Captain James Cook himself gave them that title—but he studiously avoided the islands. He was not only a superb seaman, he was a very prudent gentleman.

At the Fiji Museum, all the lithographs and household goods

I might be in a situation similar to Hans Staden's, a German naval gunner in the employ of the Portuguese (ominous coincidence: my specialty in the navy was also gunnery!).

Staden was captured in 1552 by the Tamoio, a branch of the Tupinamba inhabiting lands now moaning under the concrete canyons of Rio de Janeiro and São Paulo. He was alone hunting when a group of them appeared from the forest, surrounded him, and took him to their cannibal chief. Asked to partake in one of the chief's meals, Staden protested that even wild animals didn't eat their own kind; to which the chief laughed and explained that he was a jaguar, therefore different from humans and entitled to eat them.

—Petru Popescu,
Amazon Beaming

have captions in Fijian and English. The cannibal section daguerreotypes of slaughtered missionaries, cooking pots, throwing clubs—have no Fijian explanations at all.

"Was this," I asked an Australian sugar-planter on the island of Taveuni, "out of embarrassment?"

"Publicly, yes. But the people who work for me can give actual recipes of what their grandparents ate."

"Okay, I write about food. Let's have it."

"First of all," the Aussie said, "don't get the wrong idea. Fijians are Christians, and I have no doubt that they don't eat human flesh any more."

"Come on, the recipe," I insisted.

"Okay. When they clubbed the victims—sometimes sailors, sometimes tribesmen from a different island, because they were always invading each other—they tried not to kill them. Then they would have these pits, where today they roast pigs. The pits would always be slow burning with wood.

"Now if they had time, they would skin the victims. But according to one of my workers, the old women simply couldn't wait, and they would dig in and eat the flesh raw. That was their prerogative.

"I think that Fijians loved meat because they had no indigenous animals on the land. So they were very careful in their preparation.

"They had two methods. One was the quick-grill method. They would chop up the bodies and put them in clay cooking pots, and stick them on a log fire. Here, I'll show you. I have them in my garden....

"But the real gourmets took the bodies and wrapped them in taro leaves, and would leave them to slow-burn in the pits. It took eight hours, and they would sit and drink *kava* until sundown and then have the big meal."

Now a few days later, I had taken a dinghy to another island (Fiji has about 300, most nameless), and I was invited for a *kava* session that night.

Kava, by the way, has all the punch, pungency, and efficacy of mild novocaine. After four hours, you might feel a bit of tingling. But it does open up the memories of its drinkers. All night they drink and talk. I asked the head guy (the one who filled up the cup from the barrel) about whether his grandparents had eaten human flesh.

Now this was fifteen years ago, and the head guy was about 70 then, and he asked me not to tell people, but it's probably okay now.

"Hey," he said. "It don't matter what they did. Listen. The Japs came here during the war, and first they was winning. Then the English came. And the Japs start losing. And when they start losing, then the English gave us the prisoners.

"'For what?' I ask them. But they don't say nothin'. They just leave the Japs with us. So we sit down with 'em, and maybe six or seven, they sit there grinnin' at us. And I don't speak Japanese, but I hear 'em talk about crazy Fiji people. So we lock the door and go out and have some *kava* and come back, and I take out my knife and tell this small Jap to take down his trouser, which he does, and I quick slit down his thigh with my knife, and he faints, and the others I think are gonna throw up.

"So I take a piece of his thigh, cut it out, and he's bleedin'. And it looks real good, and I wait till he starts to wake up, and I cut the thigh in half and my friend and I eat it.

"Didn't taste of nothin'. We just decided to do it."

The others were nodding at the story.

"What happened to the prisoners?" I asked.

The head guy doesn't bother to answer. He just laughs and fills up the *kava* cup, and he talked about the tall buildings of New York for some reason. *Kava* does that.

I returned to Taveuni and told the story to the planter, feeling myself a combination of Robert Louis Stevenson and James Beard.

"Look," I said, "everybody likes the Fijians. They're smart, savvy, they love a good time, they're great sportsmen. They're patriotic. Is all of this history?"

"It's hard to say *what* they think about it today. But we show video cassettes for their entertainment here, and I put on a cassette last week. It was of *Alive,* where the survivors eat their teammates after a plane crash.

"Well, my planters were shocked, really shocked. Then they asked me to repeat the film the next night. Just to express how shocked they were. And the night after that. I've shown it about six times, and each time they tell me how troubled they are."

The Aussie looked out over his verandah onto the silvery waters of Taveuni.

"I believe them," he said. "I feel perfectly safe in Fiji."

Harry Rolnick is a Grand Prize winner of the Pacific Asia Travel Association and the author of fifteen books on Asia. Based in Hong Kong, he is a regular contributor to The Asian Wall Street Journal *and a colum-*

nist for the Bangkok Post. *An accordian virtuoso, he has enthusiastic fans in Damascus, Herat and Pyong Yang.*

★

Strange to see how a good dinner and feasting reconciles everybody.

—Samuel Pepys

Liberation Day

Is necro-amor-phagia a word?

WE REACHED TAORMINA ON YOUR SILVER WEDDING ANNIVER-
sary. The hotels were booked solid. It was Liberation Day. You
were leaving your wife for me. We drove through the winding
streets, desolate. Then, from around a curve, we spotted an ancient
villa a hairpin turn off the main road. You drove down the steep
driveway and parked. I went in. An old gentleman with white hair
and bruised eyes hobbled arthritically out of the interior and positioned himself behind the reception desk.

"Yes?" he said without smiling. I was sure he thought me a
vagabond hippie or a loose woman in my jeans and tank top.

"We," I said, enjoying the feel of the word in my mouth, "we
would like a double." I followed him as he made his way down a
long hall whose hardwood floor was carpeted with a threadbare
Oriental runner. He unlocked the door of a modest chamber that
held two single beds covered with simple white spreads.

I asked if he had anything with one large bed. He shuffled to
the next door and unlocked it. It had a double bed, but it looked
out on the driveway. I asked if, by any chance, there was an ac-
commodation with a double bed and a view. He limped across the
hallway and unlocked a spacious, high-ceilinged room that looked

out on a broad tiled terrace, beyond whose sandstone balustrades lay the Mediterranean. After we checked in, I went off to scout out restaurants while you went to the travel agency to book tickets to Malta. I came back half an hour later as we'd agreed but you weren't there.

> "*So we left that country and sailed on, sick at heart. And we came to the land of the Cyclopes, a fierce, uncivilized people...*" Thus Odysseus on reaching what legend says is Taormina.
>
> —RS

"'e is gone to dee bank for lira," the beautiful travel agent said, her dark hair falling across her cheek. Her hands were graceful, the fingers long and tapered, her skin without pores. I was grateful you were elsewhere. I wandered up and down the street looking for you, and when I couldn't find you, I convinced myself that you were off calling your wife to wish her happy anniversary. There was a florist shop a few blocks from the agency. I knew you understood the ins and outs of transatlantic phone calls. I must have startled the Signora as I sneaked up, trying, to no avail, to catch you in the act of wiring flowers. I went back to the travel agency and waited for you, trying not to chew my nails.

"Per'aps 'e 'as found 'imself a nice Sicilian girl," the beautiful travel agent said, her smile rippling like the air above a flame.

That night in Giardini Naxos, in a restaurant overlooking a valley filled with wildflowers, we waited until midnight to be seated for dinner. Plump little boys in neckties and dark trousers flung themselves across narrow tables to spear cutlets from their mothers' plates and little girls in bouffant dresses flitted like giddy pastel butterflies between kitchen and dining room.

"Do you think the travel agent is pretty?" I asked while we were waiting for the menu.

"Sort of," you said, planting a slab of butter on top of the bread and popping it in your mouth.

"On a scale of one to ten."

"Let's talk about something else."

"Why do you do that?"

"Do what?" you said, slicing off another hunk of butter.

"Eat your butter without spreading it?" The waiter brought our menus. I tried to concentrate while he hovered in my peripheral vision. Taking a gulp of wine, I said, "Who do we know that's a ten. You're allowed to include movie stars."

"I'm not going to get into a fight with you over this. It's too nice a night."

"You're right," I said. "I know I'm crazy." You refilled our wine glasses. "You were so cute eating those quails in bed last night," you said. "Everytime I started to drift off, I'd hear you crunching the little bones with your teeth."

"Did I wake you?"

"Not until you got to the radishes."

When I opened my eyes at 8:30 the next morning, you were standing at the foot of the bed, map in hand, dressed in your polyester pants and buttondown shirt, three pens lined up in your breast pocket. You had already been out on your pre-dawn exploration. You wanted to eat breakfast downstairs in the dining room. There might be a surcharge if we ate on the terrace outside our room, you said.

"We picnicked all day yesterday and slept in a cheap room without a bath for two nights in a row. So what if there is a surcharge?"

You set your jaw.

"Take it out of my half," I said. That seemed to satisfy you. Still, you stood at the foot of the bed, staring down at me as if I were an inscrutable Zen puzzle.

"Let's see," you said, cupping your chin, "you slept fourteen hours last night. You couldn't be staying in bed because you're tired. It must be to try my patience. Why don't I go down to the lobby for an hour while you primp and paint your face?" You were back in forty-five minutes. I was dressed. Breakfast hadn't yet arrived.

The phone rang. It was the room service waiter. "Signora Veinti Tre, how do you take your *café*?"

Moments later, there was a knock on the door. *"Scusi, Signora,"* the ancient chamberman said, handing me a rose with shaking fin-

gers. We waited for the table to be ready. You did your daily tally
of our expenses in your ledger, entering the cost of breakfast in my
column, I noticed as I headed for the bathroom, where I arranged
and rearranged the single rose in the empty Chianti bottle. When
the waiter left, we went outside to the terrace. The table was
draped with white linen. There were branches of loquats, and tan-
gerines from the garden next to our plates, and a bowl of clotted
cream as thick as butter. I sat with my back to the sun. When I
leaned forward, I could see Etna, a giant inkwell with a quill of
smoke trailing from its cone, its slopes striped with snow. On a veranda below, a nun in a white wimple pressed coins into a tele-
scope and stooped to look through the lens at half-naked bathers
on the beach. The cream melted into irridescent puddles in our
coffee. You seemed absent.

"I need to call home," you said.

"You mean call your wife?"

"Stop listening so hard. I've got an office, too."

When you came back from the phone, you seemed stunned.

"Are you okay?" I said. You looked at me and past me as if I
weren't there. I knew something was terribly wrong.

"She misses me," you said, as if the possibility had never occurred to you.

So there it was. You'd thought she hated you, that she'd be relieved to have you gone. And now you knew you'd made a terri-
ble mistake. You were on the verge of dividing up your community property (that was the yardstick by which you measured your
loss) for one who loved you no less than the other, and it rankled.
I thought of something you'd said two years ago when we'd met.
You'd driven up into the gorges that saw-toothed the coast of
Cinqueterre—where Michaelangelo cut his marble from, you said.
At dusk, we'd stopped at a restaurant you knew of in Forti dei
Marmi. You fed me calamari with your fingers. You'd been here
many times. With a woman you'd met in Genoa.

At dusk, you parked the car and we stood in the back of a glade
listening to a choir of men singing *a capella*. Their voices were pure
and sweet and their faces were like angels. The moon was white-

hot, like magnesium and the breezes made a soft, sighing sound. Fireflies signaled one another in the humid air.

"Did you know that fireflies live for only one day, and in that day they mate, and then they die?" you whispered, fumbling for my hand in the dark.

That night you came to my room with a book in one hand and a bottle of Chianti in the other. You lay at the very edge of the bed, propped on one elbow, reading stories to me in halting Italian, your finger marking your place in the text. Your voice was as delicate and light as a boy's. The story you read me was about a *lucciola,* a firefly.

"Did you love your wife?" I said. You were silent awhile. Then, looking out the shuttered window, you said, "What I loved never happened."

After the phone call, you stared off into the middle distance, somewhere just to the left of my head, your cobalt eyes like twin frozen lakes. When they looked at me at all, they seemed narrowed in appraisal and I read in them that I was not who you wished I were.

Not that you were who I wished you were—a man of integrity and humor and generosity of spirit, but my requirements had been tempered by fifteen years in the single world. I managed to block out your mirthless laugh when you cut off a driver, your miserly ways. I was neither turned off nor on by your inept, albeit enthusiastic lovemaking. You filled the seat beside me in the car, the place next to me in bed, the chair across the dinner table. The rest was fluff. The odd thing was that as our disaffection grew, so did our appetite. Our alienation was like a Perigord goose that we stuffed to bursting with garlic-infused *brodos* and hearty *minestras;* crisp *frittatas* of eels as delicate and slender as threads, and tiny quail striped by the wood fire; with *calzones* oozing hot gorgonzola, and *orrichietti* drizzled with basil-scented oil. We filled the cavity with cylinders of goat cheese slim as a thumb, strewn with rosemary and thyme; and *sanguinelli,* the flesh the color of pomegranate; and olives as bitter as regret. We gorged on translucent slices of swordfish bathed in lemony oil; on fleshy peppers and smokey eggplants; on octopus and razor clams and scallops in their fluted coral shells; on tiny *uccelletti* the size of coins, popping the whole birds in our mouths bones and all. We ripped into ragouts and stews and *salpicons;* filled the long silences with reeking cheeses and rustic wines; packed the maw with fleshy figs, the sticky milk oozing from the stems and icy cones of *granita,* the whipped cream setting on top of the coffee crystals like a chef's toque; and wedges of watermelon, the colors of the Italian flag. We devoured roasts and braises and sautees and broils; lit into rumps and hocks and flanks and haunches; munched and gobbled and guzzled and crunched on moist, unctuous, macerated, marinated, broiled, braised, roasted, toasted, larded, and barded comestibles and—scattering crumbs in our wake like lost children—we came up hungry for more. Our discontent crouched between us bloated as a tapeworm.

It is an unspoken hunger we deflect with knives.

—Terry Tempest Williams,
An Unspoken Hunger: Stories from the Field

We were headed back toward Taormina, retracing our steps through miserable Catania. You had left your credit card with the beautiful travel agent there by mistake.

"This son of a bitch isn't going to let me go," you said. You were following inches from the bumper of a diesel truck, waiting for a chance to pass. The sky was the color of lead erupting frequently with lightning.

"You're tailgating," I said, gripping the edge of the seat, my knuckles white.

"Poor dear," you said, patting my hand.

As you pulled out from behind the truck on a blind curve, an oncoming car came speeding toward us, horn wailing. I sucked in my breath and braced my foot against the floorboards.

"Don't," you warned, as you squeezed back into our lane by a hair.

"Stop censoring my survival instinct! It's involuntary."

"I have a question," I said, when the adrenalin had subsided. "If we keep on passing trucks and then we stop for lunch, and all the

trucks we've passed get ahead of us while we're eating, then...?"
You rubbed your chin. It felt like a reproach.

"The answer is, we don't stop for lunch."

We sped through olive-shaded hills crenelated with Saracen fortresses, past crumbling walls and weeping rocks sprayed with innocent graffiti—*DIO CE* and *TI AMO, MARIA GRAZIA*. White houses lay on the hills like bleached bones.

"Do you think leaving your credit card behind had some Jungian meaning?" I said, reaching into a bag in the back seat and taking out some sausage and flatbread.

"What?" you said absently, squinting at the sea.

"Leaving your credit card in Taormina with the beautiful travel agent," I said, slicing up the sausage and cutting out the fat. I handed you a flatbread sandwich. "Don't you think so?" You bit into your sandwich with a loud crunch.

"I can't hear you. I've got toast in my mouth." I cupped my hand to my mouth and yelled, "I said, DON'T YOU THINK IT WAS JUNGIAN?"

"NON PARLA INGLESE CON MI. PARLA IN ITALIANO," you shouted suddenly, whacking the steering wheel.

We were decanting our luggage for the mini trip to Malta, taking only what we needed for the few days. We had finished all our provisions except for the lemon vodka. You didn't want to lug it with us. You were naked, swigging from the bottle, the small egg of your penis peeping from its nest of skin.

"You'll be drunk on the hydrofoil," I said. "Let's leave it behind or take it with us."

"Get off my case. If I want to finish the vodka, I'll finish it."

"You know what I think?" I said very quietly. "I think you've been sabotaging everything since your anniversary. You want to make absolutely sure we'll have a lousy time so you'll have a reason to go back to your wife when we get home."

You lifted the vodka bottle to your lips and polished it off. "Don't give me your pop-psych crap."

"You know what else? I think you've ruined every life you've touched. What do you think about that?" As in a cartoon, I saw the arrow leave my mouth and fly across the room, watched the tip bury itself in your flesh. Slowly, very deliberately, you screwed the cap on the empty vodka bottle, held it for a moment, then lobbed it into the wastebasket. Then you picked up my handbag—it was the nearest thing of mine—and heaved it across the room. The strap of the bag tore and the guidebooks and currency converter and Swiss army knife and makeup case hit the dresser and fanned out against its base shattering my compact and sending bright shards of mirror across the floor.

That evening at dinner we sat opposite each other in silence like couples do who have been together for a long time. Behind you, the last vestige of sun limned your head and settled on your shoulders, blocking out your features.

You paid attention to the menu, pointing to each item with your index finger, engrossed in appearing fully engrossed, then transferring your absorption to the buttering of the bread, from there to the backs of your hands. I skimmed the ice from the water, placed it on my butterplate, watched it melt into a lazy puddle. I picked up crumbs from the tablecloth with my fingertip and transferred them to my tongue. Across the room there was the ring of crystal against crystal as the waiter filled a water goblet, the tintinnabulation of cutlery as he cleared a table.

I did not know what to say to you. The boundaries of civility had been crossed and there was no turning back. A single word would have pulled the plug from the dike plunging us into the midst of the maelstrom. I thought of that old joke where someone calls out a number and everyone laughs—or, as in this case, a word that would cause the two of us to detonate like land mines, spewing shrapnel. At a corner table sat two young lovers, the man with his back to the view, scarcely eating, feeding his sweetheart choice bits from his plate. She chewed each morsel slowly and deliberately. Then she swallowed. He watched her with a doting smile, never taking his eyes from her as if mesmerized by the miracle of her gustatory process.

"That man is hardly eating," I broke the silence to say.

"Maybe he's in love," you said, slicing off a hunk of meat and shoveling it into your mouth.

Kelly Simon, author of Thai Cooking, *has been published in* The Washington Post, The Quarterly, Ellery Queen, *and several anthologies. She has traveled for years and is currently at work on a series of stories about the darker side of travel and the lighter side of degradation.*

*

Is the unspeakable slowly growing in your mouth?
—Rainer Maria Rilke, *The Sonnets to Orpheus,*
translated by Steven Mitchell

LARS EIGHNER

Dumpster Diving

Like the Biblical Ruth, the author finds dignity
amongst the leavings of others.

LONG BEFORE I BEGAN DUMPSTER DIVING I WAS IMPRESSED WITH Dumpsters, enough so that I wrote the Merriam-Webster research service to discover what I could about the word Dumpster. I learned from them that it is a proprietary word belonging to the Dempster Dumpster Company. Since then I have dutifully capitalized the word, although it was lowercased in almost all the citations Merriam-Webster photocopied for me. Dempster's word is too apt. I have never heard these things called anything but Dumpsters. I do not know anyone who knows the generic name for these objects. From time to time I have heard a wino or hobo give some corrupted credit to the original and call them Dipsy Dumpsters.

I began Dumpster diving about a year before I became homeless.

I prefer the word scavenging and use the word scrounging when I mean to be obscure. I have heard people, evidently meaning to be polite, use the word foraging, but I prefer to reserve that word for gathering nuts and berries and such, which I do also according to the season and the opportunity. Dumpster diving seems to me to be a little too cute and, in my case, inaccurate because I lack the athletic ability to lower myself into the Dumpsters as the true divers do, much to their increased profit.

I like the frankness of the word scavenging, which I can hardly think of without picturing a big black snail on an aquarium wall. I live from the refuse of others. I am a scavenger. I think it a sound and honorable niche, although if I could I would naturally prefer to live the comfortable consumer life, perhaps—and only perhaps—as a slightly less wasteful consumer, owing to what I have learned as a scavenger.

While Lizbeth [my dog] and I were still living in the shack on Avenue B as my savings ran out, I put almost all my sporadic income into rent. The necessities of daily life I began to extract from Dumpsters. Yes, we ate from them. Except for jeans, all my clothes came from Dumpsters. Boom boxes, candles, bedding, toilet paper, a virgin male love doll, medicine, books, a typewriter, dishes, furnishings, and change, sometimes amounting to many dollars—I acquired many things from the Dumpsters.

I have learned much as a scavenger. I mean to put some of what I have learned down here, beginning with the practical art of Dumpster diving and proceeding to the abstract.

In the Old Testament, Ruth was a young widow who could support herself and her mother-in-law only by working as a "gleaner." At harvest time men wielding scythes brought in the bulk of the grain crop. The gleaner followed on hands and knees, picking up individual grains that were dropped and left behind. In finding dignity, faith, and love in the course of her struggles, Ruth's is one of the most beautiful stories in the Bible.

—RS

What is safe to eat?

After all, the finding of objects is becoming something of an urban art. Even respectable employed people will sometimes find something tempting sticking out of a Dumpster or standing beside one. Quite a number of people, not all of them of the bohemian type, are willing to brag that they found this or that piece in the trash. But eating from Dumpsters is what separates the *dilettanti* from the professionals. Eating safely from the Dumpsters involves three principles: using the senses and common sense to evaluate the condition of the found materials, knowing the Dumpsters of a

given area and checking them regularly, and seeking always to answer the question "Why was this discarded?"

Perhaps everyone who has a kitchen and a regular supply of
groceries has, at one time or another, made a sandwich and eaten
half of it before discovering mold on the bread or got a mouthful
of milk before realizing the milk had turned. Nothing of the sort
is likely to happen to a Dumpster diver because he is constantly reminded that most food is discarded for a reason. Yet a lot of perfectly good food can be found in Dumpsters.

Canned goods, for example, turn up fairly often in the
Dumpsters I frequent. All except the most phobic people would be
willing to eat from a can, even if it came from a Dumpster. Canned
goods are among the safest of foods to be found in Dumpsters but
are not utterly foolproof.

Although very rare with modern canning methods, botulism is
a possibility. Most other forms of food poisoning seldom do lasting harm to a healthy person, but botulism is almost certainly fatal
and often the first symptom is death. Except for carbonated beverages, all canned goods should contain a slight vacuum and suck
air when first punctured. Bulging, rusty, and dented cans and cans
that spew when punctured should be avoided, especially when the
contents are not very acidic or syrupy.

Heat can break down the botulin, but this requires much more
cooking than most people do to canned goods. To the extent that
botulism occurs at all, of course, it can occur in cans on pantry
shelves as well as in cans from Dumpsters. Need I say that home-
canned goods are simply too risky to be recommended.

From time to time one of my companions, aware of the source
of my provisions, will ask, "Do you think these crackers are really
safe to eat?" For some reason it is most often the crackers they ask
about.

This question has always made me angry. Of course I would not
offer my companion anything I had doubts about. But more than
that, I wonder why he cannot evaluate the condition of the crackers for himself. I have no special knowledge and I have been wrong
before. Since he knows where the food comes from, it seems to me

he ought to assume some of the responsibility for deciding what he will put in his mouth. For myself I have few qualms about dry foods such as crackers, cookies, cereal, chips, and pasta if they are free of visible contaminates and still dry and crisp. Most often such things are found in the original packaging, which is not so much a positive sign as it is the absence of a negative one.

Raw fruits and vegetables with intact skins seem perfectly safe to me, excluding of course the obviously rotten. Many are discarded for minor imperfections that can be pared away. Leafy vegetables, grapes, cauliflower, broccoli, and similar things may be contaminated by liquids and may be impractical to wash.

Candy, especially hard candy, is usually safe if it has not drawn ants. Chocolate is often discarded only because it has become discolored as the cocoa butter de-emulsified. Candying, after all, is one method of food preservation because pathogens do not like very sugary substances.

All of these foods might be found in any Dumpster and can be evaluated with some confidence largely on the basis of appearance. Beyond these are foods that cannot be correctly evaluated without additional information.

> *All people are made alike. They are made of bones, flesh and dinners. Only the dinners are different.*
>
> —Gertrude Louise Cheney

I began scavenging by pulling pizzas out of the Dumpster behind a pizza delivery shop. In general, prepared food requires caution, but in this case I knew when the shop closed and went to the Dumpster as soon as the last of the help left.

Such shops often get prank orders; both the orders and the products made to fill them are called bogus. Because help seldom stays long at these places, pizzas are often made with the wrong topping, refused on delivery for being cold, or baked incorrectly. The products to be discarded are boxed up because inventory is kept by counting boxes: a boxed pizza can be written off; an unboxed pizza does not exist.

I never placed a bogus order to increase the supply of pizzas and I believe no one else was scavenging in this Dumpster. But the people in the shop became suspicious and began to retain their garbage in the shop overnight. While it lasted I had a steady supply of fresh, sometimes warm pizza. Because I knew the Dumpster I knew the source of the pizza, and because I visited the Dumpster regularly I knew what was fresh and what was yesterday's.

The area I frequent is inhabited by many affluent college students. I am not here by chance; the Dumpsters in this area are very rich. Students throw out many good things, including food. In particular they tend to throw everything out when they move at the end of a semester, before and after breaks, and around midterm, when many of them despair of college. So I find it advantageous to keep an eye on the academic calendar.

Students throw food away around breaks because they do not know whether it has spoiled or will spoil before they return. A typical discard is a half jar of peanut butter. In fact, nonorganic peanut butter does not require refrigeration and is unlikely to spoil in any reasonable time. The student does not know that, and since it is Daddy's money, the student decides not to take a chance. Opened containers require caution and some attention to the question, "Why was this discarded?" But in the case of discards from student apartments, the answer may be that the item was thrown out through carelessness, ignorance, or wastefulness. This can sometimes be deduced when the item is found with many others, including some that are obviously perfectly good.

Some students, and others, approach defrosting a freezer by chucking out the whole lot. Not only do the circumstances of such a find tell the story, but also the mass of frozen goods stays cold for a long time and items may be found still frozen or freshly thawed.

Yogurt, cheese, and sour cream are items that are often thrown out while they are still good. Occasionally I find a cheese with a spot of mold, which of course I just pare off, and because it is obvious why such a cheese was discarded, I treat it with less suspicion than an apparently perfect cheese found in similar circumstances. Yogurt is often discarded, still sealed, only because the expiration date on the carton had passed. This is one of my favorite finds because yogurt will keep for several days, even in warm weather.

Students throw out canned goods and staples at the end of semesters and when they give up college at midterm. Drugs, pornography, spirits, and the like are often discarded when parents are expected—Dad's Day, for example. And spirits also turn up after big party weekends, presumably discarded by the newly reformed. Wine and spirits, of course, keep perfectly well even once opened, but the same cannot be said of beer.

My test for carbonated soft drinks is whether they still fizz vigorously. Many juices or other beverages are too acidic or too syrupy to cause much concern, provided they are not visibly contaminated. I have discovered nasty molds in vegetable juices, even when the product was found under its original seal; I recommend that such products be decanted slowly into a clear glass. Liquids always require some care. One hot day I found a large jug of Pat O'Brien's Hurricane mix. The jug had been opened but was still ice cold. I drank three large glasses before it became apparent to me that someone had added the rum to the mix, and not a little rum. I never tasted the rum, and by the time I began to feel the effects I had already ingested a very large quantity of the beverage. Some divers would have considered this a boon, but being suddenly intoxicated in a public place in the early afternoon is not my idea of a good time.

I have heard of people maliciously contaminating discarded food and even handouts, but mostly I have heard of this from people with vivid imaginations who have had no experience with the Dumpsters themselves. Just before the pizza shop stopped discarding its garbage at night, jalapeños began showing up on most of the thrown-out pizzas. If indeed this was meant to discourage me, it was a wasted effort because I am a native Texan.

For myself, I avoid game, poultry, pork, and egg-based foods, whether I find them raw or cooked. I seldom have the means to cook what I find, but when I do I avail myself of plentiful supplies of beef, which is often in very good condition. I suppose fish becomes disagreeable before it becomes dangerous. Lizbeth is happy to have any such thing that is past its prime and, in fact, does not recognize fish as food until it is quite strong.

Home leftovers, as opposed to surpluses from restaurants, are very often bad. Evidently, especially among students, there is a common type of personality that carefully wraps up even the smallest leftover and shoves it into the back of the refrigerator for six months or so before discarding it. Characteristic of this type are the reused jars and margarine tubs to which the remains are committed. I avoid ethnic foods I am unfamiliar with. If I do not know what it is supposed to look like when it is good, I cannot be certain I will be able to tell if it is bad.

No matter how careful I am I still get dysentery at least once a month, oftener in warm weather. I do not want to paint too romantic a picture. Dumpster diving has serious drawbacks as a way of life.

I learned to scavenge gradually, on my own. Since then I have initiated several companions into the trade. I have learned that there is a predictable series of stages a person goes through in learning to scavenge.

At first the new scavenger is filled with disgust and self-loathing. He is ashamed of being seen and may lurk around, trying to duck behind things, or he may try to dive at night. (In fact, most people instinctively look away from a scavenger. By skulking around, the novice calls attention to himself and arouses suspicion. Diving at night is ineffective and needlessly messy.)

Every grain of rice seems to be a maggot. Everything seems to stink. He can wipe the egg yolk off the found can, but he cannot erase from his mind the stigma of eating garbage.

Be a fearless cook. And never apologize.
—Julia Child

That stage passes with experience. The scavenger finds a pair of running shoes that fit and look and smell brand-new. He finds a pocket calculator in perfect working order. He finds pristine ice cream, still frozen, more than he can eat or keep. He begins to understand: people throw away perfectly good stuff, a lot of perfectly good stuff.

At this stage, Dumpster shyness begins to dissipate. The diver, after all, has the last laugh. He is finding all manner of good things that are his for the taking. Those who disparage his profession are the fools, not he.

He may begin to hang on to some perfectly good things for which he has neither a use nor a market. Then he begins to take note of the things that are not perfectly good but are nearly so. He mates a Walkman with broken earphones and one that is missing a battery cover. He picks up things that he can repair.

At this stage he may become lost and never recover. Dumpsters are full of things of some potential value to someone and also of things that never have much intrinsic value but are interesting. All the Dumpster divers I have known come to the point of trying to acquire everything they touch. Why not take it, they reason, since it is all free? This is, of course, hopeless. Most divers come to realize that they must restrict themselves to items of relatively immediate utility. But in some cases the diver simply cannot control himself. I have met several of these pack-rat types. Their ideas of the values of various pieces of junk verge on the psychotic. Every bit of glass may be a diamond, they think, and all that glitters, gold.

I tend to gain weight when I am scavenging. Partly this is because I always find far more pizza and doughnuts than water-packed tuna, nonfat yogurt, and fresh vegetables. Also I have not

O Lord, grant me good digestion, and something to digest.

—Arab prayer

developed much faith in the reliability of Dumpsters as a food source, although it has been proven to me many times. I tend to eat as if I have no idea where my next meal is coming from. But mostly I just hate to see food go to waste and so I eat much more than I should. Something like this drives the obsession to collect junk.

As for collecting objects, I usually restrict myself to collecting one kind of small object at a time, such as pocket calculators, sunglasses, or campaign buttons. To live on the street I must anticipate my needs to a certain extent: I must pick up and save warm bedding I find in August because it will not be found in Dumpsters in November. As I have no access to health care, I often hoard essential drugs, such as antibiotics and antihistamines. (This course can be recommended only to those with some grounding in pharmacology. Antibiotics, for example, even when indicated are worse than useless if taken in insufficient amounts.) But even if I had a home with extensive storage space, I could not save everything that might be valuable in some contingency.

I have proprietary feelings about my Dumpsters. As I have mentioned, it is no accident that I scavenge from ones where good finds are common. But my limited experience with Dumpsters in other areas suggests to me that even in poorer areas, Dumpsters, if attended with sufficient diligence, can be made to yield a livelihood. The rich students discard perfectly good kiwifruit; poorer people discard perfectly good apples. Slacks and Polo shirts are found in the one place; jeans and t-shirts in the other. The population of competitors rather than the affluence of the dumpers most affects the feasibility of survival by scavenging. The large number of competitors is what puts me off the idea of trying to scavenge in places like Los Angeles.

Curiously, I do not mind my direct competition, other scavengers, so much as I hate the can scroungers.

People scrounge cans because they have to have a little cash. I have tried scrounging cans with an able-bodied companion. Afoot, a can scrounger simply cannot make more than a few dollars a day. One can extract the necessities of life from the Dumpsters directly with far less effort than would be required to accumulate the equivalent value in cans. (These observations may not hold in places with container redemption laws.)

Can scroungers, then, are people who must have small amounts of cash. These are drug addicts and winos, mostly the latter because the amounts of cash are so small. Spirits and drugs do, like all other commodities, turn up in Dumpsters and the scavenger will from time to time have a half bottle of a rather good wine with his dinner. But the wino cannot survive on these occasional finds; he must have his daily dose to stave off the DTs. All the cans he can carry will buy about three bottles of Wild Irish Rose.

I do not begrudge them the cans, but can scroungers tend to tear up the Dumpsters, mixing the contents and littering the area.

They become so specialized that they can see only cans. They earn my contempt by passing up change, canned goods, and readily hockable items.

There are precious few courtesies among scavengers. But it is common practice to set aside surplus items: pairs of shoes, clothing, canned goods, and such. A true scavenger hates to see good stuff go to waste, and what he cannot use he leaves in good condition in plain sight.

Can scroungers lay waste to everything in their path and will stir one of a pair of good shoes to the bottom of a Dumpster, to be lost or ruined in the muck. Can scroungers will even go through individual garbage cans, something I have never seen a scavenger do.

Individual garbage cans are set out on the public easement only on garbage days. On other days going through them requires trespassing close to a dwelling. Going through individual garbage cans without scattering litter is almost impossible. Litter is likely to reduce the public's tolerance of scavenging. Individual cans are simply not as productive as Dumpsters; people in houses and duplexes do not move so often and for some reason do not tend to discard as much useful material. Moreover, the time required to go through one garbage can that serves one household is not much less than the time required to go through a Dumpster that contains the refuse of twenty apartments.

But my strongest reservation about going through individual garbage cans is that this seems to me a very personal kind of invasion to which I would object if I were a householder. Although many things in Dumpsters are obviously meant never to come to light, a Dumpster is somehow less personal.

I avoid trying to draw conclusions about the people who dump in the Dumpsters I frequent. I think it would be unethical to do so, although I know many people will find the idea of scavenger ethics too funny for words.

Dumpsters contain bank statements, correspondence, and other documents, just as anyone might expect. But there are also less obvious sources of information. Pill bottles, for example. The labels bear the name of the patient, the name of the doctor, and the name of the drug. AIDS drugs and anti-psychotic medicines, to name but two groups, are specific and are seldom prescribed for any other disorders. The plastic compacts for birth-control pills usually have complete label information.

Despite all of this sensitive information, I have had only one apartment resident object to my going through the Dumpster. In that case it turned out the resident was a university athlete who was taking bets and who was afraid I would turn up his wager slips.

Occasionally a find tells a story. I once found a small paper bag containing some unused condoms, several partial tubes of flavored sexual lubricants, a partially used compact of birth-control pills, and the torn pieces of a picture of a young man. Clearly she was through with him and planning to give up sex altogether.

Dumpster things are often sad—abandoned teddy bears, shredded wedding books, despaired-of sales kits. I find many pets lying in state in Dumpsters. Although I hope to get off the streets so that Lizbeth can have a long and comfortable old age, I know this hope is not very realistic. So I suppose when her time comes she too will go into a Dumpster. I will have no better place for her. And after all, it is fitting, since for most of her life her livelihood has come from the Dumpster. When she finds something I think is safe that has been spilled from a Dumpster, I let her have it. She already knows the route around the best ones. I like to think that if she survives me she will have a chance of evading the dog catcher and of finding her sustenance on the route.

Silly vanities also come to rest in the Dumpsters. I am a rather accomplished needleworker. I get a lot of material from the Dumpsters. Evidently sorority girls, hoping to impress someone, perhaps themselves, with their mastery of a womanly art, buy a lot of embroider-by-number kits, work a few stitches horribly, and eventually discard the whole mess. I pull out their stitches, turn the canvas over, and work an original design. Do not think I refrain from chuckling as I make gifts from these kits.

I find diaries and journals. I have often thought of compiling a book of literary-found objects. And perhaps I will one day. But what I find is hopelessly commonplace and bad without being, even unconsciously, camp. College students also discard their papers. I am horrified to discover the kind of paper that now merits an A in an undergraduate course. I am grateful, however, for the number of good books and magazines the students throw out.

In the area I know best I have never discovered vermin in the Dumpsters, but there are two kinds of kitty surprise. One is alley cats whom I meet as they leap, claws first, out of Dumpsters. This is especially thrilling when I have Lizbeth in tow. The other kind of kitty surprise is a plastic garbage bag filled with some ponderous, amorphous mass. This always proves to be used cat litter.

City bees harvest doughnut glaze and this makes the Dumpster at the doughnut shop more interesting. My faith in the instinctive wisdom of animals is always shaken whenever I see Lizbeth attempt to catch a bee in her mouth, which she does whenever bees are present. Evidently some birds find Dumpsters profitable, for birdie surprise is almost as common as kitty surprise of the first kind. In hunting season all kinds of small game turn up in Dumpsters, some of it, sadly, not entirely dead. Curiously, summer and winter, maggots are uncommon.

The worst of the living and near-living hazards of the Dumpsters are the fire ants. The food they claim is not much of a loss, but they are vicious and aggressive. It is very easy to brush against some surface of the Dumpster and pick up half a dozen or more fire ants, usually in some sensitive area such as the underarm. One advantage of bringing Lizbeth along as I make Dumpster rounds is that, for obvious reasons, she is very alert to ground-based fire ants. When Lizbeth recognizes a fire-ant infestation around our feet, she does the Dance of the Zillion Fire Ants. I have learned not to ignore this warning from Lizbeth, whether I perceive the tiny ants or not, but to remove ourselves at Lizbeth's first *pas de bourée*. All the more so because the ants are the worst in the summer months when I wear flip-flops, if I have them. (Perhaps someone will misunderstand this. Lizbeth does the Dance of the Zillion Fire Ants when she recognizes more fire ants than she cares to eat, not when she is being bitten. Since I have learned to react promptly, she does not get bitten at all. It is the isolated patrol of fire ants that falls in Lizbeth's range that deserves pity. She finds them quite tasty.)

By far the best way to go through a Dumpster is to lower yourself into it. Most of the good stuff tends to settle at the bottom because it is usually weightier than the rubbish. My more athletic companions have often demonstrated to me that they can extract much good material from a Dumpster I have already been over.

To those psychologically or physically unprepared to enter a Dumpster, I recommend a stout stick, preferably with some barb or hook at one end. The hook can be used to grab plastic garbage bags. When I find canned goods or other objects loose at the bottom of a Dumpster, I lower a bag into it, roll the desired object into the bag, and then hoist the bag out—a procedure more easily described than executed. Much Dumpster diving is a matter of experience for which nothing will do except practice.

Dumpster diving is outdoor work, often surprisingly pleasant. It is not entirely predictable; things of interest turn up every day and some days there are finds of great value. I am always very pleased when I can turn up exactly the thing I most wanted to find. Yet in spite of the element of chance, scavenging more than most other pursuits tends to yield returns in some proportion to the effort and intelligence brought to bear. It is very sweet to turn up a few dollars in change from a Dumpster that has just been gone over by a wino.

The land is now covered with cities. The cities are full of Dumpsters. If a member of the canine race is ever able to know what it is doing, then Lizbeth knows that when we go around to the Dumpsters, we are hunting. I think of scavenging as a modern form of self-reliance. In any event, after having survived nearly ten years of government service, where everything is geared to the lowest common denominator, I find it refreshing to have work that rewards initiative and effort. Certainly I would be happy to have a sinecure again, but I am no longer heartbroken that I left one.

I find from the experience of scavenging two rather deep lessons. The first is to take what you can use and let the rest go by.

I have come to think that there is no value in the abstract. A thing I cannot use or make useful, perhaps by trading, has no value however rare or fine it may be. I mean useful in a broad sense—some art I would find useful and some otherwise.

I was shocked to realize that some things are not worth acquiring, but now I think it is so. Some material things are white elephants that eat up the possessor's substance. The second lesson is the transience of material being. This has not quite converted me to a dualist, but it has made some headway in that direction. I do not suppose that ideas are immortal, but certainly mental things are longer lived than other material things.

Once I was the sort of person who invests objects with sentimental value. Now I no longer have those objects, but I have the sentiments yet.

Many times in our travels I have lost everything but the clothes I was wearing and Lizbeth. The things I find in Dumpsters, the love letters and rag dolls of so many lives, remind

A story from the village school that Yves, my son, tells me:

It's autumn in the orchard. A rosy apple falls to the grass near a cow-pat. Friendly and polite, the cow-shit says to the apple: "Good morning, Madame la Pomme. How are you feeling?"

She ignores the remark, for she considers such conversation beneath her dignity.

"It's fine weather, don't you think, Madame la Pomme?"

Silence.

"You'll find the grass here very sweet, Madame la Pomme."

Again, silence.

At this moment a man walks through the orchard, sees the rosy apple, stoops to pick it up. As he bites into the apple, the cowshit, irrepressible says: "See you in a little while, Madame la Pomme!"

What makes shit such a universal joke is that it's an unmistakable reminder of our duality, of our soiled nature and of our will to glory. It is the ultimate lèse-majesté.

—John Berger "Muck and its Entanglements: Cleaning the Outhouse," *Harper's*

me of this lesson. Now I hardly pick up a thing without envisioning the time I will cast it aside. This I think is a healthy state of mind. Almost everything I have now has already been cast out at least once, proving that what I own is valueless to someone.

Anyway, I find my desire to grab for the gaudy bauble has been largely sated. I think this is an attitude I share with the very wealthy—we both know there is plenty more where what we have came from. Between us are the rat-race millions who nightly scavenge the cable channels looking for they know not what.

I am sorry for them.

Lars Eighner has been described as the "Thoreau of Dumpsters," and as a "Latter Day Candide." He and Lizbeth were living under a shower curtain in a stand of bamboo in a public park when he began this story, which was excerpted from his book Travels with Lizbeth. *They now have a roof over their heads in Austin, Texas. I wish them well.*

★

When we pass the village produce market, which is usually sold out by eight in the morning, we notice three vendors still standing in the broiling sun.

"Mister! Food here, mister," one dealer says, beckoning.

Dressed only in a tattered jumper, she stands over several rows of rotten produce; the bananas, fermenting inside blackened skins, are bloated and threatening to burst. Her neighbor's yams have shriveled like prunes, and the lemons are brown and mushy.

Innocent takes me aside. Begging, he says, is unthinkable here or in any rural district in the Congo. Instead, the impoverished pretend to have something to sell, and people pretend to buy it from them. The family, not the tribe, village, or state, takes care of those unable to support themselves, and these women must have lost their families.

We buy out the market for six dollars and turn to leave.

"Mister. These belong to you now."

Innocent helps me heap the rotten produce on an old piece of plywood, and we carry it to a village goat pen. The owner of the livestock waves us off, flicking a switch in the air.

"That will ruin tomorrow's milk!" He points to the jungle wall. "Feed it to the ants."

—Rory Nugent, *Drums Along the Congo: On the Trail of Mokele-Mbembe, the Last Living Dinosaur*

PART FIVE

THE LAST WORD

Pilgrims All

Dust to dust.

As Ginger and I came over the mountains from Valdichiasco and into Valfabricca, we purchased some *lupini* and fava beans cured in brine and sat for a moment, munching them, on the edge of the plaza. It was a *piazza centrale* that still functioned to link local residents together, especially the old-timers. There, they swapped stories and lies, laughing and arguing with one another, each of them part preacher, part politician, part librarian of local facts.

They must have spotted Ginger and me immediately when we entered the plaza, for after we went into a small grocery store and came out, disoriented, one of them yelled, "Over here!" There, on the corner of the plaza by the main cross street, stood seven old-timers with their canes, potbellies, gestures, and stories. I went up to the closest one and asked him for directions to the official Strada Francescana.

"We're pilgrims. Which is the way that pilgrims have taken when walking to Assisi?"

Before my contact could answer, arms shot out, pointing in every direction. Seven different answers came at once out of seven different mouths, and as they heard each other's recommended directions, their faces filled with color and expression.

"What do you mean, turn left at the next street? The bridge on that street has been closed down for months now!"

Disgusted, another man waved them all off, grabbed Ginger and me by the shoulders, and marched us out into the middle of the main street, where he hobbled along with us until we arrived at the lane where he wanted us to turn. He patted me on the back and grumbled, "There it is, my friends, now go, before the others try to change your minds."

I looked back at his six cronies, and they were still arguing, waving their arms, shaking their canes, and making dramatic gestures to one another with their hands. I had to laugh; we had asked them too large and weighty a question for an afternoon in the week before the Festa di San Francesco: "What is the true Franciscan Way?"

While they argued over the answer, we struck out for the mountaintop village of Pieve di Nicola. Three hours later—after passing vineyards, olive groves, and flocks of hooded crows—we began the long descent into Assisi. Nine and a half hours after starting out that morning, we dropped our packs from our backs on a small lane below the basilica where Saint Francis was buried. In my dreams that night, old men passionately argued with one another: "Which is the way? Which is the way?"...

From Valfabricca, the massive range that included Pieve di Nicola, Monte Subasio, and Monte di Croci, was the only barrier between us and our destination of Assisi. We tried several footpaths that we presumed were parallel to the paved Strada Francescana, but each time we departed for more than a quarter of a mile from the pavement, we dead-ended in someone's ridge-top grain field. We reluctantly returned to the paved way, for it was already three in the afternoon; we had miles to go before we slept, most of them uphill.

There were cyclones of blackbirds swirling and piles of pumpkins on the roofs of barns as we reached the road's summit. From Monte di Croci down to Assisi, we did little talking; the endorphins killing the pain in our calves and feet numbed our tired bodies. We hobbled the last four miles down to Assisi in the dark, and at the junction of highways below the cathedral, began to ask for directions to the country lodge where we would stay. One driver finally looked at both of us tired souls, shook his head, and said, "Get in—I'll take you there."

It is no overstatement to claim that we were immediately asleep as soon as we put our packs down, took our shoes off, and lay down on our beds. We were much too exhausted after nine days of hiking to muster the strength to absorb all of Assisi's grandeur.

For two days, we recuperated on a small farm at Capodaqua, above the valleys southeast of Assisi in the Subasio foothills. We watched birds, washed clothes, and drank wine from the farm's vineyard; we were still shy about rushing over to Assisi and lunging into its heart, because we had arrived a few days prior to the Feast of Saint Francis. We wanted to see it in full dress, not in its bathrobe as it readied itself for the feast. We would wait for the appropriate moment to dance down its streets.

In the meantime, I arranged for a reprieve. In the days before the feast, Ginger would catch up on other interests, while I would go to the ancient village of Sacrofano an hour from Rome, to help my friends Pepé Esquinas and Rosanna Galvani with the *vendemmia,* the bringing in of the vintage, and the initiation of wine making in a cave below both their houses, a wine cellar that had not been used for more than thirty years.

The morning of the harvest, Pepé was ill, so Rosanna and I left around seven to drive to some vineyards near Monte Pocchio. She had arranged for us to pick white grapes at a friend's vineyard, under the inspection of an uncle who lived there. We were to work six long rolling rows of grapes that had turned from pale green to blush, most of them already at or slightly past the peak of ripening. Insects, molds, and fungal growths were everywhere. As Rosanna and I began to select only those bunches that had not been burst by juice-sucking insects and covered with a woolly coat of microbes, the old uncle protested, "Take all of them, goddamn it! Don't leave the row half-picked! How are we supposed to make any money off you if we charge you by the amount you pick but you leave the rows in such a mess? No one else will want to glean from your *half-picked* rows, so how will we profit? Anyway, how do you expect to make a full-bodied wine if you don't have some bugs and molds adding to the flavor? I tell you, the little crap that falls into the vats is what gives wine its taste!"

As we reluctantly began to take all the grapes, spoiled and unspoiled, the juices from the grapes already burst by bees and wasps dripped down our hands and arms. We became more and more sticky so that the insects began to swarm all over us, not biting but feeding on the sweet syrups drying on our limbs. I counted a dozen different kinds of insects, present in unbelievable numbers, hovering around the bunches of grapes, our vats, and our bodies. The *vendemmia* was not just a significant harvest event for humans but a ceremony for the attendant fauna as well.

Rosanna and I worked opposite sides of a row, talking to each other in a mix of Italian and Spanish. We shared family histories, jokes, and favorite stories about Pepé Esquinas, our mutual friend. In no time, we had picked six fifty-gallon drums full of grapes and stems, and insects catching rides with them. I remembered David Price's observation that true culture is transmitted through stories told during times of collective labor by hand and "testifies to the survival of the ancient world...binding vines, cutting the olives, chopping bamboo with handsaws and axes—these are aspects of a traditional knowledge unsurpassed...[by that which rides on] borrowed or half-owned tractors. And these skills are still a family patronage." As long as communal work parties are needed, the stories that reinforce the values of the community are needed just as much.

Rosanna and I drove back to Sacrofano, were her family and neighbors helped us roll the barrels of grapes up the narrow cobblestone walkways in their village. We washed out other wooden vats, cleaned out the cavern that served as the wine cellar, crushed the grapes through a hand-cranked masher, removed the stems from the juice and pulp, and mixed the batches of juice into other barrels. We found ourselves stained and sticky up to our armpits; tired, we returned to her house, where her family had a six-course meal ready for us. We cleaned up, then sank into our seats as Pepé poured us some wine, and the family toasted our work. Then, four of them burst into story simultaneously, telling of the last times they had participated in the *vendemmia*.

I sighed with pleasure as they spoke, for I felt as though I were landing after a long flight away from family. I finally had the sense that I had arrived in an Italian community, for I had worked with the grapes and vats and grinders long enough that day to have my outsider's status suspended for the moment. My contribution to their communal work had broken down any notions they may have had about me as a "typical" foreigner of holiday. Now, it seemed, I was considered worthy of hearing their oral histories.

Their stories led out from the ancient wine cellar—a cavern hidden deep beneath their village—through the cobblestone passageways that connected home after home into neighborhood and down through the lineages of wine drinkers who had worked the vats in the cellar, before the wars and after. Their stories moved from favorite vintages and wine makers out into the vineyards that surrounded the village, rising onto the best locations for grape growing and dipping into the ones that they had to fall back on, brushing through the good years and the bad, suffering and yet enduring all the freezes and the plagues and the droughts that they could remember, if not through their own experience, then through the tales of their elders. Their stories noted when certain wine varieties had first come within their range, but they also marked the times when certain families had come and gone, when each had had its heyday, its vintage years, and what had become of its legacy. At first, I thought these were stories about just grapes, but then they were transformed into wine by those crafty alchemists culture and time, and the wine had passed into the bodies of my hosts and become their flesh and the flesh of their neighbors with whom they had shared each batch; and that amalgam of neighbors, who had first come together by happenstance or by hidden necessity, had somehow turned into community; and that community had flowed out of the ancient stone homes, back onto the land, where it began.

We finished off the last of the freshly baked bread and the last of one bottle of wine and moved from the table to the sofas and chairs where more wine was poured and more stories told. Here, I thought, here in the sharing of bread and wine and story, was where history had its deepest roots. I could not imagine how the winds of change would ever topple such a community.

Gary Paul Nabhan is a plant conservation biologist and a fellow of the MacArthur Foundation. His literary works include Coming Home to Eat, Gathering the Desert, The Geography of Childhood, *and* Songbirds, Truffles and Wolves: An American Naturalist in Italy, *from which this story was excerpted.*

★

Books for Further Reading

We hope *Travelers Tales Food: A Taste of the Road* has inspired you to read on. A good place to start is the books from which we've made selections, and these are listed below along with other books that we have found to be valuable. Some of these may be out of print but are well worth hunting down. General guidebooks are also worth reading, and the best have annotated bibliographies or sections on recommended books and maps.

Ackerman, Diane. *A Natural History of the Senses.* New York: Vintage Books, 1991.

Boyles, Denis. *Man Eaters Motel and Other Stops on the Railway to Nowhere: An East African Traveler's Nightbook.* New York: Ticknor & Fields, 1991.

Brillat-Savarin, Jean Anthelme. M. F. K. Fisher, trans. *The Physiology of Taste.* Washington, DC: Counterpoint Press, 2000.

Chatwin, Bruce. *The Songlines.* New York: Elizabeth Sifton Books, 1988.

Cummings, Joe. *Thailand—a travel survival kit.* Australia: Lonely Planet Publications, 2001.

Daley, Robert. *Portraits of France.* New York: Little, Brown, 1995.

Dana, Richard Henry. *Two Years Before the Mast.* New York: The Modern Library, 2001.

Davidson, Alan. *A Kipper with My Tea: Selected Food Essays.* San Francisco: North Point Press, 1990.

DeWitt, Dave and Arthur J. Pais. *A World of Curries.* Boston: Little, Brown and Company, 1994.

Doling, Annabel. *Vietnam on a Plate.* Hong Kong: Roundhouse Publications Ltd, 1996.

Dumas, Alexandre. Louis Colman, trans. *Alexandre Dumas' Dictionary of Cuisine.* New York: Avon Books, 1958.

Eighner, Lars. *Travels with Lizbeth: Three Years on the Road and on the Streets.* New York: Fawcett Books, 1994.

Esquivel, Laura. Carol Christensen and Thomas Christensen, trans. *Like Water for Chocolate.* New York: Prentice-Hall, 1994.

Fisher, M.F.K. *The Art of Eating.* New York: Hungry Minds, 1990.

George, Susan. *How the Other Half Dies: The Real Reasons for World Hunger.* New Jersey: Allanheld, Osmun & Co. Publishers, Inc., 1977.

Goodman, Richard. *French Dirt: The Story of a Garden in the South of France.* New York: HarperCollins, 1992.

Gottlieb, Alma and Philip Graham. *Parallel Worlds: An Anthropologist and a Writer Encounter Africa.* Chicago: University of Chicago Press, 1992.

Gruber, Mark, O.S.B. *Wounded by Love: Intimations of an Outpouring Heart.* Latrobe, Pennsylvania: Saint Vincent Archabbey, 1993.

Hafner, Dorinda. *I Was Never Here and This Never Happened: Tasty Bits & Spicy Tales from My Life.* Berkeley, California: Ten Speed Press, 1996.

Harris, Marvin. *Cannibals and Kings: The Origins of Cultures.* New York: Vintage Books, 1991.

Henderson, Bruce Griffin. *The Chefs, the Cooks, and the Churlish.* New York: Plume, 1995.

Jacobs, Jay. *A Glutton for Punishment: Confessions of a Mercenary Eater.* New York: Atlantic Monthly Press, 1991.

James, Peter and Nick Thorpe. *Ancient Inventions.* New York: Ballantine Books, 1995.

Jordan, Michele Anna. *The Good Cook's Book of Tomatoes.* Cambridge, Massachusetts: Perseus Press, 1995.

King, John S. and Bradley Mayhew. *Lonely Planet Pakistan.* Australia: Lonely Planet Publications, 1998.

Levy, Paul. *Out to Lunch.* London: Chatto and Windus, 1986.

Loftus, Simon. *A Pike in the Basement: Tales of a Hungry Traveler.* San Francisco: North Point Press, 1987.

Mayes, Frances. *Bella Tuscany: The Sweet Life in Italy.* New York: Broadway, 1999.

Mayle, Peter. *Toujours Provence.* New York: Vintage, 1992.

Moehlmann, Kristin, ed. *Affordable Italy.* New York: Fodor's, 1993.

Nabhan, Gary Paul. *Songbirds, Truffles, and Wolves: An American Naturalist in Italy.* New York: Penguin USA, 1994.

Neruda, Pablo. Alastair Reid, trans. *Extravagaria*. New York: Farrar, Straus, Giroux, 1975.

Nin, Anaïs. *Delta of Venus*. New York: Pocket Books, 1990.

Nin, Anaïs. *Little Birds*. New York: Pocket Books, 1990.

Nugent, Rory. *Drums Along the Congo: On the Trail of Mokele-Mbembe, the Last Living Dinosaur*. New York: Houghton Mifflin Company, 1993.

Off The Beaten Track: Italy. New York: Moorland Publishing Company Ltd., 1988.

Osborne, Lawrence. *Paris Dreambook: An Unconventional Guide to the Splendor and Squalor of the City*. New York: Vintage Departures, 1990

O'Rourke, P. J. *All The Trouble in the World: The Lighter Side of Overpopulation, Famine, Ecological Disaster, Ethnic Hatred, Plague and Poverty*. New York: Atlantic Monthly Press, 1995.

Pfister, Patrick. *Pilgrimage: Tales from the Open Road*. Chicago: Academy Chicago Publishers, 1995.

Popescu, Petru. *Amazon Beaming*. New York: Viking Penguin, 1991.

Porter, Darwin, Arthur Frommer, and Danforth Prince. *Frommer's Scotland 1996*. New York: Prentice Hall Travel, 2000.

Rawicz, Slavomir. *The Long Walk*. New York: The Lyons Press, 1997.

Reichl, Ruth. *Tender at the Bone: Growing Up at the Table*. New York: Broadway Books, 1999.

Robbins, Maria Polushkin. *A Cook's Alphabet of Quotations*. New York: A Dutton Book, 1991.

Rombauer, Irma S. and Marion Rombauer Becker. *The Joy of Cooking*. New York: Plume, 1997.

Rosenblum, Mort. *A Goose in Toulouse and Other Culinary Adventures in France*. New York: Hyperion, 2000.

Shacochis, Bob. *Domesticity: A Gastronomic Interpretation of Love*. New York: Penguin Books, 1995.

Shaw, Timothy. *The World of Escoffier*. New York: St. Martin's Press, 1995.

Singh, Sarina. *Lonely Planet India*. Australia: Lonely Planet Publications, 2001.

Sokolov, Raymond. *The Jewish American Kitchen*. New York: Stewart, Tabori & Chang, Inc., 1989.

Sterling, Richard. *Dining with Headhunters: Jungle Feasts & Other Culinary Adventures*. Freedom, California: The Crossing Press, 1995.

Stevenson, Robert Louis. Osbourne, Lloyd, ed. *In the South Seas: A Footnote to History.* Charles Scribner's Sons, 1922.

Thubron, Colin. *The Lost Heart of Asia.* New York: HarperCollins, 2000.

Trager, James. *The Food Chronology: A Food Lover's Compendium of Events and Anecdotes, from Prehistory to the Present.* New York: Henry Holt and Company, Inc., 1997.

Warner, William W. *Beautiful Swimmers.* Boston: Little, Brown & Company, 1994.

Wells, Patricia. *The Food Lover's Guide to France.* New York: Workman Publishing Co., 1987.

White, Edmund. *Our Paris: Sketches from Memory.* New York: Borzoi Books, 1995.

White, Theodore H. *In Search of History.* New York: Warner Books, 1978.

Williams, Terry Tempest. *An Unspoken Hunger: Stories from the Field.* New York: Vintage, 1995.

Xianliang, Zhang. *Grass Soup.* Lincoln, Massachusetts: David R. Godine Publisher, Inc., 1995.

Yeadon, David. *The Back of Beyond: Travels to the Wild Places of the Earth.* New York: HarperCollins Publishers, 1991.

Index

Index of Contributors

Acknowledgements

I wish to send my thanks to Professors Charles Muscatine and Maxine Hong Kingston who taught me the art of letters; to Dave DeWitt, creator and Editor Emeritus of *Chile Pepper* magazine who was my first publisher, always liked my stuff, and is a most artful eater; to Sean O'Reilly for aiding and abetting me; to Raj Khadka for innumerable services well rendered; to George Wright, Sue Kinder, Cynthia Lamb, Kathryn Heflin, Kristen Throop, Judy Anderson, Nina Stewart, Keith Granger, Cindy Collins, Deborah Greco, Trisha Schwartz, Jennifer Leo, Jeff Brady, Paula Mc Cabe, Wenda O'Reilly, Tim O'Reilly, and they all know why. And to the Travelers' Tales factotum, getter-of-things-done, Voice of Reason and Voice of Reality, Susan Brady. She would humbly deny it, but she has actually been known to walk on water.

And a special thanks to James O'Reilly and Larry Habegger, who came to dinner one night and listened to a few of my tales about how I cooked this or ate that while on the road.

"You know," they said, "you oughtta write that stuff down."

"So should we all," said I.

"Apron Strings" by Pamela Michael reprinted by permission of the author. Copyright © 1996 by Pamela Michael.

"Feast of the Pig" by Theodore H. White excerpted from *In Search of History* by Theodore H. White. Copyright © 1978 by Theodore H. White. Reprinted by permission of Harper-Collins Publishers, Inc. and the estate of Theodore H. White.

"A Language for Food" by Edmund White excerpted from *Our Paris: Sketches from Memory* by Edmund White. Copyright © 1995 by Edmund White. Reprinted by permission of Alfred A. Knopf, Inc. and Macmillan Publishers Ltd.

Books, a division of Random House, Inc. and Bloomsbury Publishing, Ltd.

"A Waltz at the End of Earth" by Paula McDonald reprinted by permission from the November 1995 issue of *Readers Digest* and by the author. Copyright © 1995 by Paula McDonald.

"Pass on the Primate" by Carla King reprinted by permission of the author. Copyright © 1996 by Carla King.

"Even Their Eyes are Hungry" by Zhang Xianliang excerpted from *Grass Soup* by Zhang Xianliang, translated by Martha Avery. Reprinted by permission of David R. Godine, Publisher, Inc. Copyright © 1993 by Zhang Xianliang, translation copyright © 1994 by Martha Avery.

"The Laughter of Rul" by Garrett Culhane reprinted by permission of the author. Copyright © 1996 by Garrett Culhane.

"There Was a Train" by M. F. K. Fisher reprinted with permission of Macmillan USA, a Simon & Schuster Macmillan Company, and Lescher & Lescher, Ltd., from "The Flaw" as found in *The Art of Eating* by M.F.K. Fisher. Copyright © 1943 by M.F.K. Fisher. Copyright renewed © 1971 by M.F.K Fisher.

"To Serve Man" by Harry Rolnick reprinted by permission of the author. Copyright © 1996 by Harry Rolnick.

"Liberation Day" by Kelly Simon reprinted by permission of the author. Copyright © 1996 by Kelly Simon.

"Dumpster Diving" by Lars Eighner excerpted from *Travels with Lizbeth: Three Years on the Road and on the Streets* by Lars Eighner. Copyright © 1993 Lars Eighner. Reprinted by permission of St. Martin's Press, Inc. and Pushcart Press.

"Pilgrims All" by Gary Paul Nabhan excerpted from *Songbirds, Truffles, and Wolves: An American Naturalist in Italy* by Gary Paul Nabhan. Copyright © 1993 by Gary Nabhan. Reprinted by permission of Pantheon, a division of Random House, Inc.

Additional Credits (arranged alphabetically by title)

Selection from "Alas, Poor Opah" by Meredith Moraine reprinted by permission of the author. Copyright © 1996 by Meredith Moraine.

Selection from *Alexandre Dumas' Dictionary of Cuisine* by Alexandre Dumas, translated by Louis Coleman, reprinted by permission

Copyright © 1969 by Anaïs Nin, © 1977 by the Anaïs Nin Trust.

Selection from "Diet Tips from the Barbi Twins" by Matt Maranian reprinted from the Fall 1995 issue of *bOING bOING*. Copyright © 1995.

Selection from "Dinner in the Outback" by Mark Lamana reprinted by permission of the author. Copyright © 1996 by Mark Lamana.

Selection from "Dinner on the Rio Dulce" by Dorothy Aksamit reprinted by permission of the author. Copyright © 1996 by Dorothy Aksamit.

Selection from *The Divine Comedy* by Dante Alighieri, translated by John Ciardi. Translation copyright © 1954, 1957, 1959, 1960, 1961, 1965, 1967, 1970 by the Ciardi Family Publishing Trust. Reprinted by permission of W. W. Norton & Company, Inc.

Selection from "Don't Eat the Shellfish" by Alison Wright reprinted by permission of the author. Copyright © 1996 by Alison Wright.

Selections from *Drums Along the Congo: On the Trail of Mokele-Mbembe, the Last Living Dinosaur* by Rory Nugent. Copyright © 1993 by Rory Nugent. Reprinted by permission of Houghton Mifflin Company. All rights reserved.

Selection from *Fodor's Guide to Italy* edited by Kristin Moehlmann copyright © 1993 by Fodor's Travel Publications, Inc. Reprinted by permission of Fodor's Travel Publications, Inc., a subsidiary of Random House, Inc.

Selections from *The Food Chronology: A Food Lover's Compendium of Events and Anecdotes, from Prehistory to the Present* by James Trager. Copyright © 1995 by James Trager. Reprinted by permission of Henry Holt and Company, Inc.

Selection from *The Food Lover's Guide to France* by Patricia Wells copyright © 1987 by Patricia Wells. Reprinted by permission of Workman Publishing Company, Inc. All rights reserved.

Selection from *French Dirt: The Story of a Garden in the South of France* by Richard Goodman. Copyright © 1991 by Richard Goodman. Reprinted by permission of Algonquin Books of Chapel Hill, a division of Workman Publishing and Darhansoff & Verrill.

Selection from *Jewish Literacy* by Rabbi Joseph Telushkin copyright
© 1991 by Rabbi Joseph Telushkin. Used by permission of
William Morrow and Company, Inc.

Selections from *The Joy of Cooking* by Irma S. Rombauer and
Marion Rombauer Becker reprinted by permission of
Macmillan USA, a Simon & Schuster Macmillan Company.
Copyright © 1964 by The Bobbs-Merrill Company, Inc.

Selection from "Jungle Stew" by Thomas J. Lakey reprinted by permission of the author. Copyright © 1996 by Thomas J. Lakey.

Selection from *A Kipper with My Tea: Selected Food Essays* by Alan
Davidson reprinted by permission of Macmillan London Ltd.
and A. P. Watt. Copyright © 1990 by Alan Davidson.

Selections from *Like Water for Chocolate* by Laura Esquivel, translated
by Carol Christensen and Thomas Christensen. Copyright ©
1989 by 7th Dimension Entertainment Co., Inc., English
translation copyright © 1992 by Doubleday, a division of
Bantam Doubleday Dell Publishing Group, Inc. Used by permission of Doubleday, a division of Bantam Doubleday Dell
Publishing Group Inc., and Transworld Doubleday.

Selection from *Little Birds* by Anaïs Nin reprinted by permission of
Harcourt Brace Company and Gunther Stuhlmann. Copyright
© 1979 by Rupert Pole as trustee under the Last Will and
Testament of Anaïs Nin.

Selection from *The Long Walk* by Slavomir Rawicz reprinted by permission of Lyon & Burford Publishers. Copyright © 1956,
1984 by Slavomir Rawicz.

Selection from *Man Eater's Motel and Other Stops on the Railway to
Nowhere: An East African Traveler's Nightbook* by Denis Boyles
copyright © 1991 by Denis Boyles. Reprinted by permissions
of Ticknor & Fields/Houghton Mifflin Company and
Phoenix Literary Agency. All rights reserved.

Selection from "The Marine Wonders of Kenai Fjords" by Larry
Habegger reprinted by permission of the author. Copyright
© 1996 by Larry Habegger.

Selection from "Mix and Unmatch" by Rajendra S. Khadka
reprinted by permission of the author. Copyright © 1996 by
Rajendra S. Khadka.

Selection from "More Spices from Off the Beaten Path" by Annette

Selection from *Provence: From Minstrels to the Machine* by Ford Madox Ford published by J.B. Lippincott Company. Copyright © 1935 by Ford Madox Ford.

Selection from *Roughing It* by Mark Twain published by Signet.

Selection from "Sake on Tap" by Russell Shorto reprinted from the June 1991 issue of *Travel & Leisure.* Copyright © 1991 by Russell Shorto.

Selection from "A Scottish Food Primer" by Reed Glenn reprinted by permission of the author. Copyright © 1996 by Reed Glenn.

Selection from *Snake Poems: An Aztec Invocation* by Francisco X. Alarcón. Reprinted by permission of Chronicle Books. Copyright © 1992 by Francisco X. Alarcón.

Selection from *The Songlines* by Bruce Chatwin. Copyright © 1987 by the Estate of Charles Bruce Chatwin. Used by permission of Penguin Books USA Inc. and Random House UK.

Selection from *The Sonnets to Orpheus* by Rainer Maria Rilke, translated by Stephen Mitchell, reprinted by permission of Simon & Schuster, Inc. Copyright © 1985 by Stephen Mitchell.

Selection from *Thailand - a travel survival kit* by Joe Cummings reprinted by permission of Lonely Planet Publications. Copyright © 1995 by Lonely Planet.

Selection from *Toujours Provence* by Peter Mayle excerpted by permission of Hamish Hamilton Ltd. and Alfred A. Knopf, Inc. Copyright © 1991 Peter Mayle.

Selection from *Traveling Well: A Comprehensive Guide to Your Health Abroad* by W. Scott Harkonen, M.D. published by Dodd, Mead and Company. Copyright © 1984 by W. Scott Harkonen.

Selection from "Traveller's Tales" by Nury Vittachi reprinted from the *Far Eastern Economic Review.* Copyright © by Nury Vittachi.

Selection from *The Travels of Marco Polo* by Marco Polo published by Orion Press.

Selection from "Turning the Tables—Table Manners Around the World" by Sara Hare reprinted by permission of the author. Copyright © 1996 by Sara Hare.

Selection from *Two Years Before the Mast* by Richard Henry Dana copyright © 1936 by Random House, Inc. Reprinted by permission of Random House, Inc.

About the Editor

Richard Sterling is a writer, editor, lecturer, and insatiable traveler. Earlier in life he was a Silicon Valley engineer, but stability and respectability lost out over wanderlust. Since taking up the pen he has been honored by the James Beard Foundation for his food writing, and by the Lowell Thomas Awards for his travel literature. He is based in Berkeley, California, where he is often politically incorrect.

Other Books by Richard Sterling

Travelers' Tales Food: A Taste of the Road
The Adventure of Food: True Stories of Eating Everything
The Ultimate Journey: Inspiring Stories of Living and Dying
The Fearless Diner: Travel Tips and Wisdom for
Eating Around the World
World Food: Vietnam
World Food: Spain
World Food: Hong Kong
World Food: Greece
Unofficial Guide to San Francisco
The Eclectic Gourmet Guide to San Francisco
and the Bay Area

NOTES & RECIPES

Notes & Recipes

TRAVELERS' TALES

THE SOUL OF TRAVEL

Footsteps Series

THE FIRE NEVER DIES
One Man's Raucous Romp Down the Road of Food, Passion, and Adventure
By Richard Sterling
ISBN 1-885-211-70-8
$14.95

"Sterling's writing is like spit-fire, foursquare and jazzy with crackle...."
—Kirkus Reviews

LAST TROUT IN VENICE
The Far-Flung Escapades of an Accidental Adventurer
By Doug Lansky
ISBN 1-885-211-63-5
$14.95

"Traveling with Doug Lansky might result in a considerably shortened life expectancy...but what a way to go." —Tony Wheeler, Lonely Planet Publications

ONE YEAR OFF
Leaving It All Behind for a Round-the-World Journey with Our Children
By David Elliot Cohen
ISBN 1-885-211-65-1
$14.95

A once-in-a-lifetime adventure generously shared.

THE WAY OF THE WANDERER
Discover Your True Self Through Travel
By David Yeadon
ISBN 1-885-211-60-0
$14.95

Experience transformation through travel with this delightful, illustrated collection by award-winning author David Yeadon.

TAKE ME WITH YOU
A Round-the-World Journey to Invite a Stranger Home
By Brad Newsham
ISBN 1-885-211-51-1
$24.00 (cloth)

"Newsham is an ideal guide. His journey, at heart, is into humanity." —Pico Iyer, author of Video Night in Kathmandu

KITE STRINGS OF THE SOUTHERN CROSS
A Woman's Travel Odyssey
By Laurie Gough
ISBN 1-885-211-54-6
$14.95

— ★ ★ ★ —

ForeWord Silver Medal Winner
— Travel Book of the Year

THE SWORD OF HEAVEN
A Five Continent Odyssey to Save the World
By Mikkel Aaland
ISBN 1-885-211-44-9
$24.00 (cloth)

"Few books capture the soul of the road like The Sword of Heaven, a sharp-edged, beautifully rendered memoir that will inspire anyone." —Phil Cousineau, author of The Art of Pilgrimage

STORM
A Motorcycle Journey of Love, Endurance, and Transformation
By Allen Noren
ISBN 1-885-211-45-7
$24.00 (cloth)

— ★ ★ ★ —

ForeWord Gold Medal Winner
— Travel Book of the Year

Travelers' Tales Classics

COAST TO COAST
A Journey Across 1950s America
By Jan Morris
ISBN 1-885-211-79-1
$16.95

After reporting on the first Everest ascent in 1953, Morris spent a year journeying by car, train, ship, and aircraft across the United States. In her brilliant prose, Morris records with exuberance and curiosity a time of innocence in the U.S.

TRADER HORN
A Young Man's Astounding Adventures in 19th Century Equatorial Africa
By Alfred Aloysius Horn
ISBN 1-885-211-81-3
$16.95

Here is the stuff of legends —tale of thrills and danger, wild beasts, serpents, and savages. An unforgettable and vivid portrait of a vanished late-19th century Africa.

THE ROYAL ROAD TO ROMANCE
By Richard Halliburton
ISBN 1-885-211-53-8
$14.95

"Laughing at hardships, dreaming of beauty, ardent for adventure, Halliburton has managed to sing into the pages of this glorious book his own exultant spirit of youth and freedom."
— *Chicago Post*

UNBEATEN TRACKS IN JAPAN
By Isabella L. Bird
ISBN 1-885-211-57-0
$14.95

Isabella Bird was one of the most adventurous women travelers of the 19th century with journeys to Tibet, Canada, Korea, Turkey, Hawaii, and Japan. A fascinating read for anyone interested in women's travel, spirituality, and Asian culture.

THE RIVERS RAN EAST
By Leonard Clark
ISBN 1-885-211-66-X
$16.95

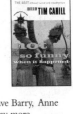

Clark is the original Indiana Jones, relaying a breathtaking account of his search for the legendary El Dorado gold in the Amazon.

Travel Humor

NOT SO FUNNY WHEN IT HAPPENED
The Best of Travel Humor and Misadventure
Edited by Tim Cahill
ISBN 1-885-211-55-4
$12.95

Laugh with Bill Bryson, Dave Barry, Anne Lamott, Adair Lara, and many more.

THERE'S NO TOILET PAPER...ON THE ROAD LESS TRAVELED
The Best of Travel Humor and Misadventure
Edited by Doug Lansky
ISBN 1-885-211-27-9
$12.95

Humor Book of the Year
—Independent Publisher's Book Award

ForeWord Gold Medal Winner—Humor Book of the Year

LAST TROUT IN VENICE
The Far-Flung Escapades of an Accidental Adventurer
By Doug Lansky
ISBN 1-885-211-63-5
$14.95

"Traveling with Doug Lansky might result in a considerably shortened life expectancy...but what a way to go."
—Tony Wheeler, Lonely Planet Publications

Women's Travel

A WOMAN'S PASSION FOR TRAVEL
More True Stories from A Woman's World
Edited by Marybeth Bond
& Pamela Michael
ISBN 1-885-211-36-8
$17.95

"A diverse and gripping series of stories!" —Arlene Blum, author of
Annapurna: A Woman's Place

A WOMAN'S WORLD
True Stories of Life on the Road
Edited by Marybeth Bond
Introduction by
Dervla Murphy
ISBN 1-885-211-06-6
$17.95

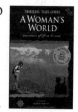

——— ★ ★ ★ ———

Winner of the Lowell Thomas Award for Best Travel Book—Society of American Travel Writers

WOMEN IN THE WILD
True Stories of Adventure and Connection
Edited by Lucy McCauley
ISBN 1-885-211-21-X
$17.95

"A spiritual, moving, and totally female book to take you around the world and back." —*Mademoiselle*

A MOTHER'S WORLD
Journeys of the Heart
Edited by Marybeth Bond
& Pamela Michael
ISBN 1-885-211-26-0
$14.95

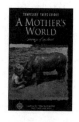

"These stories remind us that motherhood is one of the great unifying forces in the world" —*San Francisco Examiner*

Food

ADVENTURES IN WINE
True Stories of Vineyards and Vintages around the World
Edited by Thom Elkjer
ISBN 1-885-211-80-5
$17.95

Humanity, community, and brotherhood comprise the marvelous virtues of the wine world. This collection toasts the warmth and wonders of this large, extended family in stories by travelers who are wine novices and experts alike.

FOOD (Updated)
A Taste of the Road
Edited by Richard Sterling
Introduction by Margo True
ISBN 1-885-211-77-5
$18.95

——— ★ ★ ★ ———

Silver Medal Winner of the Lowell Thomas Award for Best Travel Book—Society of American Travel Writers

HER FORK IN THE ROAD
Women Celebrate Food and Travel
Edited by Lisa Bach
ISBN 1-885-211-71-6
$16.95

A savory sampling of stories by some of the best writers in and out of the food and travel fields.

THE ADVENTURE OF FOOD
True Stories of Eating Everything
Edited by Richard Sterling
ISBN 1-885-211-37-6
$17.95

"These stories are bound to whet appetites for more than food."

—*Publishers Weekly*

Spiritual Travel

THE SPIRITUAL GIFTS OF TRAVEL
The Best of Travelers' Tales
Edited by James O'Reilly and Sean O'Reilly
ISBN 1-885-211-69-4
$16.95

A collection of favorite stories of transformation on the road from our award-winning Travelers' Tales series that shows the myriad ways travel indelibly alters our inner landscapes.

THE WAY OF THE WANDERER
Discover Your True Self Through Travel
By David Yeadon
ISBN 1-885-211-60-0
$14.95

Experience transformation through travel with this delightful, illustrated collection by award-winning author David Yeadon.

PILGRIMAGE
Adventures of the Spirit
Edited by Sean O'Reilly & James O'Reilly
Introduction by Phil Cousineau
ISBN 1-885-211-56-2
$16.95

———— ✦✦✦ ————

ForeWord Silver Medal Winner — Travel Book of the Year

A WOMAN'S PATH
Women's Best Spiritual Travel Writing
Edited by Lucy McCauley, Amy G. Carlson & Jennifer Leo
ISBN 1-885-211-48-1
$16.95

"A sensitive exploration of women's lives that have been unexpectedly and spiritually touched by travel experiences…. Highly recommended."
—Library Journal

THE ROAD WITHIN
True Stories of Transformation and the Soul
Edited by Sean O'Reilly, James O'Reilly & Tim O'Reilly
ISBN 1-885-211-19-8
$17.95

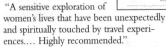

———— ✦✦✦ ————

Best Spiritual Book—Independent Publisher's Book Award

THE ULTIMATE JOURNEY
Inspiring Stories of Living and Dying
James O'Reilly, Sean O'Reilly & Richard Sterling
ISBN 1-885-211-38-4
$17.95

"A glorious collection of writings about the ultimate adventure. A book to keep by one's bedside—and close to one's heart." —Philip Zaleski, editor, *The Best Spiritual Writing series*

Adventure

TESTOSTERONE PLANET
True Stories from a Man's World
Edited by Sean O'Reilly, Larry Habegger & James O'Reilly
ISBN 1-885-211-43-0
$17.95

Thrills and laughter with some of today's best writers: Sebastian Junger, Tim Cahill, Bill Bryson, and Jon Krakauer.

DANGER!
True Stories of Trouble and Survival
Edited by James O'Reilly, Larry Habegger & Sean O'Reilly
ISBN 1-885-211-32-5
$17.95

"Exciting…for those who enjoy living on the edge or prefer to read the survival stories of others, this is a good pick."
—Library Journal

Special Interest

365 TRAVEL
A Daily Book of Journeys, Meditations, and Adventures
Edited by Lisa Bach
ISBN 1-885-211-67-8
$14.95
An illuminating collection of travel wisdom and adventures that reminds us all of the lessons we learn while on the road.

THE GIFT OF RIVERS
True Stories of Life on the Water
Edited by Pamela Michael
Introduction by Robert Hass
ISBN 1-885-211-42-2
$14.95
"The Gift of Rivers is a soulful compendium of wonderful stories that illuminate, educate, inspire, and delight."
—David Brower, Chairman of Earth Island Institute

FAMILY TRAVEL
The Farther You Go, the Closer You Get
Edited by Laura Manske
ISBN 1-885-211-33-3
$17.95
"This is family travel at its finest." —*Working Mother*

LOVE & ROMANCE
True Stories of Passion on the Road
Edited by Judith Babcock Wylie
ISBN 1-885-211-18-X
$17.95
"A wonderful book to read by a crackling fire."
—*Romantic Traveling*

THE GIFT OF BIRDS
True Encounters with Avian Spirits
Edited by Larry Habegger & Amy G. Carlson
ISBN 1-885-211-41-4
$17.95
"These are all wonderful, entertaining stories offering a *bird's-eye view!* of our avian friends."
—*Booklist*

A DOG'S WORLD
True Stories of Man's Best Friend on the Road
Edited by Christine Hunsicker
ISBN 1-885-211-23-6
$12.95
This extraordinary collection includes stories by John Steinbeck, Helen Thayer, James Herriot, Pico Iyer, and many others.

THE GIFT OF TRAVEL
The Best of Travelers' Tales
Edited by Larry Habegger, James O'Reilly & Sean O'Reilly
ISBN 1-885-211-25-2
$14.95
"Like gourmet chefs in a French market, the editors of Travelers' Tales pick, sift, and prod their way through the weighty shelves of contemporary travel writing, creaming off the very best."
—William Dalrymple, author of *City of Djinns*

Travel Advice

SHITTING PRETTY
How to Stay Clean and Healthy While Traveling
By Dr. Jane Wilson-Howarth
ISBN 1-885-211-47-3
$12.95

A light-hearted book about a serious subject for millions of travelers— staying healthy on the road—written by international health expert, Dr. Jane Wilson-Howarth.

THE FEARLESS SHOPPER
How to Get the Best Deals on the Planet
By Kathy Borrus
ISBN 1-885-211-39-2
$14.95

"Anyone who reads *The Fearless Shopper* will come away a smarter, more responsible shopper and a more curious, culturally attuned traveler."
—Jo Mancuso, *The Shopologist*

GUTSY WOMEN
More Travel Tips and Wisdom for the Road
By Marybeth Bond
ISBN 1-885-211-61-9
$12.95

Second Edition—Packed with funny, instructive, and inspiring advice for women heading out to see the world.

SAFETY AND SECURITY FOR WOMEN WHO TRAVEL
By Sheila Swan & Peter Laufer
ISBN 1-885-211-29-5
$12.95

A must for every woman traveler!

THE FEARLESS DINER
Travel Tips and Wisdom for Eating around the World
By Richard Sterling
ISBN 1-885-211-22-8
$7.95

Combines practical advice on foodstuffs, habits, and etiquette, with hilarious accounts of others' eating adventures.

THE PENNY PINCHER'S PASSPORT TO LUXURY TRAVEL
The Art of Cultivating Preferred Customer Status
By Joel L. Widzer
ISBN 1-885-211-31-7
$12.95

Proven techniques on how to travel first class at discount prices, even if you're not a frequent flyer.

GUTSY MAMAS
Travel Tips and Wisdom for Mothers on the Road
By Marybeth Bond
ISBN 1-885-211-20-1
$7.95

A delightful guide for mothers traveling with their children— or without them!